Transformations in Consciousness

D12899904

Transformations in Consciousness

The Metaphysics and Epistemology

FRANKLIN MERRELL-WOLFF

Containing His *Introceptualism*

Foreword by
Ron Leonard

STATE UNIVERSITY OF NEW YORK PRESS

Published by
State University of New York Press, Albany

© 1995 State University of New York

All rights reserved

Printed in the United States of America

No part of this book may be used or reproduced in any manner whatsoever
without written permission. No part of this book may be stored in a retrieval
system or transmitted in any form or by any means including electronic,
electrostatic, magnetic tape, mechanical, photocopying, recording, or
otherwise without the prior permission in writing of the publisher.

For information, address State University of New York Press,
State University Plaza, Albany, N.Y. 12246

Production by Marilyn P. Semerad
Marketing by Nancy Farrell

Library of Congress Cataloging-in-Publication Data

Merrell-Wolff, Franklin.
    Transformations in consciousness : the metaphysics and
epistemology : containing his Introceptualism / Franklin Merrell
-Wolff ; foreword by Ron Leonard.
        p.   cm.
    Includes bibliographical references and index.
    ISBN 0-7914-2675-0 (hc). — ISBN 0-7914-2676-9 (pb)
    1. Altered states of consciousness. 2. Self-realization.
3. Metaphysics. 4. Philosophy, Modern—Controversial literature.
5. Knowledge, Theory of. 6. Mysticism. 7. Knowledge, Theory of
(Religion) I. Merrell-Wolff, Franklin. Introceptualism.
II. Title.
BF1999.M483 1995
191—dc20   95-13896
                                                                              CIP

10 9 8 7 6 5 4 3 2

Contents

Editor's Foreword

The most profound part of human aspiration seeks to resolve ultimate questions. We strive to discover and understand the true nature of reality, and determine the means and scope of knowledge. These metaphysical and epistemological concerns are central to philosophical inquiry. However, authentic motivation for such a project must transcend intellectual curiosity insofar as new insights may transform our lives through an existential response to what is revealed. Therefore, it involves not only the ethical issue of how we should live, but also the religious quest for the ground from which to live.

Whereas philosophical speculation has been shown to fall short of an adequately grounded knowledge of ultimates, we have yet to fully explore the resources of mystical experience.* We may define it provisionally as direct, unmediated awareness of transcendent reality. To avoid begging any metaphysical questions, let us restrict the definition to the phenomenological sense, as the essential meaning of the mystics' accounts apart from any presuppositions or interpretations. Since they report that it is ultimately ineffable—that is, it cannot be captured in words or concepts—we should regard only elements that are clearly phenomenal, such as a feeling of bliss or peace, as literal descriptions. However, it is the nonphenomenal dimension that mystics generally contend reveals the inward nature of reality not accessible to empirical investigation, and with a sense of objectivity that persists even after the episode. By establishing a deeper ground within his consciousness, it transforms the mystic personally, along with his world view.

Serious questions naturally arise regarding experiences and states of consciousness that are both rare and highly valued, that seem diverse, yet are reported in virtually all cultures throughout history. What is the nature of mystical consciousness? What role does it play in reli-

---

*The term *experience* is misleading here because it is usually confined to sense experience. On the other hand, some mystical states are entirely devoid of sensory content, and even when present, it is irrelevant to what characterizes an awareness as mystical.

gion? Is it a source of metaphysical knowledge? What are the philosophical implications?

Franklin Merrell-Wolff* is uniquely qualified to illuminate such issues because he is a twentieth-century Western mystic trained in philosophy and science, particularly mathematics. Furthermore, his background includes religion and psychology, so he is able to provide an interdisciplinary† understanding of his mystical Realizations, as well as mysticism in general. Additionally, his study of analytic psychology sharpened his introspective skills and impressed him with the importance of recording relevant psychological subject matter. Consequently, he has taken pains to compose and include statements of his Realizations (mystical experiences), which allows the reader to assess subsequent interpretations and his derived philosophy. These records are invaluable, for mystics rarely chronicle, or have the skill to accurately formulate, this sort of primary psychological data.

Let us consider these Realizations, which are of central importance to the character and grounding of his formal philosophy, in the context of a brief biographical sketch. Franklin Wolff was born in Pasadena, California, in 1887, and was raised in San Fernando as the son of a Methodist minister. Although he abandoned orthodox Christianity as a teenager, since it failed to provide satisfactory answers to his probing questions, his upbringing had already awakened a deep, abiding religious and ethical concern that would pervade his life. In 1920, when he married Sarah Merrell, his first spouse, they joined their surnames to symbolize equal partnership in an ongoing spiritual work.

While he was studying mathematics and philosophy at Stanford and Harvard, the work of Immanuel Kant began to inspire Wolff to attempt to resolve the problem of metaphysical knowledge. He accepted the Kantian position that such knowledge would be impossible if our sole cognitive faculties are sense perception and conceptual cognition. However, Kant left open the theoretical possibility of another way of consciousness that might reveal a noumenal reality underlying phenomena. Wolff found evidence in Eastern literature that this cognitive function was not merely theoretical, but actual, motivating him to verify it personally. However, he felt that it was necessary to renounce his promising academic career so as to devote sufficient focus and energy to succeed in his quest.

---

*He was christened "Franklin Fowler Wolff," but uses "Merrell-Wolff" as his nom de plume.

†Wolff notes that philosophy, religion and psychology (and science generally) correspond to the three fundamental modes of human inquiry: meaning, value and fact, respectively.

In 1936, after more than twenty years of self-directed effort and self-devised means, leading to several mental realizations, his project culminated in two highly noetic Fundamental Realizations.* Wolff's initial breakthrough occurred on the evening of August 7, after reading the section on Liberation by Shankara in Paul Deussen's *The System of the Vedanta.*[†] It suddenly dawned on him that he had been making the mistake of striving for a new subtle object in meditation, but that the intended state involved no essential relation to objects of any kind. Thus, in a sense, because nothing may be attained, there is nothing to be sought, so he relaxed the effort. Instead, he attempted to abstract and focus on the subjective pole of consciousness.

> This was the final turn of the Key that opened the Door. I found myself at once identical with the Voidness, Darkness, and Silence, but realized them as utter, though ineffable, Fullness, in the sense of Substantiality, Light, in the sense of Illumination, and Sound, in the sense of pure formless meaning and Value. The deepening of consciousness that followed at once is simply inconceivable and quite beyond the possibility of adequate representation.[‡]

He characterizes it as an immediate awareness of identity as the Self, or Pure Subject. This accords with Shankara's technique, discriminating the self from all that is not-self, to attain Liberation by Realizing the Self.

For Wolff, it resulted in a permanent transformation of consciousness such that he began writing from a new, more profound base. Shortly thereafter he started *Pathways Through to Space,*[§] his first major work, which is primarily autobiographical. It details the events that structured his path, including the Realizations themselves, and records

---

*In contrast to mental realizations (for example, Archimedes' flash of intuitive insight that a substance may be identified by the relation between its mass and volume, which prompted his "Eureka!"), Fundamental Realization (Wolff's term for mystical experience) essentially transcends adequate formulation in words or concepts.

[†]Paul Deussen, *The System of the Vedanta*, trans. with a preface by Charles Johnson (Chicago: Open Court, 1912).

[‡]Franklin F. Wolff [Franklin Merrell-Wolff], *The Philosophy of Consciousness without an Object* (New York: Julian Press, 1973), 37; reprinted in *Franklin Merrell-Wolff's Experience and Philosophy* (Albany: State University of New York Press, 1994), 263.

[§]Franklin F. Wolff [Franklin Merrell-Wolff], *Pathways Through to Space* (New York: Richard R. Smith, 1944); reprinted in *Franklin Merrell-Wolff's Experience and Philosophy* (Albany: State University of New York Press, 1994).

his experiences while writing the book. Also, as various philosophical ideas and issues would spontaneously arise, he would treat them from this new perspective. Most remarkably, he found his expression becoming partially or entirely poetical.

Unexpectedly, thirty-three days later, a second Fundamental Realization autonomously took place, transcending the first in much the same way that a higher order of infinity transcends a lower order. Wolff designates it the "High Indifference" for the reason that, even though the preliminary phase could be characterized as complete Satisfaction beyond all desire, the state progressed to one of supernal Equilibrium. He found himself neutral, not apathetic, but superior and aloof regarding all polarities (such as hot-cold, pain-pleasure, beauty-ugliness, etc.). He was aware of unlimited power to actualize any of them, but had no inclination to choose one rather than its opposite.

The tertiary phase was also transcendent, but in a different sense. The previous Realization had been of the Self as Pure Subject, where the subject-object structure of consciousness remained, even though the object pole was empty. The High Indifference ultimately dissolved the subject-object structure altogether as a nondualistic Primordial Consciousness, or Field Consciousness, or, as Wolff calls it, "Consciousness-without-an-object and without-a-subject."

> There finally arrived a state wherein both that which I have called the Self and that which had the value of Divinity were dissolved in a Somewhat, still more transcendent. There now remained nought but pure Being that could be called neither the Self nor God. No longer was "I" spreading everywhere through the whole of an illimitable and conscious Space, nor was there a Divine Presence all about me, but everywhere only Consciousness with no subjective nor objective element. Here, both symbols and concepts fail.*

He reports that the attenuated relative consciousness continued in a parallel mode,† within the forms of time, space and causality. Hence, language still applies, but only Silence is strictly appropriate to the pure mystical state. Even so, Wolff considers that the value of communicating what might be possible concerning the Realizations worth the risk of defective formulation.

---

*Wolff, *Consciousness*, 73; *Experience and Philosophy*, 288.
†Relative consciousness was extinguished only in the terminal phase of mystical penetration.

In any case, this new ground made necessary a radical revision of his philosophy, a task he undertook in a manuscript that originally comprised both *The Philosophy of Consciousness without an Object* and *Introceptualism*.* There he endeavors to construct a more systematic version of his philosophy of introceptualism. The name is derived from his term *introception*, by which he designates the third function of cognition.

Transformations in Consciousness consists of Wolff's analysis of the nature of introception and its philosophical significance. To properly integrate introceptualism into the development of Western philosophy, he begins by critiquing each of the familiar schools (naturalism, neorealism, pragmatism and idealism) extant at the time. He argues that none of the four may justly claim to furnish a comprehensive world view, for they all fail to deal adequately with the potentials of human awareness inherent in introceptual consciousness.† Introceptualism is needed because its foundation is the most inclusive of the total range of human awareness. It is able to synthesize the positive values of the other schools with its own indispensably unique contribution.

Introceptualism is grounded in a nonordinary function of consciousness, apart from perception and conceptual cognition, that is a source of noetic value. Introception is the noetic aspect of mystical experience, as an immediate, nonphenomenal awareness. Strictly speaking, neither introception nor consciousness itself is definable, though Wolff proposes a definition that serves as a direction for how one might make it active. Introception is "the Power whereby the Light of Consciousness turns back upon Itself toward Its Source."‡ This implies that it may be, at least partially, a matter of volition. Consciousness is naturally object-directed, its energy spontaneously bound up in fascination with the object. In theory, if not in practice, a person may become self-reflectively aware of this dynamic, suspend the habitual commitment to the object, and reverse or invert the direction of attention. It is crucial to avoid focusing on the idea of the Self or Subject, for this merely becomes a new subtle object—one that is particularly deceptive. We must not confuse introception with introspection, which is the scrutiny of objects of inner perception. One may thus initiate the introceptive process at

---

*This is the original title of the present volume. The original manuscript, written at the time of World War II, is now part of the Wolff archives.

†Although more recent approaches to philosophy (for example, the analytic and phenomenological) eschew traditional system-building, they too would have to meet this challenge.

‡Wolff, *Pathways*, 228; *Experience and Philosophy*, 197. Literally, it is "to take within," from the Latin *intro* (within) and *capere* (to take).

will, as it is possible to control the orientation of consciousness to the subjective or objective pole. However, final success is never guaranteed. There are subtle pitfalls along the way, and its attainment requires self-giving, rather than control.

Even when successful, it must further be established that introception is a source of knowledge. Wolff advances this Noetic Thesis, supported by his invaluable firsthand account of the process. Introception reveals an autonomous, self-moving thought that is wholly other than the laborious, self-directed thought that employs words and concepts. Nevertheless, even though this mode of consciousness exceeds conceptual form, it is noetic in character. Between these two kinds of thought, but participating in both, lies a third kind that is transcriptive in nature. The transcendent thought affects the relative thought in such a manner as to precipitate articulate, but highly abstract concepts. Consider by analogy how certain chemical compounds dissolved in solution will form crystals having a definite pattern when the liquid is cooled. The same substance may precipitate in innumerably different forms, but each form represents the identical substance. Hence, we should understand each of the various formulations resulting from introception as a symbolic pointing, not a conceptual mapping. Nor is it a shortcut to scientific discovery.

Nonetheless, besides the immediacy of noesis, Wolff contends that introception constitutes knowledge in three ways that are rationally arguable:

1. the fact that there is a mystical thought of such a nature
2. becoming aware that the relative state of phenomenal awareness is nonultimate, akin to the recognition of an illusion as an illusion
3. the shift in the base of consciousness, analogous to the shift of base in mathematics, and the knowledge that base is relative.

These items are sufficient to justify the Noetic Thesis.

Beyond this, the critical issue is whether introception is a source of metaphysical knowledge as traditionally understood. Wolff insists that the various expressions resulting from the transcriptive process are not metaphysical descriptions. Even so, he considers them metaphysical in the sense that each authentically symbolizes the transcendent state from which it was precipitated. Because diverse conceptual formulations may function in this manner, none may be deemed to be exclusively true. In this case, truth is not a correspondence with determinate facts; rather, it is the relation of a symbol to that which is symbolized. This implies a metaphysical relativism, which Wolff rightly acknowledges, so he advances his specific philosophical thesis nondogmatically.

One of the strengths of introceptualism is its capacity to balance the proper, perhaps complementary, domains of science and religion. Wolff shows how religion is essentially grounded in Fundamental Realization and how its apparent diversity derives from various introceptive insights. From this standpoint we may view religious language as reflecting and symbolizing transcendent states of consciousness. Doctrine and ritual may be understood in relation to this original source. In addition, the primary function of religious practice is to orient the consciousness of the practitioner to this ground. Yet, even the elite within a religious tradition may fail to grasp the crux of its nature.* As a result, there is a tendency to interpret literally the pronouncements, and ensuing doctrines, that are based on Realization, and for religious practice to become little more than empty ritual. Almost inevitably, mistaking the accidental form of a religion for its grounding leads to claims of exclusive truth, and intolerant rejection of seemingly incompatible claims by other religions, on one hand, and science, on the other. Wolff is clear that the feeling of assurance present in introception does not legitimately transfer to the literal truth of any verbal expression. Consequently, introceptualism implies an attitude that not only tolerates, but genuinely appreciates the multiplicity of religious forms.

Religion deals with the meaning of human existence, but its methods and orientation are ill-suited to the tasks of science. Introceptualism upholds the integrity of science, whose empirical methodology is designed to determine the facts, rather than the significance, of human experience. Science is concerned with the methods and standards by which to acquire knowledge, in the widest sense. As actually practiced, however, it may also err in regarding some elements as essential that are merely accidental. In particular, modern science has relied on the Cartesian dualism of mind/matter for its dramatic advances. Treating physical reality as a self-contained realm, independent of mental or spiritual elements or influence, allows phenomena to be quantified and rationalized according to mathematically formulated natural laws. This has made possible an unprecedented degree of prediction and control and the development of a high order of scientific technology.

Notwithstanding its practical success, science overreaches when it regards its presuppositions (whether metaphysical, methodological or normative) as established truth, when it regards its approach to reality as entirely and exclusively adequate. A crucial challenge to science is to devise a satisfactory treatment of consciousness, the mental side of Descartes' proposed dualism. Obviously, consciousness, per se, is not quantifiable. If science requires quantification, and if only matter is essen-

---

*No doubt, other aspects of religion, superstition, magic, institutional orthodoxy, etc., may very well become preeminent in actual practice.

tially quantifiable, then it would seem that psychology (as the science of the psyche) would be impossible. However, there is no good reason to suppose that a single methodology will be fruitful in the investigation of all aspects of reality, no matter how effective it has proven in one sphere. Psychology would do well to determine its own appropriate principles and methods, rather than attempt to apply those of natural science.*

Furthermore, the philosophical proposal that would reduce mind to matter as a remedy for the difficulties of metaphysical dualism is misguided. Our greatest certainty lies in the immediacy of our subjective awareness, which is intrinsically different from any object of which we are aware. If we view matter as phenomenal, that is, as the appearance of different physical substances having certain definable characteristics, then it would be objective, presupposing, and standing in contrast to, the consciousness to which it appeared. However, if matter is conceived metaphysically, as a wholly unobservable substratum that theoretically underlies and supports all phenomena, then it is only a speculative construct beyond all possibility of verification.

A second difficulty concerning consciousness arises from within science itself. In quantum physics, a fundamental domain within traditional science, it is now acknowledged that the consciousness of the observer enters into the determination of physical reality, at least at the subatomic level, as an irreducible factor. Consequently, neither dualism nor reductionism is satisfactory, so a strictly scientific world view that presupposes either of them is problematic.

Introceptualism has no conflict with empirical science concerning discovered facts about the physical universe, but also embraces an authentic psychology. The function of introception would not be captured by either in the relative sense, though it is not beyond all verification. However, this would require personal attainment by the investigator. Wolff emphasizes the need for each individual to activate this function for oneself. Otherwise there is danger of excessive credulity by the naive "true believer," accepting claims second hand without sufficiently understanding, testing or grounding them.

However, the opposite extreme of maintaining a strictly detached objective attitude, such as the scholar or scientist might believe necessary to avoid losing critical perspective or professional demeanor, acts as a barrier to Realization. Wolff has found that the attitude of self-giving is essential to access introception. Consider by analogy the case of attending the performance of a symphony orchestra. A strictly scholarly or scientific attitude would virtually preclude the appropriate aesthetic

*The recent development of phenomenological psychology and transpersonal psychology is promising in this regard.

experience. More decisively, if we take the activity of love-making, this involves a mutual ecstatic communion between two human beings, a state that is impossible if one partner remains detached in a mode of observation and analysis. It is common knowledge that a certain self-giving is a prerequisite in such cases.* Moreover, no permanent loss of objectivity results. It is always possible retrospectively to provide objective descriptions and analyses of the experiences, and in manner vastly superior to that of a strictly secondhand approach.

Introceptualism is in a favorable position for developing a synthetic and comprehensive philosophy, for it explicitly avoids one-sidedness and metaphysical hypostatizing. It tests its adequacy by reference to the totality of human experience, not merely the so-called normal range.† In addition, a synthetic approach to philosophy must not only consider the widest scope of human awareness as *subject matter*, but as *grounding*. Hence, no school of philosophy is truly synthetic that ignores the transcendent ground inherent in introception.

The task of editing this text has been uniquely challenging for several reasons. As already mentioned, the material comprises the last half of a much longer manuscript, and is itself bifurcated. The first part critiques several schools of philosophy, which would appeal primarily to the academic philosopher, whereas the latter portion deals with mysticism more directly, so would appeal more to the spiritual seeker. It is thus a chief concern that the final version be clearly readable to a general public without compromising its logical rigor.

Since becoming a nonacademic, Wolff produced his writings using a portable typewriter, along with the limited resources of his personal library. For the most part, this accounts for several undocumented quotations. Most likely, he believed them sufficiently well known to be in the public domain, but did not remember where to find the original source. Where subsequent research has not located it, and where nothing of philosophical importance is at stake, these items are included without reference.

The central difficulty, however, derives from the nature of the subject matter. Wolff's critical exposition of naturalism, neorealism, pragmatism and idealism is discursive in nature, to a degree rarely found in his works.

---

*These examples make the point most forcefully because scholars and scientists presumably have already experienced these activities firsthand.

†Other things being equal, the person best able to assess the relative merit of diverse philosophical approaches is whoever is personally acquainted with the most inclusive range.

Then, as he begins to treat the introceptive factor, in itself and in relation to these other developments, his mode of expression becomes partially or wholly transcriptive. This is by necessity, since introception inherently overflows words, concepts and logical form. Its meaning is better captured by poetry and aphorism, which suggests more than it can describe. Thus, in spite of his intention to provide a systematic philosophy, he acknowledges that development from the introceptual consciousness quickly grew beyond any preconceived scheme of logical organization. Fearing that any extensive revision would sacrifice substance to form, he made only minor modifications to his original draft. Indeed, he cautions against editing any of his work, not only to preserve the integrity of transcriptive thought, but to avoid distorting the conception of the subtle elements of his philosophy.

Nonetheless, the original manuscript was able to benefit from careful editing and revision, particularly as the early twentieth-century language and style would have posed unnecessary barriers to contemporary and future readers. I believe that at this time no one is better qualified to have performed it. In the course of writing a doctoral thesis on his philosophy, I have become intimately acquainted with it, and with Franklin Wolff personally, during the last few years of his life.* Furthermore, I have sought to acquire an extensive philosophical background along with a special focus on mysticism.

The editorial process continually required resolution of the dynamic tension between fidelity to the original expression and the clearest communication to the contemporary reader of the grounded meaning of Wolff's philosophy. Wherever there was uncertainty whether a possible change would obscure or distort his precise meaning, Wolff's original wording was retained. However, where his personally idiosyncratic features of style or content would inhibit clear grasp of this meaning, the language has been altered in harmony with his overriding intention.

Specifically, I have undertaken to correct and modernize spelling, hyphenation and use of italics. The quotations Wolff cites have been rectified to appear as in the original source. Otherwise, words from other languages that have now become accepted in English are no longer italicized, and diacritical marks are used sparingly. Contemporary foreign terms are still italicized, except for Sanskrit words, which are capitalized, according to Wolff's general preference. For emphasis, he also occasionally italicizes English terms.

Special terms (such as Kant's *Categories*) are capitalized, according to accepted style. More notably, Wolff capitalizes words that he intends to convey transcendental significance (for instance, *Realization* and *Self*), but whose referents, nevertheless, are to be found in actual conscious

---

*Wolff lived in retirement in the foothills of the Sierra Nevada near Lone Pine, California, until his death in 1985.

awareness beyond the normal range, not mere speculative constructs. In particular, he distinguishes between *gnostic*, in the generic sense of *inspired intuition*, and *Gnostic*, referring to 'Gnosis' as the 'full Realization of identity with Transcendent Wisdom, or Knowledge'. Capitalization of *Gnostic* and *Gnosticism* here has nothing essentially to do with the corresponding historical religious movement, its sects, doctrines or practices. Furthermore, a word that is entirely capitalized indicates the supernal order of transcendence lying beyond even symbols. Such literary devices may seem extravagant to the casual reader, and provocative to the academic, but they are necessary to suggest exceptional meanings.

The most pervasive editing modifications involve grammar and word usage. I have streamlined awkward and convoluted constructions for readability, and altered some sentences from passive to active voice. I have deleted redundancies and unnecessary use of the definite article. Also, the use of the pronouns *that* and *which* now consistently distinguishes between restrictive and nonrestrictive clauses. In addition, occasionally I have judiciously introduced synonyms to amplify the meaning of excessively repetitive terms and substitute for terms that are archaic, cliché or slang. It has also been desirable to smooth some transitions between sections and chapters and modify some transitional expressions, especially to avoid beginning sentences with conjunctions.

Furthermore, I have followed contemporary practice in adhering to gender neutrality wherever appropriate. Also, it has been helpful to rewrite some passages in the timeless present when they deal primarily with the philosophical positions themselves, rather than specific events concerning their histories.

Insertions appearing in square brackets are Wolff's whenever they occur within the quotations he introduces. They are mine whenever they occur within Wolff's text, or in footnotes. Apart from their traditional use as editorial comment, they have been necessary for the purpose of defining special terms that Wolff introduces without explanation, or whose explanation he gave only in the first part of the original manuscript. For the sake of readability, I have minimized their use. Furthermore, all footnotes are now consistently formatted according to modern style.

Finally, I believe that Wolff could have significantly improved logical organization had he chosen to make substantial revisions in a second draft, even without benefit of a word processor. I am sure that his access to the introceptual grounding would have infused any reformulation with the same substance that he was concerned to preserve. Undoubtedly, even though it would have grown to some extent beyond whatever new framework he intended, the revised structure would have constituted a worthwhile improvement over the original.

Of course, no one but the author could have successfully undertaken such a project. However, even though the editing process has remained within the given structure, two modifications were made based on anticipated revisions of a further draft. First, Wolff included a few statements that are founded neither on his introceptive faculty nor on empirical fact, but instead are borrowed from unreliable secondary sources. Inasmuch as they have nothing essentially to do with his philosophy, and the reader would find them perplexing or distracting, they have been omitted.

Wolff also had difficulty devising titles for his works that are sufficiently descriptive to guide the reader not already acquainted with his thought. Thus it has been helpful to revise the book title, as well as several chapter headings. I have also introduced subheadings within most chapters to help orient the reader in advance to the specific subject matter. Admittedly, this device is somewhat artificial, for these subheadings are derived second hand and after the fact, rather than reflecting the writer's outline.* Nevertheless, I consider that their utility justifies insertion into the text.

In conclusion, Franklin Merrell-Wolff is a fascinating figure who nonetheless wished to be remembered for his philosophy, rather than his personality. This emphasis is correct, for his contribution is one of exceptional content and enduring value. In his life and work, he manifests the spirit of philosophy as "love of wisdom," a mode of inquiry that is also a path of transformation. However, Wolff also honors the role of the critical intellect. Accordingly, he invites careful scrutiny and evaluation of his philosophical thought, for neither blind rejection nor blind acceptance serve any worthwhile purpose. My intention is to present this text in as clear and accurate form as possible so as to allow the reader to assess its merit.

Ron Leonard
UNLV

---

*Only chapter 12 originally contained any subheadings, referring to the mysticism of Christ, Buddha and Shankara, respectively.

Introduction

Philosophy, psychology and religion are three orientations of human consciousness that, in their total range and meaning, embrace fields of interest or attitude that are identical, in considerable measure, though each extends into zones that are more or less disparate. Thus the distinctive quale of religion remains forever outside the domains of philosophy and psychology, so long as the latter are conceived in their purity as abstracted from the concrete totality of consciousness. It is no less true that much of psychology is concerned with psychical and psychophysical fact and process that is of entirely neutral concern with respect to the religious attitude, and, likewise, has little or no value for philosophic integration. Finally, philosophy expresses a mode of consciousness that is not reducible in its inner content to any possible psychology, however greatly the functions it employs may be of psychological interest, and that is in many respects quite neutral concerning the religious quale.

Nevertheless, there is a common area of human attitude and interest wherein these three fields overlap and interrelate. It is precisely in this intersection that we find the most vital and persistent problems and concerns that have compelled the attention of humanity in all times and places. We are probably quite safe in saying that all problems and interests lying outside this common zone merit, relatively, only transitory consideration and secondary significance. Hence, if humanity conceivably was to solve all of these secondary and transitory problems, but failed in dealing with the concerns of the common field, then we would have failed in the most profound sense. We would find our successes empty and futile, for while they might mean conquest of a world and the preservation of a vital animal existence, yet the adjustments necessary to a healthy and happy soul would be lacking, and the basis for a higher culture would be lost. Therefore, such achievements would be merely a vain success. A world thus conquered and possessed, and a vital life thus maintained, would be empty and valueless, with nothing to offer for inner adjustment or to serve the yearning soul. So, before and beyond all other considerations, we must face and master, if possi-

ble, the great common concerns that lie equally before philosophy, religion and psychology, while giving to other affairs the residual attention
that is their due. Succeeding in this, we may die early or late, rich or
poor in outer possessions, with much or little knowledge, but in any
case victor in the larger issues.

In *The Philosophy of Consciousness without an Object*,* I described at
some length, and in considerable detail, an instance of a transformation in
consciousness. Unquestionably, this sort of transformation is most central
to the religious problem as it is understood by the greater religions. Moreover, it is of equally profound concern for that phase of psychology that
some call "metapsychology." Finally, because it implies a theory of
knowledge and a metaphysics, it therefore affords a subject matter for
philosophy. Thus this transformation satisfies the conditions that place it
within the zone of coalescence of religion, philosophy and psychology,
and gives to it a value that may well prove to be of central importance.

In the present work I shall devote the primary attention to the
philosophical implications, with the psychological and religious aspects
occupying only a subsidiary position. There is no intent to depreciate
either the religious or the psychological values and attitudes in any
ultimate sense, merely to subordinate them for the present purposes.
The question as to which of these three frameworks deals with the most
fundamental problems, interests or attitudes is not raised at all. Their
relative valuation probably never can be separated from human subjectivity, so that, at any particular time, some will value one more than
the other two, while others will have a different preference.

Perhaps it is germane to an evaluation of the whole present discussion that the writer should acknowledge that personally the problem
of transformation has always appeared as primarily a question for philosophy, with the religious quale present as undertone. The pertinent
psychological interest in the transformation developed mainly after the
event. The factors that played the leading part in the individual consciousness before the event were primarily philosophical, so that philosophy enters the picture as an effective agent, not exclusively as subsequent interpretation. However, spontaneous—that is, not individually
and consciously willed—factors entered into the total picture, with the

---

*Franklin F. Wolff [Franklin Merrell-Wolff], *The Philosophy of Consciousness
without an Object: Reflections on the Nature of Transcendental Consciousness* (New
York: Julian Press, 1973). [Wolff first recorded this material in his more autobiographical *Pathways Through to Space: A Personal Record of Transformation in Consciousness* (New York: Richard M. Smith, 1944). These two works have recently
been combined into a single volume as *Franklin Merrell-Wolff's Experience and
Philosophy* (Albany: State University of New York Press, 1994.)]

result that a final world view emerged that is not identical with the one that helped to initiate the transformation process. In some sense or degree, there is incorporated or permitted within the present system of thought something of all the leading current philosophical schools, whereas the earlier orientation was almost exclusively idealist. Yet, despite this broadening and modifying effect, the idealist orientation was most largely confirmed. Nonetheless, my present philosophy does not seem to be completely congruent with any other extant system. Thus, for example, the present system is nonrelative in its profoundest ramifications. However, it may not be called "absolute," if the latter term is to be understood as predicating that the Ultimate is an absolute *Being*. The Root of All is conceived, not as an Absolute, but as an unconditioned Nonrelative, which we may view as an Absoluteness that is ever unknowable to relative consciousness, but which may be Realized through a process that essentially cancels relative cognition.

No proper philosophical orientation may ignore or disparage the functions of logic. However, philosophy is more than bare logic for the reason that it deals with content that in some sense is not exclusively identical with pure logic. The formal or logical relations that unite variables are necessary, but not sufficient, for the formation of a real philosophy. Of necessity, a real or vital philosophy must give to these variables some particular or general valuation or meaning that cannot be derived by logic operating exclusively by itself. Something more is required. This additional factor transcends the necessities of logic and may well open the door to all those human yearnings and needs that would be closed if the necessitarianism of logic alone were valid. When both are correctly understood, religious need and human purpose do not require the repudiation of logical necessity in order to realize their proper freedom. We can build conceptual figures that unite apparently incompatible lines of development, or forms of experience, and logical requirements by introducing the notion of multiple dimensions. Thus, within its dimension, logic has the final say and wields an unequivocal authority, but the variables that enter into logical relations may have any degree of extralogical development within other dimensions. Hence, it is quite conceivable that certain attitudes, interests or modes of consciousness may focus themselves in dimensions wherein logic is quite irrelevant. Even so, this fact would not at all render necessary a repudiation of the authority of logic within its realm. However, an attitude to which logic is irrelevant is simply not philosophy, though it may form part of the subject matter of philosophy. The philosopher, perforce, must think and produce within the framework of logic as one of his determinants, though he may carry into this structure extralogical components of unlimited richness and variety.

The content, quality, mode or way of consciousness that is the ultimate product of the previously reported transformation process will supply here the particular valuation or content given to the logical variables, insofar as such material may be conceived as an instance of terms in relation or of implicative development. All of this is a content or material given through immediacy, that is, in unmediated awareness. Admittedly, whereas the immediate material that enters into the preponderance of philosophic literature is of the nature of experiential data of quite wide general occurrence in the consciousness of human individuals, it must be recognized that much of the material that is introduced here is not part of our extensive common experience. To be sure, much of it is not without representation in extant and even current literature. Unfortunately, these literary references are, relatively, far from numerous, and they are often somewhat obscure and baffling to the rational mind. Much of the immediacy that is here the primary referent is not a sensible datum, but rather implies the activity of some function of consciousness other than the four that supply most of the content of modern analytic psychology.*

As a consequence, we are faced with a practical difficulty. The typical content of philosophy is not a self-determined whole. There is, in the formulation, an inevitable reference to a meaning that derives its content from the congruence of experience common both to the writer and to the reader. Philosophy is not written like rigorous and formal mathematics wherein all implicit intuitions are thoroughly expunged. The reader understands a philosophy—so far as he or she does understand it—because of a content immediately known and beyond the *word*, and that is known as well, and in the same sense, by the writer. This, together with logic, supplies the common domain of discourse essential for the uniting of the writer and the reader. In contrast, when the philosophical content becomes available only through a psychical function that is not commonly active, then, almost invariably, the philosophical writer and the reader will not hold much more in common than the logical structure of the discourse. This, in turn, places the critic at a real disadvantage, for although he may be able to critique the purely formal logical structures, he often will prove unqualified to evaluate the immediate content itself. Since, for him, the affirmed content is not known immediately, the material—as distinguished from formal or logical relations—must therefore fall short of being wholly clear. Thus, if the requisite psychical function is not in some measure active in his own consciousness, he can neither affirm nor deny the actuality of the immediate content in other than arbitrary or dogmatic terms.

---

*Carl G. Jung, *Psychological Types*, trans. by Godwin Bayes (New York: Harcourt, Brace & Co., 1926).

Much of the criticism of philosophic idealism centers in the contention that this philosophy has developed into an airy abstraction wherein nothing but a formal statement without real content remains. In terms that William James has made famous in philosophic literature, idealism has seemed to many to have become so "thin" that it has lost all substantiality whatsoever. This would imply that James views idealism as a formal philosophy without real content. No doubt, if we were to view all content as necessarily being of a sensible or experiential nature, then there is much justice in James's criticism. Idealism in its ultimate and most rigorous formulation is, in high degree, empirically empty. However, there remains the question whether *empiric emptiness implies* emptiness in every sense. My thesis is that such is not the case; rather, it is that through a latent psychical function, nonempiric but substantial content may be realized in a sense that is not less compelling than immediate experience. We should understand that the word *experience* is limited in its reference to a psychical state or modification of consciousness produced by sensation in the time stream. To one who is oriented to conscious content transcending experience in this sense, the apparently empty abstractionism of rigorous idealism may become transformed into an abundant fullness and "thickness." In contrast, it is precisely the empiric philosophies that tend to seem empty, shallow, and "thin." Since I have known this to be the case in my own private reading of idealist philosophies, I feel justified in suspecting that the idealist philosophers—or, at least, some of them—refer to a content that is not explicit in their systems. In a word, it appears that there is more behind these systems than the formal logical structure that is available for any reader's critical evaluation. Thus, idealism may be an expression that is true to its own substantial and immediately Realized meaning, and so have a value in the supermundane sense greater than that of any other school of Western philosophy.

Some proponents of objective absolute idealism have endeavored to establish their thesis as a necessity that may be made manifest by a sufficiently acute analysis of the common elements of consciousness, but criticism seems to have established very clearly that this endeavor has failed. It does not appear that it is possible to derive from the common features of a mundane consciousness either the actuality or the necessity of a supermundane consciousness. The attempt to do so is an analogue of inductive reasoning, which never can prove the universal validity of its generalizations. From the base of a transcendent consciousness it may be possible to infer the actuality or, minimally, the possibility of a derived mundane consciousness, but from the latter as an initial premise it is impossible to deduce a more comprehensive source. Hence, one either knows the transcendental Reality immediately or not at all. Consequently, such a Reality is not discursively provable from the ground of common experience. It can be speculatively affirmed, but this is less than knowledge, though consequences may be deduced from the affirmation that may be verifiable. It must be Realized to be known. Therefore, the effort to establish the thesis of idealism by dialectics alone is bound to fail.

At this point, if the dialectical proof of idealism fails, we are left with but two alternatives: Either we must abandon the thesis entirely, or we must ground it upon the authority of direct Realization that is an outcome of a transformation in individual consciousness. We are thus forced to face the question whether it is a valid endeavor to formulate a philosophy oriented to a private Realization that is held in common by a few fellow human beings. No doubt this issue is debatable. Clearly, if the private Realization had no chance of receiving a sympathetic response in the heart or mind of any other person, there would be little reason for producing a philosophic formulation, save as an act of artistic production. Promisingly, if one searches the appropriate literature, one will find that this private Realization is not so private as at first it may appear, for there are others who have written from the base of comparable Realizations. Consequently, that which some among the human whole have Realized is, by the sheer fact of the Realization itself, shown to be a possibility of the human psyche as such. To learn of this possibility may surely be enough to supply the impulse toward further instances of Self-Awakening, or may strengthen the assurance of those who have had partial glimpses of a Beyond, but are not yet well grounded on the new Base. To be sure, this purpose may be achieved through art, poetry, religious practice and other nonphilosophic means. Yet it still remains true that for some natures the Path to Self-Realization, or to the Higher Consciousness, is through philosophy. These facts would seem to justify an affirmative answer to the question.

In any case, if it is once granted that there is, or may be, another way of consciousness outside the field of common experience, then this is a matter of great concern for any psychology or philosophy that seeks to achieve a comprehensive view of all the possibilities of consciousness. Of course, it is possible to construct diverse systems of philosophy and psychology upon the bases of arbitrary assumptions that exclude from the outset the possibility of the Realization of a transcendent Reality, but this would be valid only as a conceptual exercise. For instance, we may say, "Let us assume mechanism as a universally and comprehensively valid principle and see what consequences follow." From this we would derive some form of naturalistic philosophy, which might prove to be an interesting and, in some measure, useful excursion. It is quite another matter when one, instead of assuming, dogmatically affirms mechanism as universally and comprehensively valid. Such a standpoint is at once seriously challenged when any individual says, "I have immediate knowledge of that which cannot be comprehended within the limits of mechanism." Likewise, one may assume the standpoint that affirms the categories of empiric life as fundamental, and from this derive the anti-intellectual instrumentalism of pragmatism. The resultant philosophies are unquestionably valid for considerable sectors of experience and thought. However, when such presuppositions are taken as universally and exclusively valid, they arbitrarily rule out standpoints from which mechanism and pragmatism are seen to have only derivative and partial validity. Affirmation of acquaintance with such larger perspectives at once challenges the universal validity of the lesser standpoints. Thus, if there is a perspective from which the whole of empiric life may be viewed as derivative, and merely a partial manifestation of a larger Reality, then pragmatism would have only a pragmatic validity, that is, as a mere stepping stone to something more durable. Finally, it is possible to assume that ultimate reality is such that it makes no difference whether it is known or not. In accord with the neorealists, one may say that this reality can enter into relations with consciousness or can be considered in relation to consciousness and yet be treated as quite independent of consciousness, its nature in either case remaining unaltered. Here we have little more than a logical exercise relative to an essentially unknown and unknowable somewhat, since knowledge cannot be derived from beyond the field of consciousness. To be sure, this point of view may well have some pragmatic utility, but it does not wield metaphysical authority. As a universal and exclusively valid philosophy, it would deny forever all hope to those who yearn for certainty, giving in its place the inflated and unsecured currency of a mere probable or possible truth. He who says, "I Know," challenges all this.

In what follows, I shall not attempt to *prove* a point of view as the only possible or valid one. We may grant that human beings may be scrupulously logical and still think otherwise. However, I do insist that a Realization in Consciousness that finds no place or adequate recognition in other systems proves the inadequacy of these. Any universally valid system, if such may ever be found or created, must embrace the rarer states and contents of consciousness as well as those that comprise the mass of common experience. I propose to present the outlines of a system that, while not excluding the contents of the more familiar experience, also embraces the wider ranges opened by the Door of Realization. As a preliminary step, to prepare the ground and to make evident the need of a further formulation, I shall briefly survey the principal schools of modern Western philosophy to show wherein they fall short of adequacy as a philosophic form for the present purposes.

PART I:
FOUR SCHOOLS OF
MODERN PHILOSOPHY

1

Toward a Synthetic Philosophy

When human consciousness at some time in the unknown past reached that point in its development where it turned a reflective vision upon its experience, taken as a comprehensive totality, it early discovered two seemingly opposed, yet complementary, components that are ineluctable parts, like poles, of that totality. These we know today as Spirit and Matter. Reflective thinkers, ever conditioned by individual psychology, have tended to realize and value one or the other of these components more completely. Indeed, some have seen them as interdependent, inhering in some common root; others, less integral in their vision, have seemed to find the ultimate in one or the other pole. Even those with the more comprehensive view have tended to accentuate one or the other component. Inevitably, then, when humankind became philosophically conscious, there was an inclination to polarize into schools of thought in which the common denominator of emphasis, or even exclusive recognition, was either Matter or Spirit, in whatever manner these two may have been conceived. Thus even a casual perusal of the history of philosophy leaves the student with the strong impression that there are always, in varying terms and forms, two main patterns conditioning the orientation of the world view of reflective humanity.

In modern Western terminology the division and contrast between these diverse lines of philosophical orientation are commonly represented by the schools of materialism, naturalism, and realism, standing in contrast to spiritualism, idealism and subjectivism. These divergent and opposed orientations are most forcibly represented in the modern West as naturalism and idealism, the former lying closer to science, the latter to religion. In addition to these most radically contrasting systems of philosophy, within the early part of the twentieth century, two other schools have arisen that occupy positions intermediate between the more extreme formulations. One of these, neorealism, occupies a position definitely closer to naturalism than to idealism, but conceives its objective reality as something considerably more subtle than that of naturalism. The other, pragmatism, diverges from neorealism to a viewpoint rather closer to idealism, though definitely less absolutist and more empiric than the latter. These two later schools may be said to be more humanistic than the older and more classical ways of thought, in that they more definitely restrict themselves to the actual human processes of cognition, feeling and conation, with their corresponding contents and valuations. In any case, the divisions between these various schools are sufficiently notable to justify a fourfold classification based upon a root twofold division.

All these systems or ways of thinking bring into relief by accentuation authentic elements or complexes that are to be found in actual human experience or consciousness. Therefore, none may be wholly neglected, and a truly synthetic philosophy, when and if it is ever written, must do justice to, or at least find room for, the positive values of each. Regrettably, there is a strong tendency on the part of representatives of these various schools to formulate their positions in more or less exclusive or privative terms, producing features that must be expunged if there ever is to be a synthetic system.

It is proposed here to examine the primary features—the essential or defining characteristics—of these schools, with the central purpose of showing in what respect they are inadequate for effecting an integration sufficiently comprehensive to embrace the values and knowledge derived from Gnostic Realization. The intent is to clear the ground for the formulation that will follow, as well as to show that a need for such new formulation exists. The discussion will begin with naturalism, pass through neorealism, pragmatism and idealism, and then culminate in introceptualism, the term by which I have designated my systematic contribution, which is in some sense and degree new.

2

Naturalism

Naturalism, as it is understood in philosophical usage, has three distinguishable connotations, all of which have in common the meaning of an attempted speculative explanation of every component of experience by means of entities and forces that are viewed as natural or mundane. The latter conceptions are to be understood as excluding everything that may be regarded as spiritual or transcendental. The three meanings of the term may be classified as general naturalism, materialism and positivism. Let us briefly consider them.

GENERAL NATURALISM

In its more general and less objectionable sense, naturalism is the more or less philosophical view that attempts to explain everything by reference to natural causes or processes in the sense of that which is *normal*. It thus eliminates as a factor in explanation any event or process that may be called "supernatural" or "supernormal." Consequently, it excludes any interpretation that is based upon the miraculous, mystical insight, enlightenment and generally any factor that may be viewed as transcendental. However, in this sense, naturalism does not imply an attempt to explain everything in exclusively physical terms, in particular, mechanistic physical terms. Mental and biological phenomena, as they are found to exist normally, are accepted as natural, though irreducible to ultimate physical conceptions. Thus the emphasis is upon the *norm*, rather than upon the conception of the ultimate reducibility of everything to matter and force. Naturalism, in this sense, is very widespread and appears to be the normal view among the professional classes whose orientation is to natural science, either in the pure or in the applied sense.

Naturalism, in this most general sense, can and does have positive value as long as it is viewed as no more than a heuristic principle. It often serves as a salutary protection against overly imaginative and superstitious tendencies and attitudes, which are often far from wholesome. Nevertheless, this positive value is lost such that naturalism becomes actively malicious when, instead of serving as a simple heuristic principle, it is raised to the dogmatic thesis that the natural is the all in all—capable of serving as the ground of interpretation of all elements and complexes of human experience.

The naturalistic attitude is of very wide occurrence among biologists, psychologists and sociologists of the present day, as well as in the engineering profession. In contrast, it is an interesting and very significant fact that the naturalistic tendency appears to be weakening among those who form the vanguard of physics, the most advanced natural science. Much in modern physics sounds more like transcendentalism than like naturalism. Perhaps the other professional groups may discover the implications of this tendency within a century or so.

MATERIALISM

In contrast to naturalism in the first sense, that may mean only a heuristic attitude, materialism is a metaphysical theory. It is "that metaphysical theory which regards all the facts of the universe as sufficiently explained by the assumption of body or matter, conceived as extended, impenetrable, eternally existent, and susceptible of movement or change of relative position."* In particular, materialism attempts to explain all phenomena, including psychical phenomena and the phenomena of consciousness in general, in terms of transformations of material molecules. They were materialists who said that thought is secreted by the brain as bile is secreted by the liver, and that man is what he eats. On the whole, the materialistic philosophy is so crude, undiscerning and uncritical that it scarcely rates serious philosophical attention. Today, pure natural scientists, though often naturalists in the philosophical sense, are only exceptionally crude materialists, for they know the essentially postulational character of their concepts too well to fall into the error of hypostatizing them into absolute metaphysical beings.

Although true scientists are rarely philosophical materialists, materialism is today of enormous importance in the field of sociological theory and practice. The vast current of Marxism, or so-called scientific socialism, is explicitly and dynamically materialistic. Its proponents even designate it "dialectical materialism." We should observe that this materialism is not quite identical with the mechanistic materialism of

---

*James M. Baldwin, ed., *Dictionary of Philosophy and Psychology* (New York: Macmillan, 1925), s.v. "materialism."

the previous definition; nor is it completely identical with the biological materialism that has grown out of the findings and teachings of Charles Darwin. Yet, Marxism is explicitly materialistic in three specific senses that are of philosophical importance:

1. It affirms an antipositivistic, realistic epistemology. We may render explicit the intended meaning by considering Vladimir Ilyich Lenin, who says, "For the sole 'property' of matter—with the recognition of which materialism is vitally concerned—is the property of being *objective reality*, of existing outside our cognition." Although the phrase "existing outside *our* [italics mine] cognition" does not by itself necessarily mean existing outside consciousness in every sense, the general context of dialectical materialism reveals that this is implied. Further, since the standpoint is nonpositivistic, the complete implication is of an independent self-existent matter. This is enough to define an essential materialism.
2. Marxism especially affirms a dialectical movement in nature and society that is explicitly conceived in the materialistic sense. The conception of the dialectical movement is taken from the philosophy of Hegel but given a radically inverted meaning. This is evident from the following quotation from Karl Marx: "For Hegel the thought process, which he transforms into an independent subject under the name idea, is the creator of the real, which forms only its external manifestation. With me, on the contrary, the ideal is nothing else than the material transformed and translated in the human brain."*
3. Marxism also affirms the labor theory of value, which means that value is produced by labor in such a sense that all productive activity, whether manual or mental, can be reduced to some multiple of the simplest form of manual production. This conception is not original with Marx, but he carries out its implications with the greatest consistency. It stands opposed to the psychological theory of value, in which it is affirmed that it is human desire that gives value to produced objects, an essentially nonmaterialistic position, because a factor in consciousness is regarded as the value-producing determinant. One consequence of this view is that, in the Marxist program, exercise of individual wish or preference in the consumption of economic objects tends to be curbed, insofar as the value of what is to be consumed is produced by labor, not by the desire of the consumer.

Ideological materialism, as distinguished from practical nonreflective materialism, is not an important social or philosophical force, yet in

---

*Karl Marx, quoted in *Encyclopaedia Britannica*, 9th ed., s.v. "socialism."

the Marxist form it has become an extremely important social, political and economic movement. This affords a rare opportunity for observing just what materialism in action can and does mean. The ethical characteristics of this movement, as we find them revealed, are not something extraneous added to the original idea. The student of dialectical materialism who is familiar with the propositions of Marx and Lenin is rather impressed with the consistency of the development. Indeed, we have a rare opportunity to conduct a pragmatic evaluation of materialism in action.

POSITIVISM

The most philosophically important form of naturalism is that which is known as positivism. It differs from materialism in that it does not hypostatize substantive metaphysical existence of the conceptual entities of physical science. It is no less grounded upon natural science than is materialism, but it may be said to be oriented to the *method* of science rather than to the *substantive content* of science. It is essentially

> the theory that the whole of the universe or of experience may be accounted for by a method like that of the physical sciences, and with recourse only to the current conceptions of physical and natural science; more specifically, that mental and moral processes may be reduced to the terms and categories of the natural sciences. It is best defined negatively as that which excludes everything distinctly spiritual or transcendental.*

It is thus evident, in theory at least, that positivism excludes from the realm of valid knowledge every element that is a priori or speculative. Also, since it views the terms, categories and methods of science as the exclusively valid source of knowledge, it provides no place for a kind of knowledge that may be derived from any other way of cognition.

Commonly the word *positivism* is associated most closely with Auguste Comte. However, for the more generalized meaning given here, it is not so restricted. Thus, in this wider sense, Locke, Hume and Spencer are positivists, as are several other thinkers who, while naturalistic in their orientation, are yet too critical in their thinking to fall into the naive errors of materialism. Positivism may be said to differ from naturalism in the general sense largely in that it is more systematically and philosophically developed.

---

*Baldwin, *Dictionary*, s.v. "naturalism."

Of all philosophies, positivism is probably most closely married to natural science. Even so, it differs from the special sciences in that it extends or extrapolates their methods into ultimately and exclusively valid means for the attainment of knowledge. The program of the special sciences is much less pretentious in that each merely integrates its knowledge of fact by means of hypothesized postulates that possess only a pragmatic validity that may, indeed, have no more than a transitory life. Thus the special sciences cannot lay claim to having discovered the central truth of phenomena, but only *warranted assertibility* (to use John Dewey's term). The question whether warranted assertibility is the final possibility of knowledge cannot be answered by any of the special sciences. This is preeminently a question for philosophy, but before we can hope to achieve an ultimately satisfactory answer, we must at least consider the claim that there is such a thing as a mystic or gnostic cognition falling quite outside the methodology of all natural science. At any rate, positivism is a philosophy that, basing itself upon scientific method, affirms that the warranted assertibility of science is the last word concerning all positive knowledge.

Positivism does not so much affirm that there is no metaphysical or noumenal reality as adopt an agnostic attitude concerning the possibility of such an existence. At times, as in the case of Spencer, it is simply called the "Unknowable," then dropped as irrelevant for human concerns. We can readily agree that such a noumenal reality is unknowable by the cognitive methods of natural science. If the positivist meant no more than this, he would be correct enough. However, he goes further by both dogmatically and arbitrarily affirming that the scientific form of cognition is the only possible form of cognition, and thus the unknowable for natural science is an absolute Unknowable of which we cannot even predicate substantive existence.

A critique of positivism involves more than a critique of natural science, for the latter does not resolve the question of whether the scientific form of cognition is the only possible form of knowledge. It gives a delimitation and evaluation of scientific knowledge as such, generally affording us an objective perspective regarding it. It can be contrasted with other, at least supposed, kinds of knowledge such as Gnosticism, so we are enabled to see precisely what science is. So far we have determined that warranted assertibility is the last word of natural science, but not necessarily the final possibility of all knowledge. However, it is just this question whether warranted assertibility is final that constitutes the crux of the critique of positivism and, undoubtedly, of naturalism as a whole. In general, the positivists have not dealt adequately with this question.

One may suggest that it is possible to investigate in the scientific spirit the problem of whether there is an extrascientific way of knowledge.

Would not such a procedure, compared to that of dogmatic affirmation without investigation, more conform with the fundamental assumption of positivism? Any way or means of cognition could conceivably be a proper subject for scientific study. To be sure, a positive finding, resulting from such a study, would take the form of a warranted assertion, for this is all that scientific method can give. Nevertheless, it would be a scientific recognition that some way of cognition other than scientific probably exists. Such a recognition would give the same justification, at least for attempting to devise a practical procedure appropriate to the probably existent way of cognition, that science gives for such procedure in other fields. This type of additional way of knowledge could not become part of scientific cognition without altering the form and nature of scientific knowledge somewhat radically, but in any case this would determine the factuality of other possibilities of cognition for natural science.

Interestingly, a study of the type suggested above exists today and has existed for many years. I refer to the investigation of extrasensory perception. The subject matter of this study has embraced telepathy, clairvoyance, precognition and telekinesis. Even though these supposed functions or faculties involve less than the cognition implied in the notion of a gnostic knowledge, if existent, they would transcend in their content and procedure the way of cognition of natural science. The results of this investigation to date have been strongly positive. Of course, as is quite sound, the conclusions have been reported in the mode of warranted assertibility, rather than categorical judgment. Despite this, the degree of assertibility is represented as an explicit mathematical probability, which is rendered possible by the methods employed. It is difficult to see how the results of these experiments can be seriously questioned, as long as one accepts the theory of the mathematics of probability. The final consequence of this research is that we may view the factuality of extrasensory perception as scientifically established to a degree of reliability that is not inferior to much of the body of general scientific knowledge.

What becomes of the positivistic assumption that the only possible type of knowledge is scientific when science establishes the factuality of a nonscientific type of knowledge? Doubting the factuality of this nonscientific kind of knowledge would then imply doubt concerning the reliability of scientific knowledge itself. Some have found this dilemma quite disturbing. The alternatives are either a thoroughgoing agnosticism concerning all cognition, including scientific knowledge, or the positive acceptance in principle of nonscientific cognition along with scientific knowledge.

The conclusion that seems to be constrained by the foregoing argument is that positivism, insofar as it asserts or implies the categorical denial of the possibility of a metaphysical, transcendental or spiritual knowledge, is simply unsound. It stands condemned by the voice of the science to which it appeals for its authority. Once the factuality of any sort of nonscientific cognition is established, by means of scientific method, it undeniably forces ajar the door of possibility for any other sort of nonscientific cognition for which existential claims may be advanced. This is particularly true if these are made by individuals of proven intellectual competence. However, positivism may well remain valid as a heuristic attitude, provided it is reasonably flexible. It also may render valuable service as a check against a too active and too credulous will to believe. Beyond all doubt, scientific method is a valuable monitor of human cognition, so long as it does not presumptuously arrogate to itself the voice of an authoritarian dictator.

Viewing naturalism as a whole, rather than in terms of its three specific forms, we can identify its general cardinal principle as realism. Realism in the modern, as distinguished from the medieval, sense is "the doctrine that reality exists apart from its presentation to, or conception by, consciousness; or that if, as a matter of fact, it has no separate existence to the divine consciousness, it is not in virtue of anything appertaining to consciousness as such."* Realism is the view that ultimate reality is not consciousness nor dependent upon consciousness for its existence. Yet, realism is not simply another name for naturalism, as it has a much wider comprehension. Neorealism, as well as the possibly more developed wing of pragmatism, would have to be classified with naturalism in this respect. Of the three schools, naturalism is the most obviously and intensely realistic, and thus it stands at the opposite pole from idealism. In addition, of all the types of philosophy that have developed in the West, it stands in the strongest contrast to the thesis affirmed in the second part of the present work. Therefore, it will be necessary to prepare the ground for the present philosophy by a polemical examination of these opposed realistic systems. However, inasmuch as this critique will center upon the realistic standpoint, as such, it is postponed until we take up the discussion of the new realism.

As is true of virtually all schools of philosophy, naturalism has features in which it is relatively strong, and offers a positive contribution and even attitude. However, it is no less marked by inadequacy regarding its treatment and offering in other respects. Its contribution to empiric science has a degree of positive value, provided its too cate-

---

*Ibid., s.v. "realism."

gorical and unsound generalizations are properly pruned. Nevertheless, even though it is a development grounded in natural science, naturalism fails to consider adequately the phases, aspects or perspectives
that are ineluctable parts of the total discipline or meaning that we
agree to call "science," and which are of no less importance than the
empiric or factual. Science is not simply a body of empiric fact; it is, as
well, a logically organized conceptual system, grounded upon a particular kind of orientation of consciousness. It is thus a compound of fact,
system and orientation. As a consequence, an adequate scientifically
grounded philosophy must deal with the systematic and orientational
as well as the factual aspects of the scientific totality. It must incorporate
a critique and due appreciation of the orientational and systemic, or
logical components, as well as the purely factual. This naturalism fails to
do, or at least fails to do in satisfactory terms. This does not mean that
naturalistic philosophers lack orientation or are necessarily deficient in
logical capacity. Rather, they fail, almost completely, to consider logic
and orientation as objects for critical examination and evaluation. In
this respect the three remaining schools of philosophy are more complete and, therefore, more sound.

Even as a philosophy based upon the factual side of science, naturalism, in the technical sense, is incomplete, for its general orientation is
to physical science. It would be possible for a naturalistic philosophy to
be oriented to the biological sciences, or even to the total of all forms of
science. We would thereby have a broader and more sound naturalism. We must acknowledge that there is a considerable degree of this
enriched naturalism both in neorealism and in pragmatism. To be sure,
we may view much of pragmatism as a naturalism that is primarily
based upon the biological sciences. However, in this respect technical
naturalism is highly deficient.

If we are to consider humankind in the totality of consciousness,
experience, interest, attitude, and so on, as constituting the proper subject matter for philosophy, then any philosophic system that is exclusively oriented to the scientific dimension of human interest is far from
complete. Human consciousness as a comprehensive whole cannot be
equated with that part of it that is scientific in its orientation. Humans
are vital and mental beings as well as embodied creatures, and in these
larger capacities of our nature we have interests and attitudes, both
rational and irrational, that are not comprehensively embraced by the
scientific dimension of our total interest. Thus there are perspectives
of human consciousness, such as the ethical, aesthetic, spiritual or religious, that are essentially other than science. No doubt, all these aspects
of the complete consciousness of humanity, with their objective manifestations, have been objects for scientific study. Even so, the last word

of science here is of value only as giving objective factuality, but nothing of the inner meaning.

However, philosophy is in duty bound, so far as lies in its power, to deal with this inner content as well as the objective factuality. In this respect, naturalism, in the technical sense, is almost a complete failure. There are some references to this other side of human nature in the writings of the naturalists, but not in such a way as true insight would dictate. For example, a naturalist (Marx) calls religion "the opium of the people." Undoubtedly there have been manifestations classed as religious that are little better than an opiate. Yet, to judge religion as a whole in such a way is no less ignorant than an evaluation made by a primitive who mistakes a mechanical construction of applied science for a form of ceremonial magic. In these dimensions naturalism fails, sometimes even egregiously, so even though we duly acknowledge the positive contributions of this school, we must also recognize its more notable inadequacies and incompetencies.

3

The New Realism

In a history of modern philosophy in which the systems and schools were arranged in chronological order, the new realism would be the last of the four schools discussed, since it arose mainly out of a polemic directed against the other three. However, if the treatment of the subject is based upon classification by similarity of content, evaluation and orientation, it seems quite evident that the new realism would have to be placed in a position between naturalism and pragmatism. This is because, in similarity to the former, and one wing of the latter, its orientation is quite naturally realistic. This defines a general attitude toward the office of consciousness that is, for the present purpose, the feature of most importance. Certainly there are important differences in the form and nature of the reality as conceived by the different schools, but all agree in viewing the object as transcending the subject. Furthermore, both naturalism and the new realism alike affirm the transcendence of the thing, or the existent, with respect to consciousness in any sense.

For realism, in the modern sense, there is no such thing as a physical or a metaphysical self-existent substance, so it defines a position of greater similarity to positivism than to the other forms of naturalism. Representatives of this school generally seem to have an acute feeling for the limitations concerning the empiric knowing process. Consequently, they have clearly perceived that, in its ordinary manifestations at least, cognition does not supply us with an immediate knowledge of substance in any sense, but only with relations connecting various terms. Much of its destructive analysis parallels that of the pragmatists, but it differs from pragmatism in not granting to activism the status of immediate authority. Like naturalism, it very largely discredits intuitive insight. However, unlike naturalism, its primary orientation is not to a sensual datum. As compared to naturalism, the thinkers of this school reveal a far superior philosophic acuity. As a result, it gives the claims of logic and ethics a recognition that is hardly, if at all, inferior to that given to those of physics and biology. Concerning the relative importance attached to logical entities and processes, this school occupies an outstanding position. On the whole, as a line of both critical and constructive thought, it offers much of interest and value.

The new realism, like all modern and self-conscious philosophy, begins with a consideration of the problem of knowledge. Since the time of Immanuel Kant it has been realized that it is impossible to evaluate justly the meaning of knowledge unless the thinker first becomes familiar with the nature and the limits of knowledge. In other words, knowledge as such and the knowing process must themselves be objects of study before a valid evaluation of the cognitive content can be achieved. Otherwise, one may fall into the error of projecting the meaning of the content beyond valid limits. Clearly, no part of the philosophic discipline is more important than this, because obviously it is useless to define reality in terms of knowledge if we do not know the nature of knowledge qua knowledge. Furthermore, the problem presented is not one of interest exclusively for technical philosophy, but has ramifications bearing upon the office of knowledge in all domains, including scientific, religious and pragmatic utilitarian. Thus, for example, in the case of the special sciences, even though great critical care has been employed in technical observation and theoretical construction, the question remains as to the essential meaningfulness of the knowledge produced. Does it give a substantial truth? Is it, perhaps, merely a useful symbol? Alternatively, is it an essentially meaningless formalism that is not true knowledge at all? Insofar as the great mathematician, David Hilbert, has affirmed the latter view concerning the constructions of mathematics, the most rigorous of all sciences, we cannot exclude offhandedly the possibility that all scientific constructions are no more than such meaningless formalisms. In support of such a position it might be well to note that Zen Buddhists hold a view about all conceptual knowledge that seems essentially of this sort. It is not my purpose here to suggest that Hilbert and the Zen Buddhists are necessarily correct in their evaluation, but simply to point out how vitally important the epistemological problem is. Thus, although the great driving motive of all philosophical effort is the determination, and even the Realization, of ultimate Reality, before such a search can hope to attain dependable results, there must be a critical evaluation and examination of the instruments employed in the search. Consequently, it is very much to the credit of the new realism that it recognizes the methodological primacy of the epistemological problem. Whether the solutions offered are adequate is quite another matter.

For an intelligent understanding of the new realism it is essential to comprehend the theory of external relations, insofar as this plays a vital part in the neorealist conception of knowledge and reality. The peculiar feature of this theory is the doctrine that the elements or terms that enter into various relations with each other are *not* altered in their intrinsic nature by reason of entering into the relationship. To illustrate, if an object A enters into a relationship of effect with another object B, and into a relationship of consciousness with another object C, then in both cases A remains precisely the same in its own essential nature. This gives to terms, of which A is a general sign meaning any entity whatsoever, a fixed definitive character that remains forever unaltered.

The opposing view is that terms cannot be completely separated from their relations, for the reason that the meaning and even the content of the term is in part determined by the relations into which it enters. This is the theory of internal relations, which results in an absolute monism, when it is consistently developed. In contrast, the theory of external relations results in a pluralistic world view, for the reason that the multitudes of terms would comprise independent self-existent entities. The theory of external relations is characteristic of the new realism, while the theory of internal relations plays a notable part in the development of absolute idealism.

To a large degree the theory of external relations is intimately connected to the analysis of the logic of pure mathematics, a field in which it does appear to have considerable validity. Whether, from the standpoint of the most profound understanding of the nature of pure mathematics, this theory will remain as the final truth is uncertain. It nonetheless has some measure of truth. For instance, a numerical entity, such as the number 2, may well seem to be identically itself and unaltered when it stands as an element in relational complexes that define various infinite series, either cardinal or ordinal. This seems no less true when 2 is the designation for the class of classes in which all members possess the characteristic of consisting of two terms. It would seem that in all the relational complexes of which 2 is an element, 2 remains unaltered as 2, that is, unaffected in its intrinsic character by differences in the complexes. However, is this not, perhaps, only a surface appearance? Let us consider the matter further. Of the class of classes whose number is 2, let us take two members, one of which consists of two atoms of a monatomic gas, such as helium, and the other of two animals of the same species, but of opposite sex. Can we say the total significance of 2 is precisely the same in each case? In one case, 2 remains 2 indefinitely; in the other, 2 is a dynamic potential tending toward numerical increase. Again, consider 2 as the limiting value of the geometrical series

$$1 + \tfrac{1}{2} + \tfrac{1}{4} + \cdots + \tfrac{1}{2^n} + \cdots$$

on one hand, and on the other, as the second member of the series of natural numbers

$$1, 2, 3, 4, 5, \cdots, n, \cdots \infty$$

In each case, 2 gives or reveals a meaning that is not identical with that of the other instances. In addition, in all these cases, 2 and the relational complexes in which it is a member stand in relation to consciousness, at least in the sense of the consciousness both of writer and of reader. It does not appear that the neorealist theory would deny that there are differences in the above complexes. Still, it would hold that the meaning in each case would reduce to a combination of 2 and a relation, with 2 remaining intrinsically the same—as is also true of any other term to which it is related—with nothing added over and above these unchanging meanings.

Criticism of this kind of theory is difficult, since there appears to be a reference to immediate experience that is not explicit. If the theory were in the nature of a formal mathematical exercise, the critique would consist simply of an examination of the logical development concerning terms that are explicitly defined and without immediate experiential content. However, neorealism is supposed to be a philosophy that deals with empiric actuality, which implies that the terms and relations are supposed to be real, not solely ideal. It is difficult, if not impossible, to avoid the feeling here that there is something in this thinking that is arbitrary and artificial. Something in the immediately given, before analysis, is lost—something that is like vision, that is not completely reducible to analysis and formulation. Can we say, for instance, that the total meaning of water is reducible to the chemical addition of oxygen and hydrogen? No doubt, the theory has a partial validity and utility, but only as an abstraction from the concrete actuality for certain purposes. Hence, when the neorealist goes further by claiming comprehensive validity, it is not easy to avoid concluding that the theorist suffers from a partial blindness.

As a correlate of the theory of external relations, the new realism affirms the complete validity of analysis. Analysis serves the office of breaking down given complexes of experience into their ultimate elements or terms, which are conceived as forming the wholes of experience by entering into various relationships. It would follow that, since relationships are external, the wholes of experience consist of the sum of the terms and relations and no more than that. Thus, the whole is no more than the sum of its parts. Sheer wholeness does not add any new qualitative character that vanishes in the process of analysis. Therefore, on this view, analysis is competent to find all that reality is. Consequently, there is no need for a mystical immediacy to know the final reality.

The ultimate nature of terms and relations is conceived as essentially logical. In their intrinsic nature they belong to a neutral region that is neither mind nor body, neither consciousness nor matter. Furthermore, the terms may enter into relation with consciousness or with the world of physical things, in either case remaining unaltered in their essential nature. A conscious being must come into adjustment with the terms and relations because they are real and not merely the creative projections of a consciousness.

This theory of the new realists is largely true about a fundamental experience of any mathematician, namely, that the material with which he or she works is, in some sense, highly compelling. Although the fundamental assumptions of a mathematician may be free creations—even fantasy constructions—as soon as he or she begins to deduce consequences he or she is not at all free to think arbitrarily. The consequences have the inevitability of an absolute necessity. The thinker must conform to this necessity; he or she cannot make it other than what it is. So, while some element of invention, such as the conventions of mathematical language and the formulations of the fundamental assumptions, no doubt enters into a mathematical system, the effect of constraint by an absolute necessity is a salient aspect of mathematical experience. Possibly more than in any other field of human effort, mathematics carries the thinker on a voyage of discovery, with the creative element occupying a subordinate position. The resistance of the rocks of the earth, or of the unconscious factors of the collective psyche, is less ineluctable, or, in any case, not more insistently conditioning. It is not the will that determines what mathematics shall be, once the fundamental postulates are given. Rather, it is mathematics that sets limits to the path that the will must follow if it is to orient itself to something more than a fantastic illusion. Nonetheless, while it is no doubt true that the determinations of mathematics are objective regarding the private wishful consciousness of the individual, it does not follow that these determinations are existences outside consciousness in every sense. We can conceive—and there are Realizations very strongly confirming the conception—of a primary and universal consciousness that conditions the merely private personal consciousness. So, we may consider the essence of mathematics as being of the nature of this primary consciousness, without the mathematical determination losing one whit of its authority and objective power.

Anyone who studies the new realism will be impressed by a certain congruence with naturalism. As was noted in the preceding chapter, naturalism grew out of an orientation to natural science, particularly that part of science that we commonly think of as physical. Neorealism has a similar orientation to mathematics and logic, such that what naturalism is with respect to physical—as distinct from biological—science, this realism is with respect to the normative sciences. Thus we may conclude that the neorealists are oriented to a much more profound necessity than that envisaged by the naturalists. Both these schools recognize a valid fact of experience, which is the experience of dealing with a compelling necessity—a somewhat that is more determining than any wishfulness. It is precisely concerning this experience that the vitalists give the least satisfactory answers in their philosophies. Whether it is vitalism or realism that has in this respect the more fundamental vision may be a question that cannot be answered in terms that transcend the relativity of individual temperament. I find myself in closer agreement with the realist view concerning this issue. In any case, the strength of the new realism appears to consist mainly in its treatment of logical necessitarianism. Its principal weakness is to be found in its depreciation of consciousness, another fundamental of no lesser importance.

For the new realist, consciousness is only a relation, which, like other relations, is external, in the sense that the terms that enter into consciousness do not acquire their intrinsic character or being by that relation. The realists maintain a view that is consonant with a conception developed by David Hume, namely, that the actual entities themselves enter and leave consciousness, while remaining essentially the same. When they are in consciousness we may call them "ideas," and when outside, "things," but these words are merely different names for the same persistent and unaltered realities. A fundamental implication is that consciousness does not creatively determine its contents; it has only a selective relationship to them. Some entities may be selected and others neglected, but they always remain just what they were in either case. The selection by consciousness may build compounds of elements through the selection of various relations, but the compounds are conceived as completely reducible to the various terms and relations. There is nothing left over, as characteristic of the compound, that is lost as a result of the analysis. Thus, this theory simply denies the experience of an immediate affective or noetic value in the compound, that is then lost in the analysis. Yet, does this denial have any greater significance than that of a psychological confession? The question whether the compound or complex of experience has what we may call an "overvalue" that is not captured within the analysis is extralogical. Our judgment must rest upon the testimony of immediate experience. If there are those who do not find this overvalue in their experience, then they are justified in reporting that, so far as their personal consciousness goes, it does not exist. Such introspective reports would be facts of importance mainly for psychology. However, the testimony of others who claim to have found the overvalue that was missing from the analysis would have no less validity. The issue between these two testimonies cannot possibly be resolved by any logical theory.

Since consciousness is conceived as a nonsubstantial and nondeterminative relation, it is quite natural for the new realist to develop a psychological and philosophical view in which consciousness is quite irrelevant. From this approach we get behavioral psychology, which conceives the determination of psychical fact as fully available for objective research without the use of introspective methods. It also conceives the mind as simply how it appears to be in objective behavior. Although it may be possible to proceed by this method to build a logically self-consistent schema, that is not yet enough to render it comprehensively true. The immediacy of inner consciousness does not cease being a fact simply because some methodological theory has no place for it. Again we have an issue that cannot be resolved without reference to testimony grounded upon immediate experience.

A particularly fundamental feature of the neorealist's polemic against the idealist is the contention that the latter has not proved that there can be no being wholly outside and independent of consciousness. No doubt the idealist cannot prove this, for it is essential to the very nature of proof that, in the act of proving, it carries its material into the field of consciousness. However, the idealist may very properly reverse the charge by challenging the realist to prove the independent being of a supposed *that* which is not knowable in any sense, or of a supposed *thatness* existing at any time apart from consciousness in every sense. He may also quite reasonably contend that the burden of proof rests with the realist, since the latter is affirming a thatness beyond the range of direct epistemological determination, thus involving hypostatization beyond all possible experience.

In the attempt to show that it is possible to know beyond the range of consciousness, the neorealist has given an illustration that at first seems quite impressive. We know, for instance, the general solution of the algebraic equation of the second degree because we have proved its correctness by rigorous logic. Therefore, we know that this solution provides a formula that will give a correct solution of every specific equation of the second degree by making the appropriate numerical substitutions for the letters representing constants in the general formula. *We know this even in the case of those equations of which no one has ever thought.* Hence, we know the actuality of an existence that no one ever has thought or experienced. In reply, two lines of possible criticism arise.

1. A radical empiricist might well question whether such supposed knowledge is authentic knowledge at all. One might contend that, even though the formula was found to be invariably valid in all the thousands of specific instances to which it has been applied, this gives

no real knowledge concerning the infinity of cases to which the formula has not been applied. In these cases, it may be claimed, our conviction of the validity of the formula is only grounded upon belief.

2. Even if we grant that the assurance of validity given by the general proof for the infinity of equations not actually solved is authentic and justified, this still does not imply knowledge of an actuality existing outside of consciousness, but only of one lying beyond consciousness in the form of specific thought and experience. Succinctly stated, the whole meaning of consciousness, as such, is not restricted to consciousness in the form of thought and experience.

The preceding discussion leads to a question of general epistemological interest and considerable importance that extends beyond the field of neorealist theory. It is a fundamental characteristic of the mathematical use of logic to develop proofs in general terms, which are completed within the limit of a finite apprehension. Nevertheless, these general proofs are conceived as giving an infinitely extended knowledge, since the specific cases they include are, more often than not, infinite in number. It is unquestionably true that the typical mathematician feels an assurance of validity extending over the whole infinity of special cases, and it would appear that the neorealist philosophers as a class also share this assurance. Is this assurance justified? Clearly this question is not one that can be resolved by logical proof, insofar as it is essentially a query relative to the validity of proof itself. It introduces a problem that requires for its resolution an examination of the very roots of cognition and an evaluation of conceptual cognition. This leads us into the sea of epistemological theory, involving all the variants characteristic of different philosophical schools, not to mention the vaster variations introduced by individual philosophies. This task will not be attempted here, but some suggestions will be offered.

There are at least three possible approaches that proposed answers to the question may take: empiric, formalistic and gnostic. None of these can be dialectically justified in the complete sense, which would finally dispose of the question. This is because their differences are grounded in differing points of view or perspective, which in turn are reducible to matters of individual psychology or of insight. In the end it appears that we are faced with the fact of philosophically significant psychological differences that are irreducible within the limits of present understanding. Notwithstanding this difficulty, we may with profit make a brief survey of these three standpoints.

1. The thoroughgoing empiricist typically denies that the authority of logic extends beyond the possibility of experiential verification. Logic

may be a valuable aid in a process of thought that leads on to a fuller experience, but its value is essentially conditional or heuristic. It does not wield an original or primary authority in its own right, but only one derived ultimately from experience. Hence, a finite logical process cannot give an infinitely extended knowledge. Consequently, the real justification and proof of a general mathematical formula derive from the fact that it is effective in the specific instance. In short, mathematics does not give us true knowledge of the infinite. The great difficulty with this point of view is that it fails to give us any adequate explanation for the success of mathematical thought, even in the empiric field. The vast preponderance of mathematical creation has been a pure development for its own sake, quite unrelated to empiric application. Yet, time and again, these pure constructions subsequently have supplied—often after the lapse of considerable time—the theoretical framework that organizes the data from experience. This observation has led no less a scientist than Albert Einstein to ask, "How can it be that mathematics, being after all a product of human thought independent of experience, is so admirably adapted to the objects of reality?" It is certainly difficult, if not impossible, to see how such a pure thought could reach ahead of experience if it is no more than a derivative from experience.

2. The formalist view maintains that mathematical entities, processes and conceptions are essentially meaningless, and thus the whole mathematical development is merely a formal structure. Of course, this would imply that mathematical thought does not really give knowledge at all, not even as much as the empiricist would grant. This view does not conform with the realist conception, inasmuch as mathematical entities would not be real. It fails to illuminate Einstein's question. On the whole, this theory does not appear fruitful, but it is worthy of note because Hilbert subscribed to it.

3. The third view, which I shall call the "gnostic," maintains that mathematical, and therefore logical, knowledge is essentially a priori, which means that it exists independent of experience. However true it may be that this knowledge does not arise in relative consciousness, in point of time, before experience, it is not derived from experience, despite the extent to which it may employ a language derived from experience. It is thus in its essential nature akin to mystical cognition—and hence gnostic in character—rather than similar to empiric knowledge. This view would explain how it is possible for the pure mathematical thinker to have prevision of the future in formal terms that subsequently become empirically concrete as experience gradually advances at its slower pace. It also explains the strong feeling of assurance extending over infinite implication that follows

upon the recognition of mathematical proof. Finally, it implies that mathematical knowledge is authentic knowledge, grounded upon an original authority. The full conception maintains that the root of mathematical knowledge is identical with the root of empiric knowledge, but that neither is derived from the other. Thus it is the identity at the root source that explains how pure mathematical thought can be relevant to the material given by experience.

Because these three views are barely sketched here, they are offered primarily as suggestions. However, the gnostic view is the one held by the writer, so its justification will be more fully developed subsequently. Inasmuch as the neorealist philosophers typically seem to accept the assurance of logical demonstration, the writer stands in agreement with them in this respect. However, he does not find that the neorealist theory supplies adequate justification for the acceptance of the assurance.

The outstanding peculiarity of the new realism does not lie in its affirmation of the independence of things with respect to consciousness, for this doctrine is a characteristic part of all realism in the modern sense. The differentiating contribution of the new realism is its doctrine of *immanence*. This is the theory that the actual things or terms enter into consciousness without being made over by consciousness. Thus the idea of a thing *is* the thing itself, when in the relationship of consciousness. Consequently, the idea and the thing are not two entities, but one. In this way the duality between mind and body is overcome, as is the duality between knowledge and things. All the while, the thing remains independent. To conclude, we may isolate as the cardinal principle of the new realism the idea of the 'independence of the immanent'.

Part of this conception suggests a similarity to the identity of the knowledge and the known, which is a characteristic part of mystical states of consciousness, but the theory of the independence of the immanent marks a radical divergence. The mystical state leads to a doctrine of interdependence, not only of the knowledge and the known, but of the knower as well.

To bring the more fundamental teachings of the new realism into clear relief, they are listed here in brief form:

1. The subject to consciousness, in other connections, can become the object of consciousness.
2. Mental action is a property of the nervous organism.

3. Mental contents consist of portions of the surrounding environment, illumined by the action of the organism.
4. The content of the mind is that portion of the environment the organism takes into account in the serving of its interests.
5. Ideas are only things in a certain relation.
6. In the case of immediate knowledge, the thing and the knowledge are identical.
7. In connections other than those of immediate knowledge, the thing is the thing in itself.
8. In mediate knowledge the thing thought about and the thought are both experienced, but the thing transcends the thought.
9. The thing is independent of experiencing as well as of thought.

The last thesis marks an important point of departure between neorealism and the more realistic wing of pragmatism. In both schools, the conceptions of the office of thought and of mediate knowledge do not diverge radically, but pragmatism tends to identify the real with experiencing. It is also true that the neorealist and the pragmatic tests of truth and error are not far apart. The former simply attaches less importance to the subjective factor. For both, truth is a harmony between thought and things, such that, in the one case, things are independent of experience, whereas in the other their nature is determined through the experiencing. Moreover, the test of truth is practical, that is, relative to a grouping of interest and circumstances, for the purpose of action. In neither case is truth an internal coherence of ideas or things. It follows that, in both cases, truth may be thought of as a function or a relation of a thinking consciousness, or organism, concerning something other, be it immediate experience or independent things.

The feature about the new realism that stands out with especial force is its enormous depreciation of the significance of consciousness. An examination of its itemized tenets gives the impression that consciousness is a sort of byproduct of the effort by organisms to attain adjustment in a preexisting unconscious environment. To be sure, consciousness here is not so unimportant as to be a mere epiphenomenon that accidentally happened in a mechanistic universe, for it serves the function of adjustment for organisms. It therefore makes some difference in the world of living creatures. Nevertheless, it is the lesser fact in the midst of an all-surrounding and compelling necessity.

Particularly notable in the new realism, as in naturalism, is the depreciation of the subjective component of consciousness. The subject is even viewed as potentially capable of becoming an object of consciousness in certain relations. More precisely, in conformity with the epistemology of neorealism, the subject that has become an object is not merely a symbol representing the subject, but is the actual subject itself. Here we have exemplified a very common error of the extraverted orientation in individual psychology, for concerning whatever it is that has become an object, its status as object implies a relation to a subject that is not the supposed subject that has become object. To be sure, something subtle associated with the true subject may become an object, but the subject remains the witness in a relationship of witnessing regarding this subtle object, and thus does not itself become an object. We may project the conception of a subject-object relationship, but the subject itself has not been projected in the conception. It still remains the hidden witness of the conception. This point is of extremely vital importance, and must be understood by whoever would personally attain Self-Realization, or would seek to comprehend the philosophical developments based upon Self-Realization.

In contrast to its relative superiority in the interpretation of mathematics and logic, the new realism seems somewhat less than satisfactory in its treatment of ethics and religion. Here we find much the same inadequacy that was so notable in naturalism. The reader at times has the feeling that these subjects enter into the total philosophical picture as somewhat troublesome addenda. One in whom the ethical and religious motives are strong tends to feel frustrated or belittled. This produces the impression that the real order of being is aloof and unresponsive to human purpose and aspiration. No doubt there is a dimension of being that has this character, or, rather, appears to have this character. Nonetheless, there is far too plentiful immediate insight that gives the real a quite opposite character to permit the neorealist view an exclusive validity. After all, the assurance of logic and of sense impression is not such as to deny other forms of assurance equal right to recognition. Finally, we must conclude that the new realism has offered an interpretation that is partly true, but no more than that. It has not succeeded in evolving a conception competent to circumscribe the whole of the real and possible. Furthermore, it fails to recognize important dimensions of awareness, at least some of which embrace that which large portions of humanity value above all else. Philosophy, if it is to fulfill its full office, must recognize and do justice to these dimensions of being, as well as those upon which the new realism is focused.

4

Pragmatism

Life as we know it, and as it appears to have always been, judging by the record of history, has consisted most largely of an effort by living creatures to survive in an environment that, while in part friendly, has yet been in large degree unfriendly toward that survival. The life story of humanity appears to be no exception to this rule. We find that the preponderant thought and effort of humankind have been devoted to the practical or mundane interest of securing food and protection from the elements and living creatures, including fellow humans. Exceptionally, from a day at least as ancient as the formulation of the Vedas,* there have always been a few among the human whole who have devoted a portion of their time and effort to a profounder investigation of nature. Their intent has been to resolve more ultimate questions, such as the meaning and purpose of life, the nature of being, and so on. The most profound part both of religion and of art and nearly all of what we know today as science and philosophy have developed out of this deeper and relatively detached questioning. These fields of human endeavor comprise the core of culture and contribute the larger part of the graces and values of living. Those who have led in the cultural side of life, either as originators or as maintainers, have never constituted more than a small, albeit especially significant, proportion of the human whole. While they have known their share of resentment and persecution by the misunderstanding masses, it is also true that, in the end and on the whole, they have received appreciation and recognition as forming a genuine *aristoi*, a sort of informally recognized elite class status distinct from others.

Among the bearers of culture, there have inevitably grown attitudes toward life, thought and forms of expression that tend, more or less radically, to diverge from those natural to the commonality of humankind. This has led toward a separation of interest and sympathy

---

*[From the Sanskrit "knowledge," the term refers to the earliest scriptures of India, beginning about 1500 B.C.E., yet based on a much more ancient oral tradition.]

that at times has amounted to a social bifurcation, so that the languages, as well as the attitudes, of the smaller class have tended to become strange and foreign to the collective mass. This inexorably has restricted the service that the former could render to the latter. As a result, from time to time there arises the necessity of reestablishing an integration or working relationship between the two parts.

In the field of philosophy, which most particularly concerns us here, the specialization of interest, way of thinking, attitude and language is especially noteworthy. Philosophers tend to write for other philosophers, thereby giving exclusive attention to the conceptions evolved in the detached philosophical consciousness. This is all quite understandable, since these conceptions are an inevitable development for a felt need, but only the trained philosopher is able to adequately comprehend them. Unfortunately, a large sector of human concern remains left out, which considerably narrows the practical office of philosophy. In the classical culture, the isolation of the philosophical world from the broader general human world was particularly notable. Science, such as there was, developed in the milieu of the philosopher, detached from practical life. The result was that, although the Greek mind was able enough, and theoretical understanding was well advanced, there was relatively little development of a practical technology. Abstract concepts became objects in themselves, unrelated to empiric utility. A distinction ultimately arose between two orders of consciousness: one, the more abstract or intelligible, was viewed as a higher, more divine order; the other, the sensuous or empiric, was regarded as irrational and evil. Apparently no culture has ever attained a greater conceptual purity than that which was realized in Greece at its peak of development, but it was a conceptuality unrelated to empiric life. Also, this was achieved at a severe price. At the height of the culture we find an aristocracy of beautiful intellectuality, and at the bottom, a massive slavery. This was a humanity so bifurcated that the masses received little benefit from the best.

The Greek dominated Western culture until that day in the Renaissance when the immortal figure of Galileo Galilei appeared upon the scene. In the hands of the scholastics, dialectical power had become refined and subtilized, but largely empty of substance, and perhaps even more divorced from the world of common experience than was true of the Ancient Greeks. However, with the appearance of Galileo, an old cycle was closed and a new one opened that has continued to the present time. Galileo's significant contribution was an insight that led to a marriage between a highly developed conceptuality and sensuous experience, the aspect of consciousness so despised by the typical cultured Greek. Out of this marriage was born science, in the modern spirit, and a vast extension of philosophic subject matter. Most important of all, from the practical standpoint, there came forth from this union technology in the modern sense, accompanied by vast alterations in social organization and in ways of life.

It is inevitable that in the modern world, as in the classical, the conceptions and language of technology, science and philosophy would develop with due regard to the peculiar necessities of each discipline. However, the attitude toward sensuous cognition was unavoidably radically altered, in contrast to the attitude of the classical thinker. The sensuous or empiric could no longer remain the despised portion of human cognition. Indeed, it has often become the most valued region, with conceptual theory falling heir to depreciation. Important as experience no doubt is, even experience has taught us that without adequate theory there can be no true science, not even technology. Consequently, we now know that we advance in knowledge, as has been said, by two legs—observation and theory. Therefore, we have not repudiated the sound features of our legacy from Greek culture. Instead, by adding to it that which the cultured Greek scorned, we have transcended his viewpoint both in theory and in practice.

The rapprochement between conceptuality and sensuous knowledge has naturally involved more than a technical advance. It was probably inevitable that it would also result in a parallel increased regard for the ways of cognition, interests, and attitudes of the ordinary person. This, though particularly marked in the zones of sociology and politics, has further had its effect in the more aloof field of philosophical speculation. In recent times there has arisen a whole school of philosophy, popularly known as "pragmatism," which questions the soundness and reliability of lofty conceptuality. Instead it has turned to the field of popular cognition and interest for its principal subject matter and basis of evaluation of the higher conceptuality.

In the hands of the pragmatist, the only kind of thinking known to most, and that all of us use most of the time in the relations of daily life, is given the dignity of philosophic recognition. In this sense, pragmatism is more popular than any other school of philosophy and, indeed, has been particularly associated with the democratic spirit. Even so, though pragmatism renders to the ordinary variety of thinking a dignifying recognition, it would be a serious mistake to imagine that the pragmatist is merely an ordinary thinker, or that this school is popular in its technical methods. Common thinking is an object for serious study and evaluation, as viewed by this school, but it treats the problems it considers with all the technical acuity of trained philosophers. Pragmatism deals largely *with* popular thinking as a type, but *is not itself* a form of popular thinking. Pragmatist philosophers, in the technical development of their thought, can and do become just as involved and obscure as any other kind of philosopher. They are not always easy to understand. So, despite the democratic orientation of their thought, they personally belong to the intellectual elite, like all others who think beneath the surface.

The popularity of pragmatism is quite different from that of naturalism. On the whole, the latter accepts an attitude toward the surrounding world that is quite consonant with the general naive view that is commonly held before the development of reflective analysis. In contrast, the philosophical pragmatist, like most other professional philosophers, is intelligently critical of this view. The pragmatist is well aware that thinking and the other psychological functions make a difference affecting the content of human consciousness—or, if he does not, this fact must be established by careful study. The naturalist typically thinks in terms analogous to those that have achieved success in the sciences of the inorganic, and, as a thinker, very largely forgets that he or she is a living being. However, the pragmatist considers life and the sciences of the organic as nearer to true human nature, thereby supplying a better key to the understanding of the contents of consciousness. Further, this life upon which the pragmatist focuses is not an abstract or Eternal Life, but the natural or empiric life seen all about us. It is the life of plants, animals and people—just that which the biologist and the psychologist study in its physical and somatic manifestations, respectively. To be sure, this implies that the pragmatist is also a naturalist in a way. However, rather than being a physical naturalist, the pragmatist might be called a "biological naturalist." He or she views biology, along with psychology, sociology, anthropology, politics, and so on, as essentially more fundamental than mathematics, physics and the more mathematical sciences generally. In the implied relative depreciation of logic and mathematics we find the primary point at which pragmatism departs from neorealism, although in other respects these two schools have many sympathies in common.

The core of pragmatic interest is the human world, not a supermundane Ideal or transcendent Reality. No doubt, empiric life involves more than the exclusively human, since we have constant evidence of other forms of life before our eyes. However, pragmatism does not pretend to speak for the possible standpoint of plants and animals any more than it does for a supermundane divinity. All these living, or supposedly living, beings may receive consideration in a pragmatic philosophy, but, if they do, they enter into the discussion as objects possessing an empiric human interest. Thus pragmatism is not, nor does it claim to be, a comprehensively inclusive system. Its validity, insofar as it is valid, is maintained to be such for humanity as we know ourselves here and now.

Pragmatism certainly does not pretend to be a philosophic system, but is rather conceived to be a definition of a method of approach to vital problems. It views philosophy as an aid or guide to an empiric life so that it may be lived more wisely, and on the whole more happily. Hence, it is more largely a philosophy of and for life than a system of ideas. Its metaphysics is the least systematic of the four schools.

Pragmatism has many roots that reach back into the British school of empiricism. Like empiricism, it gets its subject matter primarily from the raw material derived from or given by the senses. However, it departs from the earlier empiricism in that it is much more oriented toward activity, that is, more concerned with purposive action than with simple reception of impressions. The pragmatist's world is much more alive than the older empiricist world. Human consciousness is surely considerably richer than a mere blank tablet that is passively receptive to the impact of the environment. We have interests and purposes that lead to the selection of certain possibilities presented by the total environment. Our most general interest is to survive as an organism. Beyond this, it is manifest that we seek all sorts of objects and relationships, from the most banal up to the loftiest possibilities. It has remained for the pragmatist to isolate and accentuate this aspect of human nature as a significant factor for facilitating the growth of our self-understanding. The pragmatist claims that philosophy, even in its most abstract and other-worldly aspect, is, after all, simply an instance of human interest and purpose. It is not here suggested that the older philosophers or the representatives of the opposed schools of the present day were or are unconscious of the fact of interest, and of selections guided by interest. Nonetheless, it is quite true that they generally neglect this fact as a determinant factor in evaluating philosophic content. Here the pragmatist departs from the nonpragmatic thinker by maintaining that meaning cannot be isolated from the influence of interest.

At this point the pragmatist's characteristic attitude toward the psychological status of ideas becomes evident. Ideas enter into at least two systems. In one aspect they are recognizable as psychological facts, that is, as something having a history and standing in correlation with a group of more or less observable relations in some living mind, while in another aspect they carry a logically significant content. For the greater part, philosophy has been exclusively concerned with the logically significant content, so it has typically defined meaning in terms that are primarily logical. Pragmatism holds that this is a mistake. Even a perfect and logically complete content would only be, at best, partly competent in the determination of ultimate meaning, for the psychological factors of interest and purpose are also determinant. One gains the impression that the pragmatists characteristically as a class attach the greater importance to the psychological factors, with logic admitted only in a subordinate office.

One practical consequence of the foregoing theoretical evaluation of the psychological status of ideas is that proposed conceptions may be valued as much, or even more, by consideration of the purpose or motive of the thinker than by a regard for the logical acuity or factual accuracy of the content. Thus psychological facts true of the thinker become important in the philosophical evaluation of the thought. Certainly there are connections wherein the psychological conditioning of the thinker is determinant in such a way that involves the value of the content of the thought. This is clearly true in all cases involving statement of fact, particularly where the fact is not easily verified by other means. It is no less so in instances where subjective determinants form an important component of the content. In general, we may well recognize the psychological factors as possessing a constitutive importance in the zone of reflection where the perceptual referent is correlated with a conceptual statement. Distinctly apart from this, however, there is a large range of thought wherein the content is purely conceptual and objective. In particular, this is true in the case of the discovery and proof of a mathematical theorem, and only somewhat less so in the theoretical development of any science. In these latter instances we may evaluate the thought content in complete disregard of the thinker as a person. The thinker's character may be noble or vile, with normal or abnormal personal psychology, and with social or antisocial attitude; nevertheless, his or her thought is a presentation that can be judged as to its soundness quite independently and objectively. Thus, clearly the psychological evaluation of thought possesses only partial validity regarding the determination of the soundness of the content. The pragmatist has undoubtedly brought into focus a partial truth that is philosophically significant but appears to overgeneralize its application.

It is certainly true that the philosopher, being a person as well as a thinker, is conditioned by psychological determinants that vary rather radically from individual to individual. Equally, there can be no doubt that these factors play their part in providing the basic orientation of the thinker, and in giving form and direction to the thought. Unquestionably, criticism that is at all complete must have a due regard for these factors as well as for the more impersonal and rational elements, such as the factuality of references and the soundness of the logic. However, if too much stress is given to the psychological determinants, criticism may all too easily degenerate into the error of the *argumentum ad hominem.** As a result we may see philosophy fall from its lofty state of

---

*[Fallacious reasoning committed by attacking a person's character or circumstances to discredit their views or arguments.]

impersonal and detached aloofness. Issues that otherwise would be worked out to agreement, or agreement to disagree, on the high level of the forum, may be carried into the arena for final resolution. Logical issues are resolved in the forum; differences on the level of transcendental vision are resolved by the greater Light manifested by the more comprehensive Realization; but differences based upon psychological factors such as the purpose, interest and taste of the empiric individual, cannot be integrated either by the forum or the Light. When resolution becomes desirable or necessary, it tends to be achieved by either physical or psychological force.

An instance of the forcible resolution of philosophical difference, which is deeply stenciled on the world memory, is to be found in the case of German national socialism. Despite all the crudities of this movement, it was grounded in a philosophy. One who has read and brooded upon both *The Decline of the West** and *Mein Kampf†* can scarcely help but note practical implications in the latter that find their philosophical base in the former. The Spenglerian philosophy is one of the most consistent developments of the vitalistic orientation, which radically subordinates conceptualism to the will, and to psychological factors generally. It draws the conclusion that war is well nigh the essence of life, and there does not appear to be any ground for viewing this conclusion as something added to the ineluctable consequences of such an orientation. Logic stands as incompetent to resolve fundamental issues. The wars of creatures from plants to humans, and of groups and nations are the final determinants. Spengler most probably resented the form his thought took at the hands of Hitler. However, this would be more the resentment by one having the taste of a scholar and gentleman for the crudities of a vulgarian, who was no gentleman, than it would be for the essence of the Hitlerian philosophy. The fact is that purely vital issues are resolved by conflict. Thus the transcendence of conflict as an ultimate determinant depends upon the subordination of the vital by some higher principle, such as rationality or spirituality. In this fundamental sense, the powers that defeated national socialism upon the field of battle did not thereby overthrow or disprove the primary thesis of *Mein Kampf*, but merely denied survival to a specific interpretation of that thesis. The irrationalism of a psychovitalistic philosophy was not transcended by a rational power, acting in conformity with its nature. Rather, a specific manifestation of this irrationalism was overcome by a greater irrational power. The total effect constitutes a confirmation of Spengler's primary thesis.

---

*Oswald Spengler, *The Decline of the West* (New York: Knopf, 1932).
†Adolf Hitler, *Mein Kampf* (New York: Reynal & Hitchcock, 1940).

VITALISM

The foregoing illustration is pertinent to a discussion of pragmatism, since *pragmatism* is, in one of its aspects, but another name for vitalism. In this connection, we must understand the word *vitalism* with a broader connotation than is given the same term in more specialized biological theory. Vitalism, as the pragmatist understands it, includes a philosophical orientation that gives the categories of life priority over the categories of the mind or intellect. Furthermore, while it is true that, in some systems of thought, Life—spelled with a capital *L*—is viewed as the ontological or transcendental principle, this is not the sense that the pragmatist intends. The life considered by the pragmatist is the natural or mundane life that we experience and know with our ordinary faculties. It is the life of various organisms, which the biologist studies. In this respect, the attitude of the pragmatist parallels that of the naturalist, with the important difference that biological categories are viewed as more fundamental than physical categories, such as those that are fundamental in physics, astronomy, chemistry, and so on.

It is quite relevant to the attainment of an understanding of pragmatism to ask ourselves: What do we mean when we speak of "Life"? We find that besides the conception of Life as a transcendental principle there are at least two contrasted possible meanings. The word may be conceived as meaning a privative concept, defined to comprehend a certain kind of phenomenon. In this sense, *life* refers to an object of scientific study whose purpose would be to integrate the facts of life within the limits of intellectually comprehensible law. Anyone who views biology as essentially a special kind of manifestation of physics and chemistry takes this standpoint. The underlying assumption implied by this attitude, either implicit or explicit, is that life is no more than it is conceived to be. It is just another case of knowledge that, while it may not be complete knowledge today, is nonetheless regarded as capable of completion in principle. This implies that conceptual thought has the power to comprehend life and thus is a larger power, not merely one that exists as an effect or byproduct of life.

More subtly, we may think of the word *life* in quite a different sense. It may be viewed as no more than a sort of pointer to a reality that, in peculiar degree, can never be known in the conceptual sense. Thus, while we may know mathematical and other logical entities with conceptual rigor, life forever escapes this kind of knowing. What we really do know of life itself, as distinct from a conceptual symbol meaning life, is through an extraconceptual acquaintance, that is, through a way of consciousness that can never be fully thought. From this perspective, around every conceptual thought of life there lies a sort of penum-

bral field that is not part of the central thought. Although it may escape
clear analysis entirely, it may yet be glimpsed, however dimly, in those
moments when consciousness turns upon itself, as it were, and detects
a glimmer of a sort of fleeting shadow. This formless, impalpable zone
lies horizonally about the nuclear core of the concept, known darkly
like an intuition that defeats all definition. It may seem that this fringe,
rather than the conceptual core, carries the real secret of the meaning of
life. Many who affirm this view regarding the peripheral region would
contend that the nature of the fringe is such that no intellectual analysis,
however refined, can ever grasp its real nature. This is the case because
it is an essentially inconceivable life that so supports and envelops
thought that the latter can never by itself comprehend its living roots.
Hence, life is viewed as master, and thought as the servant. This
appears to be the general view held by pragmatism, in the sense of
vitalism, and particularly by Henri Bergson.

Doubtless, within nonphilosophic and nonscientific circles, the second view would normally seem more acceptable, since to regard life as
an object implies a relatively exceptional detachment where thought
itself, or something greater than thought and empiric life, supplies its
own base, or some foundation other than life. Far more commonly, life
appears to consciousness to be a mystical somewhat that conditions all
else, but that is not itself conditioned, or, if it is, that higher conditioning
is unknowable to the conceptual mind. For the most part, Western philosophy has not assumed this point of view, but some philosophers,
such as Spengler and Bergson, have maintained it. These thinkers are
classed today as vitalists.

While it is true that pragmatism is a form of vitalism, it does not follow that vitalism is always a form of pragmatism. In Spengler's case,
many features of his philosophy remind us of pragmatism, yet his
notion of Life embraces a good deal more than the life of the biologist.
His is an ontological notion that can really be apprehended only by
way of mystical intuition. The Spenglerian philosophy is not restricted
to the empirically given in the same sense or in the same degree as is
true of pragmatism. To differentiate the latter more completely we must
consider its development out of epistemological considerations.

Charles Sanders Peirce gives the epistemological definition of pragmatism very concisely: "Consider what effects, that might conceivably
have practical bearings, we conceive the object of our conception to
have. Then, our conception of these effects is the *whole* of our conception
of the object [italics mine]."* William James elaborates further: pragmatism is "the doctrine that the *whole* 'meaning' of a conception

---

*Baldwin, *Dictionary*, s.v. "pragmatism."

expresses itself in practical consequences, consequences either in the shape of conduct to be recommended, or in that of experiences to be expected, if the conception be true; which consequences would be different if it were untrue, and must be different from the consequences by which the meaning of other conceptions is in turn expressed [italics mine]."*

Inasmuch as Peirce and James were among the few most prominent thinkers in the early development of pragmatism as a philosophical school, we may quite reasonably regard the foregoing definition as authoritative. To attain a more precise understanding of their meaning, let us consider these quotations as presenting alternative formulations of the same definition. A careful study reveals that four words are crucial in the determination of its meaning: *practical, conduct, experience* and *whole*.

1. *Practical* is that which "covers all that is not theoretically or cognitively determined, but which involves purpose, teleology, striving, achievement, appreciation, ideals."† This meaning is akin to that of *practice*, which in turn is defined as "conduct or moral activity as distinguished from the strictly intellectual life."‡
2. *Conduct* is "the sum of an individual's ethical actions, either generally or in relation to some special circumstance."§ By this definition, conduct is differentiated from any arbitrary kind of action, as in the popular understanding of the term.
3. *Experience* is defined in two senses, psychological and psychic or mental: (1) "Psychological: consciousness considered as a process taking place in time." (2) "Psychic or mental: the entire process of phenomena, of present data considered in their raw immediacy, before reflective thought has analyzed them into subjective and objective aspects or ingredients."‖ James contributes the last part of this definition. He goes on to say that it is "exactly correlative to the word Phenomenon,"¶ as "it is used in a colourless philosophic sense, as equivalent to 'fact', or 'event'—to any particular which requires explanation."** The final portion of the quotation is from John Dewey's contribution to the definition of the word *phenomenon*.

---

*Ibid.
†Ibid., s.v. "practical."
‡Ibid., s.v. "practice."
§Ibid., s.v. "conduct."
‖Ibid., s.v. "experience."
¶Ibid.
**Ibid., s.v. "phenomenon."

4. *Whole* is to be understood in the sense of "entire" or "complete." Thus "whole of our conception" and "whole meaning" imply that there is no additional meaning attached to the conception above that given in the definition.

From the above definitions we derive a very clearly delimited meaning of pragmatism. We may clarify the conception still further by considering what pragmatism excludes in its use of the terms *meaning* and *truth*. Meaning and truth are denied to that which is exclusively determined by theory and cognition. This means, for instance, that a self-contained and self-consistent mathematical system that did not lead to anything beyond itself would not be true or have meaning. Sheer self-consistency is thus not a criterion of truth. To be sure, such a system might have an aesthetic value, in which case it would have a degree of meaning and truth. However, it would derive this from the value of the aesthetic feeling, not from the purely theoretical or cognitive relations or content. Thus, truth and meaning clearly depend upon a relation of the cognitive factor to something other than the cognitive thought itself. The word *whole* reveals the privative or absolute character of the pragmatic thesis. Truth and meaning, as understood by the pragmatist, do not have the signification given above in *addition* to other applications; rather, the practical or empiric significance is the *whole* of their signification. It follows that anyone who accepted the above definitions as substantially valid as a *partial* truth, provided the word *whole* were expunged, would not be a pragmatist.

Quite clearly, pragmatism is anti-intellectual, as has been so frequently affirmed by its protagonists. It is anti-intellectual in the psychological as well as the philosophical sense; that is, it denies the theory that the intellectual or cognitive functions are more fundamental than the affective and conative. It also rejects the view that the ultimate principle of the universe is some form of thought or reason, or the more modified view that reality is completely intelligible to thought. Pragmatism is also anticonceptual in the classic sense that universals are regarded as real *ante res*, *in rebus* and *post res*. Additionally, it is antirational both in the sense of reason being an independent source of knowledge, distinct from sense perception and having a higher authority, and in the sense of a philosophic method that, starting from elementary concepts, seeks to derive all the rest by deductive method, as is the process in mathematics.

So far as these determinations of what pragmatism is not are concerned, this school does not by any means stand alone, since the older empiricists maintained the same attitude, and most of Oriental philosophy would agree. Clearly, pragmatism is empiric or aesthetic (grounded in the sensible domain) and essentially nominalistic. However, in taking its orientation upon the base of experience, defined as a process in time and restricted to the raw immediacy of the senses, it departs from the Oriental aestheticism, which embraces atemporal and nonsensuous aesthetic elements. Further, in its assertion of anti-intellectualism and anti-rationalism, pragmatism has much in common with the voluntaristic branch of idealism and finds considerable support in Kant's final position. Still, pragmatism departs from the general thesis of the older empiricism by placing emphasis upon conduct and the practical. The earlier school held a relatively static view of Being, whereas for pragmatism real being approaches the meaning of activity or becoming, agreeing to a large extent on this matter with Spengler's philosophy. Pragmatism stands in contrast to voluntaristic idealism, both in that it is much more realistic and because it is antitranscendental, in the sense that the whole meaningful content of conceptions consists in a reference to experience and conduct. The antithesis of pragmatism is to be found in the rational idealism of Hegel, and even more so in the exceedingly pure conceptualism of Spinoza.

The relative human consciousness manifests through three fundamental modes that we may designate "thinking," "feeling" and "doing," or, more technically, "cognition," "affection" and "conation." In the history of philosophy, each one of these modes has, at one time or another, been given primary valuation—not merely with regard to a peculiarity of individual psychology, but even in the ontological sense. Thus, the main body of Greek thinkers, the Western rationalists and the rationalistic wing of idealism, give to cognition a prime and even ontological status, regarding which the other modes stand in either derivative or subordinate relationship. Likewise, for the voluntaristic idealists and the vitalists, conation generally occupies the position of primacy, and even, as in the case of Schopenhauer, is viewed as ontologically identical with original Being. Logical consistency would seem to allow the possibility of a school of thought that we might call "affectionism," which would assign the primacy in importance to the affections. Such a school does not appear in the mainstream of Western philosophic thought, but one is found in India. Wherever the hedonic tone of a state of consciousness is given prime valuation, the proper philosophic formulation would be some form of affectionism. In the exceptionally comprehensive and capable philosophy of Sri Aurobindo Ghose we find precisely this kind of valuation. To bring out in clear relief an orientation that is virtually unknown in Western philosophy, let us consider a quotation from Aurobindo's essay on Heraclitus.

But there is one great gap and defect whether in his [Heraclitus's] knowledge of things or his knowledge of the self of man. We see in how many directions the deep divining eye of Heraclitus anticipated the largest and profoundest generalizations of Science and Philosophy and how even his more superficial thoughts indicate later powerful tendencies of the Occidental mind, how too some of his ideas influenced such profound and fruitful thinkers as Plato, the Stoics, the Neoplatonists. But in his defect also he is a forerunner; it illustrates the great deficiency of later European thought, such of it at least as has not been profoundly influenced by Asiatic religions or Asiatic mysticism. I have tried to show how often his thought touches and is almost identical with the Vedic and Vedantic. But his knowledge of the truth of things stopped with the vision of the universal reason and the universal force; he seems to have summed up the principle of things in these two first terms, the aspect of consciousness, the aspect of power, a supreme intelligence and a supreme energy. The eye of Indian thought saw a third aspect of the Self and of Brahman; besides the universal consciousness active in divine knowledge, besides the universal force active in divine will, it saw the universal *delight* [italics mine] active in divine love and joy. European thought, following the line of Heraclitus' thinking, has fixed itself on reason and on force and made them the principles toward whose perfection our being has to aspire. Force is the first aspect of the world, war, the clash of energies; the second aspect, reason, emerges out of the appearance of force in which it is at first hidden and reveals itself as a certain justice, a certain harmony, a certain determining intelligence and reason in things; the third aspect is a *deeper* [italics mine] secret behind these two, a universal delight, love, beauty which taking up the other two can establish something higher than justice, better than harmony, truer than reason,— unity and bliss, the ecstasy of our fulfilled existence. Of this last secret power Western thought has only seen two lower aspects, pleasure and aesthetic beauty; it has missed the spiritual beauty and the spiritual delight. For that reason Europe has never been able to develop a powerful religion of its own; it has been obliged to turn to Asia. Science takes possession of the measures and utilities of Force; rational philosophy pursues reason to its last subtleties, but inspired philosophy and religion can seize hold of the highest secret, *uttamam rahasyam*.*

---

*Sri Aurobindo Ghose, *Heraclitus* (Pondicherry: Sri Aurobindo Ghose Ashram Press, 1941), 70.

It is thus a fact that corresponding to the three primary modes of relative human consciousness there have been systems of philosophy that have given primacy of accentuation to one or another of these modes. The two schools previously discussed, namely, naturalism and the new realism, quite clearly give primacy to cognition, either perceptual or conceptual. However, pragmatism clearly subordinates conceptual cognition to empiric or perceptual cognition, and, by emphasizing practice and conduct, gives preeminence to the conative mode of consciousness. Perhaps it values affection above cognition, but on this point I am unable to arrive at a definite decision. At any rate, conation receives the ascendant evaluation.

EMPIRIC VOLUNTARISM

Pragmatism, then, may be classed as an *empiric* voluntarism, in contrast to transcendental voluntarism, such as that of Schopenhauer. As a form of voluntarism, the general implications, both positive and negative, of a voluntaristic attitude, follow. There is a definite support and strengthening of those human tendencies that express themselves in performance, such as conquest of nature, missionary zeal, meliorative activities and movements, progressive education, promulgation of propaganda of all sorts, selling, promotion, building, and so on. We may well agree that much of this is all to the good, but there is another side to voluntarism that is its own ultimate law. The will may and has successfully sought to impose its idea upon other individuals, groups or nations, either for, or not for, their good. It is of the very nature of voluntarism to deny that there is any moral maxim, conceptual law or transcendental order that can serve as a supreme court for the review of its volition. Whatever willed objective is successfully brought about is, by reason of that success, morally and otherwise justified. Thus a successful national socialism would be righteous simply because it was successful. It stands today repudiated, but on purely voluntaristic grounds. That repudiation does not rely upon moral, religious or intellectual considerations; it rests simply upon the fact that, in the trial by willed force, national socialism was overthrown. According to a strict voluntarism, had the Nazis been strong enough to succeed, they would have been justified.

It is quite understandable and in conformity with expectation that, given the premise of pragmatism, there should follow the doctrine of the will to believe as a justified form of cognition. However, the will to believe, which, in the hands of William James, a cultured gentleman of superior tastes and ethical values, could eventuate in a statement with which we can feel much sympathy, is subject to no guiding modulus. It both could and would mean something very different when developed by a person of quite different character and taste, such as Joseph Stalin. Here the successfully effectuated will becomes the final authority. The good is that which the will accomplishes, and only that. This is the great dilemma of the voluntarist. On one side, will is completely free, not subject to the review of any higher authority—at the price of chaos; on the other, we have a moral and rational guiding modulus—at the price of a curtailed freedom. Howard H. Brinton, in his *The Mystic Will*,* has shown how Jacob Boehme, the greatest of all voluntaristic mystics, was troubled when he became conscious of this dilemma. As a result, he wrote at times like a rationalist. Although Boehme incarnated in his soul the spirit of nonviolence to such degree as to be the very fountainhead of the nonviolent tendency in the West, he was likewise the fountainhead of that voluntarism that is the ultimate base and justification of all violence!

The difficulties involved when pragmatism is understood as an orientation to pure activism have not escaped the attention of C. S. Peirce, the first modern pragmatist, causing him to feel some doubts. Because Peirce's mature account of pragmatism embodies some rather trenchant self-criticism, it deserves to be quoted at length, especially since it comes from the pragmatist's ranks.

> This maxim [quoted earlier] was first proposed by C. S. Peirce in the *Popular Science Monthly* for January, 1878 (xii. 287); and he explained how it was to be applied to the doctrine of reality. The writer was led to the maxim by reflection upon Kant's *Critic of the Pure Reason*. Substantially the same way of dealing with ontology seems to have been practiced by the Stoics. The writer subsequently saw that the principle might easily be misapplied, so as to sweep away the whole doctrine of incommensurables, and, in fact, the whole Weierstrassian way of regarding the calculus. In 1896 William James published his *Will to Believe*, and later his *Philos. Conceptions and Pract. Results*, which pushed this method to such extremes as must tend give us pause. The doctrine appears to assume that the end of man is action—a stoical axiom which, *to the present writer at the age of sixty, does not recommend itself so forcibly as it did at thirty*. If it be admitted, on the contrary, that action wants an end, and that that end must be something of a general description, then the spirit of the maxim itself, *which is that we must look to the upshot of our concepts in order rightly to apprehend them*, would direct us toward something different from practical facts, namely, to

---

*Howard H. Brinton, *The Mystic Will* (New York: Macmillan, 1930).

general ideas, as the true interpreters of our thought. Nevertheless, the maxim has approved itself to the writer, after many years of trial, *as of great utility in leading to a relatively high grade of clearness of thought.* He would venture to suggest that it should always be put into practice with conscientious thoroughness, but that, when that has been done, and not before, a still higher grade of clearness of thought can be attained by remembering that the only ultimate good which the practical facts to which it directs attention can subserve is to further the development of concrete reasonableness; so that the meaning of the concept does not lie in any individual reactions at all, but in the manner in which those reactions contribute to that development. Indeed, in the article of 1878, above referred to, the writer practiced better than he preached; for he applied the stoical maxim most unstoically, in such a sense as to *insist upon the reality of the objects of general ideas in their generality* (italics mine).*

Certain striking modifications of the original conception of pragmatism are revealed in the italicized portion of the above quotation.

1. Since activism appeals more to the person of thirty than of sixty, it implies that this emphasis is no more than a matter of individual psychology, and thus may not be validly converted into an ontological principle.
2. It appears that the essential meaning of the maxim is not necessarily activistic, but consists in the evaluation of the given conception by its upshot—a view that contrasts with evaluation by the source. (This would seem to be the most fundamental feature of the pragmatic method that remains.)
3. It appears that the maxim is merely useful in guiding empiric thought, but is not, therefore, necessarily an absolute criterion of truth. It is thus reduced to a mundane heuristic principle.
4. There is quite clearly an insistence upon the reality of general ideas in their generality. This would seem to bring us back to the standpoint of the conceptualist, with the consequence that the distinctive quale of pragmatism qua pragmatism very largely vanishes.

With pragmatism modified in this manner, it seems that we have left only a useful method of heuristic or pragmatic value. It follows that the idea that the *whole* meaning or truth of a conception is necessarily

---

*Baldwin, *Dictionary*, s.v. "pragmatism."

found in consequences in terms of conduct, the practical and the empiric, would have to be abandoned. In that case pragmatism would hardly have any reason for existence as a philosophic school. With pragmatism reduced to the status of a useful modulus of procedure in the movements of mundane consciousness, there does not appear any reason why a protagonist of any school of philosophic thought could not and should not also be a pragmatist in some phases of thinking. Standard pragmatism, however, by reason of the excluding restriction implied by the word *whole* in the maxim, narrows the office of conception in the sense already discussed. Even more seriously, it excludes the use of conception in relation to a transcendental meaning. This matter is of particular importance to us.

In conformity with pragmatic epistemology, *if there is a consciousness that is not conceptual, or not merely conceptual, not in time, not an immediate presentation of phenomena and not related to conduct as action, then the relationship of conception to such a consciousness cannot be classified as truth or meaning.* The immediate content of some mystical or gnostic states of consciousness has, or at least purports to have, such an immediate atemporal and nonsensuous character. It follows that the pragmatic epistemological theory either (1) implies denial of the actuality of such a mystical content, or (2) grants that such a content exists, but then affirms that the relationship of a conception to it does not qualify as "meaning" or "truth." This constitutes the second zone in which truth and meaning are denied to a conceptual relationship—the first, it will be recalled, is the zone of the relationship between concepts in an exclusively conceptual system, such as that of pure mathematics. Historically, as well as currently, the notion of 'truth' has been important, even very important, in both zones. Therefore, the pragmatic theory must imply that both of these uses of truth are without validity, and, because of this, that both of these types of conceptuality are without meaning. Neither the philosophical mathematician nor the philosophical mystic is likely to find this conclusion acceptable.

It is not here suggested that pragmatism, as such, or that all pragmatist thinkers, necessarily deny the actuality of mystical experience. On the contrary, James has treated the subject very sympathetically in his *The Varieties of Religious Experience*,* and has claimed that it deserves much more serious study. This is so, for the reason that mystical consciousness appears under two aspects: in one sense it is an experience; in another, it is an immediate content. As an experience, it is an event happening to some subject or self in time, so, as such, it falls within the

---

*William James, *The Varieties of Religious Experience* (New York: Longmans, Green & Co., 1912).

range of psychological, physiological and even physical observation. Further, the event may produce changes in the conduct of the individual involved, which may be noted and, in some measure, objectively evaluated. In this sense, mystical consciousness is a somewhat that may fall within the range of pragmatic evaluation. However, the matter is quite different when we come to consider the inward or immediate content—the psychical, as distinguished from the psychological aspect—of the mystical state. This lies beyond the range of external observation, as is also true of the immediate psychical value of any experience, such as the immediate quale of the experience blue, for instance, and can be known only by those who have realized the state. It is certainly true that historically such inward or psychical content has constituted the meaningful reference of philosophies, particularly in the Orient. Even so, the pragmatic epistemological theory rules out this sort of truth reference.

Anyone who granted the validity of the mystical or gnostic content, and of a truth relation or meaning relation on the part of a conception to such a content, but who at the same time accepted as valid the pragmatist definitions of truth and meaning in other relations, would not be a pragmatist in the sense of the definitions previously quoted. This would be true because the *whole* meaning of a conception, or of conception as such, would not be manifested in practical consequences in terms of conduct and experience. At least *some* of the meaning would be of a different sort. Superficially, one might imagine that the removal of the word *whole* from the definitions would resolve the difficulty, but this is not the case, since the independence and existence of pragmatism as a school depends upon that word. As a rather pointed example, we can easily conceive of an absolute idealist who, provided the word *whole* were removed from the definition, would say, "I also accept the pragmatic epistemology as an adequate description of conceptual cognition in its relation to the relative realities of appearance, but not in its relation to Absolute Reality." In such a way absolute idealism could assimilate the pragmatic epistemological theory as a part truth, leaving no room for pragmatism as an independent school. However, the historical fact is that epistemological pragmatism was born as the result of a polemic directed against absolutism. Thus its possibility as an independent existence lies in its emphasis on the word *whole* in its definitions. It seems somewhat ironic that pragmatism, in order to establish a position opposed to absolute idealism, needed to invoke a rather lefthanded absolutism of its own!

The argument in support of absolute idealism, as against that of pragmatism, opens a rift within the defenses of the latter whereby the former may possibly once again establish itself, if it can show to any degree, however small, that the use of the word *whole* in the pragmatist's definitions is not valid. This is the analogue of James's own thesis that pluralism is established if it can be shown, in even the smallest degree, that there is something not contained in the Absolute One. Thus, if a conception can *mean* a mystical content, and this content is neither a time-conditioned consciousness nor a perceptual experience, in the sense of the raw immediacy of sensuous presentation, then a breach is established in the walls of pragmatic epistemological theory. To be sure, this does not necessarily imply the negation of the instrumental theory with respect to the office of the concept, only that if the instrumental theory is retained, or insofar as it is retained, the concept would have at least a twofold instrumental office. One would be that which pragmatism has developed so well, wherein the conceptual idea is instrumental to an experience or practice that always includes some degree of the perceptual quale. The second instrumentality would be oriented to an immediate content that is nonexperiential—in the sense of the given definition—and nonconceptual. This latter content we may call the "transcendental" or "spiritual," in the East Indian sense of the term. The polemic of pragmatism against absolutism would prove effective to the extent that it establishes that the thesis of the latter cannot be maintained on the ground of pure conception alone. Conception would have to be differentiated from the transcendental content as well as from the perceptual. The intellectualist thesis that the fundamental and ultimate principle of the universe is some form of thought might well have to be abandoned. Whether or not the intellectualist psychology, which places cognition above affection and conation, would be retained, still the intellectual and conceptual would stand below the transcendental. In any case, the pragmatic thesis that conception is derived from perception no longer could be maintained as exclusively valid, for it is at least possible that the concept has a hidden father in the transcendental, as well as a revealed mother in the perceptual or experiential. Moreover, it is untenable on a priori grounds that the nature of the concept is necessarily in closer affinity with the mother than with the father. Recognition of the actuality of the father, and further, the realization that his nature is not less native to the son-concept than is the mother-percept, is all that the transcendental idealist needs.

PERCEPT AND CONCEPT

The instrumental interpretation of intellectual thought or conception, as developed by pragmatism, is based, in considerable measure, upon the thesis that the concept is derived from the percept, and serves solely as an office for the latter. In this connection, the percept is not to be construed as derived exclusively from sensation. Rather, its origin is something sufficiently comprehensive to include a complex of feeling and intuition as well as sensation.* Perception thus comprehends the material given by all the psychological functions except conceptual thinking, as Jung lists these functions. The pragmatist holds that perception is prior to conception, both in the sense of time and in the sense of epistemological value. With respect to the notion of 'priority in time', the study of biology, under the assumption of organic evolution, builds a very strong presumption in support of the thesis. Investigation of the psychical life of animals, particularly in the case of the higher animals, provides convincing evidence that they do have a perceptual consciousness in which there is some form of sensation, feeling and intuition. However, there is little or no reason to suppose that animals think in the conceptual sense. Thus, in biopsychology, the qualitative differentiation of humankind from all other animals inheres in the development or presence of the function or faculty of conceptual thinking. People are distinctly human because, and to the extent that, we think conceptually. From the standpoint that regards the theory of organic evolution as an all-sufficient basis of interpretation, *humanity* and *conceptual thinking* are simply the latest terms in the natural evolutionary series. If, then, we view humankind solely as a biological entity, on the whole, we clearly have achieved the most comprehensive adjustment to the environment, when compared to that of any other animal. We command the stage of life as does no other creature: We can survive under far greater diversity of conditions; and, in spite of the relative atrophy of functional capacities that are strong in other animals, we dominate the entire animal world; in addition, we have advanced far in the conquest of the inorganic sphere. Despite many remaining and new problems, humans constitute an advance over the purely animal kingdom in the art of adjusting life to environment. The key to this unique achievement clearly lies in the possession of the faculty of conceptual thinking. Therefore, there can be no doubt that the concept serves an office for life.

Does it logically follow that this is its total significance? Even though we grant that the given outline of the biohistorical genesis of the concept is substantially correct, this question remains. Here it is quite germane to point out that the biohistory to which we refer is itself a conceptual construct, not a pure perceptual fact. The history known is a history for thought, whatever else it may be. As a consequence, the ref-

---

*William James, *Some Problems of Philosophy* (New York: Longmans, Green & Co., 1911), 48n.

erence to biological evolution does not supply us with a pure preconceptual root from which the concept is supposed to be derived. The material with which we are working is so compounded that the concept is an inextricable part of it, so the problem of the inherent nature of the concept simply reappears in a new form.

The thesis that historic genesis supplies the key to significance is, itself, no more than a conceptual hypothesis, a theory of interpretation. History can be interpreted in such a way that it loses all ontological value. Thus it is possible to view all events as merely supplying occasions that arouse recognition of truth without being their source. In such a case the biohistorical process would have only the value of a sort of phantasmagoria having only catalytic significance. A consistent interpretation of history along this line is merely a question of skill. As a result, we could quite easily conclude that the primacy of perception in time casts no effective light upon the fundamental nature of conception. Consequently, the facts of biology do not prove that the total significance of conception is that of an instrumental aid to life or experience, nor that its principal significance is such. All that we can positively say here is that conception does facilitate the adjustment of a living organism, though it may have quite other relations that may be far more important.

As far as I can see, the vitalists have not established their thesis concerning the derivation of the concept, though, if they had, the conception of the exclusively instrumental value of the concept with respect to life might well follow. Yet, although the vitalist attempt may have failed, this does not imply that the instrumentalist theory may not otherwise be established. The psychological line of approach leads to substantially the same conclusion. In my opinion, insofar as it carries much more weight, it is worth our consideration.

The introspective observation and analysis of the actual quale and functioning within consciousness can lead to a philosophic statement. This seems to be the most distinctive approach to pragmatism as exemplified by James. While one is immersed in a state of consciousness, or engaged in a psychical process, it is possible to shift one's attention from the immediate enjoyment of content to the observation of the state or process itself. This step is sometimes quite difficult, as the shift of attention may, very easily, destroy the state or erase the content, but with care it can be done. In this kind of effort James was undoubtedly endowed with exceptional skill and has unquestionably made highly valuable discoveries. Not only did this sort of research contribute an important part to his psychological theory, but it also formed a significant part of its philosophical base. His theory regarding the nature and functioning of perception and conception appears to be very largely grounded upon such research. It is this phase that concerns us most particularly here.

We may best give James's root finding in his own words directly quoted from his *Some Problems of Philosophy.*

> If my reader can succeed in abstracting from all conceptual interpretation and lapse back into his immediate sensible life at this very moment, he will find it to be what someone has called a big blooming buzzing confusion, as free from contradiction in its "much-at-onceness" as it is all alive and evidently there.
>
> Out of this aboriginal sensible muchness attention carves out objects, which conception then names and identifies forever—in the sky 'constellations', on the earth 'beach', 'sea', 'cliff', 'bushes', 'grass'. Out of time we cut 'days' and 'nights', 'summers' and 'winters'. We say *what* each part of the sensible continuum is, and all these abstracted *whats* are concepts.
>
> *The intellectual life of man consists almost wholly in his substitution of a conceptual order for the perceptual order in which his experience originally comes.**

In a footnote James acknowledges the obvious fact that this account of the "aboriginal sensible flux" directly contradicts that which Immanuel Kant gave. As this contrast is historically of prime philosophical importance, and implies quite diverse interpretations of the function of conceptuality or understanding, I shall quote Kant's statement on this subject from the *Critique of Pure Reason*:

> But the conjunction (*conjunctio*) of a manifold in intuition never can be given us by the senses; it cannot therefore be contained in the pure form of sensuous intuition, for it is a spontaneous act of the faculty of representation. And as we must, to distinguish it from sensibility, entitle this faculty *understanding*; so all conjunction—whether conscious or unconscious, be it of the manifold in intuition, sensuous or nonsensuous, or of several conceptions—is an act of understanding. To this act we shall give the general appellation of *synthesis*, thereby to indicate, at the same time, that we cannot represent anything as conjoined in the object without having previously conjoined it ourselves.†

---

*Ibid., 50-51.
†Immanuel Kant, *Critique of Pure Reason*, trans. J. M. D. Meikeljohn (London: Dent, 1934), 93.

James goes on to say, not quite consistently, but I think correctly: "The reader must decide which account agrees best with his own actual experience."*

Despite James's virtual acknowledgment in the last quotation that there may be a relativity of individual psychology involved in the differences in the formulations of the sensibly given, as between himself and Immanuel Kant, he proceeds in his subsequent philosophic development as though his personal findings were universally established fact. Thus he would seem to be guilty of the "psychologist's fallacy"—his own designation—which he defines as "the *confusion of his own* [the psychologist's] *standpoint with that of the mental fact* about which he is making his report."† It may, quite possibly, be admitted that, given the perceptual base that James found through the examination of his own psychical processes, much, if not all, of his epistemological theory pertaining to the office of percepts and concepts follows reasonably enough. Even so, can an epistemology of universal validity be established in this way? Have we perhaps a statement that is valid for an individual or a psychological type, but not valid as a general truth? Both Hume and Kant most certainly found the given of sensibility in quite other form, and this fact cannot be swept casually aside. The contrast is radical: for James, a *continuum* of "much-at-onceness" in which manyness is given, fused in an original unity of perceptual flux into which the conceptual power casts "cuts" that are extracted as discreet entities, both static and timeless; for Hume and Kant, a manifold of atomic elements that, for Kant, are conjoined into unified wholes by the conceptual understanding and the transcendental unity of apperception of the Self. For James, the conceptual function introduces separation into discrete elements by abstraction from an original unified totality, while, for Kant, the conceptual understanding conjoins into the object from an originally given discrete manifold, and thus is a synthesizing function. From such contrasted bases quite different epistemologies must follow, as well as correspondingly different metaphysical conceptions.

Neither the descriptive picture of Kant nor that of James stands unsupported by other testimony. It is a historical fact that Kant's view was largely accepted by Western philosophy, but James's experience of the pure perceptual appears highly consonant with the view that holds the predominant place in the Orient. We are indebted to F. S. C.

---

*James, *Problems of Philosophy*, 51n.

†Baldwin, *Dictionary*, s.v. "psychologist's fallacy." See William James, *Principles of Psychology* (New York: Holt, 1890), 1:196; see also 2: Index, s.v. "fallacy."

Northrop for bringing this characteristic of Oriental thought and valuation into clear relief in his *The Meeting of East and West.** Indeed, Northrop builds a convincing case for the thesis that just in this valuation of the pure perceptually given we find the prime differentiation in Oriental and Occidental psychical outlook. Therefore, we cannot in a quick or offhand manner decide that either view is exclusively true, for here we do not have a conceptually deduced conclusion available for objective logical analysis. We also lack an objective datum checkable by scientific method, since the given datum is psychic in the sense of a conscious process apprehended by itself, rather than psychological in the sense of being apprehended by another. The self-observing consciousness gives material that is mostly beyond the reach of criticism because it is subjective, and so, at least provisionally, we must accept it as valid for the individual reporting what he finds. Unquestionably, we must recognize a difference in competency in the self-examination. Yet, regardless of whether the competency is limited or large, the finding must be personally determinant for the individual. As a consequence, the epistemology and general philosophy founded upon the psychic material may possess a substantial validity for the individual, and for those of similar psychological type, yet fail to authenticate an extrapolated general epistemology. We must assume that other self-determination of the psychic character of the pure perceptual supplies an equally valid ground for a quite different theory of knowledge and philosophical development.

In my own finding with respect to the perceptually given, prior to the experience of the transformation process reported,[†] the material seemed of identical nature with that described by Kant. Subsequently, upon reading James's report, I made a reexamination and found the perceptual material to be consonant with his statement. However, repeated subsequent examinations have resulted in either the continuum or the manifold, and I do not consider myself able to determine that the one view is more profound or truer than the other. This fact has forced adoption of the provisional view that the finding is conditioned by individual psychology and that the ultimate or objective nature of the pure perceptual is such that it possesses both characters at the same time. This seems like a contradiction and probably is a paradox, but it is scarcely more difficult to accept than the physicist's experience of the phenomena of light, which requires a description in terms both of corpuscles and of undulating waves.

---

*Ferdinand S. C. Northrop, *The Meeting of East and West* (New York: Macmillan, 1946).

[†]Wolff, *Consciousness*, 19-90.

We derive from Kant and James two radically contrasting theories of the origin, office and nature of conceptual understanding. For James, the concept is derived from the percept, is at all times dependent upon the percept for its ultimate meaning, and, in the end, fulfills itself by eventuating a perceptual state of consciousness or experience. For Kant, the conceptual order is a priori, that is, not derived from perceptual experience, and though not known by the relative consciousness prior to experience in time, is, nonetheless, transcendental in its nature and thus prior in its essence. It integrates the raw perceptual material and depends upon it for the predication of actuality, but not for the determination of the form of understanding. There is a considerable area of agreement between Kant and the pragmatists in that they both view the office of the concept as related to the perceptual material. Note that the first statement of the pragmatic theory grew out of Peirce's meditation upon the implications of certain portions of the Kantian thesis. Naturally, we can hardly conclude that this interpretation is true to the whole meaning of the Kantian philosophy, since modern idealism stems from this source, both in its rationalistic and in its voluntaristic forms. Truly, Kant conceived a puissant and pregnant philosophy! It is true that the Kantian treatment of the concept is moderately pejorative when compared to the view of the older rationalists, but much less so than James's account, since the latter views the concept as no more than a dependent attachment to the perceptual order. For Kant, the concept has a transcendental genesis, and, therefore, a degree of authority that is independent of the perceptual order. James does concede that the concept possesses a great practical utility in its operation in connection with percepts, since it possesses powers lacking to the latter, but that are valuable for the empiric consciousness and life. He acknowledges that the concept may operate for considerable stretches in conceptual terms exclusively, as is particularly demonstrated in mathematics, but insists that the ultimate reference must be to the perceptual. Otherwise, many conceptual problems arise that cannot be solved, such as those that have become famous and perennial in technical philosophy. James even recognizes that concepts have a substantive as well as a functional value, though he seems to view the substantive value in essentially perceptual terms and regards the functional value as definitely more important. However, the concept has a character so different from the percept that, when it builds a portrait of the world, it produces a falsification of the reality that is supposed to be of the nature of the perceptual. It serves a valid office as a pointer to the latter, but is not a representation of truth when developed in conformity with its own law in abstraction from the perceptual order.

Conceptual thought can develop a system in its own terms, employing concepts liberated from all perceptual reference, as is done in the most formal and most pure form of mathematics. In this case, the terms have been considered "meaningless" and certainly appear as such if "meaning" is restricted to a perceptual referent. In James's view, the pure perceptual continuum forms an order in itself that has no need of the intromission of any conceptual element in order that it may have existence. This order, according to James, has no meaning but is simply itself, or its own meaning, if we may so speak. "Meaning," in James's sense of the word, is an attribute or quality of the concept when it serves the office of pointing to perceptual order, or some portion of it, and the terminal value of the concept lies in the perceptual experience to which it points. He holds that there are two interconnections between the conceptual and the perceptual: (1) the birth of the concept out of the perceptual matrix, and (2) the relationship of pointer, on the part of the concept, to the perceptual, in relatively or ultimately terminal phases. That the concept can and does serve the office of pointer to a perceptual experience is not questioned here, so long as this meaning of the concept is not taken in the privative sense. However, can we truly say that the concept is born out of the perceptual matrix? If it is in some sense produced from that matrix, can we derive its complete character and nature from the perceptual source? We shall go on to examine these questions.

If the conceptual were something exclusively derived from the perceptual, and dependent upon the latter for its possibility, as the tail of a dog is dependent upon the dog, then self-contained conceptual systems would not be possible. Nevertheless, we do have such conceptual systems. Further, when we consider the inner form or organization of the conceptual systems, and of the perceptual order, we find radical discrepancies. One is not the duplication of the other, as James himself has shown at some length. Attempts to build a conceptualist philosophy that would embrace the totality of the perceptual have failed, broken by the dilemmas of many apparently insoluble problems. This we shall illustrate by one instance, specifically, that of the characters of the conceptual and perceptual continua. The conceptual continuum consists of an infinity of terms, no two of which may be selected in such a way that there will not be an infinity of other terms between them, yet each term is static and completely determinate. There are no gaps in the continuum, but also no flow or flux, and thus no becoming. In contrast, the perceptual continuum consists of no completely determinate terms, but only of parts that stand out in the sense of more or less. These are all interconnected by a stream of becoming, such that no term is identical with any other—in a sense, not even with itself—and none stands in a fixed, unchanging relationship to any other. Clearly, these two continua are radically different. We cannot set up a two-term relationship between the elements or parts of one and those of the other. We cannot do this, as suggested by Northrop, even though the two term relationship is conceived as freely in the form of one-one, one-many, and many-one. If the perceptually given were in the form of a manifold, as Kant found it to be, such a two term relationship might be quite conceivable, but we are presently viewing the perceptually given in the form which James gave it. In this form it is a flow or flux, and thus does not consist of determinate terms with which a two term correlation is possible. We must conclude that the inner form or organization of the conceptual systems is qualitatively different from the perceptual order—not merely different in degree, but diverse, in the sense of being incommensurable.

However, although the conceptual and the perceptual are orders or systems incommensurable with each other, so that the one is ineffable with respect to the other, they unquestionably do interact. Something in the conceptual system is derived from the perceptual order. Of this there can be no doubt. However, the fact that something contained in the conceptual is derived from the perceptual does not imply that the conceptual, in its total or its essential nature, is derived from the perceptual. Rather, what we have is the meeting of two powers or modes of the total consciousness that are, in their surface manifestations, alien to each other, however much they may be fused in their root source. What is being suggested here is a fusion or identity in a common root, combined with parallel manifestations, rather than a causal connection on the surface. Because of the commonality of the root, interaction is possible, but because of independence in essential development, each according to its intrinsic law,* there is an ineluctable incommensurability in the inherent character of conception and perception. We can illustrate the interaction combined with essential incommensurability by conceiving of the perceptual flux as a stream or a sea of flowing currents into which the conceptual enters as a determinate vessel that brings forth a portion of the perceptual water, as it were. The concept, in its impure or mixed form, consists both of the water and of the vessel. The water is derived from the perceptual, while the vessel is not. Pure conceptuality is a development in terms of the vessel alone, without the water.

When Kant asserts that "though all our knowledge begins with experience, it by no means follows that it all arises out of experience,"† he makes one of the most profound observations in the history of philoso-

---

Swadharma [the innate principle according to which each thing unfolds or functions within the universal order].

†Kant, *Critique of Pure Reason.* "Knowledge" here is to be understood in the sense of *conceptual* knowledge.

phy. The implication is that in the conceptual and perceptual we have two orders, neither of which is derived from the other. As a result, each is capable of independent or autonomous development in accordance with its nature. The perceptual does not need the conceptual in order that empiric life may survive, as is abundantly demonstrated by the lower forms of organism. Likewise, however much it may be true that within our ordinary experience the conceptual order does not manifest until brought into contact with experience, the conceptual is capable of operating in its own terms and in accordance with its own law, in high disregard of all perceptual elements. It does not even need the Kantian transcendental forms of perception—namely, space and time—as is demonstrated in the development of formal mathematical systems. We do not need to decide that one order gives truth while the other does not, or that truth attaches exclusively to a relationship between the two; nor do we face the necessity of concluding that one is real while the other is unreal. Perhaps we are not yet able to answer questions of this sort in the ontological sense. Even so, we can recognize that, relative to individual psychology, the one or the other order carries the greater, or even the exclusive, reality value and truth value. This opens the door to a larger mutuality of understanding and consideration.

Conceding that the perceptual and conceptual orders are, as they stand manifested to our relative consciousness, of distinct nature, neither, in its essential character, being derived from the other, we may still well inquire as to the innate character of each. Is one substantive while the other is only functional, or is each both functional and substantive, or does some other status obtain? Clearly, for James, primary substantiality attaches to the perceptual, insofar as it is both the source and the terminal of the conceptual. The conceptual enters into the picture preponderantly as a function or active agent that is valuable mainly as it leads to something beyond itself—a something that is always perceptual. Nonetheless, the conceptual is granted a degree of substantive value, apparently in the form of vague images that are associated with some—but not all—concepts and that can be objects of contemplation. Most assuredly, however, a "vague image" is not itself of conceptual character, but a form of percept, so we are forced to conclude that James did not grant to the conceptual order a conceptual substantiality qua conceptual. Rather, the conceptual qua conceptual appears as only functional. It is quite otherwise with the perceptual. It would seem that James considered the perceptual primarily, if not wholly, substantive, for he asserts, "The perceptual flux as such . . . *means* nothing, and is but what it immediately is."* Yet, there are interpretations of the percep-

---

*James, *Problems of Philosophy*, 49.

tual that vary radically from this viewpoint, as in the case of theories wherein the percept is regarded as merely the occasion that arouses the conceptual understanding into waking consciousness. Obviously, from this perspective the perceptual serves a functional office, either as a part or as the whole of its significance. Similarly, there are interpretations of the conceptual that give it a substantive value, even in the sense of prime or exclusive substantive value, for example, in the philosophy of Spinoza. There are important differences here, of interpretation or of insight, that require our further consideration.

What do we mean by function and substance? Of these two, the meaning of function is reasonably straightforward. As used in this discussion, we may understand "function" as an activity, process or constituent that is dependent for its value, significance, and so on, upon something else. "Substance," or the "substantive," is that which we may understand as the self-existent, in some measure, and the substrate of properties or processes—thus terminal, or relatively terminal, with respect to values, significance, and so on. Some philosophies abandon the notion of 'substance' entirely, as in the case of Hume's phenomenalism, much of positivism, and a great part, if not the whole, of Buddhist philosophy. However, we need not discuss this actualistic theory at this time because it does not appear to conform to the meaning affirmed by James. Practically, from the psychological or psychic standpoint, we may view the distinction between the substantive and the functional as being such that the substantive may be an object of contemplation for its own sake, more or less completely, and thus relatively or absolutely terminal, whereas the functional is not such a contemplative or terminal object, but is only a means for reaching such.

In the history of thought, rationalism or intellectualism has affirmed substantialism and the estate of contemplation as the final state of blessedness, as is notable in the philosophies of Spinoza and Leibniz. Again, we find it in the approach of Aurobindo: "For it is asserted to us by the *pure reason* [italics mine] and it seems to be asserted to us by Vedanta that as we are subordinate and an aspect of this Movement, so the movement is subordinate and an aspect of something other than itself, of a great timeless, spaceless Stability, *sthāṇu*, which is immutable, inexhaustible and unexpended, not acting though containing all this action, not energy, but pure existence."* In contrast, empiric insight has led to the nonsubstantialistic or nihilistic view that there is nothing but the movement, inhering in nothing else, as exemplified by Hume and the Buddhists.

---

*Sri Aurobindo Ghose, *The Life Divine* (New York: Creystone Press, 1949), 70.

Even though the vast rationalist tradition affirms a substantive Existent that is not revealed by sensuous experience, no matter how profoundly empiric insight may be developed, the question arises as to whether this existent is real, something more than a speculative construct. Further, if it is real, is its nature conceptual? That there is a real Existent that is not given to the sensuous consciousness, however acutely developed, is affirmed by more than pure reason. Aurobindo contends that

there is a supreme experience* and supreme intuition by which we go back behind our surface self and find that this becoming, change, succession are only a mode of our being and that there is that in us which is not involved at all in the becoming. Not only can we have the intuition of this that is stable and eternal in us, not only can we have the glimpse of it in experience behind the veil of continually fleeting becomings, but we can draw back into it and live in it entirely, so effecting an entire change in our external life, and in our attitude, and in our action upon the movement of the world. And this stability in which we can so live is precisely that which the pure Reason has already given us, although it can be arrived at without reasoning at all, without knowing previously what it is,—it is pure existence, eternal, infinite, indefinable, not affected by the succession of Time, not involved in the extension of Space, beyond form, quantity, quality,—Self only and absolute.[†]

Here we find affirmed a substantial Base, confirmed by pure reason, intuition and mystical Realization. However, it is definitely not a Substance composed of conceptual stuff any more than it is of a sensuous perceptual nature. So, while on the whole the Western rationalists, who assert the reality of the nonsensuous substantial, give the impression of meaning a conceptual sort of substance, this may be an error of interpretation, even of understanding, on their part. In other words, the intelligibly or rationally given of which they speak may be Reason plus something more. This I am convinced is the case. What they saw clearly was that there is a somewhat that has no part in sensuous experience, most definitely is quite other than that, but that is given with certainty to profound insight. It would follow then that if there is nothing other

---

*"Experience," as used by Aurobindo, is not restricted to the raw immediacy of the senses, or a time-conditioned process, but embraces the ways of consciousness that I have called "Realization," "Recognition," "Enlightenment," etc.

[†]Ghose, *Life Divine*, 73-74.

than perceptual and conceptual knowledge, this somewhat must belong to the conceptual order. However, it is possible that it belongs to another more transcendental order of consciousness that is isolated only with difficulty. Provisionally, we may then say that the pure Existent is neither conceptual nor perceptual.

Whether or not there is a conceptual substantiality, of a nature not reducible to percepts or a transcendental order, is a question we shall leave open here. The essential point of the present critique of the pragmatic epistemology in general, and that of William James in particular, is the thesis that the conceptual order is not completely derivable from the perceptual, and that its meaningful relation is not exclusively to an ultimately perceptual referent. There remains at least a possible a priori referent that the concept may mean, even though, one way or the other, the whole office of the conceptual order may be that of instrumentalism.

PRAGMATIC SCIENCE

There can be no doubt that the fundamental maxim of pragmatism is of authentic utility in many applications. This is particularly true in the case of natural science, but "science" in this sense means a particular way or form of knowledge, not knowledge in every possible sense. Natural science is a body of knowledge delimited by its methodology. It is governed by three heuristic principles:

1. The data or material of scientific knowledge is grounded in sensuous observation and restricted to the generally possessed sensory equipment and scientific instrumentation.
2. The organizational concepts or theories introduced to transform the mass of selected observation into a conceptually thinkable system are invented or intuited postulations.
3. The interpretative postulates must be of such a character that it is possible to infer consequences of such a nature that they may be verified or disproved by means of an indicated observation, either with or without a devised experiment.

Such a methodology uses concepts in a way that satisfies the pragmatic prescription. Surely science in this sense is *for* a program or purpose, not a detached presentment of the real as an object for pure contemplation. Theory is an instrument employed toward a practical end, in the philosophical sense of the term, although, of course, this practicality is not necessarily to be limited to the sense of a narrow utilitarianism.

Natural science is unavoidably a source of truth only in the pragmatic sense, owing to the limitations imposed by its methodology. Nonetheless, an analysis of the attitudes revealed by at least some scientists suggests a feeling for knowledge in a more ultimate sense, such as that of the Gnosis. Why else is there a preponderant preference for pure science, as contrasted with applied science, shown by the greater scientific thinkers? Here we have revealed an orientation to truth, not as a means to some practical accomplishment, but rather as an end or value in itself. Most assuredly a conceptual formulation of truth is less than Gnostic Truth, and the Gnosis is not grounded in a sensuous realm, as is natural science. Yet the feeling for truth as a value in itself, albeit inadequately conceived, is the sign of an interest that is more than pragmatic. It is a principle well recognized among pure research thinkers that a motivation guided by a consideration of possible practical utility acts as a barrier to successful research. The pure quest for truth, whatever it may be, is the royal road to fruitful results, not alone in the development of detached theory, but even in laying the basis for future utilitarian applications. We may even say that the pure scientist, to whatever extent he or she may be constrained to employ a pragmatic methodology, nonetheless is motivated by a love of truth as a terminal value. Thus the pragmatic theory of cognition is insufficient to explain the whole of the scientific process, just as the logistic interpretation of mathematics is inadequate to achieve an understanding of mathematical creativeness.

The degree to which our scientific disciplines confirm the pragmatic theory of knowledge varies among the sciences. Those sciences most closely related to empiric life—namely, the biological sciences and psychology—most largely confirm the pragmatic theory. This might well be anticipated, since this school is most closely oriented to this division of science. However that may be, this theory is progressively less adequate concerning the other sciences as they become increasingly mathematical, and fails most notably in the interpretation of pure mathematics—the field in which the new realism has its greatest strength. If pure mathematics consists only of conceptual elements, it certainly is freed from admixture with the perceptual, and thus is not subject to the methodology of the empiric sciences. Consequently, the pragmatic theory has only a restricted validity even in the field of science itself.

The general thesis of pragmatism, that there is a nonintellectual form of knowledge or awareness, is one that we can hardly question. However, the further thesis that this form is more fundamental and comprehensive does not necessarily follow—or it may be true in some respects, but not in others. Additionally, the pragmatists classify this other form as perceptive in the sense of being experiential, with experience defined as "the entire process of phenomena, of present data considered in their raw immediacy."* If we take a concept from a part of the perceptual flow, then it is clear that the total flux is more than the concept, but the latter in its universality has an extension reaching far beyond any particular concrete experience. Thus, in one sense the perceptual is more comprehensive than the conceptual, but in another sense the reverse is the case. We may never all agree concerning which kind of comprehension is vaster, since the relativity of individual psychology and insight is determinant here. Again, regarding the question as to which is the more fundamental, much depends upon the theory that the thinker entertains about the origin of the concept and the percept. If the conceptual is viewed as wholly derived from the perceptual matrix, then clearly the latter is more fundamental. However, if both are viewed as derived from a common source, but not the one derived from the other, then there does not appear any simple way in which we could determine that either is more fundamental in the ontological sense.

Pragmatism is not only anti-intellectual, it is also prosensational, or provital, or proexperiential. This means that sensational experience and life are more fundamental and more bedded in the Real than the concepts of the intellect, or the intellectual order as such. One may agree with pragmatism concerning its anti-intellectualism in the sense that intellectualism means the identification of things with what we know of them in reflective thought—with nothing remaining. Even so, we may diverge from the pragmatic viewpoint on vitalism and sensationalism. There is a Gnostic or Supramental Knowledge that is quite other than sensational cognition, vital intuition or perceptual intuition, yet this Knowledge is truly more fundamental and comprehensive than the conceptual order. Pragmatism is not only anti-intellectual, but also anti-transcendental. The primary focus of the present critique is aimed at the latter feature.

GNOSTIC REALIZATION

Transcendentalism may be no more than a postulate of reason, in which case it is a speculative construct not grounded in experience or any other form of immediacy. However, it may also be a conceptual construct based upon direct Realization, which may be known as Gnostic or mystical Enlightenment. For a consciousness that has no acquaintance with direct Realization, the notion of a 'transcendental Reality'

---

*Baldwin, *Dictionary*, s.v. "experience."

tends to appear fantastic, since it does not seem to be a content of common experience. It also does not seem to be a necessity for the reasoning process, except, perhaps, in the restricted Kantian usage of the notion. From this latter point of view, the hypothesis of a transcendental Existent, however greatly it may facilitate a philosophic formulation, suffers from the defect that it can never be authenticated by common experience. Thus it seems more in the spirit of natural science to abandon the notion entirely and proceed to the construction of philosophic interpretation exclusively with concepts that mean elements, complexes, relationships or processes lying within the limits of experience. In contrast, for a consciousness that possesses direct acquaintance with Gnostic Realization, such procedure inevitably appears arbitrary and inadequate. The latter may grant that, if we were to isolate that section of total consciousness that we may call the "human empiric" and "conceptual," then the pragmatic epistemology and general philosophy forms a substantially accurate interpretation. Nevertheless, it would be ultimately incomplete and could not satisfy more than a part of human need, since a portion of the total human need requires the Transcendental for its fulfillment. From this standpoint, pragmatism is inadequate, and even in some measure malicious, insofar as its orientation to the empiric is exclusive or privative.

One may contend that mystical or Gnostic Realization is a form of experience, in which case it could be embraced within the pragmatic meaning of the term and therefore be a possible referent in the forms of pragmatic epistemology. The expression *mystical experience* does occur in literature, for example, in the writings of both William James and Sri Aurobindo. Even so, to validate such usage the meaning of the term *experience* must be widened substantially beyond that given in Baldwin's *Dictionary*, and which appears as the sense directly affirmed or implied in pragmatic philosophy. Certainly, mystical states of consciousness do occur as *events* in the life of an individual, so to this extent we are dealing with a process in time, such that the event itself is a phenomenon. To this degree we may validly speak of a mystical or Gnostic experience. However, it is quite otherwise when we consider the meaningful content of the states. At least some of these states—and all that are authentically Gnostic—have a content that is timeless and noumenal, and thus fall outside the definition. I believe the definition of the word *experience* as given is perfectly correct and is in conformity with the general understanding of the term. However, if we restrict experience in this sense, then it becomes necessary to recognize other forms of immediacy, such as Gnostic immediacy.

A Gnostic immediacy may be the referent of a body of conceptual thought, in which case we may regard the conceptual or reflective thought as significant only in the instrumental sense. Yet, it would not be instrumental to an empiric immediacy, and therefore not identical with the instrumentalism of pragmatic epistemology. Although this is clear where the Gnostic Realization is sharply defined as neither thought nor experience, as in the case of preparatory meditation in which both intellective and sensuous process is silenced, there remains the sphere of Gnostic insight that is not pure, but mixed with conceptual or empiric elements, or both. Here confusion in interpretation may arise. The actual state of consciousness of an individual may seem pure or simple, whereas sufficiently profound criticism will reveal that it is a complex of functions or faculties. The Gnostic and the empiric may be so fused as to appear to be of one sameness with sense experience. Furthermore, this fusing may occur between the Gnostic and intellective thought, with the result that the whole complex seems simply to be the pure Reason. Here lies the source of the self-evident truths and innate ideas, which formed so important a part of rationalist thought before the time of Kant. Kant made it clear what the pure reason qua reason is, and adopted a pejorative attitude toward the Transcendent in the Gnostic sense, thus tying reason to experience in the narrow sense. In spite of Kant's treatment, the Reality for Gnostic Realization does not therefore cease to be, nor does the fusion of a partial gnostic insight with the faculty of reason cease to carry authority. In this respect, by isolating reason qua reason, he did not thereby invalidate the insight of the rationalists and Platonists.

Whether Platonic ideas, self-evident truths or innate ideas are grounded in pure reason, or a combination of the Gnosis and reason, once the insight is given, the rationalist method remains valid as a philosophic process. Philosophy can be, in some range of its activity at least, a deductive development analogous to mathematics. As such, it would be no more necessary for this kind of philosophy to justify its conclusions by reference to a narrow empiricism than it is for pure mathematics. We are not at all justified in assuming that all Truth is correlated with the empiric, in the narrow sense of the definition.

What I am suggesting here is that the alternative to empiricism is not *necessarily* intellectualism or rationalism in the sense of a pure reason, *in the Kantian meaning of the term*, as a source of knowledge independent of sense perception. The alternative may be a philosophy grounded upon a third form of cognition that is more fundamental, more primitive, and more authoritative than either sense perception— and likewise perceptive intuition and vitalistic intuition—or conceptual cognition. The present work is by no means unique in that it is a formulation of a philosophy of that sort, as can be verified by reference to the main streams of Indian philosophy, and at least the philosophy of Plotinus among the Greeks. This standpoint is presented very clearly in Plotinus's letter to Flaccus.

> External objects present us only with appearances. Concerning them, therefore, we may be said to possess opinion rather than knowledge. The distinctions in the actual world of appearance are of import only to ordinary and practical men. Our question lies with the ideal reality that exists behind appearance. How does the mind perceive these ideas? Are they without us, and is the reason, like sensation, occupied with objects external to itself? What certainty could we then have, what assurance that our perception was infallible? The object perceived would be something different from the mind perceiving it. We should have then an image instead of reality. It would be monstrous to believe for a moment that the mind was unable to perceive ideal truth exactly as it is, and that we had not certainty and real knowledge concerning the world of intelligence. It follows, therefore, that this region of truth is not to be investigated as a thing external to us, and so only imperfectly known. It is within us. Here the objects we contemplate and that which contemplates are identical—both are thought. The subject cannot surely *know* an object different from itself. The world of ideas lies within our intelligence. Truth, therefore, is not the agreement of our apprehension of an external object with the object itself. It is the agreement of the mind with itself. Consciousness, therefore, is the sole basis of certainty. The mind is its own witness. *Reason sees in itself that which is above itself as its source; and again, that which is below itself as still itself once more* [italics mine].
>
> Knowledge has *three* [italics mine] degrees—Opinion, Science, Illumination. The means or instrument of the first is sense; of the second, dialectic; of the third, intuition. To the last I subordinate reason. It is absolute knowledge founded on the identity of the mind knowing with the object known.*

We have recognized three forms of knowledge: Opinion, or perception (in modern terms); Science, or conceptual cognition; and Illumination, or transcendental cognition—introception (in the terminology of the present work). Reason, science or conceptual cognition occupies

---

*Plotinus, "Letter to Flaccus," quoted in Robert A. Vaughn, *Hours with the Mystics* (London: Gibbings & Co., 1895), 79-80.

a position between the other two, but is seen as having its source in what is above, Illumination, and stands in a relationship of hierarchical superiority to sense perception, which lies below. Plotinus's philosophy is grounded upon Realization, not mere inventive speculation. Therefore, we have a relationship in the hierarchy of knowledge that is found by self-examination. Thus it is grounded in a self-searching similar to that upon which James grounded his theory of the relationship between concept and percept, though the discovered relationship is radically antithetical. What are we to conclude about such disagreement? Is one competent and correct, while the other is incompetent and in error? If not, shall we assume equal competency, but with difference of results growing out of difference of perspective? I think that an affirmative answer to the last question will afford the most just view. At any rate, assuming that the answer is affirmative, then it would follow that James's position that concepts are born exclusively out of percepts is a partial truth, valid only if the word *exclusively* is expunged. The authority of Illumination is too great to be disregarded.

If reason—that is to say, the intelligible or conceptual order—is derived from a source above it and is at the same time in hierarchical transcendence with respect to the perceptual order standing below it, then it will most naturally have affinity with the Illuminative order of cognition, greater and more immediate than the affinity between the latter and perceptual cognition. Still, there is abundant ground for recognizing that a correlation of this sort, which bypasses reason, does exist. However, the difference between these two types of relationship is analogous to the distinction in military communications known as "communication through channels" versus "around channels."

A certain important consequence follows from the interrelationship of the three types of cognition, as given by Plotinus: specifically, the universal of the conceptual order is in closer affinity with the Illuminative Cognition than is the particular. In other words, the general concept is that which appears from the standpoint of concrete sense perception as abstraction away from the immediately given. However, when viewed from the perspective of Illuminative Cognition, it is closer to the immediately given—and is closest when the concept is most general, and therefore most universal. Since it is from general or universal concepts that the largest deductive development is possible, it follows that a philosophy grounded upon the Illuminative Cognition would elaborate itself mainly as a deductive system. Such systems do not derive their authority—however much they may derive illustration—from sense perception, perceptual intuition or vital intuition. Here we can see the possibility of a mathematics that is not mere logicism or formalism, but, rather, a revelation of truth as it is behind appearance or phenomena.

These considerations should illuminate Spinoza's philosophy, with respect both to its form and to its substance. His system purports to be a necessary development, in mathematical form, of certain fundamental conceptions, so that the truth of the consequences depends upon the truth of the antecedents, with no need of any other kind of dependence. Truth in this sense may be viewed as a legislative authority with respect to experience. Naturally, for a consciousness that is grounded solely in perceptual immediacy, a development of this kind seems peculiarly irrelevant, but to a consciousness that commences with a mystical or Gnostic immediacy of the type reported by Plotinus, the situation is quite different. In the latter instance, the knowledge with which the system begins is known originally and immediately, with far stronger assurance and authority than anything given through perception. From this standpoint a critique of Spinoza would consist of the following three phases:

1. Is the initial insight based upon the Reason alone, or is it grounded in some other power of consciousness?
2. Are the initial conceptions correct formulations of an adequate insight?
3. Is the logical development correct?

The question would not arise as to whether the conclusions were authenticated by experience. They might or might not conform to conclusions drawn from experience, or, what is more likely, they might in part conform, in part contradict and in part have no relation to common experience. The only important practical or ethical question would be: Do they serve to orient consciousness in such a way that it tends to develop toward, or awaken to, the initial Realization? There is something in this that reminds us of the pragmatic maxim, in that the practical test of any truth is by leading consciousness to a somewhat that is other than a concept, but this novel application would involve an inverted pragmatism.

We assume that the pragmatist has been successful, or at least may be successful, in showing that there is no knowledge that has its original source in the concept, or pure conceptual order, and that no ultimate terminal lies in this order. Yet, this achievement, by itself, is insufficient to prove that the sole origin and the sole terminal lie in experience, in the sense defined. To completely justify the maxim, the pragmatist must demonstrate, at the very least, that there is no such thing as Illuminative Cognition in the sense Plotinus has formulated. It is difficult to see how this possibly could be done, any more than could a hypothetical non-sensory being prove to our satisfaction that there is no such thing as sensation. The intellective power is simply not competent to disprove the actuality of any immediacy. The fact that a given individual, or a large class of individuals, has not known a certain type of immediacy is irrelevant so far as its factuality is concerned. This constitutes the essence of the present critique of pragmatic epistemology.

IDEALISTIC PRAGMATISM: SCHILLER

Our discussion of pragmatism would be incomplete if we failed to consider the idealist wing of pragmatism as represented by F. C. S. Schiller. The view he develops, while in fundamental methodological agreement with the conceptions of Dewey and James, differs from that of the latter philosophers in that it abandons their naturalistic realism, a characteristic that is quite explicit in John Dewey's *Logic*.* Schiller starts with a fact that has been of prime importance for all idealism since Bishop George Berkeley. He expresses it explicitly as follows: "The simple fact is that we know the Real *as it is when we know it*; we know nothing whatever about what it is apart from that process."† This fact of cognition is, for Schiller, as for the idealists generally, the foundation stone of ontology, the theory of the nature of Being. Here we have a principle of philosophic procedure that is of primary importance to many philosophers, so we may profitably devote some consideration to it in its general form before proceeding to the discussion of the special form of Schiller's treatment.

It is a fact recognized by the more thoughtful realists, as well as insisted upon by all idealists, that all we ever cognize is an existent in consciousness. Whether this existent is regarded primarily as a conception, a perception or a volition—differences of view that have led to the classification of idealists into subschools—in every case we meet this existent as a fact in consciousness. The realist, who acknowledges all this, would say that this fact is merely an incident characteristic of the cognitive process, which leaves the real Existent, as it is, unaffected. However, the idealist insists that the characteristic of Existence, as it is in consciousness, is the characteristic of Existence as it is in itself, or per se. Certain idealists have attempted to prove this thesis logically, but with respect to this effort the realist's criticism, under the headings of the "fallacy of definition by initial predication" and the "fallacy of the ego-

---

*John Dewey, *Logic* (New York: Holt, 1918).
†Friedrich C. S. Schiller, *Humanism* (Freeport, NY: Books for Libraries Press, 1903) 11n, quoted in Ralph Barton Perry, *Present Philosophical Tendencies* (New York: Longmans, Green & Co., 1912), 217.

centric predicament," does seem to be effective. It will profit us to consider these critiques.

"Definition by initial predication" means the defining of any idea, fact or thing by the circumstances of its first manifestation to our cognition. Thus my first cognition of gravity might be the experience of seeing an organic object, such as an apple, fall from a tree. If I subsequently defined gravitation in such terms that being an organic object was essential to the notion, I would have defined by initial predication. There is an obvious error in such a definition, since other than organic objects are clearly subject to gravitation. Any valid statement of the law must be such as will account for all instances, while excluding everything that is not essential to the conception. In the case of idealism, this criticism applies in the sense that the appearance of the existent in consciousness is only the accident of the first appearance and may not validly be made a determinant of the Existent as such. Therefore, it has not been shown that the Existent is an Existent for consciousness and only for consciousness. The force of this argument may well be granted, even though all that it has achieved is a refutation of proof in the logical sense. It has not disproved the existence of the fact whose significance the idealist continues to maintain. Further, there is a fundamental weakness in the argument in that there is no second or other subsequent appearance or experience of the Existent that contrasts with the initial experience in this respect. In the illustration of the falling organic object, the case is different because we do have additional experiences of falling inorganic objects. This fact makes a very important difference. The error made by the idealist in this matter is attempting a logical demonstration where his real ground lies in immediacy, just as the greenness of a green object subsists in immediacy and cannot be proved.

The so-called fallacy of the egocentric predicament is akin to that of initial predication. It is a fact that it is impossible to conceive of anything apart from consciousness. In particular, in terms of relative consciousness, it is impossible to cognize anything that does not stand in a conscious relationship to a knower, witness or subject. As usually conceived, this knower or witness is regarded as the ego, so we have the primary fact of relative consciousness that all cognition stands in relation to a conscious ego. By ordinary, nonmystical means we cannot escape this. Thus, if we try to compare the object of consciousness with what we may suppose it to be apart from all relation to an apperceiving ego, we are stymied at the very beginning of our effort. We may compare an object as it is for pure perception with what it becomes for conception, but in neither case do we get something outside consciousness in every sense, nor do we find anything that is not in relationship to a cognizing subject. The critical realist acknowledges the factuality of the predicament, but denies that this is sufficient to justify the claims that only ideas exist or that only objects for consciousness exist. Again, we may accept the validity of the criticism so far as the matter of logical deduction or induction is concerned. We may quite well grant that in formal, logical terms the idealist does beg the question. Nevertheless, this criticism carries force only if the realist can produce a conceptual system that does not involve an analogous error of equal or greater magnitude.

On this issue, however, the realist does beg the question much more egregiously than does the idealist. If we do predicate that there is an Existent outside consciousness in every sense, then we are making a statement concerning that of which we can never know anything whatsoever. As a matter of knowledge, we cannot validly affirm even bare existence of such an Existent. If we believe in it, then that is an act of violent will to believe that can hardly be surpassed by the most superstitious religious belief. Further, what possible meaning attaches to the notion of a forever unknowable unknown for every possible form of cognition there may be? How can we possibly distinguish between such a supposed existence and absolute nothingness?

The idealist is on quite unassailable ground if he affirms only that which he knows, which therefore is an existent for consciousness, and makes no affirmation or denial concerning the existence of the supposed unknowable unknown, but simply points out that the notions of 'existence' and 'nonexistence' of an eternally unknowable unknown are quite meaningless. The predication of this sort of unknown may have a pragmatic value as a convenient fiction, Schiller quite rightly notes. However, it is the *predication*, not the supposed unknown, that has the pragmatic value, and predication is an act within and of consciousness. Still, if we can dispense with predication and replace it with another conception of such a nature that it is in principle verifiable, and that has an equal or greater pragmatic value, then we shall have established our philosophy upon a sounder base than that known to any form of realism. Such a conception will be offered later in this work.

So far, I believe the position taken by Schiller is the soundest of all the pragmatists, but as we follow his thought further, serious difficulties arise. In basic conformity with the other pragmatists, Schiller restricts, or seems to restrict, consciousness to the notion of 'experience'. We now find, in addition to the general criticism of this aspect of pragmatism given, that in the case of idealistic pragmatism there are further problems. The experience treated by Schiller and other pragmatists is the experience of empiric human beings, not a total experience of an Absolute. How does this kind of experience become organized into a unity, social or otherwise? For the realistic pragmatist, there is a possible unity provided by the commonality of the supposed real order outside experience, but this order does not exist for the idealistic pragmatist. Absolute idealism provides the organizing modulus either of a Transcendental or of an Absolute Consciousness, but such a modulus does not exist for Schiller. As a result we are faced with a relativism of specific experiencings that are not unified by any rational or transcendental principle. Schiller derives an ethical metaphysic, but scarcely provides any means for choosing from among the empirical ethical orientations of the social body, save that of successful social imposition. If the ethics of Hitler were successfully imposed by the sword, then Hitler would have won the empiric argument. There would be no higher court to justify an adverse moral judgment. Schiller's strength is his idealism; his weakness lies in restricting consciousness to the experience of the empiric human being.

TEST BY CONSEQUENCES

It is neither part of the writer's present purpose to develop a comprehensive exposition or critique of pragmatism, nor any other current school of philosophy. The point is rather to clear the ground for his original formulation, which involves certain incompatibilities with many current views. Beyond this restricted project, there is no intention to attempt to prove that any extant system or philosophic orientation is completely false or unsound. It seems to the writer that most philosophies constitute a cogent formulation, in at least some measure, of genuine insight into being or knowledge, or of acquaintance with fact or experience. For the most part, error arises through giving a too sweeping, or even exclusive, extension to systems of thought that are only partial. Full recognition of their partial validity is freely offered, along with the critique of important defects.

The writer feels that pragmatism has made a durable contribution to philosophic thought, one that any future philosophy cannot disregard if it is to establish itself upon a sound basis. Thus the pragmatic analysis of the percept and the concept, including their interrelations, is a valuable continuation and advance upon the criticism provided by Kant, and, like the work of the latter, must be taken into account in any future metaphysics. However, pragmatism adheres to an exclusive orientation to experience, so conceived as to close the door to the Transcendental, and the type of cognition that renders the Transcendental available to human consciousness. Consequently, pragmatism so enormously restricts the field of human consciousness as to close the gate to those values that form the most essential part of higher religion and religious philosophy. As a philosophy that is oriented exclusively to mundane interests, pragmatism has a great deal to offer as a modulus in the field of action, but this is not the whole of human existence. There are rich values to be known only in a state of contemplation, and there comes a time, at least to some, when one feels a need for values that transcends the desire for action. Here the orientation is to the substantive, rather than the activistic or functional. It is quite likely, as Peirce testifies, that pragmatism is a philosophy more suited to the needs of youth than to the spirit of age and maturity. Eventually, we must all face the mystery of death and the dissolution of at least a phase of organized consciousness. The philosophy that provides the greatest preparation for this transition, so that it may be faced with confidence, trust and even assurance, would seem to have met the greater need. After all, the cycle of material activity plays but a small part in the vast reaches of Eternity.

No doubt the supreme criterion of pragmatic philosophy is the principle of *test by consequences*, which stands in contrast to *test by source*. Equally, there can be few qualms that in many situations the test by consequences is the only available method by which empiric humanity can evaluate proffered conceptions. This is an application of the old maxim, "By their fruits you shall know them," but raised to the status of a universal and exclusively valid principle. However, with all its unquestionable utility, this criterion has serious limitations. A given empiric consciousness, even the whole of empiric consciousness as a type, may fail to apprehend the full range and bearing of the consequences. As a result, a judgment of soundness, desirability, "warranted assertibility," or the opposite, may be made, whereas a fuller knowledge would reverse the judgment. We may illustrate the difficulty by considering Plato's allegory of the cave.* The prisoner who escapes from the cave and finds the light world, then returns with conceptions based in the light world, would most likely find that his conceptions would not be acceptable to the dwellers in the cave, whose cognitions have been confined to the shadow world. Conceivably, some of those conceptions might be verified, in some degree, by the test of consequences within the terms of the shadow world, but to the largest extent they would fail such attempts at verification. Undoubtedly, for the most part they would seem like rank heresy, with all the implications that follow. Tested by consequences exclusively, such ideas would have little or no positive value for those who would choose to remain bound in the cave consciousness. Suppose, though, that among the cave dwellers

---

The Republic of Plato (514a-517a), trans. with an introduction and notes by Francis MacDonald Cornford (Oxford: Oxford University Press, 1945).

one or more accepted as an avatar—a divine descent from a transcendent order—the person who returned. Let us further suppose that whoever did so also accepted in faith the conceptions offered, because of their assumed source, then proceeded to think and act in conformity with the implications of these new and strange notions. The probable outcome would be eventual escape from the cave, which would allow subsequent verification of the conceptions.

The great limitation of verification by consequences lies in the fact that it assumes the understanding and insight of the present, existing empiric human being as the power or standard for the evaluation of the consequences. It is easy to see how the greatest ultimate good and truth could appear from the perspective of the present empiric consciousness as something unattractive, unsound, and even malign. There may be conjunctures in human history when disaster can be avoided only by the hieratic imposition of certain truths, with their implications. Any change wrought in the human consciousness by this means can have the effect of rendering the given consequences attractive, sound and benign. In the two situations, the test by consequences leads to quite divergent evaluations.

To be sure, pragmatists do quite generally accept the notion of 'evolution' as an active operating principle resulting in the development of human consciousness. Indeed, for Dewey, the development is a fundamental conception. This implies that the valuation based upon consequences is subject to progressive modification. However, this development is, quite naturally, viewed as a continuum in the evolving empiric consciousness. Yet, while one may recognize a degree of validity in this conception, the difficulty remains that it can be finally valid only on the assumption that the sole process in the transformation of human consciousness is as a continuous evolutionary development in the empiric field. If it is true that the total process in the transformation of human consciousness is in the nature of multiple continua in discrete relationships of transcendence with respect to each other—as may be illustrated by the notion of 'multiple dimensions'—then the conception of development exclusively within the terms of one evolutionary continuum is inadequate. It is reduced to an incomplete truth, which, by being insisted upon too exclusively, can retard the realization of the higher possibilities of humankind.

A study of the history of Gnostic transformations renders quite clear that here we are dealing with alterations of states of consciousness and of self-identification that involve relationships of discrete transcendence. These states are often, if not generally, incommensurable. Here, then, we have at least one field in which the test by consequences fails.

The test by consequences, when viewed as the sole criterion of truth and soundness, tends to the enthronement of the *consensus gentium** as supreme authority, and, in the absence of universal consent, to the general exaltation of majority opinion and evaluation. This tends to drag culture down to the dead level of mediocrity, since the valuation of the majority tends to be that of the medial intelligence, character and taste. Superiority of truth-insight, moral standard, level of taste, and so on is neither initially nor naturally part of the medial level of human consciousness. These things are instead the contribution of the few who stand or march in the van of human progression. The valuations of the latter tend to fare ill before the *consensus gentium* at the time of their presentation, notwithstanding the degree to which they may slowly percolate into the common consciousness through the passage of time. The result is that the test by consequences, when too greatly exalted as a criterion of truth and value, tends to retard the development of the higher possibilities in human consciousness. If the goal of humankind is for each to exceed oneself, if this goal is such that we must leave behind what we are at present in order that we may become a something more, which as yet we cannot understand and properly value, then the test by consequences is insufficient when applied by the general acceptance of the majority. It is here that pragmatism fails.

---

*Baldwin, *Dictionary*, s.v. "consensus gentium." [Taken from the Latin, meaning "universal consent, common consent, or catholicity, considered a proof or test of certain principles."]

5

Idealism

Does consciousness exist? No question is more fundamental than this, because a thinker will develop her philosophy and orient her life in conformity with the form and substance of her answer. To many, the writer among them, the question seems redundant, since nothing appears more self-evident and certain than that consciousness does exist. Still, serious and able thinkers, including William James, who have questioned its existence ultimately arrived at a negative conclusion. This causes one to pause and ask just what is meant when the existence of consciousness is doubted and even rejected. That some should deny, while others affirm, the existence of the world is easy to understand, but that the existence of consciousness should be in all seriousness disbelieved seems to be the ultimate in fantasy. Surely, for certain states of consciousness, the world appears to be no more than an essentially meaningless phantasmagoria, yet the existence of consciousness remains as an indubitable and ineluctable fact. A very important sector of Oriental thought takes its stand upon this view, not upon the basis of mere speculation, as often happens with Occidental philosophers, but upon the ground of direct Realization. In any case, that a number of serious philosophers have given negative answers to the question compels us to carefully consider the issue.

What do we mean by "consciousness"? A profound study of the subject reveals that here we are dealing with a somewhat that is essentially indefinable. It is that which is presupposed even in the possibility of definition, but is never itself the object defined. Nevertheless, it is possible to indicate or point to what we mean by consciousness by bringing this state into contrast to a state of another sort. For a first approximation, this has been done rather well in the following words:

> "Whatever we are when we are awake, as contrasted with what we are when we sink into a profound and dreamless sleep, that it is to be conscious. What we are less and less, as we sink gradually down into dreamless sleep, or as we swoon slowly away; and what we are more and more, as the noise of

the crowd outside tardily arouses us from our after-dinner nap, or as we come out of the midnight of the typhoid fever crisis," that is consciousness (Ladd, *Psychology, Descriptive and Explanatory*, 30).*

No doubt the experience described is quite common, though we do not know enough to say that it is universal. Therefore, we generally know, with greater or lesser adequacy, the distinctive reference of the notion of 'consciousness'. However, a careful study of this experience as we actually pass through it raises considerable doubt whether we have secured an essential contrast between consciousness and a real and complete unconsciousness. Thus awaking may be from out of a dream experience, where a shifting in the mode of consciousness, with a possible fading of the dream into irrelevance and even complete disappearance from memory, is sharp and clear, with the apperceptive mass of the waking state suddenly replacing the dream. Yet both states, with all their divergence of content, affective quale and conative attitude, nonetheless, are united in the common feature of being conscious. Again, as one wakes from dreamless sleep, the moment of transition, plus a usually brief interval while waking consciousness progressively assumes dominance, may be marked by a residual hedonic tone of delight, which may well lead one to regret the awakening. There can be a somewhat clear feeling of movement from delight to relative pain, even though the relative hedonic tone of the waking consciousness at the time is of a superior and positive sort. Because of this, the contrast, even in the awakening from dreamless sleep, is not between consciousness and an absolute unconsciousness. It appears, rather, as a contrast of one conscious state with another, within a whole or common denominator of consciousness. Therefore, Ladd's descriptive definition more correctly isolates a state of consciousness, rather than pure consciousness, as such. There is a wide, if not universal, custom in Western philosophy and psychology of attributing to the word *consciousness* the meaning suggested by Ladd. However, no matter how greatly this may be justified from the standpoint of a superficial psychology, it tends to produce a restriction in understanding that renders incomprehensible the very foundation of idealistic philosophy. Consequently, we must delve into the sense in which some have made the judgment that consciousness does not exist.

In the following excerpt from Ralph Barton Perry's essay "The Philosophy of William James," the sense in which consciousness is denied existence is brought out fairly clearly.

---

*Baldwin, *Dictionary*, s.v. "consciousness."

If by a thing's existence you mean its separate existence, its existence as wholly other than, or outside of, other things, as one planet exists outside another, then consciousness does not exist. For consciousness differs from other things as one grouping differs from another grouping of the same terms; as, for example, the Republican party differs from the American people. But this is its true character, and in this sense it exists. One is led to this conclusion if one resolutely refuses to yield to the spell of words. What do we find when we explore that quarter to which the word 'consciousness' directs us? We find at first glance some particular character, such as blue; and at second glance another particular character, such as roundness. Which of these is consciousness? Evidently neither. For there is no discoverable difference between these characters, thus severally regarded, and certain parts of nature. Furthermore, there is no discoverable community of nature among these characters themselves. But continue the investigation as long as you please, and you simply add content to content, without finding either any class of elements that belong exclusively to consciousness, or any conscious "menstruum" in which the elements of content are suspended.[*]

The idea presented in this quotation seems to be that consciousness exists in the nature of a selection of one or more things, which then form the content of consciousness, out of the totality of all things that exist. These things are what they are and unaltered by reason of existing inside consciousness or outside it. Among all the things that one can select, he cannot find one thing or group of things that may be designated consciousness, in contradistinction to other things. In addition, it is affirmed that one cannot find "any conscious 'menstruum' in which the elements of content are suspended."[†] To summarize, consciousness exists only in the sense of a selection or relationship, within the existent, but does not exist as a constitutive substance supporting things, or as a menstruum or field in which contained things or objects are suspended.

The conclusion attained is reached through a critical examination of experience in the form of a scrutiny of the mental or psychic states or activity that the thinker actually finds within himself. Thus it is grounded upon something more fundamental than dialectic, namely, an immediate finding. However, such discoveries are relative to the cognizing individual, and may not be safely universalized into a general

---

[*]Perry, 352-53.
[†]Ibid., 353.

judgment. It certainly is a psychological confession that may have validity only for a particular psychological type. In any event, it cannot rule out the possibility that a self-searching by an individual of a different type, or of a different kind of power, may lead to quite different results. Indeed, other searches in this zone have led to quite diverse conclusions. We find supporting testimony in the following Oriental sources.

In the general exposition of the philosophy underlying the Tantric works, *Sat-chakra-nirupana* and *Paduka-panchaka*, as given by Arthur Avalon in *The Serpent Power*, we find the following statement: "The ultimate or irreducible reality is 'Spirit' or Pure Consciousness (Cit, Samvit) from out of which as and by its Power (Sakti) Mind and Matter proceed."* Again, from the great work of Aurobindo, the present-day leading exponent of the Indian Vedanta—a different philosophic system from the Tantra—the following quotations are extracted from a number of statements of similar import:

It then becomes apparent that what we see as consciousness must be a Being or an Existence out of whose substance of consciousness all is created.†

It is true that there is no such thing as an objective reality independent of consciousness; but at the same time there is a truth in objectivity and it is this, that the reality of things resides in something that is within them and is independent of the interpretation our mind gives to them and of the structures it builds upon its observation. These structures constitute the mind's subjective image or figure of the universe, but the universe and its objects are not a mere image or figure. They are in essence creations of consciousness, but of a consciousness that is one with being, whose substance is the substance of Being and whose creations too are of that substance, therefore real. In this view the world cannot be a purely subjective creation of Consciousness; the subjective and objective truth of things are both real, they are two sides of the same Reality.‡

These quotations from Indian sources are of particular importance for the reason that typical Indian philosophy is not of the nature of mere speculative constructs, but is made up of formulations based

*Sir John Woodroffe [Arthur Avalon], *The Serpent Power* (Madras: Ganesh & Co., 1924), 26.
†Ghose, *Life Divine*, 643.
‡Ibid., 645.

upon Realizations or immediate insights. Quite pointedly, the results are so different from that given in Perry's quotation as to lead to incompatible interpretations. Here is an issue generated from divergent immediate findings; therefore, it cannot be resolved dialectically. Mutual recriminations between the two parties would be even less fruitful. Then, if we are to assume, as I think we must, that the findings of both parties are authentic, as far as the searching extended, then the remaining possibility of a resolution of the difference lies in determining whether one insight is more comprehensive than the other and reveals a zone within which the latter has partial validity. The second quotation from Aurobindo meets these specifications. Here the essential statement is that though there is no objective reality independent of consciousness, from the perspective of the surface human mind, and therefore of the relative consciousness, there is an independent objectivity. Truly, consciousness restricted to the latter sense is not a "'menstruum' in which the elements of content are suspended."* If the consciousness of the idealist is to be understood exclusively in this restricted sense, then James's critique carries substantial force. However, for one who knows consciousness in the deeper sense, the figure of the menstruum carries considerable validity, for there are levels of direct Realization in which one finds a field of consciousness quite capable of dissolving the objects or contents suspended within it. Thus, we may conclude that there are fractions or forms of consciousness that do not have existence, in the sense that James denied their existence. Yet, in a deeper sense, there may be a Consciousness that is the substance and support of all things. At any rate, the thesis that such a Root Consciousness is the ultimate Reality is the cardinal principle of idealism.

IDEAS: PLATO TO KANT

The word *idealism* is not in all respects the best term for the designation of our present school, since its ultimate etymological reference is to the "idea." However, not all systems of thought that are classified as idealism—for example, the philosophy of Schopenhauer—are primarily oriented to the *idea*. The common feature of idealism is an orientation to consciousness, in some sense, or to some element, elements or complexes whose nature is part of consciousness. Therefore, in the technical sense, all these philosophies are to be classified as spiritual because the common meaning of the term *spirit* is "the conception of that which is

---

*Perry, 353.

conscious."* Thus it would appear to be a better practice to designate the school, when considered as a whole, as "spiritualism," taking care not to confuse this meaning with the popular conception of communication with disembodied entities, whether supposed or real, by means of a medium. Unfortunately, even this term, as commonly employed in Western philosophic thought, is hardly broad enough to embrace all philosophic orientations that find ontological primacy in consciousness in some sense. This is due to the generally held view that spirit is that of which consciousness is an attribute, rather than consciousness itself being spirit. It is for this reason that I have been unable to classify my system simply as idealism, and instead have coined the term *introceptualism*.

As distinct from this, I suggest that we use the term *spiritualism* to refer to the whole school of thought that has oriented itself to conscious being, regardless of the phase of consciousness that is given primacy. Meanwhile, let us reserve "idealism" for the subclass wherein primacy is given to the idea in some sense. Spiritualism is negatively defined as the orientation that stands in strongest contrast to materialism, naturalism and realism, where the latter school is understood in the modern, rather than the medieval, sense—which is a form of spiritualism. Common to materialism, naturalism and realism is the conception that ultimate reality is a nonconscious existence—not in the sense of Von Hartmann's Unconscious—and that consciousness arises as something derivative that may be quite irrelevant, or may be selective, but is neither creative nor constitutive. We shall attend first to the form of spiritualism that most strictly may be called "idealism."

The roots of idealism, so far they are as traceable in the history of Western thought, are to be found in the early or pre-Socratic philosophy of the Greeks. However, at this stage of reflective thinking, the idealistic and realistic tendencies are so far intermingled that the sharp cleavage that is so notable today is lacking. The first clear statement we have of philosophic materialism was given by Leucippus and developed by Democritus, his better-known pupil. Paralleling this development we have the first sharp delineation of the idealistic tendency in Democritus's younger contemporary, the justly famous Plato. One finds the primary reality in the notion of 'body'; the other finds it in eternal Ideas [the Forms]. Although these two orientations are traceable as the expressions of complementary attitudes to the present, the predominant influence for religion and philosophy is unquestionably that of Plato.

With Plato we have the clear emergence of the conception of ideal elements as ontologically significant and determinant. For example, we

---

*Baldwin, *Dictionary*, s.v. "spirit."

have such conceptions as 'tree', 'table', 'goodness', 'truth', 'beauty', 'justice', and so on, about which, in the history of philosophy, there has been extended discussion as to their real status, but without final resolution. Are they notions corresponding to real existence, or are they merely abstractions of common features from concrete and particular experiences? It is unquestionably true that, so far as sensuous experience is concerned, we do not deal with treeness, as such, or goodness, as such, for example, but with particular trees, good acts or persons, and so on. If one's feeling of reality is exclusively associated with these particular experiences, then he or she would be disposed to view the general conceptions as only nominalistic abstractions. They might be valuable for communication or manipulation, but they would neither be realities in themselves nor correspond to such self-existent realities. In contrast, for some individuals the feeling of reality is associated, predominantly or exclusively, with the general or, rather, universal qualities. In this case, the universals seem self-existent and substantial, whereas the concrete presentments of experience seem like shadows or mere phenomenal appearances of the preexistent universals. Persons of either type may develop a philosophic world view in conformity with the nature of their reality feelings. However, while argumentative conflict arising from this divergence of viewpoint may motivate, and has resulted in, the mutual perfecting of these respective systems, it has generally failed in the conversion of the individual of one type over to the view of the other. The significance of this is that, although the representatives of both types employ the same logic, they diverge in their primary insight and reality feeling, which is essentially extralogical and of the nature of aesthetic immediacy. Then, if we are to come to an understanding of the truth contained in these conflicting views, and achieve a just appreciation of their significance, we must find some other approach than that of dialectic. In modern analytic psychology, we have a means to this end that goes far toward the resolution of the problem.

Before we can properly appraise the contribution of modern analytic psychology, we must step across the centuries from Plato to Immanuel Kant, who gave to the essential Platonic conception its most important modern formulation. Moreover, to understand the significance of Kant's contribution, it is necessary to realize something of its office in the course of philosophic development. At the time Kant appeared on the scene, the stream of philosophy was divided into two divergent, though fundamentally complementary branches, commonly known today as "rationalism" and "empiricism." Rationalism, founded by René Descartes, had culminated in the dogmatism of Christian Wolff, who endeavored to derive everything by a method of deduction paralleling the processes of mathematics. This resulted in a system that was very largely unrelated to the material of actual experience. The other, or empiric, branch of the stream had flowed in opposition to Descartes, through John Locke and Bishop Berkeley to David Hume. Here we arrive at the conclusion that the sole reality consists of a sequence of sense impressions and inner introspective states, without any material or mental substrate, and without any basis for supposing the sequence to be governed by either natural or logical law. On one side, we find a dogmatism where there is an abundant emphasis on a principle of organization and order, yet no relationship to actual experience. On the other, there is a skepticism that, while closely bound to sensuous immediacy, and thus fully recognizing the force of brute fact, affords no security or certainty with respect to those values most vital in human consciousness. These include uniformity and measurability of nature, the reality and persistence of the Self, and the actuality of the Divine. Thus philosophy had come to a dead end that could satisfy the needs neither of a theoretical or systematic science nor of the religious consciousness.

The high valuation that Kant has generally been assigned by the philosophers who succeeded him is no more than just, if for no other reason than that it was he who found the way out of the impasse that philosophy had reached. This remains true, even though *all* his specific conceptions may have to be modified in the light of a later and fuller comprehension, insofar as he was the force that drew together the divided, though essentially complementary, streams of thought and gave new direction and vitality to future thought. Furthermore, Kant is significant in a considerably larger sense than that of synthesizing the Western philosophic stream, for it was he who opened the way to the bridging of understanding between the Western and the Oriental minds. This latter service was not so much contributed directly by Kant, who was not, and never claimed to be, a metaphysician, as by the main stream of philosophy that was founded upon and received impetus from his most fundamental conceptions, namely, German idealism or, rather, spiritualism. One who is familiar with the thought of Kant, and with the rational and voluntaristic spiritualism that it engendered, can turn to Buddhist and Vedantic philosophy without finding it wholly strange and meaningless. To be sure, important differences remain, due to the pervasive grounding of the matter of Oriental philosophy in Gnostic Realization. Western philosophy is more largely, though not wholly, guided by a logical modulus, as indicated by the influence of Meister Eckhart and Jacob Boehme upon Hegel. Nevertheless, the parallelism of the ultimate conceptions in these Oriental and Western developments is sufficiently close so that a conceptual crossing without undue intellectual strain is possible. This we owe in a profound sense to the labors of Kant, who thus may be the greatest synthesizing or integrating force in the whole history of thought.

Kant develops his synthesis of the two philosophic currents by the acceptance of the determination as to fact that Hume had formulated, along with an equal acceptance of the recognition of principle, or law, that was the primary vision of the rationalists. Kant, as a physical scientist concerned primarily with theoretical development, is well aware that neither factor nor component could be disregarded without destroying the possibility of any such science. However, Hume's analysis shows that on the basis of experience through the senses alone we can have no knowledge of law or assurance of an order in the universe. Yet, despite all this, science, especially in the form of the Newtonian development, builds theoretical constructions that fit with remarkable reliability the matter subsequently given through the senses. Clearly, there is some law or order, conforming in high degree with our logical thinking, that somehow governs the material supplied through the senses or by sensuous intuition, to use Kant's term. If law or principle is not given by pure experience, and yet is known with an assurance not inferior to that of experience, and, in addition, is even empirically vindicated by the power of theoretical science to prognosticate future experience, then from whence do we derive this knowledge of law and principle? Kant's answer is that our knowledge of law, principle or order—in short, of all truth, as distinguished from knowledge of fact—is innate or a priori. That is, we carry in the subjective dimension of our consciousness predetermining forms that, while they may not condition nature as it may be supposed to be apart from consciousness, nonetheless determine the form of our possible experience of that nature. We are not born as John Locke imagined, with minds in the state of blank tablets upon which the realities of the objective are written just as they are. Rather, we carry a framework in our minds, as it were, that fixes in advance the limits of possible experience. Insofar as there may be supposed to be a nature, or phase of nature, that could leave no impress within the terms of these forms, we could never know of its existence. However, we can know the conditioning forms of our experience (transcendental aesthetic) and of our thinking (the logical forms of the understanding) because they are already present in the mind, even when newborn. Thus it is possible to build a theoretical science that is reliable with respect to the phenomena given in experience, but we can predicate nothing with respect to nature or the thing as it is in itself. In a sense that is not individually voluntary, we legislate the law and order governing possible experience, and therefore can know it. It is of little moment, as Kant contends, that we do not actually cognize these forms and law temporally prior to experience. The essential point is that instead of deriving them *from* experience, experience is the *occasion* on which knowledge of them is born. In short, they are logically prior to all experience, notwithstanding that actual cognition of them may be chronologically subsequent to experience.

We need not enter into the detailed development of the idea, which is very complex and often difficult to follow, for we now have a conception of how a human individual could have an ordered experience and could know necessary governing laws, *so far as he or she individually is concerned*. Admittedly, so far this provides us with only a private or solipsistic field of ordered phenomena. If we are to conceive of humankind as a community of actual individuals, and not merely phenomenal appearances within my unique and private consciousness, then more is required. To meet this difficulty, Kant contributed what may be his most important conception, specifically, the idea of a transcendental Self or Ego, which may be called "objective" with respect to the empiric or psychological ego of the individual, since it conditions the latter. Here "objective" is not to be understood as objective in the sense in which we apply this notion to the not-self, or nonego, or content of a consciousness apperceived by a self or ego. Rather, it is to be understood as an impersonal and universal Subject, such as an Absolute Self or Subject. In some way the Transcendental Self lays down the forms of possible experience and thought such that the private or individual subject is as much conditioned inwardly by this as it is by the matter of external experience. Thus we have a basis for cognizing forms and laws that are not merely private, but that are generally valid for all individuals. Indeed, we now see the possibility of communication with mutuality of understanding, and that is not wholly dependent upon a commonality of the aesthetic component of experience. In contrast, on the basis of the Humean position, intellectual communication would be impossible. The only possibility of conveying anything would be by evoking, as by an appropriate use of art, similar aesthetic states of consciousness. In refutation, in fact we can communicate intellectually, and in the purest forms of this communication, as in mathematics and logic, there may be a complete absence of aesthetic evocation. The full Kantian conception provides an explanation of how all this is possible. Thus Kant leaves us with a conceptual framework that effected a vaster integration for understanding than had ever been provided before.

That Kant's philosophy is not complete and, in the sequel, proved in certain respects unsound, detracts little, if at all, from its importance. It opened the way to the most fruitful speculative thought that has ever been known and, whether the subsequent thought was built upon the foundation of his philosophy or by an adverse criticism of it, Kant has been, in either case, a philosophical stimulus of the highest power. There is some basis for believing that no conception has ever been produced, or ever will be produced, that will be eternally and immutably valid. Whether this is true or not, ideas that widen and broaden the stream of thought and understanding are to be regarded as among humanity's most precious possessions. In this respect, at least, Kant's legacy has a lofty and enduring value. It deserves no less honor than the earlier achievement of Plato. Further, it is permanent in its effect, even though every particular Kantian conception may be ultimately surpassed and even forgotten in the foreground of philosophic enterprise. Even though the steps by which we climb the cliff of consciousness may in time erode or break away below us, but for those steps we would not be where we now are. So, the steps that are gone are, in a profound and occult sense, permanent and enduring.

Kant's two most primary conceptions—namely, the forms or ideas that underlie experience, and the Transcendental Self—are crucial determinants in the development of the spiritualistic philosophy that grew out of his thought. Of these, we shall give first consideration to the Idea.

Kant and Plato agree in attaching an a priori primacy to certain Ideas that are of an extraordinary universality, but there is a characteristic difference in the way they view these Ideas. For Plato they appear as *metaphysical* self-existences, whereas for Kant they appear as *epistemological* predeterminants. Plato did not clearly distinguish between the judgments of knowledge and being, whereas Kant recognizes that metaphysical reality, as it is in itself, is something other than our knowledge of it—at least concerning our common nonmystical forms of cognition. Despite these significant differences, however, the basic agreement that there are fundamental preexistent Ideas establishes a far more important ground of commonality. Consequently, the primary issue that we must address in the valuation of the authenticity of idealism is whether such Ideas really exist, and how we may determine this.

One might easily imagine that these real or supposed preexistent Ideas exists only in the sense of a speculative construct or postulate, introduced for the theoretical handling of a problem, in the way that is common in modern science. In that case, the only test of their validity would be the pragmatic trial by consequences. However, they may be knowable directly through insight, in which case they are much more than speculative constructs and have a more or less ineluctable character, analogous to that of well-attested facts of experience. It is upon the question of the status of these Ideas that light is now shed by analytic psychology.

THE PRIMORDIAL IMAGE: JUNG

Just as humans are born with a characteristic anatomical structure that differentiates our species from other animal creatures, so also do we enter embodied life with a psychical organization that predetermines the general form in which our consciousness may develop, irrespective of the extent to which the *specific* form of that consciousness may be conditioned by environmental factors. Modern analytic psychology, through the development of methods adapted to the study of this kind of subject matter, has afforded us a means for an empiric investigation of psychic material so that we are not entirely dependent upon the insight of Platonic or Kantian genius.* These conditioning psychical forms, as reported in the works of Jung, differ from the Abstract Ideas of Plato, and the Categories of Kant, in that they appear as concrete, collective images that, because of the latter characteristic, Jung designates as "primordial" or "archetypal." They are images that are not mere reproductions of objects, as given through the external senses, but are of a sort that arises spontaneously from an untraceable source, therefore called the "Unconscious." They find their analogue in the mythologies of various peoples, in alchemic symbols and in the mandalas that play so prominent a part in the Oriental psychology of the transformation process. Their original character is similar to perceptual images, rather than to the form of conceptual ideas, but they differ from external perceptions in that they predetermine ways of *viewing* experience, while the latter present us with *facts*. Just as one becomes conscious of external fact by an extraverted movement in consciousness, so one may animate and bring above the threshold of consciousness the primordial images or archetypes by a process of unusually profound introversion. We have, thus, a means of research in this subjective dimension that, in some measure at least, frees us from a somewhat blind acceptance or rejection of the general conception that there are predetermining Ideas, as enunciated by Plato and Kant.

The primordial images of Jung differ from Platonic Ideas, not alone in the sense that they are in their initial form quite nonconceptual, but in the further respect that they are not truly eternal. They are indeed very ancient, representing, as it were, the view of a million-year-old consciousness for which the phenomenon of the passing moment would be rather improbable, but they are conceived to be a deposit in time. With respect to the fleeting elements or complexes of experience, they are

---

*Carl G. Jung, *Psychology of the Unconscious*, trans. with a preface by Beatrice M. Hinkle (New York: Dodd, Mead & Co., 1927); see also *Psychological Types*, particularly the definitions of "image," (554-60) and "idea," (547-51).

truly hoary; nevertheless, because they are deposits in time, albeit a vast time, they are less than eternal. Thus they enter into the total picture of the empiric consciousness in a sense that is analogous to the parameter in mathematics: they are relatively permanent with respect to the current experience of any embodied individual, but are not ultimately permanent. Jung does not give, nor does he pretend to give, a description of the ultimate derivation of the relative consciousness of humankind, since he restricts himself to statements that can be empirically verified. Even so, he has isolated by empiric means imaginal factors that serve the office of predeterminants, or a priori components, in the present concrete consciousness. In so doing, he has gone some distance in confirming the primary thesis of Plato and Kant.

That Jung speaks of "primordial images," whereas Plato and Schopenhauer speak of them as "Ideas," and Kant calls them "transcendental forms of aesthetic intuition" or "categories of the understanding," does not constitute a distinction of fundamental consequence. What is of paramount importance is that, in any case, they are a priori or preconditioning factors. It follows that the psychically received and accepted world is not the world as it might be known to an absolutely pure consciousness—a consciousness unconditioned by being an object for a subject—but is a world that is mirrored in the relative consciousness, and the mirror has a shape or character largely defined by the a priori components.

Jung views the autochthonic primordial images as the maternal soil from whence arise the general conceptual ideas that have the abstract, definitive and rational character that is the typical mark of a conceptual system. Hence, the Idea, thus conceived, possesses solely a secondary or derivative character. Here Jung stands in essential agreement with Schopenhauer's thesis. We are also reminded of the view advanced by James, with the difference that James appears to be speaking exclusively of externally derived perceptions, or images derived from the concrete and particular object. Jung, however, insofar as he is speaking of the Idea derived from the primordial image, means a perceptual matrix that is subjective, but even though this matrix is also concrete, it is nonetheless universal. The Jungian archetype, like the fundamental and essentially Platonic Ideas of Schopenhauer, is a concrete universal that stands as the source of the abstract conceptual universal. One may agree with Jung and James that in some sense the primordial image and the particular percept, with objective reference, both constitute material soils underlying the concept—in the one case, the more general ideas; in the other, the ideas with more particular and objective reference. Yet it remains true that the concept, whether more general or more particular, has features in its total character that are not reducible to either matrix, such as being more or less completely definitive. In both cases, between the concept and the primordial or the particular percept, there is a relationship of incommensurability as well as of meaningful reference. The matrix, in either case, is aesthetic or irrational, yet the most notable characteristic of the engendered "child" concept is rationality. We must conclude that something is added in the concept itself that is not reducible to the matrix.

It becomes evident that we must look further if we are to complete the derivation of the abstract and rational or the conceptual ideas, whether in the sense of the a priori universal concept or the a posteriori concept having objective perceptual referents. Though the primordial image and the external percept together are doubtless sufficient to maintain an embodied consciousness, that consciousness would be something less than that which we actually find manifested in the human being. It would be an exclusively perceptual consciousness, having a sense mind, but not an intellectual mind. Briefly, the being would not be capable of reasoning, though a perceptual, and probably autonomous, thought would be possible for it. The surface consciousness would be engaged in external perceptions, but the subliminal mind, bearing the primordial images, would remain hidden in impenetrable unconsciousness. We can see how this equipment could be adequate for meeting the task of adjustment between a living organism and its environment, for animals that have abundantly proven their ability to survive are clearly endowed with this sort of organization of consciousness. It is quite conceivable that an evolutionary development of this type of organization could lead to the establishment of entities far in advance of animals as we know them. They might very well have a capacity for quite superior states of consciousness—even states of consciousness that, in the purely spiritual sense, could far transcend those attained by most humans. However, despite all this, we would not have human beings anywhere in the evolutionary series, since the power of rational thought and of conceptual communication would not have arisen. Likewise, there would be lacking the power to turn and objectively reflect upon the states of consciousness for their analysis and ultimate mastery.

Before going on to the derivation of the rational component, which is the distinctive sign of the human qua human, it may profit us to reflect further upon what is achieved by the addition of the primordial image to the external perceptual equipment to which Hume reduces human cognition. He leaves us with a wholly unpredictable and anarchic play of insubstantial images, without any possibility of integration in terms of form or law. This feature is corrected by the introduction of the primordial image to the extent that it now becomes possible to see how a perceptual order or dependability is possible. Part of the task that Kant performs is thereby effected. The conscious entity functions within a framework of order and a kind of reliability within its world of experience, though it would be lacking the powers of understanding, discrimination and judgment, and could never construct a science, nor even produce a Humean philosophy. Even allowing for all this limitation, which would eliminate the whole rational dimension of our consciousness so that there would be no science, mathematics, philosophy or art of the characteristic Western sort, a purely aesthetic art of the type of the Zen Buddhist's constructions might conceivably remain. What is more important, a kind of enlightenment would remain a possibility, so the potential for a religious motif would not be excluded. To be sure, a careful study of Chinese Taoism and Buddhism, particularly in the Ch'an or Zen form, suggests that a central aim of that discipline is the elimination of the rational component from consciousness, so that we have left a consciousness composed exclusively of the outer and the inner perceptual factors. In terms of these, the religious objective is the shifting of identification from the external perceptual factor to the inner, or primordial, and then transcending the latter as image. Becoming conscious in this final stage is Enlightenment. From the study of these Chinese sources, the Western reader may well derive the impression that the writers viewed the development of a rational power in humanity as unnecessary, even a mistake. Nevertheless, whether or not the possession of a rational power, either as a faculty or a function, is necessary and desirable in the total constitution of a person, there can be no doubt that one side of human nature is rational, and that this characteristic is of considerable importance. Accordingly, the determination of the status of this function or faculty is of prime concern for whoever would know the nature and significance of human knowledge.

REASON AS NOUS AND LOGOS

In the history of Greek thought, the principle of Reason, in the profoundest sense, is represented most commonly under the notions of 'Logos' and 'Nous'. Although the sense in which these terms are employed varies, probably the most mature usage regards 'Nous' as an ontological or Divine Reason, while 'Logos' enters into the picture in the sense of the 'Word', or the Reason become articulate, organized and manifested. Initially, the metaphysical and the epistemological were not clearly differentiated, so that 'Logos' can mean 'Word' as well as 'Idea', and is even personified in some developments. Yet, it is easy to see in 'Logos' the original predecessor of the modern 'concept', and all that is now understood under the designation of 'logic'. This would naturally lead to the identification of 'reason', in the more common sense of modern usage, with the notion of 'Logos'. This is 'reason' conceived as a ratiocinative *process*, that is, reasoning. In addition, the Greeks also conceived of 'Reason' in a more ontological sense—as is also evident in the modern thinker, Hegel. In this more profound meaning, it is identical with the notions of 'Law' or 'Order' conceived as governing, both teleologically and structurally, the whole Cosmos. Reason, in this sense, is identical with 'Nous' and, apparently, also identical with the Indian conception of Buddhi, taken in the sense of a Cosmic principle. Within the limits of human cognition, the distinction between 'Nous' and 'Logos' seems well represented by the differentiation indicated by 'apprehension' and 'comprehension', understood in the more rigorous sense. Apprehension carries the meaning of simple cognition, or what James called "knowledge through acquaintance," whereas 'comprehension' is the definitive "knowledge-about."

In conformity with the foregoing discussion, Reason, in the sense of Nous, is not identical with the subjective ratiocinative process of human thinking, but is rather a part or phase of higher Nature, and therefore objective. Ratiocination would be a stepped-down correlate or reflection in the relative consciousness, where the relationship to knowledge would be one of seeking. Reason as Nous is preexistent with respect to the relative consciousness. In this sense, Reason does not stand in contrast to intuition—as is the case with ratiocination—nor with other forms of higher cognition, such as Vision, Direct Cognition, and Knowledge by Identity, as differentiated by Aurobindo. A perfect Rational Intelligence would, for instance, embrace the whole of extant and future mathematics as a unified totality without passing through reasoned steps as a process in time.

Reason as Nous must be conceived as preexistent with respect to all experience, unrelated to the degree to which the ratiocinative reason, or Logos, must wait upon experience before it can be manifested. Thus, however much the concepts of the latter are dependent upon experience—either with respect to the primordial images or to the particular images with external reference, for their substantive content—the concept is not exclusively derived from the percept, but has as well a source in the primordial Reason. This provides for a dimension in knowledge that is other than experience in its root, although actual knowledge, as we know it in the relative field, is so far an intermixed mass of empiric and pure rational components that their separation is a task of great difficulty.

Provisionally, assuming the picture so far delineated, we are in a position to deal with a defect in the primordial image, as presented by

Jung. This image does not appear as an eternal or a timeless archetype, and thus absolutely a priori. It is rather a deposit over a vast temporal range of experience, or the way a million-year-old consciousness would perceive. It is only relatively a priori. We may view it as the conditioning factor in current particularized experiencing, that is itself a deposit from all past experience, but does not provide the form whereby the initial experience was possible. The root form, making possible the initial experience, cannot be itself a deposit from experience. This form we find in the notion of 'Reason as Nous'.

For the consciousness of the extraverted empiricist, and even for the introverted sensationalist, the question quite naturally arises as to how a pure Reason can be cognized, since it is not given by experience, in the restricted meaning of the term. To answer this query we must assume the actuality of ways of cognition other than the empiric. For the purposes of formal discourse, once we assume or postulate the appropriate cognitive means, then we can accept, in principle, the possibility of direct apperception of a pure Reason, or of a Reason that is preexistent with respect to experience. Admittedly, if we go no further than this, then the discussion is only of academic interest. To advance beyond that point requires the immediate actuality of the specific cognitive power. There are those who have, or at least claim to have, immediate acquaintance with cognitive powers that are not active in everyone. This implies that, when such individuals formulate philosophies, grounded more or less upon these powers, verification by strictly empiric means is impossible. Thus the effective critique of these philosophies cannot be performed by those who are strangers to the necessary cognitive resources. Therefore, the ultimate and vital question is whether or not these cognitive powers exist. It is the same problem that arises in evaluating the states of consciousness of the mystic. In this case, however, it occurs in connection with the cognition of Reason itself. Of course, no attempt will be made here to *prove* the actuality of means of cognition that are not generally active, for such proof is quite unnecessary with respect to those who possess these powers, and it is impossible in the case of those who lack them. It is merely pointed out that the existence of such powers must be assumed if a primary understanding of idealism is ever to be attained.

We now possess a schema whereby the development of universal conceptual ideas may be seen as possible. These ideas are the product of the combination of primordial images and pure Reason, whereby we derive concepts that unite a perceptual context with a logical order. Both components are necessary, since, on the one hand, without the substantive content supplied by the primordial image, the logical form would lack all relation to experience, while, on the other hand, without the rational component, the primordial image could never supply the notion of 'law and organization'. Because of these two factors, we are enabled to cognize the externally given as a Cosmos, not merely as an indeterminate Chaos.

Having reached this point, the question arises as to whether we have discovered a truth concerning the nature of the world or universe, as such, or only determined conditions of human knowledge. Clearly Kant considers his analysis valid solely in the latter sense, because he explicitly states that it never occurred to him to question the existence of a real world, in the sense of an existent beyond all consciousness. He even calls himself an "empiric realist," though he acknowledges that he is also a "transcendental idealist." More precisely, he views the intuitions of the senses, in their concrete contents, as determined by an external somewhat, or the thing-in-itself, which, in its nature as it is in itself, is unknowable to human cognition. In this respect, he remains realistic, in his own opinion at least. However, the actual form of our experience he conceived as determined by transcendental forms that are preexistent in the knower. In this regard, he was frankly idealistic.

6

*Introceptual Idealism**

The idealist affirms the primacy of consciousness along with its subject. This is not to be regarded as merely an arbitrary affirmation nor as a working hypothesis, but as a direct or immediate recognition, something that is beyond all doubt for the thinker personally. This is so fundamental that the idealist finds it confirmed in the very denial by the denier, since the denial itself is an act of consciousness. That which is wholly unconscious simply could not deny anything. So, when the realist opposes the thesis of the idealist, he must invoke, however unwillingly, the very quality that the idealist affirms *is*. It never occurs to the idealist to charge the realist with being unconscious, so he is perhaps temperamentally incapable of getting the realist's point of view. To convey his argument effectively, the realist should insist more explicitly on his own unconsciousness. In this way he might avoid adding fuel to the idealist's fire.

Once one has the initial certainty of the subject or self and its consciousness, the basic problem of philosophy takes a characteristic form. So long as one focuses attention inwardly, she has an immediate realization of perfect freedom. One's will and thought are under no external constraint. Their activity is perfectly free. However, when the focus of consciousness is turned outward, the freely willed act becomes an objective deed, which is confronted by all sorts of constraints. The deed is an action of what we commonly call an "organism" that cannot simply do

---

*From the standpoint of one who appreciates systematic organization, the material in the present and subsequent chapters will prove less than satisfactory. Here there will be found an interplay between the intellectual and introceptual functions that, at times, may seem somewhat like a contest. The one emphasizes organization, the other, flow of consciousness; the former best serves communication to the trained mind, while the latter provides the fertile ground for pregnant ideas; the first exemplifies discipline, the second, freedom. Even for the writer, criticism and reorganization of such material is difficult, and involves the danger of sacrificing substance to form. Accordingly, I decided to leave the composition unaltered, save in very minor detail. By far, the most valuable material in this book is to be found in the present and succeeding chapters.

as it pleases, insofar as it operates in a seeming environment that restricts the action of the organism in innumerable ways. In this manner the freely willed act of the pure self is confronted with resistance. Ultimately, it is true that practical paths for the will can be found, but these paths are, in part, determined by necessity, so that in the final form they are only partially the expression of pure freedom. This necessity appears as the objective world of mountains, trees, oceans, buildings, and so on, precisely that which the realist takes in some sense as the ultimate and basic Reality itself. However, the idealist knows immediately the conscious self and its freedom, so the necessitarian character revealed in the object raises a problem.

Details in the proffered solutions to the problem of necessity vary with the different idealist thinkers. Nevertheless, all representatives of this school hold one feature in common, namely, that the solution must be found in the nature of consciousness itself. Manifestly the only objective world we have is the world that exists in and for consciousness. If we say that it inheres in something independent and quite outside consciousness as such, then we beg the whole question by a speculative answer that can never be checked. This is because all verification involves a conscious act dealing with material that is already inside consciousness, as it were, and thus nothing is proved as to the existence of a somewhat absolutely outside consciousness. To be sure, one might affirm this somewhat, thereby taking a purely arbitrary and dogmatic position, but this, the idealist will say, is no true philosophic solution. The only being we know is necessarily known. That is the important fact. Therefore, being is defined as identical with being known, or as being for, in or of consciousness.

At this point the idealist is vulnerable before logical criticism, since he cannot prove that it is essential to being that it should be known or exist in consciousness. As a matter of strict logic, he begs the question. Of course, the realist is not slow to pick out this weakness and on this ground accuses the idealist of failing to prove his thesis. It is perfectly true that the primary thesis of idealism is not proven logically, so there is no logical compulsion to constrain us to accept some form of idealism as the only possible true philosophy. Even so, any opposed philosophy faces the same essential difficulty, each in a different form. Always one can find root assumptions that are not and cannot be proven logically. The realist, for instance, cannot prove the existence of his or her independent reality, and thus also begs the question.

It is a fact that humankind has not and cannot build a rigorously self-contained system wherein every element is itself logically derived. The closest realization that we have of this is to be found in some purely formal mathematical systems in which the elements are wholly meaningless terms. In any case, even here logic is always assumed, since its first principles are not proven. Proof depends upon those principles, but they are themselves beyond proof. It may be impossible to doubt them, but the ground of confidence in them is immediate and original. Nonetheless, accepting anything in this way begs the question when we assert that it carries the quality of truth. Consequently, we must be content to start with something immediate, be it experience or insight, then subsequent rigorous logical demonstration is effective, yet always relative to the original immediate ground.

We must accept that different philosophies, originating from different grounds immediately given in some way, will develop in different directions and exist side by side. Each one has at its roots a basic logical weakness, with the result that mutual vulnerability gives to all a relative right to existence. So, while logical soundness is indeed an important part of every genuine philosophy, this is not the whole story. It is even more important that every philosophy is the expression of an orientation that is extralogical. A philosophy is the expression of a view that is more primary than the philosophy itself.

As it stands, although the idealist cannot prove his or her primary thesis, and so must counter the realist by bringing the same charge against the latter, the idealist can make a particularly strong point favorable to his or her position. The idealist can call to our attention that when being is conceived as identical with being known, or with existing in and for consciousness, he or she has given a definition that has some meaning. However, the notions of 'being' and 'existence' have no intelligible meaning when they are predicated of that which is apart from consciousness in every sense. What in that case does it mean to be or to exist? Anyone who tries to give an answer to this question will only invoke a meaning that exists for consciousness. Answering, and the content of the answer, is something in consciousness. Hence the idealist may very well say that the only being and existence that can possibly have any significance are a being and existence that are for consciousness of some sort. That which is completely outside all consciousness is simply indistinguishable from nothing at all, so we may just as well disregard the whole matter.

FREEDOM AND NECESSITY

Even so, a difficulty still remains. The inward Realization of freedom is offset by an outward experience of necessity. The notion of an independent and real world does have value in explaining this, for if living and conscious beings are actually in a preexistent and independent environment, then it is quite easy to see how they would be constrained by it. This, in its turn, makes it difficult to see how consciousness could have any real freedom. The direct Realization of freedom ultimately would have to be largely dismissed as an illusion. However, those individuals who have the greater immediate certainty of freedom, and only a secondary or derived experience of necessity would not accept this view. They certainly would not sacrifice the more certainly known for that which is less certainly known, so they seek to overcome this difficulty by finding some other way of explaining the necessity.

Idealism does offer its solution, which leads us into a veritable sea of philosophic theory and discourse that many find quite difficult to follow. In the end, the idealist believes that the problem has been met in such a way as to save the freedom, so that it remains as something absolutely real and yet supplies a conceivable explanation of the necessity. In this process much conceptual simplicity is lost, as compared to the statements of the realists, but at least the baby is not thrown away with the bath. The idealist considers the baby, freedom, to be so valuable as to be worth any effort to save it.

In contrast, the realist, whether oriented to a mechanistic nature, a logic of relations, or an empiric life, seems to be lost when given too much freedom. The realist seems to secure comfort by anchoring him- or herself to something apart from consciousness. He or she may call this something "matter," "terms in relation" or "empiric life," but consciousness is held to be incidental, embraced by an enveloping necessity whose nature is other than consciousness. Of course, the realist also has the direct feeling of freedom, although it can hardly be as decisive as in the case of the idealist, and he or she generally strives to find some room for it, although it never rises to a commanding position. However, the realist has a very clear idea why we cannot always do as we please.

Obviously, an idealist can never hope to be taken seriously by merely affirming unconditional freedom, and letting it go at that. If he did, he would be very open to the charge of uncritical subjectivism. There is far too much evidence for a compulsive necessity that affects all creatures, be they idealists or not. Consequently, the idealist must take up the problem of necessity. The great idealists have given so much thought to this problem, and have written so largely concerning it, that they often give the impression of being necessitarians. However, this is only the outside view of the idealists' approach. Its real heart lies in a profound feeling for freedom. Perhaps one would have to be something of an idealist to be aware of this fact, though it is possible for anyone who will look far enough to find the evidence. I need only suggest the thought of Shankara, the greatest of all the idealists, who gives the *summum bonum* explicitly as Liberation (spelled with a capital *L*).

To the philosophically naive consciousness of most people, it doubtless will seem harder to follow the more rigorous form of idealistic philosophy than any other form of thought. One is finally led into the regions where the familiar, so-called real world is left far behind, and most of the judgments of our highly vaunted common sense cease to supply any genuine help. One may be excused if she is disposed to feel like a space traveler having no planet for grounding nor solar system for bearings. Then, too, the content of the thought may often seem as though it deals with nothing that means anything whatsoever and, least of all, has any bearing upon practical human affairs. Despite this, deeper reflection will show that the idealist does have genuine anchorage, does employ an objective modulus, and is deeply concerned with that which in the end is of the most profound and vital interest to all of humanity. The mooring of the idealist is, as already noted, the immediate fact of consciousness and its subject; the objective modulus is the logical structure of thought; and the practical interest has the deepest concern with the problem of death and immortality. On the whole, it is true, the idealist as a philosopher is not greatly concerned with the practical problems of finite life in this world. He or she finds many others who are ably engaged with these problems, and so rarely finds the call of duty in this direction. Rather, he or she sees beyond the cycle of finite life a great problem that, if it is not solved, renders the solutions of all other problems unimportant. So, I submit, there is abundant reason to bear with the intellectual processes of the idealist if he or she can offer any evidence of certainty where most people only believe darkly within a cloud of doubt.

Let us now examine the main features of the idealist treatment of the problem of necessity. If there is no world apart from consciousness, and the essence of the self is freedom, how then are we to account for the experience of external constraint? The idealist's answer to this question invariably takes us away from the material of objective experience. Except for the pragmatic idealist, the resolution of the problem invokes either the Divinity or a Transcendental Self, which stands in such a relation to the empiric self that it may be called "objective." Yet, it is not objective in the sense in which sensible objects or even ideas are called "objective." Here we have a notion that is quite subtle, and which I think is quite generally misunderstood by the critics of idealism. However, first let us see how the notion of the Divinity or the Transcendental Self can help us with the problem of necessity, leaving the problem of the reasonableness of the notion until later.

Berkeley invokes the notion of the Divinity quite simply to account for the ideas experienced. Berkeleyan ideas, it must be noted, include all experiences, such as sensations, as well as ideas in the conceptual sense. These ideas, he affirms, are not produced by something outside of consciousness, such as independent real things, but many of them have the character of being given quite independently of individual volition. How are they placed in the consciousness of the individual? His answer is that God places them there. The actuality of God is not questioned by Berkeley, nor is the Divinity a philosophical conception. He seems simply to have accepted the God of Christian faith, with the result that he left many logical problems unresolved. Thus this earlier form of Occidental idealism is mainly valuable for introducing the idealistic approach to the problem of modern philosophy, but leaves us with an unsatisfactory system.

Before leaving this passing reference to Berkeley, it seems worthwhile to note that this thinker, like Schiller and Bergson of the pragmatists, is not classified as a member of the school of German idealism. As the two pragmatists mentioned, he accepts the cardinal principle of idealism but does not accept another of their principles that is of almost equal importance. Basically, in Berkeley's sense, ideas are not concepts, but percepts. Hence his subjective idealism may be characterized as an empiric or perceptual idealism, whereas the great school of idealism gives ascendancy to the concept relative to the percept. Berkeley's thought is antirationalistic as well as antirealistic, whereas the main school of idealism is antirealistic, but highly rationalistic, even in its voluntaristic form. For Berkeley, the concrete idea or perception has a reality value that the abstract concept does not possess. He continues the psychological orientation of the nominalists of the Middle Ages. However, since the cleavage between idealism and realism is more fundamental than that between sensationalism and rationalism, there is a significant reason for classifying Berkeley with idealism in the generic sense, though not with the specific school of idealism.

There is something naive about Berkeley's invocation of the Divinity to explain the necessitarian and orderly character of perceived ideas, for this is the inherited Divinity of Christian faith. It is not the Divinity of direct Realization nor is it a necessity for reason. It is thus not the kind of God that can properly enter into any philosophical system as a true agent of integration. Rather, it is a general appeal to Providence for help when one's individual resources prove inadequate. Admittedly, it does appear that no one ever quite succeeds in building a system of thought that completely avoids an appeal to something that is the logical equivalent of Providence, though it may be called by various names, such as "Chance" or "Nirvana." This means that eventually something extrarational has to be invoked, but some thinkers have been able to extend the limits of rational thought much further than others. Indeed, this has a great deal to do with the relative valuation within the hierarchy of thinkers. The greatest intellect is whoever has been able to mentally probe furthest into the unknown. Among philosophic thinkers, Berkeley did not go very far before he met his limits. The great idealists went much further, gaining profundity, though at the price of increasing incomprehensibility. As a result, they have given us the most intellectually sound interpretation of our awareness of necessity, while also avoiding the pitfalls of realism.

INTROCEPTION AND INTROSPECTION

Continuing our primary discussion, we may confirm that, by a sufficient degree of inward penetration in consciousness, one can find the self as an immediately known reality. This is not a process of simple introspection, as is commonly used in experimental psychology. This introspection remains far too objective (oriented to objects) to lead to the discovery of the self, with the result that many psychologists never do find the true self. They do find something that they call the "subject," but they describe it in such terms as to show that they have found only a subtle object. The neorealists explicitly state that this subject may enter into the relation of an object for some purposes of thought. This simply means that such psychologists are talking of a subject of quite a different nature from the self of the idealist. This difference may be suggested by the figure of a lamp with a light within it. The subject of the more empiric psychologists is only the lamp, while the self of the idealist is the light itself. Introspection, in the usual sense, can go no further than the lamp, insofar as it is the light that illumines and makes possible the subtle observation of introspection. The light is behind the act of introspection, and only the lamp is in the foreground. This implies that in introspection consciousness has not really turned upon itself, but merely established a kind of short circuit in the psyche. To find the self of the idealist, one has to go far beyond this.

The turning of consciousness upon itself is a very mysterious process. To account for it, we have to introduce the notion of a function that is other than the four functions of analytic psychology, which are thinking, feeling, sensation and intuition. I hold the thesis that it is the activity of this function that constitutes the real base of idealism in the grand sense. Further, it is the more or less complete inactivity of this function that destroys the force of the idealist argument for so many philosophers and psychologists. Also, it would appear that, even for the idealists, in whom the function is active, there is a defective knowledge of it as a distinct function. The result is that they often try to explain by pure reason something that involves a great deal more than logic itself. It is precisely here that I would locate the greatest failure of the Occidental idealists. Nevertheless, failure in terms of presentation does not imply unsoundness of fundamental insight.

The above point is well illustrated in the case of Johann Fichte, who may well prove to be the purest example of an idealist we have in the West. From the standpoint of sheer insight, I find Fichte very convincing, but his attempt in *The Science of Knowledge** to derive that insight as the necessary underlying implication of the logical laws of thought seems strained and far from persuasive. Very possibly he has the substantially correct view as to the source of the laws of thought, but it is quite another matter to say that from the use of logical principles he has proved the source. I am quite convinced that Fichte did not discover the self or "ego," as he calls it, by the method in which he sought to prove it. I would say that he really knew the self through what we might call the "fifth psychological function," though it is entirely possible that he did not differentiate this function in his analysis. In such matters the psychical analysis of the Orient has gone much further than either the philosophy or the psychology of the West.

Elsewhere I have suggested the term *introception* to represent this function. It is to be understood as the process whereby consciousness turns upon itself and moves toward its source. It is not the same as introspection, wherein consciousness merely short circuits itself to observe more subtle psychical objects that are generally unconscious for the extraverted attitude. Introception, when successful, leads to a state such that consciousness becomes its own content, that is, a consciousness that is divorced from its objective reference. By this means, the self as source of consciousness can be Realized, without being transformed into a subtle object, as a *me*. This is identical with the East Indian notion of 'meditation without a seed', which is essential for the attainment of Liberation or Enlightenment. Buddhist use of the word *Dhyana* suggests very strongly that it refers to an analogous process. So, it may be said that by 'introception' I mean substantially the same higher psychical function as "meditation without a seed" and "Dhyana." I conceive this to be the real source of the assurance of the originating idealist philosophers and the ground for differentiating idealism proper from mere intellectualistic idealism. The latter is more a reflection of a light than an incarnation of the Light itself. Introception gives immediate content, just as perception does, but diverges at least as radically from the latter as does conceptualism. If one divides the functions of

---

*Johann Fichte, *The Science of Knowledge*, trans. A. E. Kroeger (London: Trübner & Co., 1889).

consciousness into two classes, with perception on one side, including feeling, sensation and intuition, and conception on the other, then introception would appear grouped with conception. In this case, a successful critique of conceptualism would undermine the foundations of idealism, particularly for the absolutist school. However, if the true base of idealism is the activity of a function that ordinarily is latent and inactive, then the real root of idealism remains untouched by a critique of conceptualism considered separate from introception.

Introception is most certainly not thinking, feeling or sensation. It is also definitely different from 'intuition,' as that term is generally understood, though translators from Oriental sources have often used the latter word. However, this only helps to confuse the situation, for then we think of intuition as it appears in analytic psychology or in usage such as that of Bergson. In these latter systems of thought, it involves a content coming into consciousness from out of the dark of unconsciousness. Hence we have Bergson speaking of grasping indefinite fringes around the core of conscious ideas as intuition. In stark contrast, introception is a function operating in the most intense kind of Light, wherein one is more completely conscious than ever before. Consciousness turning upon itself is a very different matter from contents arising into consciousness from the unconscious.

I submit that "turning inward," according to Fichte's usage, must be understood in the sense of introception rather than simple introspection. Thus no amount of bare introspection would be competent to challenge what Fichte found. Introception is an exceedingly profound act of introversion, and the evidence would indicate that it is quite rare. If introversion is carried very far *without the turning of the Light of consciousness upon itself*, the effect is of something inchoate feathering out into the darkness of unconsciousness. However, with the turning of the Light of consciousness upon itself, consciousness becomes vastly intensified, with the quality and ground of assurance much better established than in the case of anything derived from experience. This is something that must be remembered if one is ever to understand idealism of the grander style.

Introception renders the actuality of the self far more indubitable than any content given through perception. This is the key to the idealists' assurance and explains why all the necessitarianism that inheres in the environment takes on the quality of subordination. To be sure, the intensified Light of the introceptive process gives to all experience a dreamlike or unreal character. It is like the sun quenching the light of the moon, or like the waking state quenching the consciousness of the ordinary dream. This is not a speculation; it is something that actually happens. The shift from introception to perception is like the sun fading while the moon ascends. The memory of the light of the sun, when the moon is shining, is stronger than the memory of the light of the moon, when the sun is shining. This alone gives a determinate meaning as to which is relatively most real.

The first immediate content of successful introception is the Realization expressed by the words *I am*. This is not an inference from conscious activity, such as that of Descartes when he inferred the being of the self from the fact of thinking. The being of the self is an absolutely immediate datum requiring no further support. I repeat, the actuality of perceptually experienced content, taken in its most complete immediacy, is much less decisively certain.

The being of the self, which for introception is more unequivocal than the being or actuality of perception, is like an unsupported Light. It is "the Flame that burns without wick or oil." It is so pure as to be quite without the taint of personality. One may conceive of it as like a self-supporting Light within a somewhat differentiated lamp. The latter carries the individual characteristics of personality. There is thus something about the pure self that gives it the character of real impersonality. While in the rigorous sense it is highly subjective, it is not a personal subjectivism. This is a point of exceptional importance for philosophy, because the impersonality of the self gives it a universal value. It is the ground for something a good deal more than a merely personal philosophy.

We are quite right in valuing physical science because it gives us something more than merely the private experience of the individual scientist. It gives general truths, whether they are interpreted in realistic, pragmatic or other terms. It is for this reason that we call it "objective." To this we commonly oppose subjective judgments that are so greatly colored by personal feeling tones that they have only a restricted appeal. That which we call "objective" is believed to be in some sense true for everyone, whereas that which is subjective is not universally true and may not be true at all. The self of introception, being quite pure and impersonal, is not subjective in the latter sense. It supplies a generally valid foundation. It is thus conceived by those who know it, and, if the nonidealist is ever to arrive at an understanding of the inner meaning of the idealist, he or she must grant this point. The only possible verification is by the path of introception itself.

The previous statement implies a radical departure of the idealist theory of verification from that of pragmatism. The pragmatist dictum that a difference of truth must make a difference of fact here—that is, in the world of perception or experience—implies an exclusive one-way reference of ideas. The idea means exclusively a terminal content having a perceptual quale. Therefore, there can be no verification except through experience. However, the conceptual content of the idealist, qua idealist, is purely introceptive. If this incidentally produces a difference of fact in the field of experience, that is merely an addendum that adds nothing to the essential truth value. Introceptive verification may have repercussions upon the empiric life of the individual, with the result that the latter may, more or less widely, influence other lives. Further, these effects may be valued positively or negatively in the pragmatic sense. In any event, from the perspective of introception, all this is beside the point. Introception supplies intrinsic authority and may very well, in some of its ramifications, move into zones quite unrelated to empiric consciousness. In such cases a difference of truth would produce no difference of fact in the perceptual field. Often, we must acknowledge, a difference that is introceptively significant does have effects that are also significant within the perceptual field and may even be of momentous import. For example, the Buddhist introceptive insight has led to empiric ways of life that are notably different from common practice. The reduction in militancy is one such effect that has pragmatic value. Even so, it would be a serious mistake to regard such effects as the underlying objective of Buddhist teachings. They are, after all, only incidental. The real objective is the attainment of Nirvana. I contend that if it were true that attainment of this end implied violent militancy in the empiric field, then Buddhism would have to accept such violence.

It must be clear that the fruits of the introceptive orientation, insofar as they include effects within the empiric field, will not always receive favorable valuation from the vitalistic pragmatist. While at times the good of the one standpoint will overlap the good as viewed from the other, there are other situations in which there arises an inescapable conflict of valuation and direction. Fundamentally, introception leads away from experience and empiric life, which define precisely the field of focus of the pragmatist and the realist. That they should judge such effects adversely is not only understandable, but inevitable. From an opposed perspective, the introceptualist counters with a comparable attitude in the reverse sense. He or she views all valuation of experience and empiric life that leads to estrangement from Divinity or Spirit as a positive evil—indeed, as the only real evil. There is thus a limit to the possible reconciliation of the different philosophic attitudes. Between idealism and the other three schools there is a gulf of incommensurability that implies ineluctable conflict and choice. Whoever opens the door of introception cannot possibly be a pragmatist or a realist, save only in secondary relations as an empiric entity, that is, exclusively in those relations that he or she regards as of no primary importance.

I have introduced this discussion of introception into the general subject of idealism for the reason that I conceive it to be essential to an understanding of the true meaning of idealism. I am not writing a mere history of philosophy. If I were, I should have to consider the idealist theories of knowledge as they have been developed by their leading proponents. It must be admitted that such theories have followed the intellectualistic pattern. In following this course, the idealists have made themselves vulnerable to criticism and have given a false impression of their actual base of assurance. I believe that the great idealists, in their private hearts, would agree substantially with the position I have just presented. Perhaps they have hesitated to establish their systems frankly upon what I have called an "introceptive" base, feeling that such would be unseemly for a philosopher. It is also possible that there was a defective differentiation between intellectual form and introceptive content. The isolation of the purely logical features of mathematics has given us today an advantage over the older writers. We are enabled to see that there is a vital difference between rigorously formal mathematics and mathematics that results from the union of logic and intuition or introception. This shows very clearly that something is stripped away when pure mathematics is reduced to an exclusively logical formalism. This something is in addition to the pure concept. The bearing of this point upon idealism is extremely critical, for it means that rigorous logical system, by itself, does not give content. Content enters as something extralogical, or as indefinable in the logical sense. Logical demonstration renders explicit a truth that is initially implicit, in the original content, but does not supply the initial content. Once this is understood, all reasoning becomes relative to a reference supplied by some other means than by reason itself. If it is assumed that perceptual experience is the only possible extralogical reference, then it readily follows that all conceptual or rational thinking is instrumental to empiric content. However, the idealistic transcendentalism cannot be derived by logical implication from perceptual content. Consequently, the idealist thesis falls.

The strength of the pragmatist polemic against idealism lies in its criticism of intellectualism. The case that pragmatism builds here is very strong. If the pure concept is truly empty, except insofar as it has a reference beyond itself, then it is impossible to prove a substantial reality by concepts alone. Analysis seems to have established the soundness of this point. Nonetheless, it does not necessarily follow that perceptual meaning is the only possible reference of the concept unless it can be proven that consciousness contains no other possibility.

To be sure, the argument against intellectualism is a good deal older than current pragmatism. It is to be found highly developed in the thought of Kant, whose criticism of the Ontological Argument for the existence of God is a classic example. However, he was forced to leave a door open for extraexperiential possibilities. The following excerpt from his *Critique of Pure Reason* is of particular significance.

> Our conception of the object may thus contain whatever and how much it will; nevertheless we must ourselves stand away from the conception in order to bestow existence upon it. This happens with sense-objects through the connection with any one of our perceptions in accordance with empiric laws; but for the objects of pure thought there is no sort of means for perceiving their existence because it is wholly a priori that they can be known; *our consciousness of all existence, however, belongs altogether to a unity of experience and an existence outside this field cannot absolutely be explained away as impossible. But it is a supposition that we have no means of justifying.**

For our purpose, the crucial part of the quotation lies in the italicized words. It cannot be affirmed on purely theoretical grounds that concepts derive their existential value from perceptual experience alone. Granted that the pure concept does not give existence, that existence may be grounded in something other than perception. It is affirmed here that it is sometimes grounded in introception, and that this is the actual foundation of the idealist systems. Accordingly, the essence of idealism remains untouched by all the anti-intellectualistic arguments. This implies that the alternative of antisensationalism is not necessarily intellectualism, but may be a third way of cognition that is direct and immediate in its own right.

One may agree with pragmatism as to its general theory of the instrumental nature of concepts, but radically oppose the specific theory that the instrumental reference is *always* to a perceptual content. There may be an introceptive reference as well. Granting the validity of introception, the central thesis of idealism remains unaffected. Also, idealism has the potential to develop a theory of truth wholly at variance with the pragmatic test, insofar as the latter is exclusively related to programs in the stream of time and experience. There remains the test of the psychological determination of the factual actuality of the idealistic direct Realization of the self.

I have already argued that the pure self cannot be found by introspective methods, for introspection deals with objects, albeit subtle ones. At most, it finds a *me*, having sufficient determinate character to be an object in certain relations, as the neorealist contends. This method

---

*Kant, *Critique of Pure Reason.*

fails to exclude other possibilities, unless it can rigorously prove that the four psychological functions are the only possible ways of consciousness. This it has not done, and due to the very nature of the problem, cannot do. I submit that introception is a fifth function that renders content available that otherwise cannot be known, and I affirm that this supplies the base upon which the whole structure of idealism rests.

It has long been a custom for philosophic systems to include an outline of psychology as a component part. Among the older systems, it was frequently customary to introduce psychology as rational psychology. Today it is empiric psychology, that is, the kind that results from the application of scientific method. In introducing the discussion of introception as a way of consciousness, within the body of a philosophical exegesis, I am, therefore, proceeding in accord with well-established practice. Introception, considered as a way of consciousness, differentiated from the content rendered available by it, falls under the general heading of psychology. However, it does not fall within the limits of the common understanding of either rational or empiric psychology. We may feasibly regard it as metapsychology. In principle, the material of this psychology is conceived as being available for study, provided the right conditions exist. It is not claimed that any subject at any time supplies the material in a form available for investigation. It is simply asserted that there are instances where it has been rendered available, thereby demonstrating a possibility of consciousness as such.

Psychology is philosophically significant insofar as the existence of a way of consciousness must be assumed before the content and inner relations of consciousness can be analyzed and evaluated. The question of the actuality of a way of consciousness is, properly, a psychological rather than a philosophical problem. The importance of this problem hardly needs to be emphasized in a day when the positive appreciation of psychology is so strong as it is with us now. It is philosophy that has felt the force of relative depreciation. This attitude is an expression of the widespread superficiality of the age, for a way of consciousness is manifestly only of instrumental value to the content that it renders available. Further, the way of consciousness does not define content in other than very general terms, which are always other than the distinctive quale of the content itself. The way of consciousness bears a strong analogy to a route and method of travel—so strong that it is a general Oriental practice to speak of a way of consciousness as a "path" or "road." If we analyze a route and means of travel to some destination, we can say something about the possible values to be realized at the destination, but not very much. Here our knowledge of content is mainly negative. Thus we can know that if the route and means are exclusively those of land travel, then the content of the destination will not include values that can be reached only by sea travel. Otherwise, the actual positive content realized at the destination is not known by the route or conveyance used. Thus one could know very thoroughly the road that leads to the Grand Canyon, and all that goes into the structure and operation of an automobile, yet this would give no knowledge of the direct experience of the Grand Canyon itself. Knowledge of the route and means of travel is psychology, but the valuation of the direct content of a Realized consciousness, insofar as it is thinkable, is the concern of philosophy.

We have left the problem of necessity, as it appears to the idealist perspective, suspended in the air, as it were, for quite some time, meanwhile engaging in a somewhat extensive review of a proposed fifth function of consciousness. This seemed unavoidable for two reasons:

1. The actuality of the function, which I have called "introception," is not a generally recognized fact, so it was necessary to build some presumption for it.
2. In the failure to establish its case upon purely intellectual grounds, idealism must invoke some nonempiric and nonintellectual function if it is not to be cast aside as a vain speculation.

If the reader does not feel that the evidence in support of the actuality of introception is adequate, then I suggest that she or he assume its actuality while examining the idealist thesis to see whether this is sufficient to support that thesis in principle. If the ultimate conclusion is positive, then the problem of the status of idealism rests upon the metapsychological problem of whether introception is a valid way of consciousness besides the four generally recognized functions.

I have already defined the distinctive characteristic of introception as the *"power of the Light of consciousness to turn upon itself toward its source."* It was carefully differentiated from introspection, which is consciousness concerned with an objective content, although the content of introspection is of a more subtle nature than that of observation, which is a more outward-going consciousness. The success of introception means that at some point consciousness loses all content other than itself. Such a point, if absolute, is equivalent to the complete disappearance of the world of experience. It is also possible that the fundamental effect may be achieved by a sort of diversion of the major portion of the stream of consciousness so that it turns about toward its source, while a residual portion continues to flow toward its object, namely, the phenomenal world. In this event, objective consciousness continues in a kind of twilight in an inferior portion of the individual's total psyche. The diverted portion of the stream becomes a consciousness without objective content, but with an exclusive awareness of itself and its subject. Such a consciousness is clearly not a mere relation between two terms, a subject and an object, inasmuch as only one term remains. This point has very great epistemological importance, since it begins to undercut the whole conception of consciousness as exclusively a relation *between* terms. Introceptual consciousness is Realized in a way independent of both time and space, at least as these notions are predicated of the external world. An individual consciousness in such a state would, in particular, have no basis for time measurement. Hence there would be no basis for differentiation between instantaneity and eternity. If a portion of the stream of time continued to flow toward the object, then a correlation with a chronometer, which the cosmos is, would remain. As a result, one would Realize a conjunction of consciousness as time-conditioned with consciousness as timeless. This is a curious kind of crossing of the gulf between the seeming incompatibilities of time and timelessness.

As I am speaking primarily from a direct knowledge of an instance of introception, I am better able to state what is possible than to define the limits of possibility. I do know that, as measured by the portion of consciousness still related to the surrounding world, the state wherein the self and consciousness are the sole content can be instantaneous—followed by an immediate unfolding of another, very astonishing, content incommensurable with objective experience. As this has a very close bearing upon a central part of idealist philosophy, I propose to describe its principal feature, so far as that may be.

The immediate effect of a state of consciousness having a one-way dependence on, or relation to the subject, and no object, is that of a vast void. It is an "I" suspended in an utter voidness. At once a process of "enantiodromia"* transforms the voidness into the value of substantial fullness. This is a "thickness" that I am quite sure would much more than meet James's requirement. I know of no empiric content that in the faintest degree suggests this quality of fullness, which is the actual palpable Presence of Divinity itself. It is nothing so crude as a vast person in space, but a Presence that permeates all space, interwoven throughout the objects of ordinary consciousness, yet more completely present where those objects are not. The effect is a radical reversal of all former values, and a resolution of many of just those problems to which empiricism can give no satisfactory answer.

There is very little in an introceptive Realization of this sort that suggests the God concepts of the traditional religions. Mostly, such

*Jung, *Psychological Types*, 541-42.

conceptions seem to be little more than stylized constructs o_ human imagination. Introceptive Realization instead confirms the actuality of the Supreme Value that the general faith of humanity envisages, however defective its conceptions. For both philosophy and psychology, the various names of the Divinity have simply the significance of symbolic representations of the Supreme Value. Proof of the actuality of this Supreme Value is possible only by direct Realization. It may be reflected in the practical or moral reason, in the sense in which Kant uses these terms. However, I suspect that a careful examination of the argument for God's existence from the basis of practical reason will prove it defective just as surely as Kant shows the Ontological Argument from pure reason to be flawed. Immediacy alone supplies proof, though faith definitely may be understood as a signpost.

There is excellent evidence, to be derived from the content of the formulations based upon religious mysticism, that the above stage in the introceptive process may be relatively terminal. That is, consciousness may establish an anchorage at this point. Even so, I know that if the process is continued, there are subsequent enantiodromedal transformations that lead to considerably more profound orientations. A later stage is of vastly greater significance for the understanding of idealism than the one now before us. However, before continuing with the further development, it is important to consider the effect of the present stage upon the world view.

As was previously noted, the stage of consciousness united with a self, but with no object, proved to be nascent, as that of chemical atom just freed from one compound, which immediately thereafter enters into another combination. The self becomes united through consciousness with a new object, but one that is no longer the secular world. There is no transcendence of dualism here, but the whole field defined by the self, the not-self and consciousness is manifestly psychical. At this level there is no basis for a nonpsychical existence for consciousness. Still we cannot say of this that it is a field wholly illumined by consciousness. The Divine Otherness includes vastly more than that comprehended by the conscious self. However, one would not interpret this as an independent, nonpsychical existence in the spirit of the realist. One would speak, rather, of the Unconscious in the sense of Von Hartmann. This Unconscious is the surrogate of the realists' independent entities, which carry the necessitarian factor. In summary, we have arrived at a pattern for the interpretation of necessity that can be formulated in purely psychical terms, though we have not arrived at a complete determination by consciousness. It is thus a position of modified idealism, not absolute idealism.

SELF AND DIVINE OTHERNESS

Necessity may now be interpreted as the inherent law of the Divine Otherness, rather than as the inherent secular structure. On the level of the introceptive Realization itself, there is no problem as to the reconciling of freedom with the necessity of the Divine Law. Freedom simply becomes the liberty to surrender to the Divine Law, or to affirm the autonomy of the self. If the course of surrender is taken, it is not to be conceived as something at all difficult to do. It is an act most highly desired by the self. Surprisingly, the affirmation of autonomy requires a distinctly austere act of will. Self-surrender is sweet. The burden of problems and responsibility drops away. The universe, as it *really* is, is Divine, and just what it should be. To move in the current of this 'should be', which is, seems the most satisfactory course that anyone might desire. Freedom is not an arbitrary doing as one pleases by a finite self, but a surrendering to something far more adequate in every sense. A certain glory is felt in the depreciation of the self relative to the Divine Otherness. Anyone who is familiar with the literature of religious mysticism will recognize this psychical pattern. Indeed, the essential quale of this state leads to far richer expression in religious practices and poetry than it does in philosophy. No one who knows will ever belittle this state, but as our concern here is primarily philosophical, we must focus on the more philosophical implications.

For the reflective consciousness the problem of necessity really becomes the connection between the inherent law of Divinity and the order of sensible nature. We are not concerned here with the concrete resolution of this problem, which can readily become a whole philosophic work in itself. We are merely pointing to a possible way of solving the problem of necessity other than that offered by realism. The present approach will, of course, have its advantages as well as its difficulties, but let us note what is gained by it. In principle we have a resolution of the problem of necessity without a stultification and depreciation of the yearning for freedom; nor does it deny the actuality of freedom. Freedom is reduced to liberty to affirm the self, or to abrogate it, with the latter appearing spontaneously as the more attractive course. Union with the Divine is thus an act of freedom. The religious value is neither lost nor reduced to a mere addendum of a secular philosophical system. The Divine Otherness is not something alien or unfriendly, like the realists' world, but the best of friends. All of mankind's great problems are resolved in an aura of profound Peace, through the expansion into the Divine Otherness that comes with the completeness of surrender.

The first stabilized stage of introceptive Realization does not lead to a monistic metaphysics, and therefore is not to be classed with absolute idealism. The dualism of the individual self and the Divine Otherness is not yet reduced to a true unity. In the language of religious mysticism, such unity as there is may be conceived as the union of the Lover and the Beloved where, from the finite point of view, the lover is the individual self and the Beloved is the Divinity. However, because the relationship is mutual, the Divine Otherness also appears as the Lover of whom the object is the individual self. A noteworthy part of the satisfaction of this state lies in the fact that the dualism still remains; otherwise the relationship of love would lose its objective meaning. There is plenty of reason why this stage tends to become a point of fixation—a station on a path that reaches much further. A study of the literature would indicate that mystical states only exceptionally pass beyond this. Certainly, there is much to be said for the view that the term *mysticism* should be applied exclusively to this stage, while deeper stages may be more properly categorized as Gnosticism, in the generic sense. Clearly, if we do so restrict the connotation of 'mysticism', then mysticism is far more significant for its feeling value than for its noetic value. However, as we shall see later, this relativity is reversed in the deeper and more Gnostic state. Then in the narrower sense, mysticism is of relatively minor philosophical concern, though of vast religious importance. However, it does clearly carry philosophical implications.

If we think through what this limited mysticism entails, we find that its dualism really implies a kind of pluralism, for if the self is not conceived to be solipsistic, then we have a plurality of selves in relation to a Divine Otherness, but not united in a Supreme Self. We might say that there is a kind of unity as well as a kind of pluralism, for there is a unity in the Divine Otherness and a plurality in the multiplicity of selves. This would account for the fact that, while analysis reveals first a dualism, and then a pluralism, the predominant testimony of the mystics favors a monistic interpretation. This is true for the reason that the real orientation of the mystic is to the Divine Otherness, whose nature is monistic and is clearly Realized as such in mystical consciousness. However, the objective character of the love relation prevents the monistic character from being complete.

One well may ask what the offering is from this state to objective scientific and world problems generally. Frankly, it has no primary concern with such problems. They cease to be any longer compelling to the individual who has attained the state. Human service is simply a matter of assisting others to attain the state likewise. Attaining Realization would resolve these problems insofar as they would disappear as problems. This solution is quite adequate for all those who can be induced to accept a positive orientation to the state, but beyond this limit it naturally fails. Even so, there is no logical or moral reason why the mystic should not feel favorably toward a direct approach to scientific and world problems, and there is nothing in his philosophy to prevent him from personally participating in such work. Nevertheless, all this he would regard as simply of pragmatic value in the sense of being *only* pragmatic—a very different matter from being a philosophic pragmatist in the privative sense. Of course, there is nothing in this attitude to provide a very deep concern with scientific or sociological problems, as they have too much the character of dream problems. Yet, given the will to deal with such problems, there is no reason why a mystic should not achieve as much as, or more than, the nonmystic. To be sure, some of the best scientists have been considerably more than a little mystical.

Of more profound interest is what happens to the great philosophical problems of the nature of truth and reality. The answer is quite simple. Truth and Reality mean virtually the same thing, and they have a significance that renders it necessary to spell these words with capital initial letters. Truth and Reality are identical with Divinity, and the Realization of Truth or Reality is not other than the Realization of and union with the Divinity. Clearly, as concepts, these words do not have a truth reference in either the pragmatic or realist sense. They have a substantial rather than a sign-pointer significance. One finds the meaning, not through a successful program of action, but by a meditative or introceptive penetration into the essence of the word or concept. This may be said to be a general description of the meaningful reference of concepts, insofar as they have a mystical value. On the whole, I should say that this enhances the value of concepts, as contrasted with their value in either pragmatist or realist usage. Some words and concepts are important in such a way that both the realist and the pragmatist employment of them has the effect of serious devaluation. I do not doubt that anyone who has the mystic flair would feel a distinct cheapening of value in all three of the foregoing philosophies.*

If an individual were to have a comprehensive selection of modern works on philosophy and choose at random a few volumes for reading, the primary impression would probably emerge that philosophy is humankind's initial effort to arrive at science. Furthermore, philosophy would appear to be a child of science, in that it is conceived quite frequently in this period as a proper generalization of scientific method. However, if this individual were to peruse a selection of extant Greek and Indian contributions to philosophy, together with Western works produced around the eighteenth century, a similar reading would tend to give the impression that philosophy lies close to religion. The truth is that philosophy as a whole reflects and comprehends both the scientific and the religious motifs. However, in our present day, the scientific and

---

*[Naturalism, neorealism and pragmatism.]

worldly utilitarian spirit holds the ascendant place in the reflective domain, with the consequence that philosophy is viewed as more like science than religion. Within idealism, the scientific side is subordinated to the religious motif, but still remains so valuable that the religious element is married to thought and not exclusively to feeling. Because the present age is highly secular, with religion viewed as the weak sister, if she is recognized at all, it is understandable that philosophy should be conceived largely as secular speculation. This I contend is the underlying psychological reason for the general current depreciation of idealism as a whole. As a result of the realization of the failure of the too secular orientation—a fact that is becoming evident in the present worldwide moral debauchery*—there will be a return to a serious valuation of religion. Then once more the idealistic type of philosophy will return to the royal position it once held, for, in the broad sense, idealism alone among all the philosophies really takes religion seriously.

An acquaintance with the lives as well as the works of the great idealists is an illuminating experience. Most generally, they seem to be deeply religious natures. Berkeley, for example, was a bishop. The importance of Kant's religious side is very evident, and seems to supply the deeper motivation for countering the negative effect of the *Critique of Pure Reason* with a *Critique of Practical Reason*,[†] so that a place for religious values might still remain. Fichte comes very near to being the pure devotee, as revealed in the following quotation from *The Vocation of Man*:

> These two orders,—the purely spiritual and the sensuous, the latter consisting possibly of an innumerable series of particular lives,—have existed since the first moment of the development of an active reason within me, and still proceed parallel to each other. The latter order is only a phenomenon for myself, and for those with whom I am associated in this life; the former alone gives it significance, purpose and value. I *am* immortal, imperishable, eternal, as soon as I form the resolution to obey the laws of reason; I do not need to *become* so. The supersensual world is no future world; it is now present; it can at no point of finite existence be more present than at another; not more present after an existence of myriads of lives than at this moment. My sensuous existence may, in future, assume other forms, but these are just as little the true life as its present form. By that resolution I lay hold

---

*[Although this was written during World War II, perhaps no era can entirely escape a similar appraisal.]

[†]Immanuel Kant, *Critique of Practical Reason* (Riga: n.p., 1788; reprint, New York: Bobbs-Merrell, 1958).

on eternity, and cast off this earthly life and all other forms of sensuous life which may yet lie before me in futurity, and place myself far above them. I become the sole source of my own being and its phenomena, and, henceforth, unconditioned by anything without me, I have life in myself. My will, which is directed by no foreign agency in the order of the supersensual world, but by myself alone, is this source of true life and of eternity.*

Additionally, if we go back in time nearly two thousand years, and far across the world, we find as an important part of the Buddhist canon, the *Awakening of Faith*, by Ashvaghosha. Let us select from this the following quotation: "First as to the unfolding of the true principle. The mind has two doors from which issue its activities. One leads to a realization of the mind's Pure Essence, the other leads to the differentiations of appearing and disappearing, of life and death. Through each door passes all the mind's conceptions so interrelated that they never have been separated and never will be."† Is it not as though one spirit were speaking far across space and time, in different worlds and different cultures?

Let us now turn to the opening words of a very famous logic by Georg Hegel, the greatest of the idealist thinkers, and one of the greatest intellects the West has produced.

Philosophy misses an advantage enjoyed by the other sciences. It cannot like them rest the existence of its objects on the natural admissions of consciousness, nor can it assume that its method of cognition, either for starting or for continuing, is one already accepted. *The objects of philosophy, it is true, are upon the whole the same as those of religion. In both the object is Truth, in that supreme sense in which God and God only is the Truth.* Both in like manner go on to treat of the finite worlds of Nature and the human Mind, with their relation to each other and *to their truth in God* [italics mine].‡

---

*Johann Fichte, *The Vocation of Man* (London: n.p., 1838; repr., trans. William Smith, LaSalle: Open Court, 1965), 141-42 (page references are to reprint edition).

†Ashvaghosha, *The Awakening of Faith*, quoted in Dwight Goddard, ed., *A Buddhist Bible* (New York: Dutton, 1938), 362.

‡*Encyclopaedie der philosophishen Wissenschaften im Grundrisse* (I. Thl. Die Logik, by Georg W. F. Hegel), (Heidelberg, 1817); trans. William Wallace, *The Logic of Hegel*, 2nd rev. ed. (Oxford: Clarendon Press, 1892; repr., Benjamin Rand, comp., *Modern Classical Philosophers*, Boston: Houghlin-Mifflin Co., 1908), 569 (page reference is to reprint edition).

Who but an idealist would begin a treatise on logic in the spirit of an essentially religious subject?

Clearly, anyone who would understand idealism must have the feeling for the religious problem as most fundamental. Further, the real significance of idealism is not to be judged by its offering to the practical advance of secular science, a contribution that admittedly is inconsequential. It deals with that which is forever beyond the reach of science *so long as the latter is restricted to current methodology*. Our science supplies us with many arts and material advantages *plus a dangerous implementation of the will to war*. Perhaps the idealist has good reason to feel proud that she is exempt from responsibility for this. She may be excused if she prefers otherworldliness to a "real" world composed so largely of the irrational and insane spirit of violence. Let those who desire something better look to idealism.

When introception is carried to the stage where the self appears as small and enveloped in a vast Divine Otherness, we do not find a basis for absolute idealism, as has been already noted. At this point one could not say with Fichte, "I become the sole source of my own being and its phenomena, and, henceforth, unconditioned by anything without me, I have life within myself."* The mystical stage of introception places the source of life and being in the Divine Otherness, which is not in accord with Fichte's insight as implied above. So, we must return to consider the further development of the introceptive process.

The self, stripped of all extraneous elements, of everything that can possibly be an object for consciousness, is very small indeed. It is a bare point of Light, the mathematical zero, which forms the origin of the base of reference. It is that upon which further possibility rests, but is itself no true object of consciousness. If, at this point, the introceptive process continues, as it will on condition that the autonomy of the self is maintained as against the surrender to the Divine Otherness, then there follows a simply tremendous enantiodromedal transformation. The self as a bare point becomes an unlimited Space whose nature is Light or Consciousness. Divinity fuses with the self, thereby becoming the Self, which is at once both God and I. Again, this is not speculation—it actually happens. This changes the whole view of the nature of being and supplies, as we shall find, the true basis of absolute idealism.

Where the Divinity becomes coextensive with the Self, Light spreads everywhere. This means that the Unconscious is absorbed by Consciousness. We may conceive of this Consciousness as Thought, even though that is simply to select one from among a number of possibilities. Consciousness is Thought and more besides—but this empha-

---

*Fichte, *Vocation of Man*, 142.

sis gives the World that peculiar coloring so that it may be, for philoso-phy. The Divine Thought, which is My Thought, forms the only world there is. Thus the World is Thought, before it becomes experience.

For one born into the empiric world, experience comes first in time, thought afterward. To see thought in this sequence, and only in this sequence, leads naturally to the view that thought evolved to serve experience—and that alone. Hence we have the philosophies in which thought plays only a minor role, the house servant who has no business sitting upon the royal throne. Truly, in time, experience and percep-tion are the Mother of thought. But where there is a mother there must be a father. Mythology and the psychology of the unconscious tell us that the earliest natural humans worshipped solely feminine divinities, for the child knows first and only the mother as an immediate fact. The father is accepted later on the basis of a more or less uncertain inference. The actuality of fatherhood is an immediate realization only for mature consciousness. Much of our modern philosophy is in the state of the primitive human in its acknowledgment of Mother-perception, and its doubt or denial of the Father. For instance, pragmatism doubts that the Father is even a valid inference, much less an immediate realization. Thus pragmatism is the doctrine that parthenogenesis, or virgin birth, is the universal and final truth!

Once it is realized that thought has a hidden Father as well as a revealed Mother, it becomes evident that the concept embodies a dual character. As derived from the Mother, it leads to the object whose essence is experience, but as derived from the Father, it leads inward toward an unseen substantiality. From this there follow two quite opposed logical theories, each of which is capable of validating itself from the respective ground that each assumes. A lifetime devoted to the elaboration of one of these theories will never succeed in dethroning the other. The comprehensive view that finds a place for each is found only by consciousness moving within its roots. Mere experience can never supply the final answer.

The search for the roots of thought leads us veritably into deep waters. It is easy to say that conceptual thought is generated out of per-ceptual life by a process of abstraction. Then, having assumed such a genesis, one might go on to develop a logic wherein the conceptual order acquires significance exclusively in relationship to experience. Yet how is it possible that a living perceptual flux or manifold—view it whichever way one will—should lead to the abstracting process? How indeed does it become possible to rise out of the perceptual stream or manifold to a superperceptual order? This is by no means a simple question, and it is no more answered by invoking the name of life, as is done by the vitalists, than it is by invoking the name of God. Both responses are mystical in the negative sense, whereby there is meant a breakdown of the intelligent will to carry through to the end. In the answers to these questions, we will find the essential differences between the animal and the human kingdoms. Is the difference merely one of degree in an evolutionary scale, without a qualitative separation and addition, or does it form an incommensurable division between two orders? Is a human merely a more advanced animal, or is the total human being to be conceived as an animal nature to which something transcendent has been added, a somewhat that is more lordly and divine than anything that is possible to the purely animal, however highly evolved? These questions are implied, for perception in the broad sense includes the three functions of sensation, feeling and intuition taken together in contrast to conception, and all three of these functions can be found, well or poorly developed, in the animal soul, but conception is alien. The beasts are dumb precisely because they do not have the power bestowed by the concept. Is humankind merely the child of the animal, or something from beyond that is added to the animal? If he is only the child, then he can hardly claim the royal status in the kingdoms of living forms that would rightly be his if his fundamental nature as human is something bestowed from above. In the former case, perhaps a thoroughgoing democracy might be the last word in social relations, but it would have to be a democracy in which the animals—dogs, horses, tigers, lions and hyenas—would be our equals, having the same right of political representation. However, if the quintessential meaning of the words *human* and *man* is something transcendental added to the animal order, then the true relationship of the human to the animal is royal or hierarchical. This would be true in a progressive series from the most animalistic individual up to the most human person. So, what we find with respect to the roots of thought decidedly has manifold bearings, not alone upon the form of philosophy, but even reaching down into the determination of the true social order.

How is it possible that people can receive the stream or manifold of ever-changing experience and yet not feel completely alien? To be merely presented is insufficient to supply the presented with recognition by human consciousness. Something is supplied by the human subject so that the presentation can be recognized as a perception. Otherwise, human consciousness would have no means for rendering an alien other into something familiar, understandable, and even friendly. One who studies the psychology of the more introverted phase of human consciousness finds, as Jung has shown, that in the depths of our psyche there is a perceptual matrix of a profoundly archaic nature. This appears, at times, as a projected image, which is called "primordial" for the reason that it is not reducible to a construct from the objectively presented situation. This is something truly a priori, something of the nature of the Platonic Ideas, which lies at the root of the mind, and which renders possible, first of all, the integration of perception. As Jung conceives it, the Idea proper is derived from the primordial image by a process of abstraction by the reason. Thus the idea is not merely a construct from objective perception, but, in relation to the latter, has something of an innate or a priori character. Yet the Idea is derivative from the primordial image, whose nature is primarily perceptive. This view drives the problem to a deeper level, but still does not account for how the abstracting process of the reason is possible.

IDEAS: HEGEL AND SCHOPENHAUER

There is an impressive parallelism between the views of Jung and those of Schopenhauer. The latter, we may recall, maintains the thesis that the primary root of being is not noetic, but voluntaristic. The Will is primary, while the Idea, which composes the whole objective universe, is merely secondary, as it is essentially an objectification of the Will. However, the Idea exists in two aspects, a more objective and a more subjective. The objective Idea is subject to the principle of sufficient reason, is multiform, and is the source of all science. The subjective Idea is the primary object, existing behind and prior to the principle of sufficient reason, has a unified character, and is revealed most directly, not in science, but in art—in other words, the deed. The subjective idea is fundamentally identical with the primary Ideas of Plato, and performs a function analogous to that of the primordial image of Jung. Since the subjective Idea exists prior to the principle of sufficient reason, it is useless to hope to find a reason for it, in the sense that its form or actuality could be deduced from anything prior to it. It thus exists for reason as something immediately given.

Jung is quite right in finding in Schopenhauer's more subjective Idea a similarity to the perceptive quale of the primordial image. The Idea of Schopenhauer is very different from the Idea of Hegel, for whom it has a more original and self-existent character. Here we have the conflict between voluntaristic and noetic idealism sharply drawn—a conflict that even helped to embitter Schopenhauer's life. The more subjective Idea is like a transcendental object that is derived from a Will antecedent to the subject-object relationship. The Hegelian Idea is self-existent and primary. My view is that there is a partial truth in each standpoint, but that both are relative to an even more profound actuality that occupies a neutral position with respect to Will and Reason. This view I shall develop later.

Schopenhauer's thought is in fundamental sympathy with the perspective of all those who find a primary orientation in teleology or purpose. It seems to be quite generally true that, for those who take this orientation, there is something more fundamental in generic perception than in conception. Perception is the root source and mother of the concept and of the idea conceived as conceptual. Jung has recognized something like a dependence upon a feminine source, as instanced when he states, "The primordial image is the preliminary stage of the *idea* (q.v.) its maternal soil."* However, as already mentioned, the notion of the 'mother' always implies the notion of the 'father', so the account of the genesis of the Idea or concept remains incomplete until we find the father and isolate his function also. I would suggest that one significant way of viewing the difference between Schopenhauer and Hegel consists in interpreting the orientation of the former as being more to the feminine factor, while that of Hegel favored the masculine. The whole pragmatic-vitalistic school is closer to Schopenhauer than it is to Hegel.[†]

The present stage of our discussion leads us to the necessity of considering the relation of 'idea' to 'concept'. Notwithstanding that in a great deal of usage the notions are used interchangeably, we are forced to distinguish a real difference in the meaning. The more subjective Idea of Schopenhauer, and likewise the Idea of Hegel, have a creative power, though the creativeness is understood differently. Schopenhauer's Idea is creative in a more artistic sense, while that of Hegel implies a creative reason operating through the dialectic process. However, the concept is often, and perhaps more correctly, understood as meaning rigorously just what it is defined to mean. Such a concept would not lead to possibilities that could not be rationally inferred. A group of defined concepts will lead to implications, thereby rendering something explicit, but will give no more than was implicitly present in the beginning. In contrast, an Idea with creative potential grows more like something that is alive. It has possibilities that cannot be known by pure inference alone. As I am acquainted with both kinds of mental contents, I am thoroughly convinced of the justice of the distinction. It would follow, for one thing, that Bergson's criticism of intellectualism has a great deal of validity with respect to the concept as just outlined,

---

*Jung, *Psychological Types*, 557.

[†]This would even throw a light upon the feminine element that has been noted in the psychology of Adolph Hitler concerning his strong development of intuition relative to reason.

but it would not be valid for the Idea, since the latter has the power of growing beyond itself. However, it would be a serious misapprehension to regard Hegel's philosophy as conceptualism or intellectualism in this sense, even though he gives that impression to a merely surface view, for there is a creative potency in the Hegelian Idea.

Concepts that are taken as what they are defined to mean, and only that, stand in a position of disassociation from the whole perceptual field. They are equally to be differentiated from introceptive content. They stand in a zone neither of the earth nor of the spirit and lack that which is necessary to predicate actuality in either sense. They define forms of the possible for human consciousness in its peculiar quality as human, taken in differentiation both from that which is animal and from that which is spiritual. However, we are not justified in regarding this as a limiting definition imposed upon the possibilities of consciousness in its concrete totality without specific reference to a human way of knowing. We may know a necessity for human beings as human, but do not thereby have certainty about the nature of nonhuman kinds of consciousness, whether of a superior or of an inferior nature. To know the latter, the consciousness principle in humankind would have to be shifted to the basis of other kinds of beings. Even so, the definition of what is possible for the distinctively human kind of consciousness is, no doubt, of great importance for human beings. The study of the nature and the logic of a pure conceptual order, taken in abstraction both from perceptual reference and from introceptive content, is unquestionably a valuable work. I would be among the last to undervalue logical investigations such as that of Bertrand Russell's *Principles of Mathematics*.* Nevertheless, it would be a mistake to accept this kind of logic as the final word in reasoning.

Idealism in the noetic form has been conceived far too often as the necessary implication of Reason. Beginning with the primary thesis that Reality, whatever it may be, is not self-contradictory, an examination of the specific contents of relative consciousness apparently leads to a number of contradictions or antinomies. Stated succinctly, relative consciousness is self-contradictory, and therefore unreal. Consequently, reality must be found by transcending the whole relative world, including all finite thought. The total process by which this conclusion is reached is very elaborate and involves an extensive literature, which sometimes becomes highly recondite. We shall not here retrace steps that students of philosophy know well, but merely note the outcome. Fortunately, since the days of the great idealists we have come into a better understanding

---

*Bertrand Russell, *The Principles of Mathematics* (Cambridge: University Press, 1903).

of logical possibilities through the logical analysis of mathematics. It appears that many of the supposed contradictions of the relative field can be resolved, with the result that the idealist's argument loses its force. To be sure, the relative world may be unreal, but, if it is, that fact is not established by the formal argument from the essentially contradictory nature of all relative consciousness. Further, the assumption that Reality is not self-contradictory may be challenged, not by affirming that it may be self-contradictory, but on the ground that contradictoriness is a conceptual category that is not relevant in an ontological sense. This form of challenge is typical of the anti-intellectualists. So, in the light of these criticisms, the case for rational, absolute idealism fails insofar as it is supported only by a logical thesis.

I am prepared to grant the force of the above arguments but deny that they touch the actual ground of monistic idealism. When one reads the great idealists, such as Fichte, Hegel and Schopenhauer, one finds that there is a good deal more present than a logical necessitarianism. Particularly is this apparent in the case of Schopenhauer, who is explicitly a voluntarist, but it is also true of the other two. Without doubt, they attached great importance to the logical or rational factor, with a large degree of justification. However, beyond this there is unmistakable evidence of insight, the "temper akin to genius," according to Schopenhauer. These philosophers spoke of something they knew, but not from perceptual experience nor as a logical inference alone. It is from this something known immediately that idealism of the grand style derives its authority. Beyond perception and conception lies introception, which is the path to a transcendental immediacy. When introception is united with conception, then we have the basis of the Reason that leads to idealism.

THE SELF

In support of my present thesis, I call attention to the profound affinity between the idealism of philosophers such as Fichte, Hegel and Schopenhauer, on the one hand, and an orientation that is characteristic of the Upanishads,* on the other hand. This similarity is especially notable in the case of the philosophy of the great Indian monist Shankara. Here also, reality is supersensible and radically monistic. Additionally, one who studies his philosophy and life finds quite man-

---

*[The part of the Vedas that deals specifically with spiritual and philosophical matters. Etymologically, it means the supersensuous knowledge that liberates one from the bondage of the world.]

ifestly that the logical presentation of his system is incidental to a primary insight. His ontology is not exclusively, nor even primarily, derived from a logical deduction. There is evidence that he successfully *awakened a latent function of consciousness* resulting in immediate Realizations of an essentially nonperceptual and nonconceptual nature. From this the philosophical system followed. I have employed the term *introcept* for this kind of immediacy, and *introception* for the process.

It has already been stated that when introception is carried far enough, the self and the Divine Other coalesce in a Self having a highly transcendent character. This is a radically unitary Self of so complete an aloofness that personality simply does not exist for it. It is equally aloof from the empiric world. It is the union of the subject-to-consciousness and its content. It is not contained by space, time and the world of sensible objects, but is like a Space that contains and comprehends all these. From this state of introceptive Realization certain consequences follow:

1. The Self supports the universe, yet is not conditioned by the presence or absence of the universe.
2. The transcendent Thought of the Self is the substratum of the universe, which is *experienced* later by the empiric self, with possibilities of distortion.
3. This Thought defines necessity, whereby the freedom of the empiric self is conditioned, so that for the empiric self the inner sense for freedom attains no more than a partial realization.
4. This Thought is the noumenon of the laws of nature, which receive a statement from physical science of only a pragmatic validity.
5. The world of the empiric self, being only derivative, is no more than an illusion when it is conceived as an independent self-existence.
6. Truth is a relation of congruence between empiric thought or conception and the transcendental Thought.
7. The laws of empiric thought are part of the necessity imposed by the transcendental Thought.
8. The Thought, which is both of and identical with the Self, serves the purpose of attaining complete Self-consciousness.*
9. The Thought of the Self is pregnant with creative potentiality so that it elaborates from within itself possibilities that are more than may be formally deduced.
10. This Thought is concrete in that it is totally comprehensive, but appears as abstract when contrasted to empiric thought derived from perceptual experience.

---

*This implies that the Self has something to attain and therefore is not to be regarded as identical with Absoluteness.

11. The development of this Thought, insofar as reflected to objective
    thought, is a process of enantiodromia, insofar as it follows the form
    of the triadic dialectic.*

The above statements are not merely invented postulates from
which one might proceed to build a hypothetical system, nor are they to
be viewed as the necessary consequences either of empiric or of pure
objective thought. This is a very fundamental part of my whole thesis.
Criticism that does not bear this point in mind misses the essence of
the whole argument. *They are ideas in objective form derived from the
Thought of the Self.* They are not themselves the immediate form of that
Thought, which is inherently independent of the concepts and word
signs of objective thought. That Thought, in its essence, is forever
incommunicable in the forms of relative consciousness. Thus the primary postulates are, rather, precipitates within relative thought of a
Meaning prior to the latter. They are subject to unavoidable distortion
through processes whereby content identical to the Self is made to
appear as an object of consciousness for the empiric subject. The
Thought of the Self is not, and must not be conceived as, an objective or
empiric thought, even to the point that, if Realized by a nonthinking
being, it would not appear as Thought at all. It is a potential of many
facets, of which Thought stands out as the most significant to a predominantly *thinking* being. Doubtless, through another appropriate
facet, it could appear primarily as Willing. There is, therefore, a certain
relativity here that prevents us from reaching an objective decision as to
the primacy of Reason or Will. We may simply say that to a predominantly thinking being it appears primarily as Thought, and from that
perspective a characteristic philosophy follows. Consequently, the postulates previously stated are affirmed as true, but not as so exclusively
true as to preclude precipitation in other patterns.

In any case, whether one Realizes the Self as inherently Will or
Thought, the common implication of this stage of introception is the identification of being with conscious existence. That is, in the generic sense,
the introceptive Realization confirms the cardinal principle of idealism, but
does not necessarily develop in the form of rational idealism. However, as
implied by these postulates, it may take the form of rational idealism.

Even a brief examination of the postulates will show that they confirm the major part of the Hegelian thesis, though stripping from it cer-

---

*[First proposed by Fichte, the triadic dialectic is a process whereby the
tension between a Thesis and its implied Antithesis is resolved in a higher-
order Synthesis. This in turn becomes a new Thesis in a continuing process.
Hegel viewed this as the essential nature of Reality.]

tain features, including its privative character. The most primary thesis of Hegel is confirmed to a degree, but not wholly. Thus there is a sense in which Being is identical with Thought, yet not identical with objective or empiric thought. The Thought of the Self is the noumenal Reality underlying the sensible world, and the necessity inherent in that Thought is projected as the constraint that surrounds the empiric subject. Yet, that constraint is only partly identical with the laws of empiric or objective thought. We are dealing here with the Father of the concept, but as the Father implies the Mother, so the total character of the concept is no more given completely by knowledge of the Father than of the Mother. We have here a dual determination—the one introceptive and the other perceptive—with the result that neither perspective alone can give a complete view. Thus the fundamental criticism of the exclusivity of pragmatism applies equally, though in the reverse sense, to that of Hegelian idealism. The comprehensively synthetic philosophy requires a perspective so far neglected, at least in the Occident.

It is now evident that we must differentiate thought into three forms or aspects. In its most familiar and common form, thought is concerned with a content given through experience. In this case the relatedness of thought is to a perceptual datum, with perception, in the broad sense that includes sensation, feeling and intuition, guiding the course of the thinking. This is the only kind of thinking that is given recognition by the empiricists—including the pragmatists and the nominalists—as possessing genuine validity. It is clear that thought in this sense is of only instrumental value in relation to an experienced or perceptual content. However, there is a second kind of thought wherein the concepts are taken in abstraction from meaningful reference. Here the process begins and ends with concepts without implying a reference to anything else. The concepts do not mean anything that may be perceived or experienced, nor do they refer to a spiritual essence. There is thus no material, but only a formal content. This is the thought of symbolic logic and formalistic mathematics. In this case the truth and existence of a system lies only in its self-consistency. Such a body of thought is neither material nor spiritual, but lies in a realm between the transcendental and the mundane. It really corresponds to the neutral entities of the neorealists that are conceived as neither body nor mind. If we call the first kind of thought "empiric" or "perceptual," we may call this "pure Thought."* In this third sense, Thought does not stand apart from the thinking subject, but is to be viewed as identical with the Self. Thus there is a sense in which we may say that the Self is its own

---

*This kind of thought is strictly transcendental, so I differentiate it from the other kinds by spelling the word with a capital *T*.

Thought, and this Thought is the Self. Yet, we may employ the two notions for the purpose of emphasis—the word *Self* referring to a center of consciousness in its purity, and *Thought* to its quality as Meaning. Thought, in this highest sense, may be conceived as pure Meaning stripped from all form, whether conceptual or perceptual. Meaning, in this sense, is to be conceived as unconditioned by time, space and experiencing. It is purely transcendental and preexistent with respect to all history of process. Neither experience nor pure thought, by itself, can lead to the transcendental Meaning of the higher Thought. It can be attained only through another function, namely, introception.

UNIDENTIFIED INTROCEPTION

Manifestly, for most individuals, introception is not differentiated as a distinct conscious function, but this by no means implies that it is wholly inactive. We may conceive of it as either wholly inactive, or in some measure active without the individual being conscious of its operation. The latter case would parallel the unconscious activity of the other primary functions, which is already a known fact for analytic psychology. There is really nothing strange about the notion of an unconscious activity of a function, as this is implied in all cases where there is a content given to consciousness through a function without there being consciousness of the function itself. Indeed, this would seem to be more the rule than the exception. So, I am not positing anything strange or even unusual in affirming an unconscious activity of introception. However, when the introceptive function operates in this way, the tendency would be to identify it simply with intuition, which is merely a general name for all possibilities of psychical functions that have not yet been revealed to consciousness as distinct. I claim merely to have isolated for conscious recognition a function that has at all times operated more or less widely among humankind. It is to be regarded as truly inactive, both in the conscious and in the unconscious sense, only in the case of those who have an exceptionally mundane or materialistic understanding. When introception is not consciously isolated, and at the same time produces contents for consciousness, the effect is a fusing of this content with the content of the other functions, with the result that there is no clear understanding of the differentiated reference of the total complex content. The result is widespread confusion of interpretation.

An indistinct feeling for or conviction of a spiritual reality is an indication of the activity of introception in its unconscious mode. When introception itself has been rendered conscious, the indistinctness disappears and is replaced by a positive assurance resting upon a ground that is also known. In the latter case an inchoate knowing is transformed into a clear knowing, fortified by knowing of the knowing, and knowing the how of the knowing. Yet even the inchoate knowing that maintains a religious orientation, in the face of the sharpest kind of criticism based upon scientific enlightenment, is the strongest kind of indirect evidence for the existence of the additional function. Furthermore, when the content brought forth through introception, without knowledge of the activity of this function, is fused with the content of one or more of the other functions, then there is a general, and quite normal, tendency to attribute this content to the familiar functions. We are particularly interested in the case where unconscious introception is united with the content of conceptual thinking.

In the fusion of unconscious introception with conceptual thinking, the individual tends, quite naturally, to give to the concept a transcendental reference. This is the real ground of the Ontological Argument for the existence of God, and for the metaphysical reasoning of the scholastic and rationalist type generally. The fundamental failure of this way of thinking does not lie in the insight, but in the attribution of the authority of the insight to the concept itself. Kant's analysis succeeds in differentiating the purely conceptual factor. Based on this distinction, his criticism of the rationalist or scholastic kind of demonstration stands as valid, insofar as he shows that from the pure concept alone the conclusions of rationalism and scholasticism do not follow. Even so, Kant's criticism does not touch the real ground upon which the scholastic and rationalist insight rests. Hegel felt this when he rebuked Kant for treating the conception of God in the same way as the conception of a hundred dollars in one's pocket that possesses everything that may be thought of a real hundred dollars, but that lacks something that the empiric hundred dollars possesses. The point I would make is that the idea of Divinity, or of any other metaphysical actuality, contains this actuality *if, and only if, the concept is fused with the introcept.* Thus the error of the metaphysically oriented thought preceding Kant lies in a failure of epistemological analysis, but not of insight, at least, not necessarily of insight. Some of the rationalists may be quite correct in their metaphysical conclusions, in spite of the extent of error in the methods they employed in deriving those conclusions.

The rationalist wing of monistic idealism is virtually a restatement of Spinoza's metaphysics in the form that became necessary after the criticism of Kant. Hegel, who most forcefully continues the spirit of Spinoza, does not in the essential sense alter the original metaphysical outlook. He mainly changes the form of the statement so as to render it less vulnerable before the Kantian form of critique. The insight is virtually the same; the method of establishing the insight is different. Hegel's effort is enormously important, for Kant's treatment of the issue leaves us without ground for spiritual or metaphysical assurance. Kant himself felt this but was far too religious to like the outcome. In large measure, he tries to correct its effect by way of his *Critique of Practical Reason*, but with results that fall far short of supplying an adequate ground for genuine metaphysical assurance. Hegel, I believe, succeeds better, even though he, in turn, proves assailable by more modern criticism.

Modern analysis, like the earlier Kantian criticism, leaves us with only perceptual experience and conceptual thought, which either is related to experience or produces only an abstract construction without real content. It is thus without means for determining any metaphysical actuality, since the metaphysical is no immediate part of either the purely empirical or the purely conceptual. The result is that religious conviction has, for modern enlightened consciousness, either the value of superstitious fantasy, or else only a psychological value, in Jung's sense. Under such conditions, the best that one could possibly say of religious conviction is that it has a value for psychological therapeutics. It is subjected to a simply terrible depreciation because the content of such conviction is valued, at best, as of only instrumental significance, whereas its very soul is that its content is of terminal significance. The would-be destroyers of Hegel are, in effect, the destroyers of religious insight, regardless of whether they are Marxians, naturalists, pragmatists or neorealists.

However, we find that all of the foregoing critiques constitute a delimitation of pure conception taken in abstraction from all content. They have no bearing upon the content that may be supplied to the concept through introception. The authority of the introcept has a quite different ground from the authority of the concept. So, granting that conception qua conception can have only an instrumental value, it does not therefore follow that it is instrumental to an exclusively perceptual or experiential content. Granted that conception in its purity by itself is servant, yet that service may be related to a transcendental as well as a mundane order. Further, when conception is united to the introcept, it becomes a viceregal power in relation to the whole mundane field of perception and experience. Thus there is such a thing as a Royal Thought as well as a servant thought. The mundane philosophies know only the servant thought, and though they may ever so correctly understand the nature of this kind of thought, all of this is quite beside the point when we are in the presence of thought vested with the robes of true royalty.

THE PROBLEM OF FORMULATION

The truly Royal Thought stands above the formalism of words and concepts, though it may ensoul these. Let it be unequivocally understood that I am not here speaking in terms of a speculative abstraction, but of something that, under the appropriate conditions, may be known directly. There is a state wherein one may be clearly aware of a dual thought process within the mind that may even be present concurrently. One, the deeper Thought, moves or develops without words, concepts or images and reaches into the more objective mind only through an incipient and casual contact with conceptual fragments. It is a thought possessing tremendous clarity and sweep. Until one has had the impression corrected by subsequent experience, it seems as though this thought would be very easy to formulate, but in practice this is extremely difficult. It does not precisely fit any conceptual or word forms. A pure meaning grasped almost instantaneously is only by laborious effort partially conveyed in a form that can be written or spoken. Often very strange constellations of conceptual forms are required to suggest the primary meaning. Such arrangements are of an order that makes little or no sense in terms of the more familiar conceptual references. For example, ordinarily the notion of 'flow' implies a movement from a point here to a point there, either in space or in time. This is a fixed meaning that we habitually give to the notion of flowing. It is most certainly progressive, in some sense, rather than static. How then would one convey an immediate value or Realization wherein the static and flowing quality were equally emphatic? I used the notion of a 'life-current' constantly moving but, at the same time, so turning upon itself that there is no progress from past to future. I thought I had turned the trick in giving a lucid formulation to an immediate content, until someone gently suggested to me that it did not make sense! I caught his point of view right away. Yet, that did not change the fact that I knew what I knew. Actually, this difficulty is not so strange, for if one manages to abstract his purely perceptual consciousness from the ordinary complex of concepts and percepts that form the manifold of daily conscious content, and further tries to formulate the raw perceptual material in terms of concepts, then he or she finds that the concept and word forms do not fit in that case either. The pure perceptual quale is more like impressionistic, futuristic or surrealistic art. Anyone who tries to capture that sort of thing in terms of concepts and words so that they will make a straightforward and understandable statement will have a difficult labor.

The inner Thought is spontaneous in that it happens of itself insofar as the objective personal thinker is concerned. It is not the product of a consciously willed effort by the personal ego. Further, it is not a content that stands out as clearly differentiated from the self. Rather, the self and content are blended in identity, a state that is very difficult to conceive from the objective point of view. It follows, though, that as a result of this identity between the I and the content, there is no possibility of a content that is erroneous with respect to the self. Hence, there is a noetic certainty here, without all the problems and doubts that grow out of the trial-and-error method of empiric cognition. There is no question of knowing correctly until one seeks to achieve a formulation through the objective mind. However, the latter process can be more or less in error, and, withal, is never wholly accurate. Right here lies the reason the great idealist philosophies are always vulnerable before criticism, yet, at the same time, in their inward meaning, they are equally impregnable. The psychological, epistemological and logical hackers may tear to pieces the formal garments of systems like those of Spinoza and Hegel all they please and still never reach at any point the inner authority upon which those systems rest. This is so because philosophers like Spinoza and Hegel know what they know despite the defects of their formulations and all the attacks of lesser thinkers. One who has been There is not moved by a mountain of denials from those who have not been There, though he may be convinced that he should alter his expression.

The inner Thought *is*—whether or not it has also been thought conceptually. Even so, whether or not this is important to the inner Thought, it is certainly of the highest importance to the empiric individual that it should be brought down within the range of conceptual reach. By having been thought conceptually, the inner Thought ensouls the concept so that thereafter such concepts are powers in themselves. They are no longer merely sign-pointers to further experience in the pragmatic sense. Doubtless many concepts and words have merely a sign-pointer value in this sense, and perhaps all concepts may have such a significance as a dimension of their total meaning. To this extent, the pragmatic theory of knowledge may be acceptable, but it becomes positively vicious when it arrogates to itself exclusive validity. The ensouled concept is a lifeline from Spirit to the empiric human being— the wanderer in the confusing forest of experience. When such a concept is reduced to a soulless sign-pointer in a purely mundane manifold, it ceases to be a lifeline to Spirit.

CONCEPTION, PERCEPTION AND INTROCEPTION

Introception, conception and perception constitute three primary functional forms of consciousness, if we take perception, in its turn, as consisting of the complex psychical manifold produced from the psychological functions of sensation, feeling and intuition. From the three primary functional forms of consciousness we can derive four secondary combinations that produce corresponding fields, each having a distinctive character.

1. Introception combined with conception already has been partly discussed in its relation to rational idealism. This is Spirit descending to humanity from above and thus appearing in the transcendental relation.

2. Introception combined with perception is the foundation of mystical states of consciousness of the alogical type. In this case, the psychological functions of feeling and intuition play a much larger part than does thinking. A study of mystical literature leads to the conclusion that by far the larger portion of the mystical states are of this type. It is reasonably appropriate to speak of mystical *experience* here, whereas the more noetic quality produced by the combination of introception and conception is not properly called "experience," but requires some other term, such as *recognition*. The latter may be characterized as Spirit in the immanent relation to human consciousness.

3. Conception combined with perception. This is the familiar relationship that forms the subject matter of the vast bulk of current philosophical and psychological literature. It is entirely possible that the pragmatist's epistemological interpretation of this particular field is, in large measure, correct. The field determined by this combination is exclusively secular and practical in the mundane or utilitarian sense. In this connection the humanistic theory of value and ethics may be valid enough, but the field of consciousness produced by this combination, when taken in abstraction from other possibilities, is strictly nonreligious. Since practically all of current sociology is conceived in terms of this combination, it is easy to see why most of our social thought has an exclusively secular orientation. It is conceivable that, in this combination, primacy could be given either to perception or conception. This gives us two opposing alternatives: (1) Where perception is given primacy, conception appears as only instrumental, with the pragmatic theory of knowledge following as a natural consequence; (2) where conception is given primacy, the instrumental theory of ideas does not follow. Neorealism appears to imply the relative primacy of conception when it affirms the independence of primacy of mathematical and logical entities.

4. Introception combined both with conception and with perception naturally represents the most comprehensive field of all and supplies the most difficult problems for philosophic integration. I know

of no philosophy that deals with the problem in this complex form. It does not seem to lend itself to any single, simple epistemology. It is more likely that all theories of knowledge have a relative validity within this field. However, merely to accept this view can result in little more than an eclectic syncretism, which is far too loose to be philosophically satisfactory. The major problem would be the integration of the apparently incompatible theories into a systematic whole—certainly no simple matter.

If the three primary functional forms of consciousness are each taken in isolation from the other two, distinctive fields of consciousness are also delimited.

1. Perception taken in isolation corresponds to subhuman consciousness, such as that of the animal kingdom. This has its superior possibilities, which are evidenced in some of the behavior of the higher animals. Some animals do indeed seem to have superiority in certain directions that would shame many human beings. Nevertheless, no doubt, out of this field of consciousness no science or philosophy could ever be evolved, although something of art might develop.

2. Conception taken in isolation clearly encompasses the fields of pure mathematics and pure logic, in the modern rigorous sense. A mathematical philosophy is quite possible here, in complete detachment either from the perceptual or from the introceptual functions of consciousness. When mathematics is related to perception, we have the applied mathematics with which we are familiar. However, when mathematics is combined with introception, it carries a religious force that results from a kind of applied mathematics, though in quite a different manner. In the latter case, Truth is not an incidental notion employed by mathematics, but so largely becomes its soul that the word must be capitalized. Russell never discusses this potential of mathematics in *The Principles of Mathematics*.

3. Introception taken in isolation is pure Spiritual Consciousness in the strict meaning of the term. It is absolutely Otherworldly in that complete sense wherein the whole relative universe, with its multitude of forms and creatures, literally vanishes, just as a forgotten dream. It is the Nirvanic or Super-Nirvanic State of Consciousness, which is the objective envisaged by spiritual exemplars such as Buddha, Shankara and Christ—the religious endeavor in the grandest sense. It transcends philosophy just as it does all other relative formations, even the most abstract, though it is closer to the most abstract forms than to any concrete particularization.

Of the seven fields of consciousness, three are manifestly non-philosophical and nonscientific in their inward content, namely, pure perception, pure introception and the combination of introception and perception. The other four fields that incorporate conception do present the possibility of a philosophical problem and orientation. Our interest here falls within the range of these four fields, to the exclusion of the other three, other than to recognize them as states in their own right. One implication that follows is that an absolutely comprehensive system of philosophy or science is impossible, since it could not truly represent or portray states wherein conceptual cognition does not enter as a component part. In other words, a conceptual monism would not be a universal monism, insofar as it could not incorporate the forms of consciousness wherein there is complete absence of the concept. Yet, this does not necessarily imply pluralism because there may be an ultimate nonconceptual unity.

Of the four current philosophical schools, naturalism, neorealism and pragmatism are exclusively related to the field delimited by the combination of conception and perception. Idealism alone is oriented to the combination of introception and conception, and perhaps to some extent to the combination of introception, conception and perception. Therefore, the religious motif is dominant only in idealism, whereas with the other three philosophical schools it enters, at most, only as an afterthought. Each of these schools implies a difference of accentuation in the relative importance of the functions of consciousness, emphasized as follows:

1. Naturalism: Perception under the quale of sensation is given ascendancy over thinking, while both intuition and feeling are quite ignored, as philosophically insignificant.
2. Neorealism: Thinking is given ascendancy with sensation subordinate, though remaining an important constituent. Feeling is not wholly disregarded, since there is a neorealist theory of value, but, on the whole, intuition seems to be rather despised.
3. Pragmatism: Sensation, feeling and intuition are all recognized as philosophically significant, with conceptual thinking playing an auxiliary or servant role. The degree of importance attached to the three perceptual functions varies according to different pragmatic thinkers, though all agree in subordinating conceptual thinking. Bergson and Spengler accentuate intuition, whereas sensation apparently carries the primary value for Dewey. Perhaps James gives a larger recognition to the determinate part of feeling, as compared to the other leading pragmatists, but I would not say he gives it first place. He affirms the right of a will to believe, and of "over-belief," which implies a

high valuation of the right of feeling to play a determinant part. Schiller possibly gives as much emphasis to the constitutive part of feeling as any. Also, quite frequently, pragmatists affirm the doctrine that all thinking is wishful thinking, which implies an attribution of a predominant role to feeling, at least insofar as conceptual thinking is concerned. It does not seem to be so well recognized that there is such a thing as wishful sensation and wishful intuition as well.

4. Idealism: This school divides into two branches, rational idealism and voluntaristic idealism. My study of rational idealism leads me to the conclusion that here conception is united with, but ascendant over, introception. In my judgment, voluntaristic idealism, of which Schopenhauer is the greatest representative, combines introception, conception and perception, with perception ascendant both over conception and over introception. The Will of Schopenhauer is really a reference to the perceptive quale, with accentuation of its conative character. (This accentuation of conation is likewise characteristic of the pragmatists.) In my opinion, no modern Occidental philosopher has given primacy to introception, nor did Plato among the Greeks. However, this accentuation is to be found in Shankara, Plotinus, Buddha and Aurobindo. In our culture, the predominantly introceptualistic philosophy remains to be written.

Kant's great philosophical achievement consists of two parts, one positive and the other negative. He supplies a basis whereby we are able to have confidence in the orderliness of experience, which is the necessary condition of any possibility of science. However, on the negative side, he shows that pure reason or pure conception can never lead to a knowledge of metaphysical reality. Nevertheless, the yearning for metaphysical certainty is not only the greatest driving motivation of the philosopher, it also equally underlies the religious feeling. Clearly, Kant personally feels the desire for this certainty no less than others; he comes to his negative conclusions simply as an act of intellectual honesty. Yet, while he is forced to conclude that pure conception cannot prove a metaphysical existence, it is equally impossible for reason to prove the nonexistence of a metaphysical reality. The incompetency, in this case, is merely such as that of the pure reason operating by itself. The possibility of some other way of knowing, whereby metaphysical reality may be the certain Realization of humanity, is not excluded. Therefore, in the absence of this other way of knowing, one has a right to faith that pure reason is incompetent to deny, so long as the faith is oriented to a moral or a spiritual order. Even so, faith alone justifies only the postulating of a metaphysical reality. It is less than knowledge, and so conceivably may be grounded on nothing more than fantasy. Kant, like James, gives us a right to believe, but no real ground of spiritual security.

We may say that the great purpose of the German idealists who succeeded Kant was to secure a more adequate foundation than Kant provides for the orientation to spiritual or metaphysical reality. The idealist development was certainly not necessary for establishing the ground for a practical science, for Kant left this ground abundantly secured. Still, the greatest yearning of the human soul can never be satisfied by a practical science, however far it may be developed, for this approach never answers the question of the ultimate meaning of the whole of experience. We must acknowledge that it is possible that philosophy might accept as final Kant's conclusion as to the office of conception. Then, discrediting faith as a valid signpost to the Transcendental, continue on to the general handling of those problems that fall outside the range of particular sciences. Both neorealism and pragmatism have followed this course, while the metaphysical conclusions found in naturalism are obviously of the type that is untenable in the light of the Kantian critique. To idealism alone falls the task of finding a positive answer to the metaphysical or religious yearning of humanity in more satisfactory terms than that of a permitted faith, with a right to postulate that which one feels or intuits.

Does idealism succeed in its task? In the light of modern criticism, the answer seems to be negative. One can find places in James's writings where he says that the idealists may be right in their insight, but they have not yet established that insight. He grants the right of a will to believe, but nothing more positive than that. With neorealism, the outlook becomes even more discouraging, for here the logical outcome is a practical pessimism without hope, as expressed by Russell.* Today the philosophical standing of religion—by which I mean the orientation to a metaphysical certainty—is very shaky indeed. After all, faith is only a crutch, or a boat whereby humankind may hope to cross the stormy sea of uncertainty to the far shore of assured Knowledge. Within some reasonable time, faith must lead to transcendent Knowledge, or it must be judged as tried and found wanting. Hence, every truly religious person must feel the deepest wish for the success of the proposed enterprise of the idealist. For anyone to feel happy in finding that idealism has failed is the clearest proof that he lacks any authentic spiritual sensitivity. Intellectual honesty may compel an individual having a genuine religious orientation to acknowledge the force of modern criti-

*Bertrand Russell, "A Free Man's Worship," in *Philosophical Essays* (n.p., 1910) 60, 70, quoted in Perry, 346.

cism, but she must feel saddened by its success. Furthermore, in the face of its results, one must either feel a challenge to carry further the idealists' endeavor, or else acquiesce in devastating defeat. No vital spiritual nature will ever be satisfied with an ersatz substitute, in the form of a psychological permission to believe, for indubitable metaphysical Knowledge. Psychology offers to the religious orientation no more than a toy for quieting a wayward child. An authentic human being will insist upon the real thing or nothing. There either is a Kingly Knowledge that we can know, or life is no more than a barren waste filled with mirages wherein childish souls disport themselves and mature souls face despair, which they may meet heroically or not. Doubtless there is something noble in the heroism that can face this despair with firm, upright posture and a smile, but it is entirely futile. Universal suicide would be a more rational response.

The three mundane philosophies give us no valid reason for eschewing wholesale racial suicide as the one and only adequate solution to the problem of life. Sufficient reason for another course can be found only in carrying on the enterprise of the great idealists in the hope of correcting their technical errors. Long ago I proposed to continue that project and finally attained success. I know that the Kingly Knowledge *is*, and that it is possible for people to know it. I also know the Road by which it may be attained so completely that faith is ultimately consumed in certainty. However, the Road lies in a way of consciousness very difficult to find for whoever looks forth exclusively upon the world of common awareness, whether of sense or ideas. Yet, this Road is very close at hand, since it lies locked in every human psyche. Sought in the proper way, it can be found. Despite all of our extensive psychological and epistemological analysis, we of the West have missed the greatest secret of the psyche. Fortunately, once this Kingly Knowledge is attained, the problem of its relationship to conception and the empiric world is only one of detail. The problem may be technically difficult, but since its solution is not vital, we have plenty of time for its resolution.

In the next chapter, I propose to outline a new philosophic approach that, while it lies close to the spirit and motive of idealism, it departs from the method of the latter in certain important respects and orients itself to an Ultimate conceived in different terms. So far I have simply traced a path through the systems and ways of thought presently existing. In principle, I have removed barriers wherever they appeared and emphasized indicators to a similar goal wherever they were found. I am not here concerned with the development of extant philosophies with ramifications in directions neutral to the present purpose. There is much of relative value in each of them, and in many relations I may assume the attitudes of these other philosophies. However, all modern thought falls short with respect to the great problems that we must solve if life is to be more than the rearranging of the pieces of a meaningless jigsaw puzzle. It is not enough somehow to wriggle through the span of life through the judicious employment of innumerable games. Durable satisfaction can come only when humankind has, at last, crowned its effort with the Realization of an all-inclusive and significant Meaning.

PART II:
INTROCEPTUALISM

7

Introception

In the broadest usage of the term, *idealism* means any interpretation of being or of experience wherein consciousness, in some sense, plays the determinant part. Notably, the manner in which consciousness is determinant varies quite widely concerning different thinkers. Thus the external universe may be conceived as composed merely of ideas, in the sense of percepts or recepts, as in the case of Berkeley, or it may be a system of Reason, as conceived by Hegel, or of a Will lying behind the reason, as with Schopenhauer. Further, the empiric activism of pragmatism may be conceived essentially in terms of consciousness, as was true in the case of F. C. S. Schiller. For Kant, the idealism has an epistemological character, in that it defines the form of possible experience and knowledge without saying anything about the nature of the thing-in-itself. Idealism in this most general sense stands differentiated from realism in its broadest connotation, wherein both primary existence and the constitution of knowledge are conceived as independent of consciousness. However, idealism, in the sense of the specific philosophical school known by that name, is more definitely defined. In the latter instance, either the Reason or the Will of a universal or absolute Self constitutes the metaphysical nature of the universe. This implies that the general affirmation that consciousness is a primary determinant is not sufficient, by itself, to lead to the classification of any thinker as an idealist in the restricted sense of the school of idealism. Idealism, in the grand sense, is otherworldly, as well as being oriented to the view that consciousness is primary, while according to the more general sense of the term, the idealist can also be an empiricist.

In the philosophic view of which I am here giving an introductory outline, consciousness is again conceived as primary and constitutive, but the point of departure from the preceding philosophic theories is so considerable that a new classification seems necessary. I ground my thesis upon a new function of consciousness, which I have called "introception." It implies a way of knowledge differing both from the empiric and from the conceptualistic, as those notions are currently understood. It also implies a function more profound than the conative principle of

Will as understood by Schopenhauer. Thus I am calling this view "intro-ceptualism," in which the term *introception* is given a dual reference, (1) to a function of consciousness, and (2) to the content or state of consciousness rendered accessible by the function.

As has been already noted, the validity of the present thesis rests primarily upon the actuality of the function of introception. Without at least assuming that actuality, the thesis loses its ground as a possibility. Moreover, even if the function is granted to be real, it does not therefore follow that the theoretical statement is necessarily correct throughout. It may be correct as a matter of fundamental principle and yet fall short of accurate interpretation in detail. This is true for the reason that all philosophical interpretation necessarily involves a correlation of the primary given material with a conceptual organization. As a result, the immediate element may not always be correctly conceived, or the laws of thought may be violated in the development. The latter is a problem for human skill, wherein the thinker is limited by the relativity of his or her proficiency. It is important that the critic should bear this distinction in mind and not judge the reality of a function either by the strength or weakness of the proficiency in conceptual interpretation. I am much more concerned that introception should attain recognition as a genuine psychical function than that this system of interpretative ideas should be accepted.

The function of introception has been defined as the power whereby the Light of consciousness turns upon itself toward its source. This statement, bare and simple as it is, has profound implications. It implies that human consciousness is not exclusively of such a nature that it is dependent for its existence upon the presence of *two* terms, a subject and an object, that it unites in a relation. As I understand the neorealist theory of consciousness, it is conceived as exclusively a relation between two terms, and not a self-existence or a function of a subject taken in abstraction from all objects. Upon the basis of such a theory, the turning of the Light of consciousness upon itself and moving toward its source would be a meaningless and fantastic conception. Therefore, I am forced to deny at least the exclusive truth of the neorealist theory, though it might conceivably have a relative validity as a description of part of the total nature of consciousness.

THE FLOW OF CONSCIOUSNESS

The definition of introception further implies that human consciousness is of such a nature that it may be conceived as flowing or streaming, in part at least, from the subject toward the object. This, again, entails that consciousness is not merely a relation, for a flowing involves the notion of a something or a somewhat that is flowing. Even when we speak of the relationship of flowing we do not mean that the relation of flowing flows, but have merely abstracted a feature from the total situation. So, while consciousness conceived as no more than a relation might bind subject to object, it could not flow from subject to object. The whole notion of consciousness turning upon itself and moving toward its source thus implies that consciousness has a substantive character. This I shall later affirm on immediate grounds, not merely as an inference from a definition. In contending that consciousness is substantive, I am giving an affirmative answer to the question that James asked in the form, "Does consciousness exist?" Since he proposed a negative answer in the sense in which I give an affirmative one, it follows that here I depart radically from James's position.

If consciousness does flow from the subject to the object, then it follows that the function of the senses is not purely receptive. I am unable to exclude the possibility that there may also be a flow of consciousness from the object to the subject, in which case there would a sense or a degree in which the function of the senses is receptive. Yet, the flow from the subject to the object is the primary fact for our purposes. This implies, then, that in some sense the individual subject makes the object that he or she realizes or experiences. However, I do not mean to suggest by this that the object necessarily is a consciously willed creation of the individual subject. It would be, at least more usually, a projecting process from the subject that is unconscious to the individual ego. Indeed, there is much evidence from analytic psychology that gives substantial support to this idea. Especially do we find in primitive psychology that the unconscious projecting of subjective elements upon the object plays a highly important part in determining the nature of the surrounding world as the primitive experiences it. We have the advantage over the primitive insofar as we are now able to isolate this function for analysis, so that the world we experience is something very different from what it is for the primitive.

As has already been conceded, it is possible that there is also a flow of consciousness from the object to the subject, thereby placing the subject in the receptive position. Such a theory does exist in the Indian Tantra, but while important implications would follow from it, I shall disregard this feature for the present.

Fortunately, the idea that, at least in part, human consciousness is of the nature of a flow from the subject to the object is available to a degree of verification that can be applied rather generally. I have employed a test both to myself and others that has afforded some very interesting results. The subject of the experiment is asked to attend to some fixed object, preferably a visible object. Then, without changing the fixation of the sense impression, the subject is told to focus his or her attention upon the perceiving itself, rather than upon the object of perception. This is an effort to perceive perceiving. I find that most subjects report results having one or more of the following features:

1. The object tends to grow dim.
2. Often something like a dark shadow, which yet has a character different from ordinary darkness, begins to grow over the object.
3. The object may disappear completely.
4. A field of light may replace the object.
5. Along with this, there is very frequently a marked change of the affective state of awareness. It is a somewhat intense feeling of felicity of the general type reported from mystical experience, but not as completely developed.

Of course, I am well aware that it is possible to invent other theories to account for this kind of experience. Alternative theories for any experience whatsoever are always possible and are limited only by the imagination of the theorist. At any rate, this test indicates that the definition of introception, as a turning of the Light of consciousness upon itself so that it moves toward its source, is a functional concept. Therefore, it is scientifically useful to some degree.

The facts of introceptive Realization and experience definitely imply that human consciousness is of such a nature that, under the appropriate conditions or by the appropriate effort, it can be severed from the object and exist with no more than a one-way dependence upon the subject. This has a profound bearing upon the nature of the ecstatic trance of the Neoplatonists and of the Samadhi trance of the East Indians. If one assumes the theory that consciousness is exclusively a relationship dependent upon the *two* terms, known as *subject* and *object*, then Samadhi or the ecstatic trance would be interpreted as a state of complete unconsciousness. James Leuba, in his *Psychology of Religious Mysticism*,* has maintained this position, but his view is manifestly prejudiced by his assumed theory of consciousness and is not based upon knowledge. Both Neoplatonic and Indian literature on the subject attest that the state of ecstatic trance has a distinctly superior noetic and affective value, which is quite incompatible with the notion that it is a state of unconsciousness. The only proof here is, of course, immediate experience or Realization, and then the *proof* exists only for the individual

---

*James Leuba, *The Psychology of Religious Mysticism* (New York: Harcourt, Brace & Co., 1925).

subject. My experience has always been in the form of a separation in the flow of consciousness so that a minor portion of the stream continues toward the object, with the result that objective consciousness is dimmed, but not extinguished. The object is extremely depreciated in that it loses all, or nearly all, relevancy, but always remains as sensibly or conceptually available. In contrast, the consciousness in the state of the reverse flow toward the subject is like a Light highly intensified. All objective consciousness is, relatively, only like moonlight contrasted with bright sunlight in a dry desert. I know that the introceptive state is anything but a dimming or disappearance of consciousness; rather, it is a radical intensification of it. I must agree with the frequently recurring analogy found in mystical literature wherein the introceptive state of consciousness is likened to the rising of another Sun so bright as to dull forever thereafter the light of the physical sun. Most emphatically, this experience of intensification of consciousness is real, entirely apart from its meaningful value for knowledge or feeling. A comprehensively true psychological theory of consciousness will simply have to incorporate this fact.

So far I have not attempted to define consciousness, for the reason that I can no more define it than I can the distinctive quale of any perceptive state. One could, for instance, define a single-wave color as consisting of a given wavelength, frequency and wave form, but could not define the distinctive quale of the color seen by an individual subject. This definition gives that which a person born blind could understand, but the distinctive quale of the color is something that cannot possibly be conveyed apart from immediate personal experience. Therefore, because consciousness is of this nature, it is indefinable. We can point to consciousness by saying that it is that which becomes less and less as one sinks into dreamless sleep, and that which becomes more and more as he or she slowly returns to waking consciousness. No one who has never had this experience or its equivalent could ever possibly know what consciousness is. In other words, a state of continuous consciousness that never has stood in contrast to unconsciousness in some sense, could never be known as consciousness. It is thus conceivable that there could be a primordial consciousness that never knew its own conscious quality. Moreover, even the so-called unconscious of analytic psychology may very well simply be a consciousness of this sort.

While the starting point of the introceptive process is human consciousness, it does not follow that our search will comprehend only that domain. Human consciousness is a form or way of consciousness that is differentiated from animal and other possible kinds of consciousness. If consciousness qua consciousness is a continuum, rather than a discrete manifold, then the search may carry us to a place where we shall see humanity as simply a zone of possible forms of consciousness among others. Perhaps it is precisely the significance of Kant's work that he delimits in principle—however defective in detail—the characteristic features of a human qua human consciousness, while beyond there lie other possibilities of consciousness he either does not consider or does not know. To be sure, strange things happen when one initiates the introceptive process, things of such revolutionary implication that the radical Copernican change in astronomy or in Kant's thought is distinctly mild in contrast. The would-be investigator may well think twice before embarking upon the enterprise if he or she fears the loss of his or her gods, be they scientific or traditional, for once the door is opened, there is no turning back.

When an investigator is presented with an affirmation or evidence that there exists a psychological function that is not generally isolated so that it is commonly known, it is quite natural to question whether any means exists to render this function consciously active. This is an enormously important issue, but I shall not here consider it more than briefly. The present concern focuses primarily on the office of introception, and the significance of the content that this function makes available. The problem concerning the method by which the function of introception may be aroused into conscious activity is one of great difficulty and has vast ramifications. There is indeed quite an extensive Oriental literature on the subject, but much of it is so largely adapted to the peculiarities of a psychical development foreign to the Occidental organization that it is practically useless for the Western student. Nonetheless, even a casual perusal of these sources will convince one that the Oriental sages have given the problem very serious and profound consideration. There can be no doubt that Oriental students of the subject were as thoroughly convinced of the value of the investigation as we are of our science. There is unmistakable evidence that they attained positive results, and that they valued such results above all other achievements. The typical Western supercilious attitude toward the Oriental will not survive a serious examination of Eastern wisdom. Oriental intelligence simply developed in a different direction from our own and achieved results there that are in no way inferior to our own. Where we have progressed in the physical control of matter, they have advanced most in the understanding and control of the psyche.

The problem of method, whereby the latent introceptive function may be aroused to conscious activity, is peculiarly difficult, since the solution proves to be one that can never be completely attained by method. Moreover, effective method is found to vary with individual temperament. The means that have proven effective for an individual of one temperament may fail completely for another with a radically different psychical organization. Recent work concerning the differences of psychological types sheds considerable illumination upon this aspect of the matter. Clearly, the subject requires extensive study.

Yet, even if we knew the last word that could be uttered about method, we would then control only one side of the problem. The other part of the arousing process is autonomous or spontaneous, and is thus something that no one can command by willed effort alone. To use a metaphor in the Eastern spirit, the individual, through the faithful employment of method, merely prepares a cup, which is filled when something other, and quite beyond his or her control, acts on its own initiative. Sometimes it so happens that an individual may have unconsciously prepared the cup and then received the benefit of a spontaneous filling as a matter of complete surprise. It would follow that the conscious employment of method is neither an absolute essential nor does it provide a positive assurance of success within a prescribed time. Even so, the consensus of Oriental experience abundantly confirms the view that the application of appropriate method vastly increases the probability of success, so work in this direction is well justified.

When I was a university student, this problem came to my attention and ultimately came to occupy a central place there. I finally proved that the discovery and use of the appropriate method could eventuate in a successful outcome, though success was not attained until after more than twenty years. Yet, today, though I am aware of the office of method and the meaning of what it can achieve, I still find it impossible to define the crucial step. In the end, everything hung upon a subtle psychical adjustment that is truly inexpressible, since the very act of expression gives it a false appearance of an objective character that is not at all true to the real meaning. I found that the key consisted in attaining a moment within which there is a thoroughgoing detachment from the object and from the activistic attitude of ordinary consciousness. The simplicity of this statement hides a real stumbling block, for the degree and extent of detachment implies an uprooting of very deep-seated habits. There is a sense in which we may say that a thoroughgoing breaking of the dependence upon the object, as well as the activistic attitude, is like a conscious dying, which long established psychical habits tenaciously resist. It may take considerable work to attain the critical state.

Certain habits place the Western scholar at a peculiar disadvantage. We even have made a virtue of an attitude that operates as a fatal barrier, so long as it persists. This is the attitude of detaching intellectual understanding or apprehension from oneself. We study, think about and gather endless information about all sorts of subjects and pride ourselves in standing aloof from the content of what we study. For much material this is a justifiable and useful attitude, but it is not the way one attains a psychical transformation. One can raise a study to the status of an effective transforming agent only by giving oneself to it with the same completeness that is characteristic of the more intense religious natures. Most scientific and scholarly minds seem to be afraid of this as of the devil himself. However, this fear must be mastered or the scholar will remain a stranger to his or her most valuable inner resources. 'Knowledge about' becomes an effective agent only when it is transformed into 'knowledge through acquaintance', with the willingness to accept any practical consequences. Beforehand, one does not know whether one will lose exactly that most valued. It takes a strong attitude of faith to face this. However, what happens is a radical change in the orientation of valuation, so that a vastly greater Value replaces the old system of values. Thus it is not really *value* that is lost, but an old *orientation*, which is quite a different matter.

A secular kind of scholarship, no matter how extensively developed, will leave the scholar outside the sacred precincts, so long as the attitude remains secular. It is just the subtle change implied in the difference between secular and sacred that makes all the difference in the world. In principle, anything whatsoever can acquire the sacred value. It is simply important that the attitude of sacredness shall exist in some direction and shall absorb the predominant portion of the interest. Sacredness implies self-giving, while secularity implies self-withholding. In the transformation process, everything else is incidental to the attaining of the pure self-giving attitude. For the most part, one attains this attitude only after a desperately painful crisis, but if the individual can accept it without waiting for the crisis, he or she simply avoids a great deal of discomfort.

Having given brief consideration to the problem of method, I shall return to the issues of more specific philosophical significance. Yet we should not forget that philosophy itself becomes a part of method, provided that it is united with the religious attitude. Most of current philosophic thought tends to destroy the sacred or truly religious attitude. For instance, thought, when viewed through the pragmatist's perspective, cannot be used as an instrument of introceptive transformation. Further, a philosophy that views religion as merely a superfluous incident of human psychology, as do all three secular philosophies, does not in itself favor the religious attitude.

It is possible, in considerable measure, to consider the office of introception, and the content rendered available by introception for philosophical development, without having direct personal acquaintance with this function. Admittedly, this implies an entertaining of abstract ideas in a sense that is different from abstraction based upon perceptual experience, but the intellect has abundantly proven its capacity to do this in the development of pure mathematics. One can treat the philosophy as if it were true and then follow the implications to see if they would lead to results that can be directly evaluated.

INTROCEPTUAL PROCESS: ST. JOHN OF THE CROSS

The turning of the Light of consciousness toward its source does not mean that the subject or I is transformed into an object. If the I were an object, then it must be an object for another subject, with the result that the supposedly objectified I really is no more than an abstract construct for the real I, which now is in the position of the new subject. It is utterly impossible for the I to be an object, unless consciousness attains a transcendental position in a more comprehensive Self from which it is possible to look down upon something like a discrete self that is a reflection of the former. However, at the first stage of introception this transcendental perspective has not been attained. The process begins with the consciousness of an individual human self, and so there is no adequate base from which that self can be viewed as an object, insofar as it does its own viewing. This is a point of immense importance, since here we have one of the most fundamental differentiating features of introception as contrasted with the more familiar functions. It is extraordinarily difficult to give this part of the process a conscious recognition and then to interpret it in conceptual language. Where the process functions unconsciously, which seems to be by far the predominant rule, the individual simply finds him- or herself in the new orientation with no appreciation of how he or she got there. (There are amusing instances recorded where people have wondered about their own sanity.) The individual, in this case, is at one moment in the familiar world field, at the next, in something that seems to bear no commensurable or intelligible relation to it. The transformation just happens like an act of Providence, and then everything that was true of the old world field suddenly becomes sheer nonsense—mundane wisdom transformed into mere folly. Furthermore, if the transformed individual tries to speak of this new way of consciousness, he or she sounds nonsensical to the worldly-wise. The result is a more or less mutual contempt.

St. John of the Cross, in one of his poems, has effectively presented the inner effect of an unconscious transformation. The following excerpt illustrates this:

> I entered in—I knew not where—
> And, there remaining, knew no more.
> Transcending far all human lore.

I knew not where I enter'd in
'Twas giv'n me there myself to see
And wondrous things I learn'd within
Yet knew I not where I could be.
I tell not what was shown to me:
Remaining there, I knew no more,
Transcending far all human lore.*

It is not surprising that one who knows only the more objective functioning of the intellect should regard this sort of thing as a kind of intellectual suicide and a general breakdown of organized consciousness. Notwithstanding this sort of reaction, that people such as St. John of the Cross have been enormously influential, not before, but after and because of the mystical transformation, implies in itself that we are in the presence of a highly significant process. People of this sort wield an immensely potent power upon the consciousness and motivation of their entourage—one that is of a distinctly profounder sort than the ordinary lines of influence. Both psychology and philosophy fall short of performing according to their full responsibility if they simply avoid serious consideration of the problems and issues presented by this transformation process. Unquestionably, something does happen, even though our judgment is based only upon observable effects. It is just because of the transformation that figures like Buddha and Christ become incarnations of the most far-reaching powers known to history. Neither their personal lives nor their moral and metaphysical theories supply us with any adequate basis for interpreting their influence. Such influence operates mainly through the collective psychological unconscious, thus affecting individuals at the very roots of their consciousness and motivation. It seems to me rather foolish for the scientific mind to avoid dealing with the problem presented simply because it threatens the comfortable enjoyment of accepted presuppositions.

The quotation from St. John of the Cross is not beyond the possibility of analysis if one is familiar with the transformation process. There is no necessary breakdown of rational understanding here, provided the conceptual presuppositions are appropriately altered. Let us attempt to analyze the portion of the poem quoted: "I entered in—I knew not where—."

Clearly, here we have a transformation of base. Familiar methods employed in mathematics prove of considerable help here. The base of reference in mathematics is the beginning point of an analytic process.

---

*E. Allison Peers, trans. and ed., *The Complete Works of St. John of the Cross*, 3 vols., new rev. ed. (London: Burns, Oates & Washburn, 1934), 2:448.

The base is taken arbitrarily—in the logical sense—while the subsequent analysis follows strict logical form. However, we may change our orientation to a problem from one base to another, which changes, perhaps to a radical degree, the form of the analysis of the given problem. If one were to view the two treatments without knowledge of the change of base, the effect in some cases might be distinctly confusing, enough even to make the conjunction of the two treatments seem irrational. This situation is analogous to the effect of an unconscious introceptive transformation. One enters a new field having different systems of orientation and valuation, but has no idea of how he or she got there. One knows that he or she has entered into something, but has no idea how or where. One knows immediately a new kind of consciousness with its content, or that which replaces all content, but the connection with the old kind of consciousness is completely broken. That is, the process of transformation from one base of reference to another is unconscious, but the field defined by each is immediately Realized.

> And, there remaining, knew no more.
> Transcending far all human lore.

The "knowing no more" implies a destruction of consciousness; however, the "transcending far all human lore" implies that consciousness still is. This seems like a contradiction, but it is only a paradox. A contradiction is the affirmation that x can be both A and not-A at the same time and in the same sense,* while a paradox implies opposite affirmations when taken at different times or in different senses—one or the other, but not both. This distinction shows that we are not dealing with a breakdown of conceptual power, but rather with a new and more comprehensive kind of thought. Clearly, in the above quotation, the "knowing no more" refers to the field delimited by the base of reference of ordinary consciousness. The knowing was not in terms of the old pattern. However, the new position transcends the old. It comprehends much more and, hence, reaches far beyond "all human lore."

The next excerpt implies that not only is this superior state not unconscious, it even has positive noetic value.

> I knew not where I enter'd in.
> 'Twas giv'n there *myself* to see
> And wondrous things I learn'd within
> Yet knew I not where I could be.

---

*[Here x is a variable representing a thing, whereas A denotes a specific characteristic.]

St. John simply did not know how he got There, or where he was. This was mystery. Despite this, he learned tremendously valuable things, including the *seeing of himself*. This seeing of himself is the first most significant and distinctive fact of the introceptive process. The word *seeing*, used here, is deceptive, since it suggests a perceptual process. It is more akin to the sense of seeing an idea. This is a form of cognition that is neither perceptual nor conceptual, but is another way of consciousness. In earlier efforts to describe the process, I found myself in considerable difficulty because the available language gave an impression different from that intended. The development of the word *introceive* proved to be of substantial value once it was defined to mean a process that is reducible neither to perception nor to conception. Strictly, one should say "myself to introceive," rather than "myself to see." This is genuine acquaintance with the self or I *without transforming it into an object of consciousness*. It is totally different from a perceptual process, which is confined exclusively to contents other than the self or I. Perception is essentially extraverted and nonspiritual, even though it has relatively introverted and extraverted phases, whereas introception is a radically introverted process.

St. John affirms that he learned wondrous things within. This is an explicit affirmation that the state was not only one of consciousness, but also one possessing a noetic quale. (Of course, I am assuming that St. John was neither a fool nor a liar, but, on the contrary, an exceptionally intelligent and conscientious person.) However, the content of the new kind of cognition was beyond his powers of formulation— hence: "I tell not what was shown to me." This, of course, might be interpreted as a will not to tell, but one who is familiar with the state, or with the difficulties in expression mystics always manifest, will realize that the true reason for not telling was the inability to tell. Concepts simply do not conform to pure introceptive meaning. Equally, concepts do not conform to pure perceptive meaning. Rather, they delimit fields of possibility, in a certain way of consciousness, which may grow. They are forms, in the Kantian sense, which do not give actuality as it is apart from conceiving. Yet they provide command, and that is an office of the highest importance. We are generally familiar with its operation in relation to the world of perception, but we are almost wholly ignorant of a corresponding potential office with respect to introceptive cognition. Too few mystics are also masters of conceptual thought, so most give up the effort to communicate even that which could be told if the appropriate skill were employed. The concept does not and cannot give the distinctive perceptive quale, and the same is true with respect to the introceptive quale. Nonetheless, it has an actual or potential role in both.

The "transcending far all human lore" carries an implication of far-reaching importance. It means that a human being is capable of attaining a state of consciousness that is not strictly human. Extensive reading of introceptive literature, whether of the gnostic or of the more narrowly mystical type, reveals that such transcendence is quite generally implied or explicitly affirmed. In other words, there is a linkage between human consciousness and other kinds of consciousness such that a human self can either become more than this or can participate in a more than human kind of consciousness. Here we see why mystics are never humanists, in the modern philosophic meaning of the term, although they may be highly humane and compassionate. Humanism conceives of human consciousness as exclusively human qua human and incapable of being or becoming anything else. The content of mystical Realization is incompatible with this position and even implies that there is available to humanity a superior kind of consciousness that is much more desirable than the only human. To the mystic, the merely human problem can never seem to be vitally important, save as it may serve as an instrumental office for the arousing of the superior consciousness. Insofar as human suffering may serve as a means for awakening, the mystic would say that it is good and should not be removed until it has fulfilled its office. This gives an impression of cool detachment from human pain, but the deeper meaning is a heroic willingness to permit a pain that serves the end that is conceived as the only one that is ultimately desirable. Some physicians feel the same way about childbirth, with similar justification.

In the sense of introception, the consciousness related to the I is not a consciousness of the I. It is immediate "knowledge through acquaintance" in the most rigorous sense. One might even speak of it as a sinking into the I. However, the difficulty with all these formulations is that they suggest a connotation in the ordinary sense of language usage that is quite different from the actual meaning. 'I am I' conveys the idea with more rigor, but at the price of proffering a meaningless tautology for ordinary thinking. We might say, "I am, and I am thus without dependence upon any objective setting." I am known as I in an empty world, which is empty because I am not projected as a not-self, in the sense of Fichte, while in the introceptive state. It is I, together with consciousness that I am, immediately known and not as a mere inference. To be conscious as the pure I is to be conscious of Nothing, which yet is infinitely more valuable than any *thing*. I am the pure Light, which by illuminating everything gives to everything existence for me, and except as things exist for me, there is no meaning in predicating existence of them.

Knowledge toward the self, in the introceptive sense, may be likened to a zero state that is intensely illumined. As it were, the world contracts to a zero point and becomes pure Light. Comparatively, the old world is darkness. The immediate effect at this stage is of an absolute emptiness filled with absolute value. We are dealing here with a very profound conception where, again, it seems that only mathematics can aid us.

The single conception in mathematics that required the greatest degree of genius for its birth was that of zero. This was the great mathematical achievement of India. This notion stands for nothing, literally, yet it is the most vital unifying conception of mathematics. Zero is the foil that gives meaning to all numbers. The step from 0 (zero) to the numeral 1 (one) is a leap across a whole universe. From one and zero we may generate infinite manifolds. We construct our systems of reference upon zero, which is merely a way of saying that, with our center at nothing, we have the fulcrum for control of all elaboration in form. Zero is the bare point, having only position, but no magnitude, upon which all else in our analysis rests.

The pure I is the zero point of organized consciousness. It is the center of all systems of reference for our human kind of consciousness. When an astronomer takes the Milky Way as a base of reference, she really projects herself as a thinker to the Milky Way. This illustrates the real independence from body that is characteristic of the self or I. I am at the point where I center my thought. If I habitually center myself in the body, then I am there in an exceedingly narrow kind of bondage. (Such identification with body is the essence of materialism.) However, I break this bondage every time I think myself away from body, as to some other base of reference. We are actually doing this sort of thing all the time, but commonly without realizing its significance. Simply to realize what one is doing in all this is to take a long step in the liberating process. I literally am where I think or otherwise function.

If one sinks into pure self-consciousness and carefully strips away all habitual or inherited interpretations, one will find that there is no meaning attached to the notion of 'body'. He or she will find consciousness with various modifications, and nothing else. He or she may call certain modifications "body" and various other names, but these are merely creative or fantastic constructs. One knows only consciousness, and that consciousness is centered in its subject—nothing else. That subject is, always has been, and always will be perfectly free and unaffected by any objective conditioning. To the self, the space outside and inside a granite mountain is one and the same, and access is equally free in both cases. When a surveyor establishes a point inside a granite cliff that has been pierced by no tunnel, he or she has, in effect, placed him- or herself at that point. He or she has not placed another physical body there; he or she has placed his or her I there, and from that point inside the cliff of granite he or she can think further.

We often talk of unconsciousness; we never experience it. Dropping all inferences and habitual interpretations, and watching as closely as possible, I never find one moment of unconsciousness. I find the beginning and ending of *states* of consciousness, but I know nothing of unconsciousness. I find appearance and disappearance of contents, but no unconsciousness. Some changes of state I call "going to sleep" and "waking up"—merely a habit—but not one moment of unconsciousness have I detected. Sometimes I remember from one state to another, so that there is a cross-correlation of content, but there is no change of consciousness—only of content. If I predicate that which is true of content as also true of I, then I artificially bind myself through a fantasy. I, in reality, am quite free from content and never for one moment unconscious. Anyone can verify all this by studying him- or herself with clear discrimination.

We, who are born today into a world transformed and molded by untold millennia of thought, find it exceedingly difficult to imagine the state of consciousness wherein thought has not yet arisen. Only with great effort during the waking state do we silence our conceptual processes and abstract from all experience the modifications of content produced by thought, so that we may once more regain the ancient primitive consciousness. We acquire knowledge of this state more easily when we recall our dreams during sleep. While dreaming we are wholly in a state of pure perception or, at least, nearly so. Here we have pure experience wherein the dreamer lives in an environment projected by his psyche, and where rarely is there a thought that stands detached from the experiencing. The dreamer moves in a self-produced environment, but he knows not the nature of his production, or even that he has produced it. Consequently, he becomes the victim of the projection that seems to be not himself. Ordinarily he is quite unable to will anything counter to the circumstances that surround him, so he flows along as a conditioned pawn in the stream of his experiences. Upon awakening, the dreamer recalls his experiences with something of shame for exhibiting so little capacity of command, for proving to be such an infantile weakling in the midst of mostly trivial circumstances. The person who is awake has long ago learned to conquer and command his course of life in far more formidable circumstances than those presented in the dream. There is something appalling in the realization that the awake individual should be so strong and yet so terribly weak when dreaming.

In our memory of the dream, we have recaptured something of the pure perceptual consciousness that was the common form of consciousness of all earthly creatures before conceptual thought was born. To only perceive is to dream. To think as a primitive is to produce thoughts that are perceived—thoughts that are not yet freed from their prenatal dependency. To live thus is to live as the victim of that which happens, not as a ruler in the kingdom. This is the life in the mother's womb where the autonomous forces of life rule with unbroken sway. Through untold ages the human race dwelled as unborn infants in the womb of pure perception, and only very slowly was the birth of a self-determining will achieved. Even today, only a few have emerged, relatively, from the ancient racial womb. Most have scarcely learned more than to creep, or to walk a few steps on unsteady legs, ever ready at the first portent of crisis to return to the encompassing protection of the Mother. This is why, when contents surge from the perceptual depths of life, the masses are embraced in psychical currents over which they have no command. Whole crowds, even nations, races and humanities, are swept away by currents of feeling over which their half-born ideas have no power. Thus, and only thus, arises the folly of warring classes and nations. Only in more peaceful hours does the tender newborn life of thought possess a fragile and uncertain direction of the individual lives. So it is with the overwhelming mass of humanity. However, a few have grown sufficiently strong in the power of self-directed thought to be able to face the storms surging from the perceptual depths of life and maintain a free judgment and a free will in the midst of the hour of trial. Moreover, this power that some have attained, all may someday yet attain, for no individual can achieve anything without proving a general possibility for all.

The child becomes the adult only by leaving the home of her birth and early protection and guidance, to go forth into a strange world, there to achieve for herself a place, or to fail in the effort. The youth, standing midway between the child and the adult, is summoned forth to adventure by the call from the unknown, but still is called back by her homesick heart. As the adventure becomes the austere trial of the solitary life, which must rest upon its own unaided forces, the cry of the homesick heart becomes ever stronger. Any member of the human race, far more often than otherwise, will heed the cry of the heart and return to her former home, where for her only the Mother is known, and not the Father. In the life of a rising consciousness, the wistful yearning is for the irresponsibility and protection of the pure perceptual state. The austerity of the conceptual craving has proven too severe, the responsibility of conceptual thought too great. For when one conceives, she builds her world; she becomes the architect of her destiny. No longer does she rest securely in an inheritance provided by her source. Thus it is that often, even those who have built much from their strength, come to a time when they direct the lines of their structure so as to provide a way of return to Mother-perception. They even philosophize their way back, forgetting their love of Sophia. Great indeed must be the call of the Mother that her offspring of such maturity should feel so strongly the desire to return to the womb! Conception, viewed as only instrumental to perception, is but a philosophical apology for the longing for the womb. Thus the great labor of conception is frustrated, because its first great purpose is to build a bridge to the Realization of the unknown Father.

A person has become mature only when he or she has ceased to dream, whether asleep or awake. One has become adult when, instead of dreaming, he or she conceives and builds. To dream is the easy way—the way that grows of itself. To conceive and build is the difficult way of mature consciousness. It is true that conceptual thought is instrumental, but it is not true that its total meaning lies in finding a way to return to Mother-perception. It is also instrumental to the attainment of the Father-consciousness, Realized through introception. Finally, it is instrumental to a new-world building wherein are compounded the consciously realized forces of both the Father and the Mother. Here, through conception, humankind produces the future estate, a domain that previously had abode in privation of form as a bare possibility, awaiting the office of conception that it might become existential. I do not oppose the instrumentalism of the pragmatists as being in principle unsound, but because it is far too narrowly conceived. The instrument of return to the Mother-perception is but one possibility. When this is given exclusive recognition, a person fails to assume larger responsibilities. There is more than one kind of Truth and Meaning.

When the youth has ventured forth from his ancient perceptual home he carries an inheritance that, if used with reasonable discretion, will prove sufficient to build the bridge to the Father, where he will uncover illimitable resources. However, if he fails to make the crossing, then exhaustion will force a return to the womb, there to gather strength for a renewed trial for adulthood. Thus it is that we see human culture rising out of the matrix of life and, then, largely failing of its intended destiny, falling back into the matrix, to rise once more in a new culture, and thus continuing time after time. This is the Vision that Spengler has seen so clearly. However, he saw only the periodic rising and the Material Soil. He found nothing eternal but the Mother. This limits his Vision and renders his philosophy only a part truth. He failed to see that life below supplied the material wherewith, by appropriate usage, Life Eternal might be attained. Seeing the rising and the failure, he said this was all. He missed the occasional successes that stand as earnests of final universal achievement. Profane history is mostly a record of failure, and so does not teach the more hopeful lesson. For this reason, history may be a dangerous study if one fails to extract the small amount of hidden gold in the otherwise worthless ore. If one can find the hidden gold in history, then surely its study may prove to be highly profitable. Otherwise, it is better not to have consciousness too heavily laden with the vast record of failure. The real meaning of history is the striving of life for Life.

CONCEPTION AND THE MYSTIC THOUGHT

How is conception related to perception, on the one hand, and introception, on the other? This is a problem that ever grows in mystery the more one studies it. In the more confused states of consciousness where concepts and percepts are so interblended that no clear distinction between them has arisen, the strict distinction between the two is by no means clearly apperceived. Only such a confusion could lead to the idea that concepts are simply copies of percepts. Once conception is isolated and realized in its proper nature, it seems like a world apart having no commensurable relation with perception. There is something decidedly transcendental about conception, even though it is not wholly unrelated to the perceptual order, as is made evident by the command it wields over the latter. The conceptual meaning can be defined, whereas the perceptual cannot, insofar as its peculiar nature ever lies in that which the philosopher calls "quale." Likewise, the quale of the pure introceptual Realization, in its innate character, is equally foreign to the conceptual order. Nonetheless, despite the fact that there is something incommensurable among these three orders, it is true that somehow conception bridges the gap between perception and introception. This gulf is far too vast for a self-conscious crossing to be effected without aid. Somehow conception partakes more of the nature both of perception and of introception than do either of the latter two of each other. In some sense, conception is the child of both perception and introception, although it possesses something inherent that differs from both. Because of this dual heritage, it can serve to span the chasm between the Father and the Mother, though its own peculiar quale differs from both.

Kant's critical analysis of knowledge has greatly helped to clarify the problem of how conception is related to perception. Frequently, it has happened that philosophers and scientists, thinking in their towers of pure thought, without any concern of possible bearings upon perceptual experience, have defined the forms within which future experience developed. So impressive has this fact become in these latter days of astronomical and intra-atomic discoveries, that Sir James Jeans remarked, in his *The Mysterious Universe*,* that the universe seems like the thought of a Divine being who thought like a pure mathematician. This does, indeed, impress us as strange and mysterious when first we contemplate its significance. Yet, Kant has prepared the way for our understanding of it in principle, for the basic structure of human thought is an a priori determinant of the world that we think. It is not simply a question of thought conforming to a preexistent order in a perceptual manifold or flux, but the reverse. The perceptual order manifests to the thinker only within the forms that thought allows. Other forms would reveal other worlds and have done so, within minor limits, in the cases of other cultures. Consequently, the form of our conception is the form of *our* possible thinkable experience, whatever the experience of any other types of consciousness may be. We can predict, when we think in conformity with the laws of our thought, not because we have guessed correctly, but because we have predetermined what is possible. In a sense we have created the world we later experience, though there is something that we, as merely human, have not placed there. We cannot predetermine the distinctive quale of experience, nor can we make over the underlying structure of our thought as we please. Thus there is a sense in which we can truly say that any self-consistent system of thought possesses existence and is real. Who can say that any such system will never be filled with a perceptive content? Thought destroys something, and yet it creates something to take the place of that which is destroyed. By thought some of us have been led far away from the primitive maternal ground of perception, and, in that, we have known both impoverishment and enrichment.

In any case, if we cannot live by bread alone, then neither can we live by concepts alone, nor by both of these, no matter how richly combined. Not all yearnings are fulfilled within this compound zone. As passing time brings maturity, the unsatisfied desires grow in number and with ever greater intensity. More is needed to give the endless game of life durable Meaning, and the longer the yearning remains unsatisfied, the more empty becomes the game, and the more insistent the demand for Meaning. This longing is evidence that the total possible consciousness for humanity is more than that which we have generally realized. Humankind is more than a subhuman perceiving creature that has learned to conceive.

That which all but the few have neglected is the Father of consciousness—introception. Here is that which originally impregnated the Mother, then was forgotten in the inner depths of consciousness, and was even denied by many. It is the return to the Father that com-

*Sir James Jeans, *The Mysterious Universe* (New York: Macmillan, 1930).

pletes the first cycle of the Pilgrim on the journey to full Enlightenment. Until humankind essays this final step, there can be no true Peace, but only the return to the prenatal stage of perception when there is weariness from the labors of conceptual creation. This latter return is a kind of failure, though it may be unavoidable when weariness and weakness have become too great. Yet one who, before his or her powers have become too greatly exhausted, forces the Gate of introception, completes the first cycle of the Great Work,* and may rest, if need be.

To arouse self-consciousness is the great office of the conceptual function. Within the dreamlike state of pure perception there can be no awakening of self-consciousness. The child born in the womb is sustained by psychical forces that it does not control. It is, but does not know that it is; it is conscious, but does not know its own consciousness. The labor pains of conceiving first arouses the power of consciousness to be aware of itself. When this power of consciousness to know itself has grown sufficiently, the introceptive door may be opened and, leaving even thought behind, consciousness may still retain the power not only to be, but to be aware of itself as well. Thus the crossing is consummated over the bridge of conception. Beyond lie further possibilities—among them, the union of conception with introception.

Conception is the son of the Mother, but the daughter of the Father. Thought gives eyes to blind perception, and so leads it. In contrast, thought is led by introception and gives form to it. With respect to the transcendent realm, thought gives form to unlimited formless possibility. With respect to perceptual content, thought determines the range of possibilities. It clothes Spirit in form and illumines the matter of perception. These are the dual offices of conception in its relation to introception and perception.

When thought moves toward its roots, then it comes near to the key that will open the door to the new function. Kant approached this key, but either neglected it or did not use it properly. Those who received his mantle most directly went far on the new road. Within the writings of the post-Kantian idealists there lies indubitable evidence of Vision, in the sense of Gnosis. However, it is not at all clear that these visionary philosophers ever clearly recognized that the authority of their insight rests upon a new function. Perhaps Schopenhauer glimpsed something of the truth when he grounded his world view upon the conative principle of Will, but this position is simply the accentuation of the activistic element in consciousness, which always stands as the other of the contemplative element. There is nothing inherently more profound in activism than in contemplation. The emphasis of one

*[The full Enlightenment of all humanity.]

aspect or the other is more a reflection of individual temperament than of absolute validity of insight. Schopenhauer's voluntarism is a metaphysical interpretation of insight, not its instrument. The function of insight gives a transcendental content that, when reduced to an interpretive system, becomes subject to the relativity of all subject-object consciousness. Therefore, there can be no such thing as an infallible interpretation. Thus we must distinguish between insight and its formulation. The voluntarist doctrine is simply a formulation that gives accentuated valuation to the conative element in consciousness and depreciates the rational features. In the final analysis, voluntarism is just as relative as rationalism and is no more profound.

However, I believe that Schopenhauer did isolate the function of introception in some measure, because he speaks of the intuition of genius and the "temper akin to genius." This is clearly the function of insight, if one considers the notion in the sense that Schopenhauer employed it. It is not the ordinary kind of intuition, but intuition moving toward the transcendental. Intuition is a general notion applying to all forms of immediacy reaching from the most primitive instinct up to the highest insight. No doubt this is a collective rather than a definite notion that will become progressively differentiated the more our consciousness of the function grows. The "intuition of genius" is not just any kind of intuition, but a special kind related to the truly metaphysical side of being. It has a character that definitely differentiates it from other kinds of intuition and thus deserves a special designation of its own. In Buddhist psychology it is called "Dhyana." I have called it "introception."

While we are considering Schopenhauer, it is worthwhile to draw attention to a weakness in his system that I am able to avoid. He gives to Will a fundamental and constitutive metaphysical character such that it is the true nature of the underlying Reality. Spengler has quite correctly shown that this metaphysical conception by no means implies Schopenhauer's ethics. Spengler has carried out that particular metaphysic with fundamental consistency and derived an ethic that, I believe, is a much truer derivative from it than is Schopenhauer's. For my part, I would maintain, in opposition to Spengler, that the most profound insight of Schopenhauer is to be found in his ethics, rather than his metaphysics. The ethics starkly controverts the metaphysics, for he affirms in his ethics that the feasible way to salvation lies in the thoroughgoing denial of Will, through the denial of the will to live. The ultimate salvation is a state wherein the Will is nullified. *But if the Will can be nullified, then it is not the ultimate ontological principle.* There must be something still more ultimate. At the very end of Schopenhauer's *The World as Will and Idea*, a very significant sentence and footnote suggests this: "We freely acknowledge that what remains after the entire abolition of will is, for those who are still full of will, certainly nothing; but, conversely, to those in whom the will has turned and has denied itself, this our world, which is so real, with all its suns and milky ways—is nothing."* Thus the world that rests upon the will is *nothing*, whereas the state that results when the will has turned upon and denied itself is nothing for those who are *still full of will*. This is not the same thing as saying that it is nothing, per se. Its nature is simply a somewhat beyond all conception, yet is the root source of every possibility. Clearly, Schopenhauer reaches a somewhat that is more fundamental than Will. Here Schopenhauer and I converge to agreement, however greatly we may differ as to the relative status of the Will.

It is interesting and significant that in the second clause of the above quotation Schopenhauer uses the expression: "those in whom the will has turned and has denied itself." This is a logical parallel of the "turning of the Light of consciousness toward its source," and the recurring phrase in certain Buddhist Sutras, "the turning about at the deepest seat of consciousness." It is this *turning about* that forms the very essence of Dhyana and the function that I have called "introception." Most definitely, I am not discussing a merely private experience, but something that was recognized as crucial for both religion and philosophy at least as long as 2,500 years ago, and was, at least to some extent, appreciated by one of our leading Western philosophers. The "turning about" does involve conative factors, so it may be viewed as an inversion of the will such that it denies itself in its habitual movement toward the object. This aspect of the function of introception is certainly important (I shall discuss it later), but since I view the conative element as instrumental to noetic content, I have naturally placed the emphasis upon the latter. I conceive the turning about of the will as more significant in relation to the problem of method than it is to the question of the ultimate constitution of Reality. Schopenhauer, despite his metaphysical theory, implies this when he speaks of the will as denying itself.

At the very close of his book, in a footnote to the previous quotation, Schopenhauer makes an allusion of considerable import, specifically, "This is also the Prajna-Paramita of the Buddhists, the 'beyond all knowledge,' i.e., the point at which subject and object are no more."† In other words, that which seems like nothing to "those who are still full of will" is precisely the same as the Prajna-Paramita. This leads us to the question of just what is meant by this term. The Prajna-Paramita is the

---

*Arthur Schopenhauer, *The World as Will and Idea*, 3 vols., 3rd ed., trans. R. B. Haldane & J. Kemp (London: Routledge & Kegan Paul, 1882), 1:532.
†Ibid., 1:532n.

central core of Buddhist philosophy, and the sacred objective of its religious practice. Everything else has only a relative or derivative reality, but this is absolutely real. Through the Realization of Prajna, in the highest sense of the Prajna-Paramita, one attains Nirvana and states of consciousness that are still more profound.

I shall later discuss this subject at some length, but here let us consider briefly whether this is merely another name for absolute nothingness. Something of the meaning of both Prajna and Paramita may be derived from a study of exoteric Sanskrit sources.

> Prajna (adjective) intelligent; knowing, acquainted with. (feminine noun) information; discrimination, judgment, intelligence, understanding; wisdom, knowledge; purpose, resolve; the Universal Mind; the capacity for perception; Consciousness.*

> Paramita (feminine noun) reaching the further shore, complete attainment.[†]

> Prajna-Paramita (feminine noun) highest degree of knowledge or of understanding.[‡]

We would reach even better the Buddhist meaning of this compound term if we give "Prajna-Paramita" the value: the wisdom, knowledge or understanding attained by reaching the further shore. It is otherwise known as "Transcendental Wisdom," which is to be understood as radically different from empiric or worldly wisdom or knowledge. To be sure, neither form of wisdom implies the other, since each is attained in different ways. Yet, one individual may attain both by the appropriate effort in the two directions. The Indians differentiate between Absolute Truth or Knowledge, known as Paramartha-Satya, and relative truth or knowledge, known as Samvriti-Satya. This corresponds to the difference between Transcendental Wisdom and empiric wisdom.

Clearly when Schopenhauer uses the phrase *beyond all knowledge* in his definition of Prajna-Paramita, it is to be understood in the sense of being beyond Samvriti-Satya, that is, empiric knowledge or wisdom. It is not beyond Knowledge in the sense of Transcendental Wisdom (Paramartha-Satya)—wisdom, knowledge and understanding attained by reaching the further shore.

---

*A Practical Sanskrit Dictionary, transliteration, accentuation and etymological analysis by Arthur Anthony MacDowell (Oxford: Oxford University Press, 1924), s.v. "Prajna."
[†]Ibid., s.v. "Paramita."
[‡]Ibid., s.v. "Prajna-Paramita."

Obviously the Buddhists do not mean by Prajna-Paramita an absolute nothingness, although they often do use in this connection the term *Shunyata*, which literally means "voidness." However, the Buddhist Canon is clear on the point that the Voidness may be attained and abided in as a state for a prolonged period, as measured by objective time, then may be left. Further, the Realization of the Voidness may be the beginning of a higher kind of evolution of such a nature that it simply cannot be conceived by ordinary relative consciousness. Sometimes it is spoken of as a supercosmic evolution. All of this implies something totally different from an absolute annihilation.

No matter how much the Western student may seem to be justified in questioning whether the Buddhist sages know what they are talking about, it is nonetheless completely certain that they do not mean by Nirvana and Shunyata a state of annihilation of all consciousness. On the contrary, these terms refer to states that are, or may be, states of consciousness—definitely possessing the noetic quale. This would imply that one would arrive at a better understanding of the Buddhist meaning by taking the metaphysics of Hegel in combination with the ethics of Schopenhauer, rather than by taking Schopenhauer's metaphysics and ethics together. However, we have here only an approach to the Buddhist meaning, as the Hegelian Idea is something less than Shunyata. So far, no Western philosopher has quite made the crossing to the "Further Shore."

In my employment of the term *consciousness* in the phrase *the Light of consciousness turning toward its source*, I am implying something more fundamental than either the noetic or the conative. Consciousness, in its total meaning, includes these two aspects, as well as feeling tone and more or less undetermined other qualities. Consciousness is the common denominator of all. Therefore, it is the best neutral term.

Unquestionably, one must employ the will in the appropriate way before the "turning about" can be effected. The mystical participation in the object holds humanity in a hypnotic spell that is harder to break than bars of iron. To release this spell requires a strongly willed effort. No objective achievement requires an equal degree of intensity and persistence of will. Will, both conscious and autonomous, rules the empiric world and simply employs ideas or concepts as instruments. The result is that, in ordinary experience, the will never has to face as great a battle as when it turns upon itself for the purpose of effecting a neutralization of its long-established habit of flowing outward. Ideation is able to achieve a theoretical turning about much more easily, and, if the will has been already trained to accept subservience to ideation, the latter can lead the way in the turning about, and the struggle with the will is substantially reduced. Yet, in this case, part of the task was already accomplished when ideation achieved the subordination of the will.

Without some degree of theoretical understanding of the whole process, the turning about suggests an almost tragic climax, for, from the standpoint of conative and feeling-oriented consciousness, the turning away from the object seems like self-annihilation. The mystical participation in the object involves both will and feelings far more profoundly than it does cognition. The intellect has already had such extensive training in abstraction that it has become familiar with objects of high tenuity. This affords an enormous advantage, since the gap between an object of extreme subtlety and true objectlessness is relatively small. The labor whereby a person attains the point of working with such objects implies much of the austerity requisite for the achievement of true objectlessness.* The very "thinness" of concepts, that motivated the protest of William James, definitely becomes a superior merit when the concept is employed as an instrument for arousing introception.

Again, I am implying that the office of conceptual thought in relation to the function of introception is of instrumental character. However, this is instrumentalism interpreted in a very different sense from that of the pragmatist, wherein conception is viewed as serving solely

---

*One of my mathematics teachers once told me of the preparatory steps necessary for the production of creative work in the field of the theory of groups, a particularly difficult branch of mathematics. This preliminary work requires about three months in which one studies the subject, works on it, thinks about and dreams of it. Meanwhile, he or she religiously severs him- or herself from any diversion, especially of a type that is naturally attractive and might absorb his or her interest without great effort. Only after a protracted period of this sort of discipline, is the intellect enabled to move creatively within the tenuous field of that kind of mathematical thought. There was one case of a German professor who specialized in the same field, but who also loved the opera. He found that, if he wished to continue his mathematical work, he had to renounce the opera. His operatic interest simply drew off too much of the libido, in a way that was essentially an easy and spontaneous activity, with the result that there was a fatal weakening of the creative will in the more austere discipline.

This illustrates the fundamental meaning of the austerity required for the awakening of the introceptive function. The libido must be concentrated in the new direction until the function is awakened and established. All that these mathematicians needed to add to their effort to arouse introception was the spiritual polarization of consciousness. As it was, they stopped somewhat short of the Gnostic Goal. Otherwise, they employ essential features of the discipline necessary to break the mystical participation in the object.

the end of more experience in the perceptual field. Here both knowledge and the conceptual function are to be viewed as *relatively* terminal
with respect to experience. The kind of conception that has transcendental roots *is not derived from experience.* With respect to this kind of
conception, experience enters into the picture only as a catalytic agent
that drops away more or less completely as the conceptual process takes
hold on a totally different kind of base. One comes to value experience
for the knowledge it arouses and the conceptual process that it helps to
initiate, rather than the other way around. The pragmatist values
knowledge and knowing because of the further experience to which it
leads. Thus a radical difference of orientation is implied. In the end,
the conceptual process leads beyond itself, but, in the case of introception, the goal is a spiritual Realization, not merely more experience.
After the attainment and anchorage in the spiritual Realization, the conceptual order may serve a new office, with bearings upon the field of
experience. In this case, however, the relationship is hierarchical, with
conception serving as the lawgiver with respect to experience and the
perceptual order generally. Even so, for an individual consciousness
that does not know the latter directly, conceptual knowledge is only a
surrogate for the introceptive content.

The thinness of concepts has a twofold connotation. In one sense,
which James employs in his *Pluralistic Universe** and elsewhere, the concept is thin because it lacks substance. It is like the blueprint and specifications of a bridge, building or machine, because in this regard it is a
practical instrument for the effecting of consequences in the realm of
perceptual existence. Everything that can be conceived concerning the
bridge, building, and so on, can be conceived of the blueprint and specifications, but the corresponding perceptual existences have something
that the latter does not possess. They lend themselves to empiric use. It
is this latter functionality that constitutes "thickness," in James's sense.
In contrast, thinness takes on quite another meaning when it is understood in the sense of the Voidness (Shunyata) of the Buddhists. Shunyata is voidness only in its seeming as it appears to relative consciousness, particularly in the sense of perceptual consciousness. In its
inherent nature, it is the one and only self-existent Substance. The spiritual concept or, in other words, the concept when united with introceptual content, can be called "thin" only in the Buddhist sense. Realized in its essential nature, it possesses a higher substantiality than
perceptual experience. Thus it is entirely possible to realize greater fullness, greater substantiality, in the case of some concepts than that given

---

*William James, *The Pluralistic Universe* (New York: Longmans, Green &
Co., 1909).

by experience. Consequently, there is a sense in which the most abstract knowledge—just that which James would call most "thin"—is in reality the most concrete of all. Unless one appreciates this fact, he or she will miss the real force of transcendentalist thought.

If by the *meaning* of a concept we understand a perceptual experience, whether as an object for sensation, a program of action, an adjustment to life, or so on, then with respect to the conceptual relation to introception, we would not say that the concept enrobes its meaning. It rather points toward its meaning, in the only sense in which significance can be understood. This is not the only kind of meaning recognized. When concepts carry meaning only in this sense, they are purely sign pointers, and thus are instrumental relaters exclusively. This is meaning taken strictly in the objective or extraverted sense. However, there is another form of significance that is related to the subject, in which the relationship of the concept to its meaning acquires quite a different form. It is not a meaning objectively experienced to which the concept or idea leads. The significance lies within the concept, so that we would properly speak of the concept enrobing the meaning, rather than pointing to it in the sense of the figure of the signpost. One finds this inherent meaning, not by the appropriate kind of action, but by the correct kind of meditation, that is, by a process of introception. The difference between these two procedures is of enormous import. For one thing, one must understand that introceptive meditation is not merely a process of reflection about an object, whereby one deduces or infers consequences. It is a movement of consciousness such that a successful outcome implies a transcendence of both thinking and perception, so that consciousness enters something like another dimension. The inward penetration into the significance of a concept is the epistemological or psychological parallel of the introceptive movement toward the self, wherein the self is not transformed into a new object, but remains unaltered in its subjective character. This is not a conceptual relation considered either in pragmatic or in realist epistemology.

A given concept may have both perceptive and introceptive kinds of relations, but evidently some concepts possess more than one kind of meaning, while others are more valuable in the opposite sense. We can say with a considerable degree of generality that the more concrete the character of a concept, the more it may be taken as meaning a particularized perceptual experience, while the more abstract it is, the more the reference is to an introceptive content. In other words, increase in abstraction is a movement toward a spiritual orientation. As an illustration, we may take two notions such as 'a beautiful scene' and 'beauty', the former the more concrete, the latter the more abstract. The notion of a beautiful scene implies a judgment related to a concrete perceptual object, whereas beauty is an abstraction of a bare quality. From the standpoint of a highly extraverted concrete consciousness, there is an actual referent that corresponds to the beautiful scene, but no such real referent for the notion of beauty. The latter notion may help to further the process of thought, but, taken by itself, it has no real meaning, only something like a flavor derived from concrete experience. At any rate, from this viewpoint beauty is not a self-existence apart from beautiful objects. However, no one who has had any considerable experience with introverted penetration will agree with the above judgment. There is such a thing as a direct Realization of beauty quite apart from beautiful objects. Indeed, acquaintance with this Realization leads to the discovery that there is no such thing as objective beauty. The beauty seen is super-imposed upon the object by the observer, though generally this process is unconscious. Not only can beauty be conceived in abstraction from objective content, but it can also be Realized directly apart from all objects. This is part of what is accomplished by the introceptive function.

When a concept enrobes an inner Significance, it possesses thickness or depth. In other relations, the same formal concept may point, directly or indirectly, to a perceptual experience. In this case, it has the value of thinness. Thus the thinness of a concept, when viewed from the extraverted perspective, may be transformed into thickness when the same concept is taken in an introceptive relation. Accordingly, thinness and thickness are relative to perspective, rather than being absolute or formal properties.

As the process of abstraction is carried further and further toward the limit of tenuity wherein conceptual thought is able to function, the growing thinness, in the perceptual sense, corresponds to a growing thickness, in the introceptual sense. There eventually is reached a point where thought continues without the use of concepts or, at least, without the use of concepts that can be represented in words. In mathematics, this process has long since reached the stage where words, in the ordinary sense, are intrinsically incapable of expressing the thought, so only symbols can serve as the conceptual instruments. However, there ultimately comes the point where even symbols are no longer adequate. Thought then deals with a disembodied Meaning. At this point the thinness, in the extraverted sense, has become absolute, while the inner thickness has virtually become infinite. This is an extremely pregnant Thought, for a single Idea, in this sense, may require literally volumes for its interpretation. Indeed, it is never wholly interpreted, since no objectively thinkable elaboration can ever exhaust its possibilities. We may think of it as being, in its intrinsic nature, like the perfect summation of a converging infinite series, whereas the objectively thinkable interpretation is no more than an approximation of that summation, proceeding term by term. At any point attained in the latter process, there still remain an infinite number of terms to complete the summation. Consequently, in speaking of the inner Thought as infinitely richer than the objective thought, the words *infinite* and *infinitely* are to be taken as strictly correct.

The relative substantiality of the inner disrobed Thought may also be suggested by certain notions taken from modern physics. Today we think of matter as composed of atoms, which, in turn, are composed of protons, neutrons and electrons. The atom appears to be organized with a nuclear center, consisting of protons and neutrons, while there are electrons revolving around this nucleus. The total size of the atom is conceived as the space circumscribed by the movement of the outermost electron. Within this space, the total volume filled by electrons and protons is comparable to the space within the solar system filled by the sun, planets, satellites, asteroids, and so on. The point is that the unfilled space, even in the densest of matter found in nature on this planet, is vast compared to the filled portion. Further, if protons, neutrons or electrons were packed tight so as to rest in contact with each other, the resulting density would be almost inconceivable. In some of the heavy stars, it appears that this state is approximated in high measure, with the result that, according to calculation, a volume the size of a pea would weigh many million tons. If we liken ordinary conceptual thought to the atomic organization of matter as we know it here, then the disrobed or transcendent Thought would correspond to the tightly packed protons or neutrons. It is immeasurably more substantial.

Another way of presenting the idea is to say that the transcendental Thought consists of meaning in its purity, disassociated from all form. In this sense, even the most abstract mathematical formula must be regarded as form. Clearly, this is not thinking in the familiar sense of the word; nonetheless, it is Thought, though of another order. One is justified in calling it "Thought" for the reason that it is a content most nearly related to thought among the more familiar human functions. We may call this the "pure introceptive Thought," but it is not to be understood as identical with the whole of introceptive content. For instance, there is as well an introceptive quality that bears an analogous relation to feeling, with a corresponding degree of relative intensity.

If I have succeeded in conveying my meaning, it will be understood that Voidness, in the sense of Shunyata, is only the Suchness as it appears from the perspective of relative consciousness. When it is Realized in its inherent nature, it is absolutely substantial. This shift of value corresponds to a shift in the base of self-consciousness, as from one to another system of reference, in the mathematical sense. The transformation is effected by means of a reversal of the flow of consciousness, both in the sense of the will turning about and nullifying its normal flow, and of awareness consummating the same turn.

8

Transcendentalism

Introceptualism is a transcendental philosophy. However, since the notion of the transcendental has a number of specific meanings in both philosophy and theology, it is necessary to explicitly render the sense in which it is used here.

1. In one sense, the transcendental is conceived as Knowledge or Truth beyond the range of human conception or acquisition. In this case, the judgment that such a Knowledge or Truth exists is based upon superhuman revelation or upon universalizing rational categories beyond the range of possible experience.
2. We have as well the use of the terms *transcendent* and *transcendental* as employed by Immanuel Kant. Here the transcendental is conceived as the a priori forms that delimit possible experience and what may be thought concerning it. He sharply distinguishes the transcendent as that which lies beyond all possible experience and, in conformity with his thesis, can never be an object of knowledge.
3. Transcendental philosophy may also mean the systematic development of the view that the subjective component of consciousness stands as the determinant factor with respect to the objective. This often implies that the experienced world is dependent upon the activity of reason.
4. In a further sense, transcendentalism is "any philosophy which emphasizes the intuitive, spiritual and super-sensuous; any mode of thought which is aggressively non-empirical or anti-empirical."*

The present transcendental philosophy has much in common with all four of these uses of the terms *transcendent* and *transcendental*, yet possesses its own peculiar difference. Introceptualism affirms a Truth and a Knowledge that are not derived from experience, and that are not dependent upon experience for their being. Yet, it does not deny the existence of an inferior empiric sort of knowledge that is grounded

---

*Baldwin, *Dictionary*, s.v. "transcendentalism."

upon experience and is valuable mainly, if not wholly, in its relation to further experience. From the standpoint of introceptive Realization, empiric knowledge may be valuable exclusively as a catalytic agent that may, under some conditions, help to arouse the introceptive activity. In this case, however, the empiric factor supplies none of the content of the transcendental Truth or Knowledge, though it may supply symbolic figures of speech in connection with the problem of suggesting a spiritual meaning. Thus experience remains valuable essentially for no larger purpose than to supply a language whereby hidden and preexistent Meaning becomes objectified.

Most notably, although introceptive Knowledge transcends experience, it does not lie beyond the possibility of direct Realization by a human being. Since, in quite common loose usage, the term *experience* is often given a connotation sufficiently broad to include what I mean by the term *introceptive Realization*, it is important to remember that here experience is given a delimited meaning.

1. I understand experience to be "consciousness considered as a process taking place in time."*
2. I regard experience as the state of consciousness produced through the function of perception, into which conceptual knowledge enters only as a ministering agent.
3. Finally, I view experience as a mode of consciousness wherein the object is relatively ascendant with respect to the subject.

The latter emphasis appears to be a necessary part of all empirical philosophy and constitutes a primary differentiation between empiricism and transcendentalism.

In relation to all three phases of the definition of experience, introceptive Realization stands decisively differentiated.

1. It gives consciousness in a state such that time is not at all relevant.
2. It is not a state of consciousness based upon perception, but upon another function or way of consciousness.
3. It definitely gives the subject the position of transcendence with respect to the object.

Thus introceptive Realization is to be conceived as something that can be known by a human being, but cannot be experienced.

Pure conceptual knowledge is also a somewhat that falls outside of experience in the above sense, but it most definitely is not identical

---

*Ibid., s.v. "experience."

with introceptive Realization. The distinction is highly significant, since introceptualism, when negatively considered from the standpoint of empiricism, may appear to be identical with rationalism. In rationalism, the object for knowledge transcends the object for experience. However, it by no means follows that the subject transcends the object. Rational demonstration produces an effect that is, indeed, closer to the subject than any demonstration through experience. Even so, the most rigorous reasoned proof has yet a quality of objectivity and, therefore, of distance regarding the subject. For this reason, one cannot by pure thought alone think oneself into the transcendental state of consciousness, though he or she may attain a highly rarefied surrogate of that state—something that is far beyond the possibilities of mere experience. As a consequence, it requires more critical acuity to differentiate between this surrogate and genuine introceptive Realization than it does between the latter and experience proper. Thus, for example, we can both conceive and introceptively Realize a timeless order, but we cannot experience it, since a state of consciousness conditioned by time is an ineluctable mark of experience as such.

As will be shown more fully in what follows, introceptive Realization is a state wherein the subject and the object become so far interblended that the self is identical with its knowledge. This is a state of intimacy that pure rational demonstration alone can never attain. For this reason, the most rigorous logical proof, however far it transcends mere experience, nonetheless falls short of certainty. The subject can be absolutely certain only of that knowledge with which it is itself identical. This is characteristic of introceptive Realization, and thus differentiates introceptualism from rationalism, though there is closer affinity between these two philosophic forms than there is between either of them compared to any empiric philosophy.

Introceptual transcendentalism must not be conceived as a form of revelation beyond the possibility of verification by the self within a human being. Revelation that cannot be verified directly, and not merely pragmatically, wields no authority worthy of philosophic respect. All religions based upon this notion of revelation fall below the level of philosophic esteem. Revelation, in this sense, implies acceptance through blind belief, which is something considerably less than inner faith. Only the latter may be regarded as an intuition that has not yet fulfilled itself as full knowledge in the Light of consciousness. Introceptualism affirms no knowledge, truth or reality that may not be directly verified by the self resident within a human being. It is even more antagonistic to the attitude of blind belief than is physical science.

However, there is a sense that the Knowledge of introceptive Realization is not to be regarded as human knowledge. For this reason I use the form *verified by the self resident within a human being*, rather than simply *verified by a human being or human subject*. In the end, we will have to regard the self as transcending the condition of being human. The complete impersonality of the Light of consciousness, appearing as emanating from the self, renders meaningless the distinction between human, subhuman and superhuman. It is only after this pure consciousness has been modified by form, tone or state that we are enabled to classify it as being consciousness of one or another order. Consciousness, as it is behind the categories of human consciousness, is no longer merely human consciousness, but simply capable of assuming this form.

Critical philosophy has generally derived the conclusion that a human consciousness can know only a content that is capable of being experienced, except that it may also know the a priori forms that define the limits of possible experience. Beyond this, human consciousness has only faith or moral intuitions, which, while giving less than knowledge, yet provide an orientation to a somewhat transcending human consciousness. I am not only forced to agree with this conclusion, but would even affirm it independently if it did not already exist. Thus the possession of a knowledge that goes beyond not only experience, but also the conceptual forms that delimit possible experience, implies a consciousness that is more comprehensive than human consciousness, per se. If the self that is resident within a human being is conceived as incapable of awareness in any other than the restricted human form, then a transcendental Knowledge would have to be judged impossible. Anything derived from a transcendental order would have to be regarded as a revelation that people would have to accept or reject blindly, insofar as it could not be directly verified. However, if the ultimate organization of consciousness is such that it is possible for the self resident in a human being to transcend the limits of the human form of consciousness, then it becomes possible, in principle, for such a self to Realize a transcendent Knowledge. Consequently, to the degree that an individual establishes a correlation between the transcendent and the conceptual, he or she could give expression to this Knowledge. There would then arise the problem of how such an expression is related to the transcendent content, just as there is a problem of how conception is related to a perceptual content. Nonetheless, at least a way of correlation between transcendental content and human consciousness is established in principle. In this way it would be possible for a person to check directly the content of purported revelation, thereby sifting the true from the erroneous. It thus becomes conceivable that humanity may consume faith and belief in the Fire of Knowledge.

CONCEPTION AND INTROCEPTION

Introception is the function whereby a human being transcends the limits of the merely human. It is the way to direct metaphysical understanding, but here sound criticism must be careful to draw the distinction between the pure metaphysical understanding and the conceptual framework that symbolizes it. What a person can think conceptually is not a true portrait of the transcendent, and never can be, for a conceptual order is objective with respect to a thinking self, while transcendental Knowledge is identical with its self-aware subject. As a consequence, the process of objectification inevitably implies distortion, no matter how great the skill of the thinker. However, the conceptual order is a symbol that means the transcendent order, and a defect resident in the symbol may not rightly be predicated of that which is symbolized.

Of course, it is again clear that the conceptual form is instrumental in its relation to the introceptual content, but here the reference lies in the dimension of intensivity, rather than of extensivity,* as in the case of the pragmatic theory of knowledge. Further, a conceptual order having introceptive reference, when considered in its relation to the field of perceptual experience, is not a servant function, but a master function. It legislates laws governing the range of future possible experience. As I have said before, this kind of conceptualism is a surrogate for transcendental Realization in the field of experience for all consciousness that is not in a state of direct Realization itself. Conceptual cognition, in this sense, transcends experience and wields an authority beyond the testing of experience. It supplies the framework or base of reference of future possible experience, but such conditioned experience cannot check its own presuppositions, thereby rendering an objective pragmatic testing impossible. Transcendental insight alone is competent to test an introceptive concept, while experience can test an empiric concept by the pragmatic method. It thus follows that, from the standpoint of empiricism, the introceptive concept bears a strong analogy to a rationalist system, though its real nature is totally different from that of abstract rationalism.

---

*[Wolff introduces these terms to emphasize the crucial distinction between perception and introception, which implies a drastically different role for concepts in relation to each. The extensivity of perceptual experience (whether external or internal) is of the nature of a definite manifold, which concepts map. However, the intensivity of introceptual awareness is more of the nature of a continuum that concepts may only symbolize, but not describe.]

INNATE IDEAS

We can now develop a theory both of the doctrines of innate ideas and of natural rights. Whenever any individual from the level of an introceptual Realization gives conceptual embodiment to a transcendent content, that individual imprints this as a form within the collective psyche. Such concepts are peculiarly vital forces. They are of a distinctly different order as compared with mere working hypotheses, since the latter are merely invented constructs designed to integrate some empiric complex. Any number of working hypotheses may be designed to deal with such complex situations, and the choice among alternative hypotheses is governed by purely pragmatic considerations, such as relative simplicity of formulation and application. Such formulations are proposed, used and abandoned, either when they prove inadequate or when some alternative theory offers superior advantages. Clearly, such constructions supply little more than scaffoldings that facilitate the growth of human understanding and command of the environment. The pragmatists probably have interpreted this process correctly enough. However, a concept that is the embodiment of an introceptual Realization carries a force of quite a different nature.

If a student can so far suspend his own cultural matrix such that he may view other cultures with an attitude freed from prejudice, he will find that they have world views and sciences of a nature rather incommensurable with his own. He will find that many of the features of older cultures that formerly seemed to him merely crude or immature have a good deal more enlightened sophistication than he had imagined. It will become clear that there are simply a number of different ways of viewing the world and conceiving a science, and that all such ways that have been part of a historically significant culture have proved themselves adequate by pragmatic tests. Our science and world view may seem obvious enough to us, but quite different orientations have seemed no less obvious to other peoples and have been no less effective in achieving an adjustment between the living human being and the world. No one culture, not even our own, possesses the exclusively correct world view. What is it that causes any particular world view to appear to be obvious or natural? This is a question that leads us down into the generally unconscious determinants of the various ways of orientation possible to humankind. Some of these orientations we can trace to historic sources, thereby clarifying particular instances of a general process.

Individuals like Pythagoras and Galileo are a good deal more than scientific workers. Rather, they are agents of scientific deeds, in the sense of Spengler. They establish ways of approach of such a basic source to problems that those who follow in the respective cultures subsequently think along these lines. Our science may even be called the "Galilean" science, while that of the Greeks may be thought of as the "Pythagorean" science. It is particularly significant that the use or understanding of number in these two sciences is so vastly different that it is quite difficult for one who belongs to the current of the one kind of science to understand the number concept of the other. These thinkers established frameworks of approach that became as self-evident truths for those who followed in their footsteps. We are not merely convinced of the soundness of these truths; we rather believe them with a religious sort of conviction. Such people imprint within the human psyche of their respective cultures concepts that embody an introceptive Realization. These concepts are pregnant and living, and within their respective spheres of influence they possess those who are subsequently born so that they find it exceedingly difficult to free themselves from the feeling that these concepts are necessary.

In the field of religion, this process is even more notable. Thus, to the Christian Protestant of conviction, the Lutheran doctrine of "justification by faith" is not merely a philosophical theory to be entertained among alternative theories. Rather, it is a necessary fundamental principle that is believed by all who realize the true doctrine. To be sure, this doctrine has never been universally held, either in the historic past or at present, even among people of distinctly superior religious natures. The opposed doctrine of mediation appears to possess an even wider acceptance and seems quite as natural and obvious to those who accept it. What we have here is simply an illustration of a process wherein a person of introceptive insight impregnated a concept with that insight and thus predetermined the viewpoint of his numerous followers. Through the insight of Luther, "justification by faith" became an innate idea.

Closer to our time, Friedrich Nietzsche supplies us with another instance of this process. Nietzsche gave his own peculiar insight conceptual form in his works, with the result that it also possessed a sector of subsequent humanity within its folds. It is easy to see how much of the orientation of German national socialism is predetermined by the thought of Nietzsche. To many students, his thought may appear as merely another philosophical theory, but for those who are possessed by it, it presents itself as an innate truth, regardless of whether they have read Nietzsche.

Every significant philosopher and important social or religious leader has produced an impregnated concept from out of the hidden heights or depths. Not always are such concepts impregnated with Light, for they may also be born out of darkness, but they are always more than bare conceptual frameworks or theories. They always carry something of the nature of life within their depths, be it of a dark or a luminous sort. As a result there is, besides the explicit logical consequences, an even more vital development such that they may grow in ways not foreseen by their originators. Doubtless Nietzsche did not mean by his "superman" the "super race" of German national socialism, but this would simply mean that his impregnated concept had potentialities transcending his own private imagination. It is indeed a wise father who can foresee everything his child will become. When one gives life to anything, he or she assumes a vast amount of responsibility. One may have started something better than originally thought, but it may equally well develop into something considerably worse.

The foregoing illustrations are instances of a process within the range of historic observation. By studying instances of this kind, one may learn much of the forces that predetermine the thinking and conduct of humanity. Our consciousness operates within frameworks that quite generally we do not examine, and frequently do not even know in their nature as frameworks that stand in contrast to other possibilities. Within these structures, the possessed individuals may deal with their respective problems with greater or lesser measures of critical rationality, but the acceptance of a frame of reference is something either more or less than rational. One can easily demonstrate this point by subjecting another person's somewhat unconscious framework to criticism while in his or her presence. This almost inevitably arouses a state of consciousness highly toned with affect. One makes no headway at all with rational criticism. Furthermore, in the case of the response by less mature religious types, one runs the risk of being accused of possessing a satanic disposition. On the whole, such attempted criticism is an unwise and even dangerous procedure. Generally it is better to let people sleep within their respective world views, so long as they pose no threat to others. In this matter the East Indians are wiser than we, for they say that it is inadvisable ever to awaken someone forcefully. Rather, let the individual awaken naturally before trying to teach him.

Basic frameworks possess people and thus have the nature of *conviction*, rather than of a theory that one accepts through *persuasion*. Convictions carry the force of innate or native ideas. A psychological or introceptive insight, which has penetrated to deeper levels of consciousness than the frameworks that predetermine the consciousness and conduct of most humans, leads to a knowledge that all such frames of reference are relative. Their innateness is thus only relative—not absolute. Nevertheless, they are properly of the nature of innate ideas for those who are possessed by them, since these frameworks are not for these individuals something derived from experience, but rather underlie it and predetermine its form. It is impossible for their experiences to disprove them, since they automatically exclude all possible experiences that are not confirmatory. It is no easy matter to transcend frameworks of this sort, since the transcending implies something analogous to a dying process that precedes a new birth, either in a minor or in a radical sense. In this, the consciousness of the scientist is as greatly bound as that of the representative of any religious sect. Transcendence of any sort is never easy, but all real advance of human consciousness, that is more than mere elaboration of old possibilities, is dependent upon it.

Enlightenment is a process of transcendence of the old conditioning frameworks; it is not merely the further development of possibilities subsumed by them. For example, to continue the further development of a science delimited by the framework of Galileo's insight is not a progress to a new enlightenment, but merely an elaboration of Galileo's enlightenment. The enlightener always speaks from out of the transcendent, while the continuer merely elaborates further or sustains structures already established. This is generally true about science, religion and social orientations.

Enlightenment may proceed to any degree but always transcends something that formerly had seemed necessary and innate. Old anchorages are broken while new ones are achieved. This is serious business, for while the greatest values known have come by this road, every enlightenment is a destructive force concerning old, somewhat unconscious, presuppositions. For this reason, the enlightener is more likely than not to be an object of persecution, appearing to his milieu as the destroyer of precious established values. In this respect, one may be considered fortunate who is not understood in his or her time.

Innate ideas are not derived from experience, but have their origin either in introceptive Realization or by penetration in the shadowy depths of the psychological unconscious. They are thus not merely logically presupposed in all experience, but in reality have a source in a realm other than that covered by experience. In their higher form, they are rooted in an introceptive Realization, and therefore are truly transcendent in the very sense of a transcendent Knowledge that Kant considered impossible. Objectively, the existence of such ideas can neither be proved nor disproved. Hence they are not to be judged as either true or false, but rather as the relative standard by which the true and the false are measured. It follows that, for instance, it is impossible to determine whether the doctrine of natural rights is true or false. Rather, it is true that if this doctrine is a presupposition of a social consciousness, then a way of social thought and life follows as a consequence. There is excellent reason for regarding this doctrine as defining the distinctive meaning of the American way, since the moral ground for American autonomy was grounded upon this doctrine. Thus, if this doctrine is repudiated, then the distinctively American way is overthrown, to be replaced by something else, better or worse—probably the latter.

So far we have been investigating innate ideas as particularizing frameworks whereby different human cultures, religious sects and social movements are differentiated. Beyond these limits, humankind as a whole has still deeper roots such that intercourse and cross-understanding become possible. Various human groupings are obviously different in innumerable ways, yet the whole human family still remains one, having certain similarities of feeling, thought and action. It is because of this that we differentiate some creatures as being human. How does a human differ from an animal or other kinds of creatures of either an inferior or a superior order? The biologist would say that the differentiation lies in a distinctive anatomy. This answer is doubtless true enough as far as it goes, but it reflects the superficiality that confuses the incidental (accidental) with the fundamental (essential). A creature that possessed the anatomy normal to our species, but the consciousness and behavior of an animal, would in fact be an animal, not a human. Likewise, a creature that possessed a human type of consciousness, but the form of one of the animals, would really be a human being. It is unimportant that the term *man* should be defined as "a featherless plantigrade biped mammal of the genus Homo," but it is highly significant that the Sanskrit root *man* should mean "think" or "the thinker." An intelligent donkey would be more of a human being than a mindless humanoid. The most primitive "featherless plantigrade biped mammal of the genus Homo" that lacks the capacity to think is *not human*.

A human being is human due to the faculty of conceptual thought, not because of any other function, however highly it may be developed. Consider further that the conceptual thinker is one whose stream of consciousness is modified by the framework essential to thought as such. This framework includes the laws of thought in their totality of principles that cannot be derived from any other conception, except in the circular form of mutual implication. No one can repudiate these principles and remain a thinker, though one might continue to be conscious through the activity of other functions. These basic laws of thought are not derivations from experience, but the ground structure that renders possible the world view characteristic of the thinker. They are not necessities of "things" or of consciousness in its concrete totality. Consequently, they are of ontological importance for conceptual thought, but not for being, as a whole.

The laws of thought are thus quite properly considered innate ideas, which cannot be thought away without thinking away the very possibility of thinking. They are real and objective for the thinker qua thinker. Hence, to attain an insight that so far transcends them that they assume the character of relative determinants is to penetrate into consciousness beyond conceptually thinkable limits.

There are innate ideas truly enough, but they are themselves dependent upon a source beyond experience, which is, therefore, genuinely transcendental. Within the circumscribing limits of the framework of consciousness predetermined by them, they can only be known as "terminal" or "borderline" conceptions. They are the theoretical sum of an infinite converging series. While confined within the limits of this framework, human consciousness cannot pass beyond the borderline. However, this limitation is superseded when humankind finds a function by which it is possible to reach consciously beyond the borderline. Every such movement is an act of transcendence. What is more important, if anyone attains the point of introceptive Realization such that he or she may look down upon the most basic principles that render conceptual thought possible, then he or she has transcended human consciousness, in the rigorous sense. In East Indian symbolism, this is the transcendence of the Manu or of Vaivaswata; that is to say, it is a transcendence of the root framework of consciousness that literally is the progenitor of all thinking beings. Thus the laws of thought are the seed of Manu.

It is certainly true that no one can speculatively determine what lies beyond the deepest roots of conceptual thought. Kant's criticism concerning this point is conclusive. Speculation is valid within the framework of the thinker, but not beyond. In addition, beside speculative thought, in our total psychical constitution there is a function—generally latent—whereby we can reach above, and not merely below, thought.* This function is introception. Through its operation the self resident within a human being can know and check transcendental realities. Here is something considerably more than faith, intuition or revelation. It is also not subject to the limitations that criticism has imposed upon speculative thought. We have here the basis for a theory providing an epistemological foundation for a transcendental Knowledge.

Through introducing the notion of the introceptual function, I have avoided, at least in principle, the logical difficulties that until now have dogged the heels of transcendental philosophy. The problem of the

---

*The processes described in Jung's psychology of the unconscious mainly lead to levels below conceptual thought.

genuineness of transcendental insight or presupposition reduces to the problem of showing the existence of the function of introception, as I have defined it. This is not a problem for logic, but for psychology, in the sense of metapsychology. The actuality of the function must be determined, either by a search of the historic evidence for its existence, or by direct individual arousing of its activity. The latter method, of course, supplies the only absolutely certain demonstration that the introceptive function is a fact.

THE SUBJECT TRANSCENDS THE OBJECT

When the Light of consciousness turns upon itself toward its source, the object vanishes. It would follow that if consciousness were dependent upon the object for its existence, then the resultant state would be one of complete unconsciousness. However, we find, to the contrary, that the resultant state is quite other than one of unconsciousness; it is, indeed, a state of greatly intensified consciousness. Thus, if consciousness depends upon anything at all, it is exclusively dependent upon the subject or self. However, the vanishing of the object as consciousness sinks back into its source, as it were, thereby proves the contingency of the object. Whether there is an external world existing as a thing, outside the relation of being an object for a subject, is really a matter of no importance. To predicate existence or nonexistence of such supposed independent thinghood is a meaningless judgment, since no meaning attaches to the notion of existence apart from consciousness. Anyone who attempts to define such existence inevitably finds that the very act of defining has transformed it into an object, that is, into a somewhat that exists for consciousness. The arguments for the existence of the independent thing do not have any sounder logical basis than the old formal arguments for the existence of God that Kant criticized so effectively. The existence of the independent thing is not a necessity for thought, and that which takes place in introceptive Realization shows that it is not a necessity for consciousness. We may conclude that it is wholly unnecessary either to affirm or to deny the existence of the independent thing. It is simply irrelevant.

At the first stage of the introceptive transformation, the object vanishes, while the subject persists. This minimally implies the transcendency of the subject relative to the object—a consequence of the highest importance, not only for philosophy and religion, but also for sociology. The relationship between subject and object is not equalitarian, but hierarchical, with the subject occupying the transcendent position. Thus authority inheres in the subject. An instance drawn from history illustrates the practical bearings of this relationship.

It is reported that, during or after his conquest of India, Alexander the Great became quite interested in the strange powers of the Indian Yogins. Eventually he had the opportunity to meet one who was seated upon the bank of a river. The Yogin graciously condescended to converse with Alexander, answering his questions at some length. Alexander was greatly impressed, and wished to have the Yogin return with him to Macedonia. When he proposed this, the Yogin refused. Alexander commanded, but the Yogin still refused. Finally, Alexander threatened to employ all the compulsive means he had in his power, including the threat of death itself, but all this left the Yogin as unmoved as ever. Ultimately, Alexander retreated in defeat. Even though this great soldier could conquer a world, he could not influence the will of a single naked Yogin. Stated in psychological terms, Alexander exerted the greatest power of his time over the objective situation, but was powerless over the self, for the very essence of being a true Yogin is single-pointed identification with the self. The world ruler, no matter how great or powerful, never commands the Yogin but in all relations with the latter seeks from him what he may graciously bestow. Here the proud ruler must play the humble part.

The objective situation does not dominate because it transcends the Subject, for it is the Subject that is transcendent. The objective situation dominates only those who are weak and deluded, which, unfortunately, comprises the vast majority of humanity. Metaphorically stated, the beggar (object) in life has usurped the royal throne, while the true ruler (the self) has permitted himself to become the scullion who seeks largesse of the real beggar who appears in royal robes. One who has great compassion may pity the true royalty who imagines himself to be only the scullion. However, since the latter has no one to blame but himself, and could reaffirm his status at any time, he really merits only contempt. When all this is clearly understood, our whole conception of social organization and method will be radically altered. Today, because we have permitted ourselves to fall under the hypnotic domination of the object, we conceive of government in terms that fit only the psychology of the deluded scullion.

Philosophy has fallen far from its high estate when it sells itself to the object. That physical science should do this is not so surprising, but one expects more from philosophy. Not only do the explicitly realistic schools do this, but one even finds the pragmatists assuming the same orientation. Consider the following quotation from William James referring to Dewey, Schiller and himself: "As I myself understand these authors, we all three absolutely agree in admitting the transcendency of the object—provided it is an experienceable object—to the subject, *in the* *truth relation* [italics mine]."* The final phrase suggests that possibly the pragmatic theory does not affirm the transcendency of the object in all possible relations, but definitely it does in the preeminently important relation of truth. What does this imply?

It certainly means that truth is not a transcendent relation that exists prior to experience. The truth relation is a function of experience, not of introceptive Realization. One finds truth by an adjustment to an objective situation, not by an inner, supersensuous attunement. In the one case, one attains truth by achieving adjustment with an already existent world, even though it is merely the world that is given through perceptual experience. In the other, the Realization of truth effectively destroys the world as possessing any real independence. Consciousness, as known through introceptual Realization, is independent of the objective world, and merely permits the latter to be. Knowing the true nature of this objective world is a quintessential feature of the truth of inner Realization. Awakened self-consciousness may choose to act as though the objective world were real in itself and thus play the game on those terms. In this case there are various relationships, some of which may be called "correct" and others "incorrect," but here we have something less than the truth relation. It would be better to speak of empiric correctness and incorrectness, meanwhile leaving the loftier term *truth* for the more fundamental adjustment that determines the relationship between the subjective order and the objective order taken as a whole.

---

*William James, *The Meaning of Truth* (New York: Greenwood Press, 1909), xvii-xix.

9

Reality and Appearance

In the psychology of the transformation process, it is a known fact that the process is generally accompanied by a presentation, either in the dreaming or in the waking state, of a series of symbols that convey a particularly significant meaning to the individual. The culminating symbols tend to take certain forms, technically known as "mandalas,"* which are generally sensuous presentments or actions. Once the content of these symbols is adequately assimilated, the transforming process is complete and the individual has achieved integration at a new level. The manuals of Oriental Yoga agree with the Western psychology on the subject that these symbolic instruments are highly important. However, it is not invariably the case that the symbol takes a sensible form, either as a recept or as a sensible act. In my own psychological organization, there seems to be a distinctly limited capacity for fabricating sensible images autonomously. As a result, I personally stand in a defective position to analyze this process directly. I have never known visual or other sensible presentations of this sort during the waking state, and only rarely even in dreams. Even so, I have had acquaintance with conceptual presentations of a semiautonomous sort that proved to be of enormous importance in the transformation process.

CONCEPTUAL PRESENTATION

A conceptual presentation is not to be understood as a conceptual representation, since it enters consciousness, in part at least, in much the way a percept does. It is not more than partly a conceptual construction. Indeed, it apparently may be an almost wholly autonomous development. As I know this kind of presentation, it is marked by a complete lack of concrete perceptual or sensible elements. It is more like a newly born and fully grown idea—a birth well symbolized by the stepping

---

*[Somewhat symmetrical archetypal patterns representing the unity of the self.]

forth of Minerva fully grown from the head of Jupiter. It is highly abstract, as though coming directly from a consciousness to which what we call "abstract" is more immediate and direct than the concrete and particular. Here I must diverge from Jung when he insists that the abstract idea is exclusively a development from an essentially concrete and perceptual primordial image. As far as my acquaintance with this kind of Idea goes, it is so abstract in its original nature that any formulation at all results in at least some distortion from a process of concretion. Our language fails because it is not abstract enough. Thus the distorting effect of conceptual representation is the reverse of that which occurs when a concrete perception is given conceptual formulation. I must insist upon this point, as it has an important bearing upon one of my theses, namely, that our most abstract language is the best vehicle of ultimate Truth.

The immediate conceptual presentation is more like the manifestation of a mature consciousness than of the primitive kind of consciousness suggested by the primordial image. This leads to some rather startling implications, for it seems to imply that the collective unconscious, in its total meaning, is not merely filled with a kind of primitive primordial content. Unquestionably, there is such a content, but there is no good reason for doubting the equal existence of a deposit in the collective unconscious from ancient and unknown cultures of a very high order of maturity. History, insofar as we know it, definitely does not reveal to us a stage when the earth was without sages of a very superior order. Our current idea of a development from exclusively primitive roots is little more than a mythical construct, probably very largely the result of prejudices induced by the influence of Darwin. The archetype of the wise old man, which Jung has isolated, does not at all carry the symbolic meaning of primitivity; rather, it conveys something that is distinctly mature. It is not improbable that there were ancients who were wiser in their day than we are in ours. By no means is it a self-evident truth that the process of time inevitably implies progress in wisdom. Degeneration is also possible.

I most certainly insist that the Sage is the child of introception rather than of perception, so that Wisdom in the spiritual sense is a Root, rather than a flower growing out of perceptual experience. Thus Wisdom descends from the sky and does not ascend out of the earth, so that without the downpourings from the sky, the earth would be parched and cultured life would gradually disappear. It is for this reason that earthborn philosophies are sterile.

A conceptual presentation differs from a conceptual representation in the further respect that it carries an enormously clarifying authority. It is entirely possible that through unaided intellectual speculation an individual might develop a formulation precisely the same as that of a conceptual presentation, but the effect on the transformation process would be entirely different. The speculative construct would be only a theory, from which systematic conclusions could be drawn, but it would not yield the authority of insight. It would not make the thinker into a different person. However, a conceptual presentation carries with it a superlative order of assurance—one knows without doubt that here is Truth. The Knowledge does not seem external to the self, as it does with purely speculative constructs. One can transfer one's anchorage to the conceptual presentation with the same certainty that one formerly viewed oneself as a world-bound being. Subsequently, the influence of inherited and traditional ideas may introduce doubt, if the individual permits them to do so. In that case, the transformation process would be hindered, if not prevented entirely. Without question, mere habit and tradition must be heroically depreciated, as mere dangers that must be conquered along the way. At any rate, at the moment of the presentation itself, the authority of the insight is unequivocal. One has found a base upon which to stand against the opinion of the whole world, if necessary.

SUBSTANTIALITY IS INVERSELY PROPORTIONAL TO PONDERABILITY

In my own experience the crucial key to the transformation process lay in a sudden and highly authoritative recognition that finally took the aphoristic form, "Substantiality is inversely proportional to ponderability." At a particularly lucid moment, I simply saw that this must be true. Sensible presentments and conceptual representations in that moment acquired the value of voidness, surrounded by fullness that is forever hidden to a consciousness operating *exclusively* under those forms. In other words, I found real fullness in just those zones where sensation and conception reported absence of anything. This was a radical inversion of all habitual values, but it removed the remaining barriers to the awakening of the introceptual process.

Anyone who analyzes the aphoristic formula will find that it implies a phase in the process of turning about. With our ordinary understanding and habits, we conceive of all development and progress as a movement toward further elaboration of perceptual and conceptual content. We imagine that such content is, of course, something—indeed, something valuable. Enrichment is a process of increasing it. However, this valuation is reversed. Both perceptual presentation and conceptual representation have the significance of an empty phantasmagoria of essentially no more substantiality than dream stuff. Particularly is this true of sensible presentments, though it is somewhat less emphatically the case with concepts. Sensible fact, instead of having the greatest reality value, as with most individuals, is seen as most empty of reality. All the relationships of the sensible world are seen to have only the significance of a sort of painful game that does not lead much anywhere. In contrast, the assurance of a supersensible actuality is far more profound than any former belief in sensible reality. Here is indubitable evidence of another way of consciousness, which receives practically no recognition in our psychology and philosophy.

I conceive it to be highly significant that the transformed point of view leaves the substance of the logical processes of thought unaltered. The content of meaning given to the indefinable terms that enter into logical systems is simply given a new reference. In other words, rational thought remains the mediator between the perceptual and the introceptual orders. We can view the perceptual contents as negations, instead of positive actualities, and then proceed with the systematic development of either a science or a philosophy, as formerly. One can think as well as or better than ever before, but the valuation of the content of the thought is radically altered. As a consequence, this transformation does not imply in any way an alogical attitude. Therefore, I feel justified in affirming that there is more relative reality in logical process and form than there is in any perceptual presentment or experience. Still, even this reality is only relative.

None of this implies that experience is wholly without value, but its value is symbolic and instrumental. A negation can serve very well as a symbol of that which is negated. It is all a question of how the meaningful reference is interpreted. Experience simply is not an end in itself, nor does it mean something that can be attained by further experience. Its real reference is to that which is Realized directly only by the turning about in consciousness. Movement of consciousness in the direction of experience always ultimately leads to disappointment and frustration.* However, with the turning about, the frustration and disappointment vanish.

Of course, we also need a theory of the nature and office of experience. Experience arises out of a conative attitude of hunger or craving. In a state of complete satisfaction, there is none of the desiring or yearning that leads on to experience, whereas in the absence of satisfaction, all sorts of strivings are aroused that are oriented in whatever direction it may seem that satisfaction may be achieved. So long as consciousness is

---

*Schopenhauer's *The World as Will and Idea*, book 4, illuminates this point.

oriented toward the object, this leads to a search for ever more experience. Yet, somehow every experience is a disappointment in that it fails to supply the satisfaction sought, and so the same effort is repeated through a seemingly endless series. The content of experience is like a worthless piece of quartz rock in which there once lay a nugget of gold, but where now there remains only the mold of that nugget. It is like the gorgeous color on the inner pearly surface of a seashell, which color is no substance in the shell, but is the light as it is refracted from the surface. It is the promise of fulfillment at the rainbow's end, which ever recedes as one approaches. This is true because there is no substance in the content of pure experience.

The office of experience is to frustrate and to cheat, yet not for a malicious purpose. Experience brings pain so that consciousness may be gradually awakened to self-realization, for if consciousness flowed freely toward the object and thereby found the fulfillment of its yearning, there would be none of the shock necessary for consciousness to become aware of its own true nature. Empiric consciousness is like an alien in a distant and strange land who is yearning for all that has been lost. She seeks widely in this land for old companions, but they are not to be found anywhere in that region. To find them, consciousness must return to the source from whence it came. It is the office of experience to lash the wanderer until she finally awakens to the need for the return.

The values that experience symbolizes lie behind the outward flowing stream of consciousness and thus are, in reality, closer to the wanderer than the objects that lie before her. These specific values are never the content of any presentment, nor of any idea. They are thus symbolized by the void of unfilled space, which seems to the objectively streaming consciousness to be nothing at all. So, experience gives just that which Reality is not; it is the thin and insubstantial surface that bounds and hides the Real. The framework of empiric consciousness is such that it always pervasively veils the durable and substantial.

It is characteristic of the critical analysis of our day that it finds no substance anywhere. There is real acuity of understanding revealed in this criticism, for it is indeed true that the form of our externally oriented consciousness is precisely such that it never can give us a realization of substantial actuality. Terms in relation are truly empty, as thin as a mathematical surface, and undoubtedly this is all that experience ever gives. However, to say that this is all that there is, or all that may be realized, is equivalent to saying that the experiential kind of consciousness is the sole possibility. Whoever has once found the way to turn the stream of consciousness backward toward its source knows that this is not so; whoever has not done this is in no position to know. The denial of the actuality of substance is valid for the zone delimited by possible experience, but not for domains of consciousness beyond that.

At present, when one attempts to reintroduce the notion of 'substance' into a philosophical system, he or she is moving against the current of the times. In the older philosophies, the notion had an honorable place, but not so in our time. In part this may be explained as a result of the development of critical philosophy, and in part as a result of a change of the psychological focus of consciousness. When consciousness is oriented more to the extraverted attitude, there is a tendency to spread widely in a consciousness of surface, at the price of a loss of depth. This means that content of consciousness becomes valued only as experience or as mere terms in relation, having no underlying substantiality. The result is a state of essentially soulless consciousness separated from its roots, in the sense of a conscious correlation with the roots. In this case Knowledge as Assurance is lost. There remains either only probable knowledge or a knowledge that has only a tentative value because of its empiric working. From this point of view, that there should be something substantial behind this knowledge is an idea without weight. At best, it is an unknown and unknowable somewhat that is of no practical significance, and certainly is not logically necessary. It appears as though all we have is simply the play of phenomena, and from this it is a short step to the philosophical standpoint of phenomenalism.

I am forced to agree that if we restrict knowledge to the combination of pure reason and experience, the notion of an underlying substance is reduced to a speculative construct. Indeed, there is much to be said for the elimination of all speculative constructs that are not theoretically necessary. For many purposes, no efficiency is lost if we assume that no substantial substrate exists behind either the phenomenal object or the empiric subject to consciousness. Further, this standpoint receives considerable support from the better known doctrines of Buddhism, the most philosophical of religions. Because there is a considerable rapprochement between modern Western speculation and the phenomenology of Buddhism, we clearly face a problem that calls for careful examination.

In its more important signification, the concept of 'substance' means the substrate underlying all experience, which is not itself a direct object of experience. Since the time that the problem of knowledge attained recognition as being crucial, the notion of the 'substrate' has acquired two contrasted meanings. In one sense, it is conceived as the underlying thing-in-itself; in the other, as a supporting and constitutive subject. These contrasting substance philosophies are, respectively, realist and idealist in perspective, but both agree in predicating a reality behind the

scenes. Both also agree in affirming a somewhat that perdures throughout all change, such as the unchanging mass of matter throughout all
changes of state of matter, or a persistent self that remains identical
throughout all modifications of consciousness.

Opposed to the substantiality theory is the view that both the object
of experience and the subject to experience are merely complexes of
insubstantial elements, either material or psychical. All entities are thus
simply phenomenal effects of complexes, rather than being perdurable
substrates. It is interesting and very striking that a doctrine as modern
as this should have been formulated by the Buddha 2,500 years ago. It
was the main philosophical point of departure between Buddhism and
Brahmanism proper and seems to have been a source of considerable
bitter controversy. Since the practical ethical objective of Buddhism was
the dissolution of these complexes, it is not surprising that Buddhist
phenomenology should have suggested that the Nirvanic state was literal annihilation. For how could there be any real immortality if there is
no such thing as a perdurable self?

I am not aware of any philosophy more subtle or more difficult to
understand than Buddhism, if one is solely familiar with the more public teachings. There seems to be neither a subject nor a thing-in-itself
behind the phantasmagoric play of phenomena. However, the Sanskrit
Sutras, which were written about five or six hundred years after the
final Nirvana of the Buddha, reveal a much more positive metaphysical
teaching. There is something behind the empiric subject and phenomena that does endure, thereby giving to the Nirvanic state a positive
meaning, but it is by no means an easy task to isolate the logic of the
total teaching. I doubt that real clarity in this matter can ever be
achieved without individually passing through the process of the direct
Realization or Transformation. In any case, Buddhist philosophy* does
affirm a somewhat that is perdurable and thus does teach a substan-
tialist metaphysics that is the counterpart of the phenomenalist treatment of empiric consciousness.

The fundamental idealist doctrine, that existence is identical with
being known or otherwise determined by being in and for consciousness, would lead to the most rigorous kind of phenomenalism if knowledge were conceived as restricted to experience and pure reason alone.
In this case, the notion of 'substance' would be confined to the realist
view, which holds that there are real existences independent of all con-

---

*[The Buddha personally maintained an antimetaphysical attitude. Despite
this, some schools of Buddhism (for example Yogacara) developed metaphysical doctrines, whereas others (such as Zen) retained a phenomenalist orientation. Wolff is, of course, referring here to the former development.]

sciousness, which are, in their own true nature, different from their appearance to consciousness. However, a study of the idealist thinkers quite generally reveals either an implication of another way of consciousness, or an explicit reference to such. I have already interpreted Schopenhauer's "intuition of genius" and "temper akin to genius" as implying a kind of cognition other than either perception or conception. Friedrich Schelling is even more explicit. The following quotations from *System of Transcendental Idealism* are impressive:

> By this act of separation ["the two affirmations, *I am* and *There are things outside of me*"] when it is completed, one transports one's self in the transcendental act of contemplation, which is by no means a natural, but an artificial one.*

> The sole organ of this method of philosophizing is therefore the *inner sense*, and its object is of such a nature that, unlike that of mathematics, it can never become the object of external intuition.†

> The whole object of this philosophy is no other than the action of intelligence according to fixed laws. This action can be conceived only through a peculiar, direct, inner intuition, and this again is possible only by production.‡

> For whereas production in art is projected outward, in order to reflect the unconscious by products; philosophical production is directed immediately inward, in order to reflect it in intellectual intuition.§

It seems to me abundantly clear that the phrases *transcendental act of contemplation, inner sense, peculiar, direct, inner intuition* and *intellectual intuition* refer to essentially what I mean by introception. This "inner sense" is explicitly conceived as an *organ* and, hence, implies a function of consciousness. It is thus clear that this is not the same as introspection, for the latter activity does not imply a new organ essentially different from the functions employed in ordinary perceptual observation. Introspection is merely a kind of observation.

We have now arrived at a position such that we can define the notion of substance in idealistic terms. Substance in this sense does not

---

*Friedrich Wilhelm Joseph von Schelling, *System of Transcendental Idealism*, trans. Benjamin Rand, in *Modern Classical Philosophies*, 540.

†Ibid., 544.

‡Ibid., 545.

§Ibid.

mean an unknown substrate, in every possible sense of knowing. It means, rather, a substrate that cannot be known as an object of perceptual experience, nor can it be known through pure conceptual thought. *It is known through the introceptive function of consciousness, that is, through the process whereby consciousness turns upon itself toward its source.* There is thus a sense in which substance remains as the unknown perdurable substrate, for it is unknown so long as the introceptive function is not awakened and active. At the same time, in the more comprehensive sense, consciousness remains as the constitutive determinant of being, at least insofar as the notion of 'being' can have any conceivable meaning. Indeed, we may say that consciousness is itself the substantial substrate, but not that any given isolated phase or function of consciousness is such a substrate.

From this perspective, we are now able to define, in general terms, how it is possible that the whole of being may be constituted by consciousness and yet may appear to the empiric human as in part objectively determined. The objective world as a whole is a precipitate from Consciousness in its most comprehensive sense, but it is only partly determined by perceptual and conceptual consciousness. The precipitate from Consciousness beyond perception and conception appears as objective and independent to the empiric individual. It is what it is, despite the individual's wish and will. One must come to terms with this objective appearance and direct his or her willing through various adjustments, rather than by free action. Even so, if any individual were to become completely conscious, there would no longer be any objective world, except insofar as he or she willed it into being and voluntarily accepted a degree of binding or veiling of his or her consciousness. However, such a person would have become more than a mere private individual; that person would have become identical with the collective Self of all creatures.

Substance has the psychological value of "Depth," whereas the notions of terms in external relations and of experience imply consciousness as surface exclusively. Therefore, it may be said that substance philosophies alone have soul, though in the case of materialism, the soul would be dead, but not nonexistent. There is soul only when there is something more felt or Realized than that which appears upon the surface of consciousness alone. Thus soul never can be a part of the material available for objective analysis. Consequently, any philosophy that views its whole problem as concerned exclusively with material completely available for objective analysis in principle must be regarded as soulless. It is for this reason that a philosophy such as the new realism is more deadly to the religious feeling than even outright materialism. It is better to have a dead soul than no soul at all.

Depth, in the above sense, is not easy to define, though it may be so clearly Realized or felt that its actuality is indubitable. A positive and comprehensive definition is impossible, so the most that can be said of a definitive character is mainly negative. Thus Depth is that which is not comprehended by any concept, nor any part of experience, in the definitely delimited meaning we have given to the latter term. It is that which is always "felt," at least, in every genuine religious experience. It is that for which those who know its value would readily sacrifice their lives. It can be directly and consciously Realized only by the conscious introceptive movement, in which consciousness turns upon itself toward its source. Here there is immediate, direct and positive Realization of the Depth dimension in consciousness. This Depth quale is precisely the inexpressible element in all Gnostic and mystical Realization. Every expression that has come out of such Realization fails to convey explicitly the Depth quality. The surface meaning of all such expressions can be interpreted in such a way that there is no Depth, but in so doing the real meaning is lost. Of necessity, one must be at least a near mystic in order to understand a mystic.

The direct Realization of Depth alone gives certainty of assurance with respect to perdurability. Without this Realization, there can be no certainty with respect to immortality, however conceived. On objective grounds, the notion of 'immortality' can never be more than a speculative extrapolation that reaches far beyond its grounds. Even a real communication with disembodied entities—assuming that such a communication could be established—would not prove that such entities were perdurable. Their existence might be as much conditioned by time as embodied life in the world, and the affirmation of a disembodied entity to the contrary would be insufficient to justify any certainty. To establish the actuality of a disembodied entity would prove only that living beings can exist in such a way that they are not apparent to the normal sensorium. More is required to give the notion of immortality a positive meaning.

It is equally true that the mere event of physical death is insufficient to prove perdurability or immortality. There is no reason whatsoever to suppose that mere physical dying is enough to awaken consciousness in the Depth or transcendental dimension. One may die to find oneself still aware, with much the same kind of consciousness as while in physical embodiment. With most humans, this would still be a case of consciousness moving on the surface. It is quite significant that the Buddhists speak of the death of a Buddha as the final Nirvana, but not so in the case of other persons. The direct acquaintance with Depth not only may be attained before death, but there is also no reason to believe that there is any advantage for such attainment in an after-death state. If any individual consciousness is perdurable, then it is so *now* no less than at any future time.

Kant was quite correct in viewing the problem of immortality as belonging to metaphysics. Thus, except insofar as one has awakened the function of transcendental cognition, he can find no certain answer to this problem. Apart from this, faith may build a positive presumption, and considerations of practical psychological therapeutics may render the inculcation of belief in immortality an important heuristic method, as Jung has found in his practice. Yet, great as the psychological value of belief and faith is, they still fall far short of supplying epistemological certainty. No truly rigorous and heroic thinker can ever be satisfied with the crutch of mere belief or disbelief, nor is the standpoint of agnosticism better than a confession of defeat, if it is accepted as more than a temporary position. It is simply sound and conscientious think-ing to acknowledge frankly, after adequate search and analysis, that knowledge of the metaphysical cannot be attained by ordinary means. However, it is a moral failure to be willing to accept nescience in any dimension as a final state. The true soldier in the ranks of inquiry will never be content to rest short of grounded certainty.

A resolution of the three metaphysical problems recognized by Kant (God, freedom and immortality) is attained through the awaken-ing of the function of introception. Even so, certainty thus achieved by awakening this function cannot be conveyed merely by conceptual thought, however skillfully developed, to one who is introceptively blind. This is the analogue of the similar impossibility of conveying the immediate certainties of ordinary vision to someone who was born blind. At best one might suggest something of how it is possible that introceptive insight can provide certainty.

KNOWLEDGE THROUGH IDENTITY

A rigorous analysis of our ordinary cognitive processes reveals that this kind of knowledge does not give us certainty in any direction. Rus-sell is quite correct when he says that this knowledge gives us no more than probable truth. Why is this so? The answer is very simple. It lies in the fact that in the case of ordinary knowledge, the knower stands in a relation of distance or difference from the object of knowledge. There-fore, he or she has no ground of certainty concerning the content of this knowledge. However, in contrast to ordinary knowledge, introceptive cognition is in the form of an identity between the knower and the known. Thus the certainty-destroying factor of distance or difference is eliminated, with the consequence that introceptive cognition is absolutely certain in its original state. Undoubtedly, subsequent error may be introduced when one proceeds to a conceptual interpretation of the introceptive content, but such error does not attach to the pure introceptive cognition itself. One can secure oneself from error of the interpretative type only by carefully avoiding saying anything positive concerning introceptive content, beyond claiming that such content exists and is certain. There would then remain only the task of the destructive analysis of all relative knowledge. However, I contend that the value of a conceptual interpretation outweighs the evil of interpretative error.

The Knowledge through Identity given by introceptive cognition presents an immediate relation to a comprehensive content, which would have for ordinary relative knowledge the character of an indefensible extrapolation. Thus the notion of the 'infinite', such as the idea of the sum of all terms of an infinite series, is a borderline concept for relative thought. Ordinary conception does not strictly comprehend the infinite, but projects the notion as a logical extrapolation. In contrast, introceptive cognition may be said to begin with just such borderline concepts by way of immediate and instantaneous Realizations. The infinite is no more an extrapolation for introception than is the immediate content of ordinary vision an extrapolation for perceptual consciousness. Perhaps, for a being that completely lacked the power of ordinary vision, but had the capacity for conceptual thought highly developed, the actual content given by vision would appear as an infinite or borderline concept. The psychological significance of the notion of infinity is by no means comprehended in the formal mathematical definition of infinity. I submit that, in terms of its psychological significance, the infinite is the borderline of any function, which may become the immediately comprehended content of another function. Thus the seen world is infinitely distant from the world of sound, yet is the immediately given for sight. If one bears this point in mind, one will realize that there is no undue pretension in saying that introceptive cognition gives immediately that which for ordinary conception is the borderline notion of infinity. The immediate Realization of infinity would not be the literal step-by-step summation of an endless series—an impossible task—but would be the direct comprehension of that which *appears* as an endless, and therefore impossible, summation. This means that the notion of infinity enters into the picture simply as an interpretative device when one seeks to convey an introceptive content within the inadequate form of ordinary conception.

To ordinary consciousness, God appears as the Infinite, and immortality as an infinite extension of time. In the light of the preceding discussion, this means that we are dealing with borderline concepts for a function for which neither God nor immortality can be a direct content. Except insofar as he or she is also a conceptual thinker, the introceptively awakened being would have no need for the notion of infinity. God and immortality are simply immediate Realizations that have very little to do with our ordinary theological notions on the subject. For instance, we can say that the whole of Eternity can be Realized in an instant. In this awareness the relativity of time as an infinitely extended manifold is transcended.

From this standpoint we may see why the post-Hegelian idealists need to introduce the notion of 'infinite regressions'. They are trying to convey through conceptual thought a meaning that can be truly comprehended only though introceptive Realization. Naturally, the figure that they develop seems inconceivable if it is taken literally. It is clearly absurd to conceive of the Absolute Consciousness as actually moving through a process of infinite regression, so I do not believe that the post-Hegelians mean anything like that. They simply are dealing with a problem of interpretation by using a function that is inadequate for the content in question. It is a serious error to predicate the unavoidable defects of a symbol as defective of that which is symbolized.

The implications of the theorem *Substantiality is inversely proportional to ponderability* are indeed far-reaching and often startling from the standpoint of habitual valuations. For here, by the term *ponderable*, I mean not merely everything that can be measured in the usual sense, but everything that can be an objective content of consciousness, whether perceptual or conceptual. This means that everything objective and tangible is insubstantial and, therefore, ghostlike. The content of empiric consciousness is real emptiness. The empiric world is a mirage, though innocent enough until it is taken to be something real in itself, in which case it becomes the source of all sorts of delusion and bondage.

To be sure, the empiric human being must come to terms with his environment, since by no ordinary means can he simply imagine it as not there, and then successfully act along the lines of his imaginings. Furthermore, the meaning of this objective resistance, which forces a person to meet its terms, does not consist in a thing that is independent of all consciousness. It is rather a reflex of that portion of consciousness that has not yet been awakened and assimilated. *The extent of one's awareness of the universe is the measure of the degree of his unconsciousness.* To the degree that his consciousness awakens, to that degree the universe tends to vanish until, with complete consciousness, there is no universe left at all. This is the stage wherein, at last, complete freedom is attained. Humankind is bound by unconsciousness and is conditioned by nothing else. The completely liberated being could choose to reintegrate his universe, but this would not be a process of adding to his consciousness. Rather, it very definitely would be by a process of selective self-veiling. Becoming aware of an external world would be achieved by narrowing the field of awareness, not by expanding it.

One may object to the idea that the "extent of one's awareness of the universe is the measure of the degree of his unconsciousness" on the ground that this implies that the increase of scientific knowledge is tantamount to an increase in unconsciousness. However, if we analyze physics, our most advanced special science, we shall find that its development supports my thesis, for the content for the physicist's thought has become progressively etherealized and intangible. The ponderable universe has become very largely merely an appearance for the physicist, so there is much in this science that sounds decidedly like the Indian doctrine of Maya.* Matter is first reduced to elemental parts, such as electrons and protons, then these cease to be merely understood as small hard balls. It is found that they are essentially of the nature of electricity and that their behavior cannot be represented by any sensible model. In the end we find that the only effective description of this behavior lies in a group of differential equations that do not give a picturable meaning. Further, even the electrons and protons can be destroyed as units, to become flashes of radiation spreading indefinitely throughout space. In effect, all of this is simply a disappearance of the universe in the sense of being something real as it appears, while that which remains determinant is a mathematical statement, a somewhat that exists for thought. This simply means that our physicists have become highly conscious and thereby caused a substantial vanishing of the ponderable universe. Thus, far from discrediting my thesis, the late development of our most fundamental special science strongly confirms it.[†]

As I use the term, the *Substantial* is that which is Real, Perdurable and Self-existent. In contrast, the phenomenal is that which depends upon something other than itself as it appears. However, the phenomenal is not conceived as a direct manifestation of the Substantial, so that by a direct movement of consciousness toward the noumenal, the Substantial can be attained, if the movement is maintained far enough.

---

*[Maya is equivalent to Avidya. Avidya is the opposite of Vidya, or knowledge of reality, so Avidya is ignorance of the true nature of reality. Specifically, it is to mistake the phenomenal appearance of the world as ultimately real. In one sense, then, Maya is this illusory appearance; in another, it is the condition of ignorance concerning its true nature.]

[†][The development of quantum physics since this was originally written would lend even more powerful support to Wolff's view. Experiments confirming nonlocality and the energy of the vacuum are particularly significant.]

Rather, the phenomenon is produced by what might be called a "relative withdrawal of substance," so that a movement of consciousness toward the phenomenal is equivalent to a movement *away from* the Real. The Real is attained by a movement of consciousness in the direction opposite from that by which the phenomenon is experienced. The key to the Realization of the Real lies in the turning about of the stream of consciousness toward its source.

The movement of consciousness toward experience as an end in itself is equivalent to a growth of spiritual poverty. The ultimate effect of this movement is a state of complete slavish bondage to the object, in which the entity becomes a mere appendage to appearance. Consciousness in this state is quite without depth; that is, it is a soulless state in the sense that all the values connoted by soul are completely unconscious. Even so, the unconscious depths of the individual are by no means inactive simply because the individual consciousness is not aware of them. Thus it follows that anyone in this state is completely at the mercy of autonomous psychical forces. Individuals and nations in this state are continually drawn into impossible and tragic situations wherein what is done, or has to be done, one would prefer to have been done otherwise. The conscious individual or national will has no control over the factors that are unconscious to it.

10

The Meaning of Divinity

When we come into the presence of the notion of 'Divinity'* we face that which is the Supreme Value for all consciousness, but also, in most of its representations, the greatest source of evil. Far more often than not, when we hear someone refer to God, that person is conceiving of only a human invention that has been handed down by religious institutions and traditions. At times, however, this word is used to designate the one Reality that genuinely underlies all that is, and that may be directly known as the universal Substrate. Thus it is meaningless either to affirm that God is or that God is not, if one does not consider the specific sense in which the term is employed. The God of direct mystical or Gnostic Realization is very different from the God of theological speculation, and of priestcraft generally. So, we can define the term in such a way that it has the highest philosophical and psychological validity, but in that case we shall mean something very different from common understanding. There is a meaning centering on the notion of Divinity that I find to be of the highest importance; yet, I could equally well employ or avoid words commonly used to designate God. Either line of procedure introduces psychological difficulties. On the one hand, if familiar words are used with a specially delimited connotation, the reader's inherited presuppositions are almost certain to confuse the issue. On the other hand, the denial of any reality to traditional God conceptions is equally likely to be interpreted as a kind of atheistic materialism. Both views would lead to a false understanding of my true meaning. Therefore, it is necessary to discuss the matter further to distinguish the senses in which the notion of Divinity is sound from those which are untenable.

---

*[Wolff distinguishes between that for which adequate conceptual definition may be given and that for which it is essentially impossible. He uses the term *notion* to refer to the latter. Although notions cannot strictly describe the Reality, they may suggest something that allows us to orient toward a direct awareness, or Realization of it. By implication, he considers Divinity or God a notion, in this strict sense.]

There is one sense of the God notion that can be dispensed with very readily. Often in our history priests and political rulers have invented or modified an already existing God notion to employ as an instrument of psychological power and control over the people whom they rule. That in this we have a supreme manifestation of evil I believe to be so self-evident that it needs little supporting argument. In this connection, the author of the *Mahatma Letters* makes the same point in a manner worth quoting at some length:

And now, after making due allowance for evils that are natural and cannot be avoided,—and so few are they that I challenge the whole host of Western metaphysicians to call them evils or trace them directly to an independent cause—I will point out the greatest, the chief cause of nearly two-thirds of the evils that pursue humanity ever since that cause became a power. It is religion under whatever form and in whatsoever nation. It is the sacerdotal caste, the priesthood and the churches; it is in those illusions that man looks upon as sacred, that he has to search out the source of that multitude of evils which is the great curse of humanity and that almost overwhelms mankind. Ignorance created Gods and cunning took advantage of the opportunity. Look at India and look at Christendom and Islam, at Judaism and Fetichism [sic]. It is priestly imposture that rendered these Gods so terrible to man; it is religion that makes of him the selfish bigot, the fanatic that hates all mankind out of his own sect without rendering him any better or more moral for it. It is belief in God and Gods that makes two-thirds of humanity the slaves of a handful of those who deceive them under the false pretense of saving them. Is not man ever ready to commit any kind of evil if told that his God or Gods demand the crime—voluntary victim of an illusionary God, the abject slave of his crafty ministers? . . . Remember the sum of human misery will never be diminished unto that day when the better portion of humanity destroys in the name of Truth, morality, and universal charity, the altars of their false gods.*

Thus speaks a modern representative of Buddhism, one of the greatest religious philosophies.

I think that if we can free our minds from inherited prejudice, we must agree with this indictment. In our time, one needs but to observe the

---

*A. P. Sinnett, *The Mahatma Letters*, transcribed and comp., with an introduction by A. T. Barker (London: Unwin, 1923), Letter X, 57-58.

procedure of the totalitarian and other nations to see how false gods are invoked to arouse people to most inhuman and uncharitable action. These gods are variously called, "the Collectivity," "the Race-nation," "Shinto," "the white man's burden," and other names. In any case, the effect is always the same, to cause people to act and think unrighteously, though believing that they are righteous in doing so. Mankind's most sacred motivation is harnessed by a mundane will to accomplish the most malicious kind of objective. There is no evil greater than this. If ever a nation would make war to enforce its will with clean hands, then it must carefully avoid invoking the notion of Divinity as a means of building a fighting morale.

If divinities of the above type were the only kind of divinities there are, then it would be better that the God notion be completely eradicated from the mind of humanity. Fortunately, the God notion has a much more sincere meaning, even though, in some manifestations, we still must judge it unsound. Here, at least, we move in a field of philosophical dignity.

When sincerely, though unsoundly, believed in, God is the name of the unknown cause of effects that no one has been able to trace to their roots. In this sense, God is only a speculative conception that comprehends all that of which humankind is ignorant, but that seems to be necessary to account for that which is known to occur. Thus the "Independent Thing" of the realist functions as a God of this sort. So also does "Experience," when the term is spelled with a capital *E*. In this sense, God begins where reason and knowledge end.

It is unquestionably true that, so long as we have awakened only some of the functions of consciousness, there are problems that we cannot solve. Experience and reason alone are incapable of resolving the most ultimate questions, which can, nevertheless, arise in the rational consciousness. In the presence of such a situation there are three possible ways to proceed.

1. We may invent a speculative construct that is conceived to be such that it is the resolution of the problem, but yet is of such a nature that it cannot be directly verified. If one places unconditional confidence in such a construct, it is a God notion in an unsound and indefensible sense.
2. It is possible to conceive the resolution of the problem as unknown and eternally unknowable. This is systematic agnosticism, which is a voluntary surrender to ignorance.
3. One may honestly acknowledge that at present the resolution is unknown, and yet maintain the attitude that possibly, by appropriate means, a resolution may be found. This is simply a tentative and honest agnosticism, without implying the ultimate failure of knowledge.

All three attempted resolutions imply ignorance. The first is proud and pretentious in that it places before us a pretension to knowledge that is not genuine. The second is also proud in that the individual implies that her own ignorance must necessarily characterize everyone and not be merely the mark of the limitations of particular functions of consciousness. The third also implies ignorance, but it is frankly acknowledged and humble, thereby supplying a condition most favorable to the awakening of a superior and more comprehensive knowledge.

In the case of a speculative construct that is viewed solely as a pragmatic device for handling some practical problem, there is no objection to be raised. Such a construct only has the value of a temporary scaffolding and is known to be such. A positive evil arises when such a construct is uncritically given a transcendental authority and hence discourages a genuine search for Truth and the acceptance of self-determined moral responsibility. As a general proposition, we may affirm that the gods of theology are of this sort, so are a hindrance, rather than an aid, in human progress toward genuine Enlightenment. It is better for a person not to feel sure, provided one continues the search for certainty, than to build a structure of assurance upon the quicksand of false gods.

Nevertheless, although it is true that most God conceptions will not withstand the light of critical examination, a psychological study of the religious consciousness reveals that the general notion of 'God' points to something genuine. In contrast to the secular kind of consciousness—which most individuals possess most of the time—there is also a sacred kind of consciousness. The latter always contains some sort of supermundane content or reference. This content or reference is of a somewhat that is of very superior value when compared to any of the values of the ordinary secular consciousness. In this sacred consciousness there is that which stands as the Supreme Value, often symbolized as the Jewel beyond all price. It is entirely unnecessary to give this Supreme Value any delimiting definition in order to recognize that it exists, and is of the highest moral importance to the individual who is oriented to it. All of this, so far, is within the limits of fact available for the appropriate kind of psychological investigation, regardless of whether the introceptive function is awakened and active within the investigator or not. This Supreme Value, when Realized, may be, and generally is, given the name for the Divinity that is current in the society of which the individual is a part. When used in this sense, the word *God*, or any other name for the Divinity, not only corresponds to a reality, it points to a Reality that is far more important than anything lying within the limits of secular experience. In this sense, the introceptive

Realization has the value of an indubitable proof of the reality of God, for the individual who has awakened this function.

The God of Gnosis, or of mystical Realization, is not the God of theology or of priestcraft and political rulers. Consequently, great care must be taken not to confuse the two meanings of the word. There are God conceptions that really are no more than opiates for dulling the reason of dominated peoples. However, there are also God conceptions that are filled with the brightest and purest kind of Light. It is always possible to find counterfeits of real values, but it is ever necessary to be on guard against emotional reactions that all too easily lead the disillusioned individual to discard genuine coins once he or she has been deceived by the counterfeits. Here our means of discrimination between the true and the false coins is fairly clear. The true divinities are known to be by direct and individual Realization and do not exact from anyone blind and undiscriminating belief. The false gods rest upon inculcated and constrained belief. Furthermore, the true gods never demand that anyone should commit rational or intellectual suicide by arbitrarily believing any systematic absurdity. On the contrary, the more intelligent the devotion, the more the true Gods are honored.

The Gnostic Divinity may be quite properly known by other names than those most commonly employed. It may be with perfect justice called "Life," "Consciousness," "Truth" or "Substance," though always there is something implied in these names when thus used that reaches beyond any formal definition. The true Divinity can never be completely dissected by conceptual analysis. This is so not merely because of a failure to think clearly, but rather for the reason that more is involved than can be comprehended by conceptual process alone. Analysis is capable of accomplishing a great deal, but it still remains limited because it is a functional modification of consciousness that is, in an important respect, less than the totality of all consciousness. Whenever any individual comprehends anything through analytic power, that which one comprehends stands on a lower level than oneself. It follows that the value of Divinity cannot be given to anything that anyone can analyze, for the whole notion of Divinity implies something more comprehensive and superior than the individual. Do I possess and command Life, Consciousness, Substance and Truth, or do they possess me? If they possess and fundamentally condition me, then they stand in the relation of the Divinity to me. As some individuals possess and command more than others, it follows that the Divinities of some are equaled or even transcended by others. It is quite possible for humankind to transcend former Gods, so we are dealing here with a relative, rather than an absolute, status.

It is an idea of the more evolved religious consciousness, as exemplified in the case of true Buddhism, that humankind can attain a position superior to that of his or her gods. From this superior level he or she can even become a teacher of former gods. Thus we find the gods pictured as attending the discourses of the great Buddha, and even of others who have attained comparable status. Of course, in such a case the person has become equal or even superior to the gods, so they cease to bear the former relationship to him or her. Undeniably, all of this gives to the conception of Divinity a meaning quite different from that common to our Western theology. The gods have a relative, rather than an absolute character. However, their existence is much more than an arbitrary predication of a speculative construct. It is known by direct Realization and so rests upon solid ground.

To call Life, Consciousness, Truth or Substance the "Divinity" implies that in these notions we are dealing with something of much greater significance than mere abstractions or hypotheses. In the true sense, only that may be called "Divine" with which a person may Realize the most intimate relationship, that is, an intensely vital relationship. This is not true of a merely abstract construction. Of course, the notion of Divinity implies that the Divine is also something superior and more comprehensive, so intimacy of relationship is a necessary, but not a sufficient, condition. It may be said that we speak of life in general as a sort of abstraction, but so long as it means only that to us, it is not known as a Divinity. However, anyone who attains a state of conscious unity with universal Life would know God. Such a person would be in the Awakened or Enlightened state behind the scenes of empiric activity. This means *being conscious* in precisely the zone that commonly is quite unconscious, which in turn implies that such an individual can will and direct subtle activities, where formerly he or she was merely acted upon. Simply enormous implications follow from this, for the individual who attains this state can, from a personal standpoint that is quite rational and governed by law, produce effects that seem to be magical or miraculous, from the perspective of others who are more largely conditioned by unconscious powers. Yet, there is nothing more involved than the awakening of a latent human possibility and an activity that, on its proper level, is completely rational and governed by law. A change of perspective is equivalent to a magical transformation of the world. There is nothing here transcending the possibilities of philosophic understanding.

To be directly conscious of Life as such, of Consciousness in its unorganized purity, or of Substance as perdurable Depth is to be conscious of the Divinity, and possibly even as the Divinity. There is no question here of setting up a relationship with an infinitely distant Being that stands apart from the universe, a notion that would be quite absurd. It is all simply a matter of achieving a conscious relationship with one's supporting roots. One could even dispense with the language commonly associated with religion, provided he or she did not depreciate the significance of the roots. Often the awakened person can afford to be privately amused or saddened by some of the notions that many view as sacred. Even so, a compassionate consideration may cause him or her to veil personal feelings, because the feeling for the sacred is very important, even when it is oriented to inadequate and even inferior notions.

It is to be hoped that the foregoing discussion will supply a more intelligible and acceptable meaning to the idea of God Consciousness. Having now elaborated what I mean when I refer to the Divinity, I trust that I shall not be misunderstood in subsequent use of the term.

The chapter on idealism noted that the state of consciousness wherein consciousness is dissociated from the object, and united only with the subject, is only transitory. Almost immediately, consciousness acquires a new kind of content that is wholly of a sacred character and is not the world as formerly known. What is meant by this is very easily misunderstood, since it does not mean or, at least, does not necessarily mean that the photographic image of the sensible world is altered.

I shall attempt to clarify the distinction between the new and the old content. The transformation that I am describing has no effect upon the sensible form of the world as it appears. If an engineer were to pass through the transforming process and yet continue to function as an engineer, his methods of practical operation upon objective nature would remain the same. There would be no reason for dispensing with pragmatic conceptions that had proven to be of practical value. Superior insight might guide him to more effective conceptions and methods, but still there is no reason to expect that these would be of a radically different type as compared to those commonly used by other engineers and scientists. The transformation affects the attitude toward the sensible world, rather than its apparent form. It is the reality value that undergoes a radical alteration. We may illustrate this by a familiar experience of the geometry student. In the case of the familiar Euclidean form of geometry, we conceive of the various configurations as existing in a space that is unaffected by the presence or absence of material bodies. Straight lines will pass through the earth as little altered as when passing through so-called empty space. The surveyor constantly makes use of this principle. Obviously the employment of this conception interferes not at all with the power to perceive material bodies. They are merely irrelevant to the geometrician. They exist for the sensible person, but for the geometrician they are unreal and are in no way a barrier to thought. Here we find that the object as seen is one thing, while the object of thought is quite another. In this case, for the concrete human being, we have a practical separation of the functions of perception and conception; except for periods of special concentration, both functions are active simultaneously, but essentially independently.

In the foregoing case, we have a situation such that a problem of relative reality arises almost inevitably. Two individuals of equal intellectual ability may give to the geometric and sensible worlds diametrically opposite reality values. One may say that the sensible world is the more real, while the other may say that it is the geometric world that has reality. In both cases some form of the problem of appearance and reality arises, and each predicates a reality-maya contrast, though in reverse senses. This difference cannot be resolved, either by logical reasoning or by reference to empiric fact, for both individuals may resolve the specific geometric theorems equally effectively. Further, a discussion based upon a study of the genesis of the original geometric conceptions would not resolve the difference. Even though it is shown that geometric conceptions first arise in connection with an empiric problem, this does not imply that the geometric knowledge comes from the perceptual field. The empiric situation may be interpreted as simply an occasion that aroused into activity a latent geometric understanding. No, neither a reference to fact nor logical reasoning can resolve the difference between the two valuations. The difference is one of fundamental attitude and, hence, essentially religious. One individual is more materialistic in attitude, the other more spiritual, although their intellectual ability may be practically equal. Nonetheless, the significance of the objective world in the two cases is totally different. The problem of adjustment takes quite diverse forms.

In this instance, we have an illustration of the effect of introceptive transformation upon one's world view. The new sacred content of consciousness radically affects the reality valuation without altering the photographic image of the sensible world. The consequences that follow are enormously important, though they are of such a subtle nature that they do not readily lend themselves to description. For instance, one knows the universe to be the best possible world, and everything is as it should be, despite all the seeming disharmony and barbarism. It is Realized that the seeming out-of-joint world is an effect of an incomplete consciousness—the kind of product one receives by the collaboration of perception and conception when the introceptive function is not awakened. The latter is like the reverse side of an embroidered cloth where the effect is chaotic and there are many loose threads. However, on the other side we have a perfectly orderly design. On one side it seems that mere chance accounts for the pattern and that humankind lives in an alien world that has no inner sympathy with our purposes and yearnings, while the other side reveals a perfect

order in complete sympathetic rapport with the deepest human yearnings and aspirations. In the sacred world, one feels perfectly at home
and nothing is strange. There is no problem of melioration. There is no
problem of making a better world, since that which is already is the
best that possibly could be.

The practical moral problem is completely transformed. It is no
longer oriented to meliorating conditions or improving the world, *but to
the awakening of a sleeping human consciousness.* The transformed individual may devote herself to this moral problem in the social body with
all the energy of which she is capable. In this activity she may will to
face the severest kind of hardship. Her heart may be touched most profoundly with sympathy for human suffering. Despite this, her treatment is radically different from that of the meliorator. She knows that
mere melioration, which is not united with an effort to awaken the
introceptive function, is merely a movement down a blind alley. Indeed,
there are even circumstances such that improving external conditions
will have a delaying effect upon the awakening process. In this kind of
situation she would view the melioration as unwise and tending to
delay the real resolution of the problem of suffering. To the all-too-
human consciousness, she may even appear to be cold, though her heart
may be bleeding at the sight of what she knows to be needless suffering.
To be sure, the moral problem tends to become more vital than ever
before, but the way of resolution is totally transformed.

The sacred universe is identical with Divinity and is exclusively
Divine. There simply is nothing else. For one who has been captured by
the view that the Divinity is simply a grand sort of entity designed on
the lines of the human, almost inevitably the meaning of the Divine
universe will be misunderstood. There is very considerable testimony
that some individuals have seen appearances of vast and grand
humanlike forms, but such are much less than what I mean by the
Divinity. At present I am not discussing the meaning of such appearances, even though there is evidence, at least in some cases, that they
do have enormous significance. Rather, I am referring to a substrate
underlying all forms whatsoever. Indeed, subtle appearances of the
above type may enrobe an aspect of Divinity, but no less is such the
case regarding every visible aspect of the universe. Divinity is equally
embodied in a mountain chain or in an ocean. All of these appearances
are simply symbols of a Reality that, in its own true nature, is unseen,
although it may be introceptively Realized and thus known in the
Gnostic sense.

Clearly, what I mean by Divinity is a somewhat that is quite impersonal. Yet, this somewhat can be directly Realized by the function of
introception. When so Realized, it is found to be quite the most inti-

mate of all things. It is the fulfillment of all the deep yearnings of the human heart, and it illumines the mind with a Light that is far more brilliant than any light of the intellect, operating either in its purity or in relation to experience. This combination of impersonality and intimacy poses a real difficulty to unawakened consciousness, for we commonly associate the intimate with the personal. Yet, that which is personal is segregated into a rather differentiated cell, so that between personalities there are always separating boundaries. Mostly what we find in other personalities is, at best, but a hidden aspect of ourselves. Between us and the other there is a distance that is never crossed until mutual identity is achieved by the Realization of common roots. It is not difficult to see that we are much more intimately related to space than to any personality whatsoever, for space interpenetrates our being at every point. So it is when one comes into conscious Realization of the underlying Divinity. It interpenetrates our being with the same completeness that space does our physical manifestation. However, whereas objective space seems to us something quite cold, the hidden Divinity is warm.

To attain a direct Realization of Substance, Life, Consciousness or Truth involves vastly more than solving a scientific problem. When one has solved a scientific problem, one has mastered something of instrumental value and achieved a means for facilitating some human purpose. No doubt this is much less than the ultimate fulfillment of purpose and yearning. The growth of scientific knowledge is merely progress in a series where each last term leads on to a new problem, with apparently no end. However, introceptive Realization provides a terminal value. At one step the individual has reached the culmination of the infinite series of relative consciousness. This gives to the Realized value a unique significance. It is more than an instrumental knowledge and more than the temporary satisfying of one desire in an endless series of desires. Desire as a genus is fulfilled; the Knowledge Realized is culminating. For this reason, we are dealing with an order quite other than that of secular consciousness. Because I can find no other language that will suggest its meaning, I must call it the "Sacred Order" and speak of the content of this consciousness as Divine. Yet, the common attitude toward religious values suggests features that I do not at all intend. Thus we often associate religion with an attitude wherein discriminating thought is allowed to lapse. It is the zone wherein rational people often allow themselves to take an irrational holiday and are permitted a kind of intellectual irresponsibility. This is not at all true of the Gnostic Realization, which requires the most serious application of the will and the exercise of the keenest discrimination. What I mean is suggested by a combination of the religious motif with scientific alertness and discrimination. Thus it is, in a sense, neither religion nor science as ordinarily understood, and yet it combines features belonging to each.

For the individual who is both introceptively and perceptually awake, the universe is cognized in two ways that may be to some degree completely blended. As perceived, the universe is known to be a drama that is not itself its own meaning, but as introceived, it is known to be an effect of realities hidden to perception when functioning alone or in combination with thought. One sees the drama and yet is united with the consciousness of the director of the drama. A person has an introceptive understanding of underlying purpose even though his power of conceptual interpretation may be highly defective. He may even Know, and know that he Knows, without being able to conceive of what he inwardly Knows—for conception in these matters requires all the skill of a superior intellect, and it appears that skill of this sort is by no means a condition of introceptive awakening. Hence we have many inadequate interpretative statements from those who have attained some degree of this awakening. Perhaps, more often than not, the mystic does not possess the best conceptual understanding of his insight. I believe that this is one of the main reasons why genuine mystical consciousness is so generally depreciated by scientific and philosophical minds. Yet, rational people should make allowances for this and not condemn a content because of inadequate presentation.

The substantial substrate behind the perceptually apparent world is the soul of the Universe. Through the introceptive union with this Soul it is possible to establish an inner communion with all things. Through participation in that Soul, humankind partakes of the soul of all creatures and things. Humankind also finds a phase of consciousness underlying all objects, and in so doing finds that the universe is, in reality, neither dead nor blind. As a result, for one who has attained introceptive Realization, a mystical communion is, or may be, established with all objects. They are no longer merely lifeless values that may be substituted for x in general propositions. Rather, they are parts of a universal brotherhood that is not at all exclusively confined to human beings.

PART III:
THE PSYCHOLOGICAL
CRITIQUE OF MYSTICISM

11

Judgments of Meaning and Existence

Whenever we consider any conception, our way of viewing it may be oriented to one or the other of two attitudes, or to a combination of these. We may think of the conception as an existence in time, and thus having a history, possessing an externally observable constitution and standing in discernible relationships with other conceptions. All this may be done without an inner understanding of the significance of the conception. However, we may also think of the conception regarding its meaning or value. From this standpoint we may view it quite apart from any relation to its history and various external relationships. Thus, as an example of the former approach, if the object of interest were some important theorem in mathematics, we might be especially interested in its historical development, the psychological processes that led to its discovery, and the part that it played in its impact upon the social body. Conceivably, the historian or the psychologist might conduct a reasonably comprehensive and competent investigation of these circumstances without being able to understand the theorem itself. The theorem would be simply a somewhat having a particular history and influence upon life in general and possessing more or less determinant psychological antecedents. In contrast to all this and even in complete ignorance of these facts, the student of the theorem might be interested exclusively in its inner content, its logical development and its relationship to other parts of mathematical theory. For this purpose, it would be a matter of no moment whether the theorem had a human history or had been precipitated "out of the blue," as it were, and was somehow just *there* before consciousness. Indeed, most of the mathematician's interest in pure mathematics is of this latter sort.*

---

*An instance is afforded in Einstein's theory of relativity. An aspect of the theory leads to the formula $E = mc^2$ where E represents energy, m is mass and c is the velocity of light in centimeters per second. This formula led to the development of the atomic and the hydrogen bombs. The impact of these upon history and the mass psychology of the world is an all too painful fact. The historian and psychologist are, no doubt, abundantly aware of all this. Yet, this by no

These two ways of thinking of a conception are recognized in logic and supply judgments of different orders. The first kind of judgment may be called a "judgment of existence," and the second, a "judgment of significance or value." The former is a determination *that* a somewhat is, and traces its observable history and relations, while the latter is a determination of *what* a somewhat is, thus giving its inner meaning. We might say that the first deals with considerations of *fact*, while the second concerns *Truth* value. However, I acknowledge that I am forming an evaluative judgment as to the relations of these two types of judgment. Other philosophic orientations exist that would not support this evaluation. Nonetheless, as we all must assume, consciously or unconsciously, some philosophic orientation in the approach to the subject matter under consideration, I hold that it is better to be frank about the matter at the beginning, rather than to hide oneself under the appearance of a false omniscience. As James clearly states in the first chapter of *The Varieties of Religious Experience,** one type of judgment does not lead immediately to the other, at least insofar as our relative experience goes. Any judgment as to how one type of judgment is related to the other is itself a value judgment involving subjective factors, not an objective determination of fact.

It appears that the relationship between judgments of existence and judgments of significance is not a uniform one for all possible kinds of objects that may come under consideration. For instance, if the object is of the sort that Spengler has called "physiognomic" or "political," it is likely that the existential judgment is, in high degree, determinant regarding the judgment of significance. In this domain, a difference in history clearly effects a difference in meaning. However, in the domain of the "systematic," in Spengler's sense, the existential and meaningful judgments may be nearly, and possibly wholly, independent. Certainly the independence is very clear in the case of the mathematical theorem, for the truth value of the theorem has nothing whatsoever to do with the background of its discovery. Whether the psychophysical condition of its discoverer is judged to be pathological or normal has not the slightest bearing concerning the soundness or value of the theorem.

Great discoveries and creative developments, which so largely differentiate the life of humankind from that of the animals, are usually the

---

means implies that they have a competent understanding of the inner content of the special and general theories of relativity, of complex conceptions of simultaneity concerning bodies having different velocities relative to each other, of the increase of mass toward infinity as velocity approaches the speed of light, or of the properties of a non-Euclidean geometry.

*James, *The Varieties of Religious Experience*, 1-25.

work of genius. Yet, the study of geniuses has demonstrated that, in the sense of psychophysical existence, genius as a whole stands closer to the pathological types who occupy asylums than it does to the ordinary person. Thus, from the standpoint of the valuation that views organic adjustment to environment and fitness to survive, in the biologic sense, as the adequate measures of the worth of a person, the genius would be judged in the same way as the ordinary psychotic. In this sense, genius is a weakness and liability that might better be exposed to death in childhood, in a manner akin to the custom of the Spartans. However, from the standpoint of the valuation of one who sees the contribution of genius as affording the highest of all values for individual and social consciousness, it might well appear that the worth of the psychophysical normalcy of the Philistine is very much in doubt.

The issue we face here is whether we shall take our stand with or near those who give exclusive approval to survival and adjustment value of the psychophysical organism, or stand with those who give exclusive or primary value to the meaningful offering for consciousness. Not all agree, or can be brought to agree, as to which point of view to adopt. Some, in essential agreement with the former German national socialists, will take the position that fitness for psychophysical survival is all-important, while the contribution of genius is to be tolerated only insofar as it contributes to biological survival. Others, in essential agreement with the philosophical mystic and the pure mathematician, will affirm that enrichment of consciousness is all-important, and biophysical existence is of worth only in an instrumental sense. Unequivocally, I take my stand with the latter group and categorically affirm its superiority, since there is no logical way to prove that superiority to everyone's satisfaction. Still, I would not deny to those with the biophysical orientation the right to go to perdition by their preferred route.

The psychobiological study of genius has not generally led to a depreciation of the contribution of genius as a result of the general finding of an abnormal psychophysiological makeup in its constitution. The value of genius to the sciences and arts is a too-well-attested fact to permit serious consideration of such a judgment. Without doubt the psychological and biological sciences owe their existence far too much to the achievements of genius for such a judgment to be a safe weapon. Indeed, it would prove to be a boomerang, because if the soundness of the contribution of genius is conditional upon the soundness of the psychobiological constitution of the genius, then many of the conceptions fundamental to biology and psychology would also be vulnerable before such a criticism. Hence, the psychobiological judgment would be self-destroying. So, on the whole, this kind of study has not led to a confusion of existential and meaningful judgments. Unfortunately, in one particular field this discrimination has not been consistently maintained, namely, the study of religious genius. Here, in instance after instance, the psychophysical facts concerning their lives have been employed to evaluate the conscious value they have produced, generally in the direction of its depreciation.

Both consistency and integrity are violated in arbitrarily treating religious and nonreligious genius by divergent canons of interpretation. This arbitrary discrimination in treatment is not a manifestation of an impersonal scientific spirit. Rather, it reflects the personal prejudice of the investigators and is less than ethical, to say the least. It is simply a manifestation of wishful thinking in an antireligious direction.

Psychobiological investigation has been extended beyond the special study of genius. It is assumed, with considerable justification, that all states of consciousness, with whatever content and of whatever value, are associated with psychophysical states or modification of function. Hence, it appears, a correlation may be established between conscious attitudes and contents, on the one hand, and the psychophysical states and modification of function, on the other. There is substantial evidence to support this view as a general principle, and there is no logical reason to suppose that it is not universally true about all embodied consciousness. However, establishing the factuality of such a correlation is in no way equivalent to determining its nature. Thus, the relationship might be one of parallelism or of causal connection. If the relationship is causal, there are then three possibilities of interpretation. The causal priority may be biological, psychical, or an interacting combination of these two. Further, the question arises whether the causal connection is essential and constitutive, or is like a catalytic agent. It is no easy matter to answer these questions satisfactorily so that objective determinations become decisive. For the most part, it appears that personal predilection or, possibly, insight determines the manner in which one views the correlation.

Insofar as the psychobiological approach has been employed in the study of mystical states of consciousness, whether or not the subjects of study were geniuses, there has been a strong tendency to interpret mystical content from the perspective of observed psychical and physiological states and modifications. There is a quite considerable tendency to view the psychical and physiological as causally determinant, and the doctrine of organic evolution is widely assumed as a valid interpretative principle. As shown by the treatment of naturalism in the present work, there is much in this that is simply assumption; therefore, it is much less than proven fact. One is not less scientific for not accepting these assumptions, provided one can work from another basis with logical consistency and does not affirm a position incompatible with determinant fact.

In the present psychological critique of mystical states of consciousness, I shall assume as a working principle the primacy of conscious content to psychobiological state and function. This is equivalent to affirming that significance is primary and determinant, while fact, in the sense of objective determination, is derivative and secondary. Applying this principle to the case of mathematical production, we would begin with the theorem and its directly known value. From that perspective, we would interpret the psychical and biological facts that are observed in the study of the productive mathematician. This I conceive to be a much more significant approach than the reverse, for we are much more certain about the theorem than we are the psychical and biological facts. If there is room to doubt mathematical assurance, there is certainly much vaster reason to doubt the empiric determination of fact. Further, I would assume as a starting point the mathematical understanding of the best-developed mathematical genius and would determine such genius by the consensus of mathematicians, not that of psychologists and biologists.

I believe the foregoing principle of selection is generally recognized in the professional world as the only valid one for the valuation of special talent. I simply propose to apply this principle consistently in the field of religious mysticism.

This is genuinely an approach to the subject from the perspective of the greatest and most perfect manifestations of mystical consciousness. Therefore, it is a radical divergence from the approach of both James Leuba and William James, who explicitly begin with inferior manifestations, though arriving at divergent conclusions. It also varies from Jung's approach, but not so radically. There will be many points of agreement with the conclusions both of James and of Jung, though my conclusions and treatment will diverge fundamentally from that of Leuba.

12

Three Mystical Paradigms

It is not difficult to select three mystical geniuses to which general and competent consensus would grant the status of primacy—Christ, Buddha and Shankara.* Christendom would obviously accord such a status to Christ, and Christian mysticism agrees with this judgment. Similar status is granted to the Buddha in the vast Buddhist community, as well as by a number of Western scholars and aspirants. Shankara is afforded a comparable position within the Brahmanical tradition, especially by those who follow the Advaita Vedanta.† I am aware of no evidence that would support any claim of superior mystical profundity on the part of any generally known Sage from beyond the sphere of Indo-European culture. In the Far East, I know only Lao-tzu to be of comparable stature. Regrettably, we do not know him well enough, nor is his meaning clear enough to our Occidental minds, for him to serve our present purposes satisfactorily.

The question whether these three great religious geniuses and leaders are genuine instances of mystical Realization is easy to answer. Nonetheless, for the purpose of illustration, I shall establish the ground for classifying them as mystically awakened Beings.

MYSTICISM

As a preliminary step, it will be necessary to define mystical consciousness. The words *mystic* and *mysticism* have both a wider and a

---

*[Jesus was called "The Christ," meaning "anointed," by his followers to reflect their belief that he was the Messiah of Jewish prophecy. Gautama Siddhartha was called "The Buddha," which means the "Enlightened One." Over the centuries, both titles came to be used as proper names. Shankara was given the honorary title, "Sri Shankaracarya," where the suffix means "spiritual teacher."]

†[Vedanta (literally, "the end of the Vedas") comprises one of the half dozen or so schools of Indian thought. The approach of Advaita (of which Shankara is the greatest exponent) advances a nondualistic interpretation.]

narrower definition. There is, in addition, a loose usage in which 'mystical' is understood as meaning a reproach thrown "at any opinion that we regard as vague and vast and sentimental, and without a base in either facts or logic."* However, this usage is of no help to us. In addition, it is quite incompetent. The term as I employ it has a much more definite reference. Let us consider several definitions derived from standard sources.

The Century Dictionary gives the following: The word *mystic* means "hidden from or obscure to human knowledge or comprehension; pertaining to what is obscure or incomprehensible; mysterious; dark; obscure; specifically, expressing a sense comprehensible only to a higher grade of intelligence or to those specifically initiated."† The word *mysticism* means

1. Any mode of thought, or phase of intellectual or religious life, in which reliance is placed upon a spiritual illumination believed to transcend the ordinary powers of the understanding, and
2. Specifically, a form of religious belief which is founded upon spiritual experience, not discriminated or tested and systematized in thought.‡

The Dictionary of Philosophy and Psychology gives as the preferred meaning: "Those forms of speculative and religious thought which profess to attain an immediate apprehension of the divine essence or the ultimate ground of existence."§ This source notes, but does not recommend, a usage that defines the term *mysticism* as "any philosophy which does not limit itself to the world of 'the visible' and 'our logical mensurative faculty.'"‖ It further notes that several mystics or mystically oriented thinkers insist upon a special organ, faculty or mode of apprehension, other than the senses and discursive intellect, as the means of mystical apprehension or Realization. Thus we have the "scintilla" or "spark" of Bonaventura, the "*Funklein*" or "spark" of Eckhart, the "intellectual intuition" of Schelling and the similar requirement of Schopenhauer.

Leuba, in his *Psychology of Religious Mysticism*, defines the term *mysticism*, for his purposes, as "any experience taken by the experiencer to be a contact (not through the senses, but "immediate," "intuitive") or union of the self with a larger-than-self, be it called World-Spirit, God, the Absolute, or otherwise."

---

*James, *The Varieties of Religious Experience*, 380.
†*The Century Dictionary*, s.v. "mystic."
‡Ibid., s.v. "mysticism."
§Baldwin, *Dictionary*, s.v. "mysticism."
‖Ibid.

James, in *The Varieties of Religious Experience,** defines mystical experience by four marks, two of which are essential and sufficient, while the remaining two are generally present. The two essential and sufficient marks are

1. "ineffability" as marking the quality of the state of consciousness immediately experienced by the mystic, and
2. "noetic quality" of a sort "unplumbed by the discursive intellect."

The secondary marks, not necessary but usually present are

1. transiency of the state of mystical experience and
2. passivity of the individually directed will or activity in the presence of an overwhelming superior power.

In India the word *Yoga* carries the meaning comparable to that of "mystical Realization." Paul Deussen, in *The System of the Vedanta,* defines 'Yoga' as "preparation (for the union with the World-Spirit),"† but he also uses the term to designate the Realized state of union itself. Indian culture also affirms the actuality of a mystical organ, faculty or mode of apprehension. Thus *Samadhi* (concentration) and *Dhyana* both refer to meditation as a process, other than sensuous perception or intellective activity, that leads to Realization of the "Supreme Soul" or, according to the Buddhists, "the Prajna-Paramita," or Transcendental Wisdom. Specifically, the term *Samadhindriya* means the "organ of ecstatic meditation."

These definitions are all substantially correct regarding either some phase of the state or the thought oriented to such a state. Anyone who is familiar with the mystical state of consciousness as a type, either through objective study or especially through direct acquaintance with the state itself, will recognize this. However, the definitions are manifestly not identical. Careful study reveals definition from three points of view—religious, epistemological and psychological.

1. From the religious (also possibly the metaphysical) perspective, mystical Realization or Yoga, conceived as "union," involves the very essence of the religious spirit. This may be interpreted as "union"

---

*James, *The Varieties of Religious Experience* (New York: New American Library, 1902), 292-95.

†Paul Deussen, *The System of the Vedanta,* trans. Charles Johnson (Chicago: Open Court, 1912), 513n. [Deussen uses "All-Spirit" as equivalent to "World-Spirit" (18).]

with the "World-Spirit," the "Void," the "Absolute," the "Divinity," the "Supreme Self," or any supernal Largeness that is to the personal self as the Infinite is to the finite. This is definition by a conceptual reflection of the immediate value that the state has for the mystic personally.

2. For epistemology, the definition is by means of the instrumentality whereby the mystical consciousness is attained, not in the sense of a practice, but in that of an organ, faculty or mode of apprehension other than those of the senses and of intellectual functioning. Definition from this angle emphasizes the noetic quale of the mystical state. The consciousness is conceived as possessing an immediate, but nonsensuous, noetic value, which may serve as the fountainhead of philosophical systems. This definition does not adequately comprehend mystical states that are mainly or wholly states of feeling.

3. The psychological approach considers the state primarily as an "experience" and hence something that may occur in the lives of empiric beings as they live in time. This is not definition of the state from the perspective of the Realized content nor from that of an awakened Way of consciousness. It is rather mysticism as viewed from the outside, that is, as it can be observed by a consciousness that has no immediate acquaintance with the state. This is the objective view, but it is not restricted to the extreme objectivity of the behaviorist. It includes introspective observation, but not the introceptive insight that is essential for the study of what we may call the "metapsychology" of the process. For the most part, the definitions of Leuba and James fall into this category.

The ordinary psychological approach—excluding metapsychology—is largely dependent upon the autobiographical accounts of mystics who have included introspective material. Unfortunately, the Orientals have supplied us with almost none of this type of material. We find elaborate rules governing practice, metapsychological descriptions of the processes and interpretations in the abstract of the resultant, but almost no report in objective terms of what happened in the experience of an individual. Material of this sort provided by Western mystics is also restricted. Moreover, in the few cases where it is fairly ample, we do not find very mature development of consciousness.

The immediate purpose in developing an adequate definition of mystical states of consciousness is that of justifying the selection of Christ, Buddha and Shankara as the outstanding exemplars of such states. Sadly, inasmuch as we do not seem to have any introspective material from any of them, satisfactory identification of these figures as mystics from the standpoint of Western psychology is not easy. This is

224 The Psychological Critique of Mysticism

especially true regarding the test of the ecstatic trance, to which Leuba seems to attach chief importance.

I have found no clear evidence that either Christ or Buddha entered into the full trance state. The references in the Gospels to Christ's going into the wilderness to pray for protracted periods almost certainly imply a practice of meditation, rather than prayer in the common sense. Even so, meditation can lead to Samadhi without blackout trance. The Buddhist Sutras distinctly speak of the Master as being at times in states of deep Samadhi, particularly at the time of his initial Transformation. However, Samadhi does not necessarily imply blackout trance. Furthermore, judging by the record as given in the Sutras, Buddha regards trance as unnecessary, so he does not recommend it, though he does not repudiate it. Some incidents in the biographical account of Shankara's life do imply full trance, but in these cases it appears to have been a deliberate transference of consciousness for a specific purpose, rather than for the attainment of spiritual insight. In any case, Shankara's teachings elaborate a technique of exceptionally keen intellectual discrimination that would be strictly incompatible with the trance state.

Here is a problem of considerable import. Are trance states, of greater or lesser degree, essential to the Yogic and mystical Awakenings, even of the highest order? Leuba seems to regard this test as decisive as he develops his position, even though this criterion plays no part in his definition. He begins with cases of drug intoxication, then goes on to color the whole subject with that perspective. This constitutes a gross misrepresentation. I appreciate the methodological convenience of the test, since a trance state can be objectively determined, but such procedure is equivalent to sacrificing substance to method. It is not exactly a case of throwing out the baby with the bath; rather, it is akin to throwing out the baby and keeping the bath. I am well aware that some Yogic techniques do develop trance of extreme degree, but these techniques fall under the general approach of Kundalini Yoga.* I have found no evidence that practices of the types known as "Jnana Yoga"† and "Dhyana Yoga"‡ necessarily imply trance, and it is just this latter form of Yoga that, it is said, can reach to the highest Samadhi. Finally, my personal experience clearly confirms the view that blackout trance is unnecessary, at least as far as my consciousness reached.

---

*[Focus on the arousal and direction of energies through seven centers within the "subtle body."]

†[The way of knowledge, in the sense of spiritual knowledge, as the path to Liberation.]

‡[The path of meditation emphasizing concentration, leading through eight stages of "absorption."]

How does the state that I Realized correspond to the above definitions? Let us first relate it to James's four marks:

1. The immediate content of the state was *ineffable*.
2. It had a most positive *noetic* value.
3. The periods of penetration were temporary. (Notably, I found it necessary to restrict the length of each episode because the state does impose subtle strain upon the nervous organism.)
4. There is a flow of consciousness that is autonomous, such that even when in the personal sense I initiated a thought, it developed of itself without intellectual labor.

Judging by Leuba's test, the consciousness clearly involved union of self-identity with an Other that was larger than the personal self, though it was initially a Transcendent Self, then later transcended all selfhood and all being.

By the more philosophical standard of definition, I believe that the expression in my previous work, *The Philosophy of Consciousness without an Object*, as well as earlier parts of this work, unquestionably places the speculative treatment within the class of mystical conception. Further, I know that the most profound state, if formulated strictly, rather than symbolically, can only be represented by absolute negation of every possible conception. I confess, if I had in former years come across such a definition or description of a state, it would have seemed to me to be simply unconsciousness, for that would have been the only thing I could have imagined satisfying the description. Nevertheless, I know that it is very highly conscious, and thus the difficulty lies in the limitations of conceptual imagination.

In any case, the state goes far beyond that in which one might imagine subtle appearances of beings to be substantial realities. Yet, through all this, objective awareness of the sensible environment remained unbroken, and relative thinking continued, either in a subdued form, or even as a rather intensive activity. I know the state is possible in the presence of other persons, even on the lecture platform, and can be analyzed and discoursed upon to those who are present—without breaking the state, if care is taken. The state involves a dissociation in consciousness such that two, and even three, parts are recognizable. One must employ discrimination to keep these phases isolated. This, I think, accomplishes the essential office of trance. In addition, consciously self-directed bodily motion is possible, but generally the *dynamis** is definitely reduced in the motor sensory and intellectual

---

*[Unrealized potentiality.]

fields. Still, when compared to more familiar states, I do not find that the energy reduction in the sensory field is greater than that involved in any intense intellectual abstraction, as is required in mathematical thinking, for instance. It is not a state favorable for close objective observation, for this requires concentration in the sensory field. Yet, perhaps surprisingly, the objective sensible images, as seen, do not appear any less distinct than in the normal state. However, they are quite empty, in the sense of having no relevance whatsoever. Objects of sense perception are seen clearly, as a definitely defined mirage is seen clearly, but they have as little reality as a mirage that is known to be a mirage. Thus, there is a subtle sense in which the objective world is destroyed, but not as the realm of perceptible sensible fact.

Considering the foregoing, I am positively forced to conclude that Leuba's trance test is unnecessary. Later I shall analyze the question of its sufficiency, but anticipate my conclusion: I believe that I can show that it is not sufficient, since trance consciousness may include many states that are not truly to be classed as mystical, except in a loose sense.

Without more ado, I shall abandon the tests of Western objective psychology for justifying the inclusion of Christ, Buddha and Shankara among the mystics. I shall judge their mystical state by the evidence of their lives and teachings.

THE CHRIST

In considering the life of the Christ as represented in the available records, I shall disregard entirely the miraculous powers he is said to have possessed and manifested, for I do not intend to deal with the sensible theurgic side of mysticism. We do not yet have any way of dealing with the problem of theurgy that is scientifically adequate. For the most part, we can only accept or reject theurgic claims or reports blindly, which is not at all satisfactory. Further, I am convinced that the mystical state can be vindicated entirely apart from any consideration of sensible powers. Finally, I do not consider myself competent on this question, at least insofar as theurgy is concerned with phenomenal effects. In any case, I do not consider that the record of sensible miracles either adds to, or detracts from, the stature of the Christ.

However, the nonsensible theurgic powers are quite a different matter. They are significant. Magical effects that produce moral and spiritual revolutions in the entourage are of the highest importance. This is one of the major mystical signs, and in the case of the Christ, these effects are particularly outstanding. There is no question but that innumerable human beings in the past two thousand years have become changed as to the center of their motivation and valuation as a result of the influence of the Christ. Typically, this has been brought about in a way that is much more magical than intellectual. On the whole, the change has been in a direction of greater selflessness of attitude, together with a shift from a worldly to an otherworldly orientation. As this is definitely in the direction of the norm for the inner state of mystical Realization, we have indirect evidence of the mystical character of Christ Consciousness. This is simply a massive instance of the "leavening" or "inducing" power of the mystical consciousness. It is highly contagious.

Enhancement of moral energy in the character of the followers is further evidence of prime importance. The strength of character with which the Christians faced centuries of persecution is a great miracle in itself—one that is a good deal more significant than the feeding of the five thousand. As contrasted with what we might call the "counterfeit" or "mystoid" states, such as those induced by some drugs, true mystical consciousness leads to increased power of self-determined will—a will that is all the stronger because it does not have an egoistic centering.

One who reads the record of the life and teachings of the Christ objectively, and then goes on to integrate the whole about a single idea that shall reflect the primary significance of that whole, finds that it consists almost entirely of an ethical teaching and a personal exemplification of that teaching. One finds neither philosophical interpretation nor psychological analysis, though there is an implied philosophy and psychology. Christ did not teach the doctrine of the absolute primacy of ethics as such, but rather a specific kind of conduct and moral orientation, which he exemplified in his life in extraordinary degree. It is the *kind* of morality inculcated and exemplified that is significant for our purposes. People have promulgated various types of moral orientation, and there have been innumerable individuals and groups who quite heroically have organized their lives around one or another of these systems. The exemplars of Christian and Buddhist morality have no monopoly on moral heroism. The history of the world records numerous examples of professional soldiers who have thoroughly believed in the militarist's moral code and have made their lives conform to it as thoroughly as has any Christian or Buddhist saint to his moral orientation. The thoroughgoing militarist is not without a code, but this code is diametrically opposed to that of the Christs and the Buddhas. Certainly, morale may mean as much to the militarist as it does to the saint, but it is a radically opposed kind of morale, implying a quite different philosophy. Then, what is significant for us is the kind of ethics taught and practiced by the Christ, rather than that ethics, as such, be given prime importance.

The Christic* ethic centers around four interconnected principles or foci that are of the highest significance. Let us briefly consider them. First, the Christic morale focuses on the primary consideration for otherness, and therefore is radically antiegoistic. In this respect, it is in complete accord with Buddhist morality, which is explicitly and emphatically antiegoistic. Self-depreciation is implied in the concern for the good of others that shall at least equal concern for one's own. This exaltation of otherness has two phases, (1) the primary self-giving to the God or Transcendental Principle, and (2) the valuation and regard for one's neighbor that shall be at least equal to the valuation and regard for oneself.

Second, the Christic morality implies a denial of the will to live, or of the desire for sentient existence. There must be no thought for the morrow; no provision for one's sustenance or self-protection; and no thought or action motivated by prudential considerations. This is mystically equivalent to a will to die, and, again, is identical with the Buddhist motivation. Life is to be lived so long as the automatic *dynamis* supports it and external circumstances provide for it, but there must be no egoistic clinging to life or striving to maintain it. There is no teaching that life should be hated and, hence, destroyed. On the contrary, all manifestations of it outside oneself are to be carefully cherished. The total attitude is one of compassionate indifference. That which comes is to be accepted, but with loving compassion, not cold stoicism.

One who succeeds in living this kind of life reasonably well will find that it is full of rich compensations. The adherent will become seemingly defenseless and harmless, but really will be more secure than ever before. He or she will feel more secure with doors unlocked than locked; without weapons than when armed; when unconcerned about money than when concentrating upon accumulating it—and feel more certainly sustained. The adherent accepts whatever comes, and will be surprised to find that, while some painful experiences do occur, he or she will feel relieved of a great burden, and, on the whole, live more happily and more comfortably than ever before. He or she will also become a particularly potent force within his or her milieu. Such a person will wield a deeper influence upon those close to him or her than do any individuals having great worldly power. We have in all this the very essence of the mystic morality.

In addition, there is another effect that is of the greatest social importance, particularly in a world filled with strife. The exemplar of

---

*[Wolff coins this term to emphasize that this was the ethic that Jesus personally practiced and preached, which is not necessarily identical to that of the Christian religion as such.]

this morality will find that fear dies within him or her, which destroys the root cause of cruelty. The primary cause of the cruelty of our present dark age is really fear. The hurting of the feared object has the psychological significance of wielding power over that which is feared. However, as the real cause of fear does not lie in any object, but in the inner psyche, the wielding of power over the object never brings the security sought. There are always new objects upon which to project the fear, and thus always something to be fought and to be treated cruelly. Proceeding in this direction, there is no peace anywhere, but only periods in which it is no longer possible to fight—for a season. Yet, one who has renounced the clinging to life has destroyed fear at its source, so that nothing external is any longer capable of arousing it.

The third principle of Christic morality is orientation to otherworldliness. Christ often said, "My Kingdom is not of this world." The moral practice that is equivalent to a denial of the will to live in the objective world implies, in positive terms, a will to live another life in another world. Properly understood, Christ's attitude toward mundane reality is just as pessimistic as was that of Buddha, though the latter was more explicit. Fundamentally, Christ taught an ascetic attitude toward objective life, but not active self-flagellation. The true discipline is moral development, not bodily torture. Detachment toward the objective is the key, and detachment is the essence of asceticism. True asceticism is much less painful than joyous. Bodily self-torture grew out of literal materialistic interpretation.*

Fourth, the doctrine of otherworldliness implies the possibility and need for the "second birth." Jesus said, "Except a man be born again, he cannot see the kingdom of God."† As the doctrine of the second birth is of paramount importance as revealing the mystical character of the Christ's teaching, I shall present the complete relevant passage. When the above words aroused in Nicodemus's mind only a literal meaning, the Master said,

> Verily, verily, I say unto thee, Except a man be born of water and *of* the Spirit, he cannot enter into the kingdom of God. That which is born of the flesh is flesh; and that which is born of the Spirit is spirit. Marvel not that I said unto thee, Ye must be born again. The wind bloweth where it listeth, and thou

---

*[See Manichaeism, the influence of Zoroastrianism on early Christianity, which holds that salvation lies in extricating spirit from matter, implying the need to liberate the soul from its evil bodily prison.]
†John 3:3.

hearest the sound thereof, but canst not tell whence it cometh, and whither it goeth: so is every one that is born of the Spirit.*

The Christic morality is negative concerning life as will to live, but this is so that the *dynamis* may be given another polarization or direction. The positive meaning of the morality is found in its effect of directing the vital *dynamis* toward a new birth. The true meaning of the totality of Christ's teaching lies in the idea of the second birth. Melioration in the objective life is merely incidental. Indeed, some of the words of the Master are more than a little severe when they express his attitude toward the purely objective field, as when he said, "Let the dead bury the dead"; and again, "If any man come to me, and hate not his father, and mother, and wife, and children, and brethren, and sisters, yea, and *his own life* also, he cannot be my disciple [italics mine]."† Christ's moral teaching is not pragmatic, but uncompromisingly otherworldly.

In this there is revealed in clearest possible terms the mystical motif, for genuine mysticism is always uncompromising about fundamentals. It does not work out diplomatic deals. It cuts sharply like pure logic. One must choose mammon or God; he cannot cling to both at the same time. One must be either for or against; there is no point between that is neutral. The compromisers are the lukewarm, and Christ clearly preferred the cold ones to such.

In Christ's discourse with Nicodemus, there are two statements of peculiar significance:

1. In order to enter the kingdom of God, a person must be born of the water and of the Spirit.
2. One who is born of the Spirit is likened unto a wind that "bloweth where it listeth," and though its sound may be heard, the hearer cannot tell either its source or its destination.

The latter statement unmistakably identifies the spontaneous character of the "new birth." One who is born anew is possessed by an autonomous Power beyond his or her personal self that cannot be commanded by anyone. Those familiar with the mystical transformation will readily recognize this truth.

The being born of water and of the Spirit is a highly significant notion, which is clarified by psychological analysis. It is a fact, well known in analytic psychology, that water is one of the most important symbols of the Unconscious. In the terms of analytic psychology, the

*John 3:5-8.
†Luke 14:26.

'new birth' is viewed as the establishment of a new Self center, located in the Unconscious, that is quite other than the personal ego that rules the conscious attitude of the unregenerate person. However, I do not find that our present analytic psychology has discovered the meaning of Spirit in the pregnant sense. In *The Integration of Personality,** Jung briefly discusses the idea of a Super Consciousness, differentiated from the Unconscious, but although he does not exclude the possibility of such a Consciousness, he views its actuality as not yet empirically determined. If we turn to the psychology of the Indian Tantra, we have more light thrown upon the subject. In this system, it is easy to identify Spirit with Pure Passive Consciousness or Shiva, which corresponds to the top of the head in the subtle body. Also, water, as the feminine counterpart of Shiva, is identifiable as Shakti in the sense of Kundala, or the Power aspect of consciousness. In Kundalini Yoga, Shakti is awakened, caused to arise from her resting place in the lowest Chakra† and to ascend to the place of Shiva, thereby bringing about the union that accomplishes the new birth for the individual.

While it is true that church council theology has given to the life and teachings of Christ an externalized interpretation, thereby revealing great human ingenuity in working out artificial conceptual constructions, the truly valid interpretation is mystical. This is virtually self-evident to one who is acquainted directly with the mystical consciousness itself, but I believe, as a matter of simple logic, that the Gospel record fits this interpretation better than any other. Of course, it implies that Jesus was not a unique Son of God, in a sense that could not possibly be true of anyone else. Christ was simply an exemplar, in extraordinary degree, of that which is possible to humankind as such.

Mysticism, in the comprehensive sense, is not merely an attained state of consciousness, but includes as well a philosophy and a method. As to philosophy, Christ is silent, and he says little concerning the ultimate state, apart from a few parables. His practical teaching falls in the field of method, which is almost exclusively ethical. In emphasizing the ethical, he is in primary agreement with Buddha, but the latter provided both fuller interpretations and exceptionally keen psychological analyses. Christ does not elaborate the rationale for his ethics, nor do I find Buddha wholly clear in this respect. However, within the Vedantic teaching of Shankara, the rational ground of the morality is quite explicitly presented. This rationale becomes manifest in the light of a well-developed philosophy.

---

*Carl G. Jung, *The Integration of Personality*, trans. Stanley M. Dell (New York: Farrar & Rinehart, 1919).

†[Subtle energy centers that also correlate with locations within the physical body.]

In Shankara's philosophic form, the goal of Yoga is the Realization of the Supreme Self. The Supreme Self is related to the empiric self in a way analogous to that which correlates the sun to its image in a drop of water. The only reality possessed by the little sun seen in the drop is the great sun of which it is an image. The object of devotion of the Yogin is the Supreme Self, or Great Sun, metaphorically. To be attached to the little sun, or personal self, is a barrier to the Realization of the Great Sun. Consequently, there must be a demotion of the little personal self from the false position of royalty that, in the ordinary state, one confers upon it. All honor must be given to the Supreme Self as its original source. The Supreme Self is one with its reflection, but no more so with one reflection than with another. Thus the ultimate Self, which I am, is identical with the ultimate Self of every creature. It follows, therefore, that I cannot honor the Supreme Self truly unless I regard equally the empiric selves of all creatures. That which I really am is not different from what all creatures really are. Hence, regard for the Other is identical with regard for Myself. The good of all humans and all creatures is identical with my own good. This would be essentially consistent both with the Christic and with the Buddhist moral practices.

In treating the Yoga of Patanjali, Leuba says, "The removal of all ethical considerations would leave essential structure unaffected; for, after all, ethical considerations have no logical place in a system that aims at the breaking of all bonds connecting the individual to the physical and social world."* I regard this statement as revealing the grossest misunderstanding of the true nature of mysticism. It is certain that, in the techniques of Christ, Buddha and Shankara, practical ethics is given the highest place. Patanjali aimed at the same end, the only differences lying in methodological emphases. On the question of ethics, all four of these great religious leaders stand together, for a reason more profound than the high moral character that each possessed, specifically, that the moral practice is a *logical* part of the whole. It is rather questionable whether, without the mystical ground, there ever could be developed a true morality, that is, one that was other than mere social expediency. The mystic's morality would be just as imperative for the last person in a dying world as for someone in the midst of a living society, whereas mere sociological morality would have no ground whatsoever in the former setting. Stated in terms of the logic of classes, the mystic's attitude toward the class of the Other is the same whether that class contains members or is empty. This is so because the *attitude* is a fundamental both of the process and of the attained state, entirely apart from objective empiric considerations. If there is no objective situation, the

---

*Leuba, 45.

attitude remains the same, but is not manifested in action; if there is an objective situation, then, without any alteration of the attitude, it is manifested in practical action. I contend that this presentation adequately outlines the logic of mystical ethics.

Concerning the question of how ethics is related to mystical consciousness, I believe that we are dealing not only with an important part of the whole problem, but, most assuredly, the very heart of it. Certainly, empiric science cannot bring any indictment here, for it is not difficult to show that the real guilt lies on the other side. Authentic mysticism affirms the primary unity of all. This implies that the Liberating or Enlightening Truth can only be known to the whole person, not to a mere functional part. This applies, not only in the sense of a necessary unity between one individual and another, but equally in the sense that one psychical function needs the collaboration of its companions. Thus, a science that is grounded on the intellect and the senses, but divorced from a spiritually oriented ethics, can achieve only a distorted knowledge. All such learning lacks something *essential to the very constitution of the knowledge itself.* It is not so much that there is effected a difference in bare fact, or that the formal logic is altered, but rather that there is a change in the perspective that affects the total integration of knowledge. There is a fundamental difference in its meaning.

Outstanding examples of the separation of ethical perspective are found in the practice of vivisection and in military science. Thus, in vivisection, moral regard for the creature experimented upon is repudiated. Inevitably this results in the experimenter becoming desensitized, his feelings calloused and his vision narrowed, in an invidious sense. As a result, he cannot see the processes he studies in their relation to the whole. He may acquire considerable command over the physical manifestation of disease, yet with the result that the pathological condition will be driven into a more hidden place in the psyche. He may be enabled to free bodies from physical symptoms, but at the price of increased psychical sickness, particularly in the sense of moral blinding and stultification. From the standpoint of mystical or spiritual morality, such a condition is infinitely worse than a very high death rate and very low life expectancy at birth, combined with much physical suffering from disease. Such is the valuation that the mystical consciousness places upon morality.

In the case of military science, the situation is even worse. The practice of thinking of the most outrageous moral action in terms of cold calculation is probably the most effective way there is of destroying the moral sense. The mystic, or spiritually oriented person, would say that the physical death of an individual, group, race or nation is preferable to any survival based upon such thinking, for such survival would be at the price of spiritual death. Anyone in such a condition progressively ceases to be a spiritual and human being, and becomes more and more a mere animal with an unillumined intellect, a creature that is more a curse than a blessing to him- or herself and to others. There are values infinitely more important than physical survival.

One need only look at recent world history to see what a curse science may become when it is solely an intellectual achievement divorced from spiritual morality. It has become more an instrument of darkness than of light. No longer are we civilized. One must go back to the seventeenth and eighteenth centuries to find a reasonable degree of civilization. In this development toward degradation, our science must share a large, if not a principal, part of the responsibility. Bear in mind that this is not due to science, as such, being anything bad, but to the severance of the intellect from spiritual ethics.

It is far better to overemphasize the ethical factor than to undervalue or neglect it. There is an error in such overemphasis, but it does not produce a serious problem. Overemphasis is possible because ethics is not the whole of being. Knowledge and aesthetic appreciation, for instance, are equally parts of the whole, and, since the mystical spirit is integrative, these and all other parts must be included. At this point, the teachings of Christ, as given in the record, are open to criticism for the reason that his message is defective from the standpoint of noetic need. However, this simply means that these offerings should be supplemented. Trouble arises only by trying to make the Christ the all in all. It is neither necessary nor desirable that he should be so regarded. It is quite sufficient that he may be accepted along with other possibilities of consciousness.

THE BUDDHA

That the great Buddha was a mystic, in the most profound and exalted sense, is so evident from a study of his recorded life and teachings that no time need be given to demonstrating it. He attained Illumination under the Bodhi Tree explicitly through the mystical meditation process. His doctrine teaches the attainment of Nirvana through a righteous living, thinking and feeling that destroys the Sangsaric state. The religious method was exclusively Yogic in the highest sense. Since his time, corruption has entered into parts of the Buddhist community by the accretion of foreign elements, so that in modern Buddhism there is a great deal of Tantric ritualism. However, this is no more a true part of Buddha's doctrine than was the Inquisition a part of Christ's teaching. Authentic Buddhism is to be understood as was expressed by its founder and continued by those who attained the Buddhist Realization in the centuries that followed. In the light of these sources, Buddhism, as a religion, is the purest sort of non-Tantric Yoga. Hence, here, as nowhere else, it is possible to determine just what Yoga or mystical Realization is.

The two great factors that implement the motivation underlying the drive toward mystical Realization are love of Truth, and Compassion. Whoever is motivated by a desire for bliss will fail, inasmuch as such a motive is selfish. Desire for voluptuous pleasures may lead to practices, such as the use of certain drugs and psychophysical performances, that will induce temporary experiences of the type sought, but at the expense of intellectual and moral degradation. This voluptuous pleasure is as different from the Beatitude of true Yogic Realization as is a sensuously seductive dream different from the state of aesthetic delight realized by a mathematician when she has achieved a new integration in thought. The voluptuous state may be mystoid, but it is as different from a true mystical state as is a base counterfeit from a true coin. The Beatitude of the genuine Mystical State is a fruit of renunciation of all personal satisfaction and attainment. It is very real, but is an effect, not a legitimate objective. Compassion and love of Truth are the only proper and effective motivations. The Compassion must be utterly self-disregarding, and the seeking of Truth must be so pure that every preconception is offered up on the altar of sacrifice.

From the record of the early life of Gautama, as well as from his subsequent life and teachings as the Awakened Buddha, we know that his central motivation was Compassion. There probably never was a life less frustrated than was the early life of this prince. According to his account, he seems to have been a well-nigh complete stranger to suffering. For the first twenty-nine years of his life, he remained unaware of the suffering involved in human life in general, because his father saw to it that he should not know. Eventually, when he did learn of human suffering, he simply felt compelled to seek the means whereby it could be overcome. This entailed the search for Truth, not so much as an end in itself, but more as a means to serve the office of Compassion. He sought assiduously for seven years, including a six-year unsuccessful experiment with extreme asceticism. Finally, through mystic meditation by his own method, he attained the highest known stage of Realization of Truth. Through this Realization he organized his redeeming doctrine and devoted the balance of his life (forty-five years) to spreading it among humanity. The overriding purpose of the teaching was relieving humankind, as far as possible, from the ubiquitous burden of suffering. Since relief from suffering is a necessary consequence of attainment of Transcendental Wisdom, or Prajna-Paramita, the doctrine lends itself to the more positive interpretation of attainment in terms of the Noble Wisdom. Even so, the emphasis on Compassion is preeminent in the character of this great Buddha, although he is also the wisest of the Wise.

From the study of the authentic Buddhist Sutras, one achieves probably the best understanding of the profoundest development of mystical consciousness that is available anywhere, provided the student can understand them. Unfortunately, they are excessively obscure, so it is doubtful that anyone who is not already a mystic could possibly grasp them. Other treatments of the subject, particularly that of Shankara, are much more comprehensible to an intelligence in which the mystical door has not yet opened. This Buddha did not possess the best skill to enable adequate cross-translation for a thinking consciousness. As a result, he was not wholly successful. This is obvious in view of the fact that vast groups among his followers have misunderstood his Nirvana as meaning literal annihilation in the absolute sense, even though it is perfectly clear that Buddha did not mean that at all, if one but studies the Sutras deeply enough. Because many able Western scholars have fallen into the same error, and several other mystics, including the Pseudo-Dionysius, have fortified this impression, it is necessary to give this misconception some serious attention.

In the Sutras there are numerous descriptions of the Ultimate in the general form of the following logical pattern. The Ultimate is not-A, where A is any predicate whatsoever. Then, it is said, it is not not-A, nor is it that which is neither A nor not-A, nor is it that which is both A and not-A. If one were to define absolute nothingness, in every possible sense—that is, absolute annihilation or absolute unconsciousness, without any potentiality in it—then one would find the above definition just about perfect. Beyond question, this definition fits absolute annihilation. Nevertheless, it does not follow that it does not also fit a somewhat that is other than absolute annihilation. Just what is it that is negated in such a thorough fashion? The answer is very simple. Specifically, it is the *conception* as a type—not particular conceptions, but the thinkable conception as such. This is not a denial of Being as other than thinkable conception, unless it were proven that Being in the absolute sense is thinkable conception. However, there is no such proof of that thesis. The positive meaning, then, emerges at once: Enlightenment is transcendence of thinkable conception. It follows that, since anything that can be imagined is a thinkable conception, the State of Enlightenment cannot possibly be imagined. However, this does not preclude the possibility of Realizing the Enlightened State, provided that the means are other than relative thought, as well as other than sensation. If we conceive of a mystical function or faculty, such as the Samadhindriya, then we have a schematic clarification.

No mystic was ever more rigorous in his use of language than Buddha, but that rigor is well-nigh devastating to anyone but a near Arhat. This means that, pedagogically, Buddha was less than completely successful, but no one in the ethical dimension, not even Christ, has ever been more successful. Indeed, reports by adequate observers indicate that even to this day the followers of Buddha live more nearly consistently by Buddhist ethics than do the followers of Christ live by the ethics he taught, or do followers of other great religious and moral leaders adhere to their respective ethical teachings. It seems that Buddhists even do so when they expect to achieve absolute annihilation! For instance, through the centuries, the Buddhist community has been far less a community of killers than has been the Christian community, yet the morality of Christ, no less than the morality of Buddha, implies nonkilling. Of all religious leaders, Buddha has had the greatest success upon the visible plane, in spite of some failures.

That Buddhism is fundamentally Yogic or mystical in its method and objective is further revealed in the following quotation from the *Buddhist Catechism* of Subhádra Bhikshu:

> Buddhism teaches the reign of perfect goodness and wisdom without a personal God, continuance of individuality without an immortal soul, eternal happiness without a local heaven, the way of salvation without a vicarious Savior, redemption worked out by each one himself without any prayers, sacrifices and penances, without the ministry of ordained priests, without the intercession of saints, without Divine mercy. Finally, it teaches that supreme perfection is attainable even in this life and on this earth.*

Thus, the Buddhist redemption or attainment clearly does not depend upon external revelation or authority; nor upon the use of ritual or other formal religious practices; nor upon the intermediary function of any human agent. It is something achievable by each individual directly. While various subsidiary aids of this sort may be employed, and may be of assistance to certain or even most individuals, in principle none of these are *necessary*. This means that the essence of Buddhism is individual Realization, which is Yoga or mystical Awakening, purely and simply. Without Yoga no one would ever attain Buddhahood, nor would there be any Buddhism. Hence, whoever would know just what Yoga or mysticism is, in its essential and purest form, should study Buddhism.

---

*Subhádra Bhikshu, comp., *Buddhist Catechism* (New York: Brentano's, 1920), 61-62.

The Western scientist may object that this is impracticable because Buddhist consciousness, practice and doctrine are too foreign to the understanding of the scientist's mind, and thus supply no employable base for research. Some have suggested that since some states of drug intoxication that resemble the mystic state are closer to the understanding of the Western scientist, this affords a better starting point. It well may be that some scientists are in closer rapport to the states induced by drug intoxication than they are to Buddhism, but, for my part, I have a higher regard for the Western scientific mind, taken as a whole. At any rate, the minds of our mathematicians and modern theoretical physicists seem to me to rest in closer rapport to Buddhism than they do to the state of drug intoxication, however it may be with our more materialistic physiological psychologists. Doubtless we can learn something concerning psychical states from the study of drugged and other abnormal consciousness, but there is a fundamental danger in drawing conclusions concerning the normal and proper from the pathologic. It is the danger of distortion and of drawing unsound conclusions from improper or inadequate perspective.

Authentic Buddhist teaching and practice do not at all encourage soft or dreamy states of mind. On the contrary, they call for the keenest analytic discrimination. As little does it encourage the cultivation of an empty mind, as is quite evident from the scorn that the sixth Chinese Buddhist patriarch had for such practices:

> People under delusion believe obstinately that there is a substance behind appearances and so they are stubborn in holding to their own way of interpreting the Samadhi of specific mode, which they define as, "sitting quietly and continuously without letting any idea arise in the mind." Such an interpretation would class us with the inanimate objects; it is a stumbling block to the right Path and the Path should be kept open.

> Some teachers of concentration instructed their disciples to keep a watch on their minds and secure tranquillity by the cessation of all thought, and henceforth their disciples gave up all effort to concentrate the mind and ignorant persons who did not understand the distinction became insane from trying to carry out the instruction literally. Such cases are not rare, and it is a great mistake to teach the practice.*

True Buddhist Yoga, as well as other authentic Yoga, requires accentuation of intellectual discrimination and concentration, whereas drug

---

*Goddard, 523.

intoxication and the conditions produced by false asceticism lead to intellectual dullness and to all sorts of confusion.

In the conclusions that he draws from his study of mysticism, Leuba finds himself in agreement with Henri Delacroix and George A. Coe as to the illusory nature of the mystical claim. He then quotes the following from Coe: "The mystic acquires his religious convictions precisely as his nonmystical neighbor does, namely through tradition and instruction, auto-suggestion grown habitual, and reflective analysis. The mystic brings his theological beliefs to the mystical experience; he does not derive them from it."* There can be no doubt that much of the interpretative teaching given by mystics generally is more than a little colored by their background of instruction and tradition. Interpretative differences as between different mystics of different times and cultures, when such interpretations are in conformity with the beliefs of the milieu, indicate at least some such influence. Notwithstanding this, when we study the very great mystical geniuses, we are impressed by a reverse tendency. Such is the case with the three figures we are studying here. Each one challenged the current convictions of his milieu and, at times, diverged radically from them. By such variance, both Buddha and Christ called down active persecution upon themselves, and upon their following.

Let us consider the doctrinal divergence of Buddha. Two of the defining tenets of Brahmanism, the religious setting in which Gautama was born, are reincarnation and the doctrine of a permanent and unchanging Atman, the individual self or soul, that persists from incarnation to incarnation. It is this permanent soul that, persisting as a sort of central core, takes on the clothing of various embodiments, both subtle and gross. According to the record, when Buddha first began his search, he questioned certain Brahmin pundits who propounded these doctrines. Buddha, through the powers of concentration and meditation, penetrated into these doctrines, pronouncing one sound and the other false. He concluded that reincarnation is undeniable but there is no persistent Atman or individual soul. This is the point of most radical divergence between exoteric Brahmanism and Buddhism, both exoteric and esoteric. It proved to be a serious point of disagreement that provides one of the main reasons why Buddhism found it difficult to establish itself in the land of its birth. This doctrine is, perhaps, the most obscure feature of Buddhist psychology, but I shall do what I can to outline it. It stands as a weighty counterexample to Leuba's claim, since it is, most emphatically, not a teaching taken into the mystical state

---

*George A. Coe, "The Sources of Mystical Revelation," *Hibbert Jr.* 6 (1907):367, quoted in Leuba.

from the instruction and tradition of the mystic's milieu, but is born out of the insight.

Buddha taught that the self, or "I am," does not persist from incarnation to incarnation. To be sure, if it did, there could be no liberation from the cycle of birth and death and endless sorrow. The doctrine is thus of indispensably central importance. The individual that is born is a congeries of psychical functions or faculties that integrate an illusive personal self that lasts only as long as this congeries persists. At times the congeries separate, and then, after a period of rest, reintegrate to form a new personality having a new ego, or "I am." The following quotation from *The Gospel of Buddha*, as told by Paul Carus, presents the argument and teaching in exceptionally clear form. The words are given as the words of the Buddha.

> People are in bondage, because they have not yet removed the idea of *I*.
>
> The thing and its quality are different in our thought, but not in reality. Heat is different from fire in our thought, but you cannot remove heat from fire in reality. You say that you can remove the qualities and leave the thing, but if you think your theory to the end, you will find that this is not so.
>
> Is not man an organism of many aggregates? Do we not consist of various skandhas, as our sages call them? Man consists of the material form, of sensation, of thought, of dispositions, and, lastly, of understanding. That which men call the ego when they say "I am" is not an entity behind the skandhas; it originates by the cooperation of the skandhas. There is mind; there is sensation and thought, and there is truth; and truth is mind when it walks in the paths of righteousness. But there is no separate ego-soul outside or behind the thought of man. He who believes that the ego is a distinct being has no correct conception of things. The very search for the Atman is wrong; it is a wrong start and it will lead you in a false direction.
>
> Is not this individuality of mine a combination, material as well as mental? Is it not made up of qualities that sprang into being by a gradual evolution? The five roots of sense perception in this organism have come from ancestors who performed these functions. The ideas which I think, came to me partly from others who thought them, and partly they arise from combinations of these ideas in my own mind. Those who used the same sense-organs, and thought the same ideas before I was composed into this individuality of mine, are my previous exis-

tences; they are my ancestors as much as *I* of yesterday am the father of *I* of today, and the karma of my past deeds conditions the fate of my present existence.*

In a later discussion, Buddha uses the figure of a candle that is lighted, the flame representing the self, and the candle the congeries of Skandhas or psychical elements that make up the entity. If the flame is extinguished and lighted again, the question is whether it is the same flame. Buddha says it both is and is not. It is not, because there is a break in continuity, but it is the same in the sense that it has the same size and quality as the original flame, in that it comes from the same source. Further, if there is a group of candles of the same composition, size and shape, then their flames are and are not the same flames, for identical reasons.

Any creature, animate or inanimate, is the product of past causes, and the father of future effects, with no conceivable beginning or ending point. However, the congeries of elements that constitute these beings are eternally interweaving in a process of becoming and dying in the resultant phenomenal effects. The phenomenal effects float like mirages upon this interweaving stream. Likewise, the discrete series of personal egos are born upon this stream as the counterpart of the mirages. There is thus a subjective and an objective phantasmagoria: one, the series of personal egos; the other, the various appearances of the phenomenal universe. Both of these have no substance in themselves. The relatively durable thing-in-itself is the interweaving congeries, but the stream of congeries is compounded and therefore subject to birth and decay and the cause of all suffering. The really durable is the Uncompounded, that which lies behind the congeries as their support. The Realization of this is Liberation and Enlightenment.

We have here a conception that definitely differentiates Buddhism from all other religions and from the Western philosophies. It differs from Brahmanism in that there is a denial of a permanent Self, though there is agreement as to the illusory character of the objective universe. It diverges from Christian theology, which grants reality to the objective world and predicates a permanent soul. It differs from Western realism in that it grants no substantial existent thing, and from Western idealism insofar as that idealism centers around a persistent transcendental Subject. However, much of Schopenhauer is congruent with Buddhism, though I do not find his notion of Will as carrying the same meaning as the Buddhist "Essence of Mind," or Shunyata. In some respects Von Hartmann is closer to the Buddhist position.

---

*Paul Carus, *The Gospel of Buddha* (Chicago: Open Court, 1909).

Before the Recognition of September 1936, I had never been able to grasp the doctrine of Anatman, but as a result of it, I saw the necessity of the doctrine, and for the first time Realized the relativity of Nirvana in the simplest sense. This Recognition confirmed a conception that, only later, I found in the Sutras of northern Buddhism, which had been previously unknown to me.

The point of this rather lengthy argument is that here we have a case of knowledge not derived from instruction and tradition, but originating in mystical insight. It is not a case of taking into the mystical state the conceptions that are born forth from it. It is, in my mind, most positive evidence that the mystical Door is one from whence comes new Knowledge that makes a difference in thinkable concepts. Undoubtedly, imperfectly developed mystical states can be misinterpreted, and the sense of certainty may be incorrectly predicated of the erroneous interpretation. All of which simply means that there is a need for a critique of mystical consciousness, just as we have found a critique of the reason necessary. Similarly, just as the latter critique showed in what way we may trust the intellect, as well as in what ways it cannot give reliable knowledge, the same is true of a mystical critique. Later I shall consider this subject in more detail.

SHANKARA

Concerning these three great mystics, Shankara's life and teaching are most *explicitly* Yogic, in the technical sense. However, he deals with Yoga, or mystical Realization, exclusively in the highest sense, since he is interested solely in the final Liberation, and seems to scorn any lesser attainment. Shankara discourses upon the technical problems of method and philosophy to a degree not found in the teachings of Christ, or even Buddha, because he was qualified for this by birth and training as a member of the Brahmin caste, and he worked exclusively with a public that needed and could understand this treatment. He is the *philosopher* Sage, par excellence. Apparently, he did not attempt to reach simple minds, but was rather a teacher of teachers. In principle, Buddha spoke to all of humanity, but due to certain temperamental and intellectual barriers, was not acceptable to the more learned, with some exceptions. Christ frankly oriented himself to the lowly of this world, and thus reached some, at the price of being unable to reach others. However, the saving Wisdom is for all, not the exclusive right of the simple and lowly. Unfortunately, no single embodiment of the Sage can reach all equally, but the Divine Wisdom incarnates in many forms, which, while seemingly different, are really complementary.

Shankara does not present his philosophy as something original and *de novo*. On the contrary, he presents it as a clarification and explicit logical development of the Vedic meaning. Yet, the Veda is not to be understood as exclusively the recorded literature that goes by that name. It is even more fundamentally the innate Wisdom resident in the depths of all consciousness. Hence, by means of Yoga, the Yogin attains Realization of the Veda quite independently of all scholarship, though such attainment does not of itself imply mastery of formulation. Consequently, the best statement is the combined result of Yogic penetration, scholarship and the development of intellectual acuity and profundity. In terms of this combination, Shankara is the greatest of all exemplars.

Even so, Shankara is not wholly satisfactory to the modern Western mind. For one thing, he is not concerned with science in the modern sense; certainly there was no such science in his day. For another, he employs the scholastic form in much of his reasoning. For that matter, there is considerable scholastic coloring to be found in the rationalist language of Kant, who forms the gateway to postscholastic and postrationalist thinking. The similarity to Kant runs even deeper, for, remarkably, Shankara is also a critical thinker—living many centuries earlier than Kant. In a third respect, the modern Westerner may find Shankara not entirely acceptable in that he continually introduces references to the written Veda as an authenticating argument. It strikes us too much like the method of theological argument that justifies a thesis by reference to statements in the Bible. In this connection, however, it must be noted that Shankara spoke to a public for whom the Veda was regarded as authority, so no hearing could be attained other than by conforming with Vedic authority.

Nonetheless, Shankara is never content to rest his case on the codified Veda alone. He establishes his thesis, point by point, by reference to reason and experience independently of the written Veda. Clearly, for himself, the source that ultimately grounds his teachings is not mere scripture, but his personal Yogic Realization. Thus he writes meanings that, while reconcilable to the written Veda, could hardly have been derived from it by the methods of unaided scholarship.

We are here again confronted by the question that forms a central interest of the present volume, namely: Is the mystic Realization an authentic source of Knowledge or Gnosis? That it does provide such Knowledge is well-nigh Shankara's main thesis, after the importance he ascribes to Liberation. Emphatically, he even claims that Atmavidya (Knowledge of the Self, or Gnostic Knowledge) is not merely a means to Liberation, but *is* Liberation. To deny the validity and actuality of mystical Knowledge would be equivalent to denying all significance in the work and thought of Shankara. With no one else, so far as I know, is the noetic element in the Yogic consciousness so fundamental.

Further discussion of this question is warranted here. Von Hartmann says, "Gnosis is knowledge acquired by immediate perception (intuition) instead of by intellect."* He continues that if this direct perception stands alone, it may be so colored and dominated by a preconception that it may become quite unreliable. It needs the correction of intellectual examination and of any other source of knowledge there may be. Mohini Chatterji, in his criticism of Von Hartmann's position, admits the justice of this point, but proceeds to state that Oriental esotericism does not teach the exclusive dependence upon the "immediate perception." The test of reason is applied, and the insight of one individual is checked by that of others, just as is the case in Western science. When a body of philosophic-scientific-religious teaching or doctrine is established, it is the combined product of many highly trained minds, in all of which the mystical sense, as well as the intellect, is highly developed. It is true that in many instances the mystical insight may be prepared by previous study and the content of the insight may be in accord with that study. Nevertheless, this does not mean that the mystic merely takes out of the state that which he or she brings to it. Mystical knowledge is of another dimension.

Chatterji gives a very suggestive illustration from Western science. A mathematical astronomer might—as has actually been done—determine the existence and calculate the location of a formerly unknown planet, entirely through analytic interpretation of the perturbations in the orbits of known planets. Following the directions resulting from these calculations, the same person, or another astronomer, might then direct a telescope to the indicated portion of the sky and visually confirm that which had been predetermined by calculation. Would we be justified in claiming that the observing astronomer merely derived such knowledge from his observation as he already possessed? In the purely schematic sense, the answer might be affirmative. Even so, he acquired new perceptual knowledge, that which James called "knowledge through acquaintance." Looking through the telescope did more than simply add feeling tone to an already existing knowledge. Perceptual knowledge was added to the formal schematic knowledge of the intellectual calculation. In this illustration, the telescope represents the mystic sense, which gives a dimension of knowledge as much different from the intellectual conception as is the perception. Something is added, even though subsequent intellectual formulation might differ

---

*Eduard von Hartmann, criticism of *Esoteric Buddhism*, by A. P. Sinnett, in *Weiner Zeitung*, reprinted in *The Theosophist* (May 1885).

in no way whatsoever from already extant teaching or doctrine. Essentially, the new knowledge is as incommensurable with intellectual conception as the latter is with sensible perception. Just the same, in several ways the two can cooperate, much as the percept and concept cooperate.

Once I was the subject of a dream experience that illustrates the difference in dimension of two kinds of related sense. Many years ago a group of us had planned an extended trip through the Painted Desert of northern Arizona. Our proposed course was to take us over the Mormon Dugway, which gave access to the Lee's Ferry crossing of the Colorado River—the only crossing then in existence for a distance of hundreds of miles. This approach was one of the most nerve-wracking for drivers, due to its narrowness, its winding roughness and, most of all, the very rapid current of the Colorado River below. Formerly, I had been over this course, so I knew that it was a trial. One night, while lying in bed waiting for sleep, I was thinking of this drive, outlining the course rather clearly in my mind. During the process I fell asleep, as I found out later, but without any break in mental continuity. I simply found myself apparently driving a car over the course I had been contemplating. I was driving along nearly identically with the way I had been thinking, that is, driving slowly and carefully, as one actually would be compelled to do. In the dream, the road wound in and out, around coves and points, and climbed upward, essentially as I knew it did from my previous experience. Suddenly, as I rounded a point of rock, I saw, far up on the furthest visible portion of the road, another car coming toward me— a very strange car, such as I had not previously seen. It was extremely streamlined, very much as the designs of the race cars later used on the Salt Lake salt flats. More dramatically, this car was coming toward me at unbelievable speed, surely as fast as the fastest race car, while negotiating the turns with great precision. To my consternation, Mephisto was driving—and he was a magnificent driver. There was no place for passing and no time for me to do anything. It was inevitable that I would be struck, which then happened, the strange car and Mephisto passing right through my car and me. With that, I awakened.

I then analyzed what had happened. In the first stage, while awake, I had been thinking of a process in terms of idea. There was the normal dualistic consciousness in the mode of thinking, with an undertone of awareness of myself as an organism. In addition, there was the normal clear differentiation between a process thought about and a process performed by the activity of the organism. Then, without knowing the shift, I was actually performing the process, with the awareness of the organism lying in bed dropping away entirely. The *idea* had become *performance*, in another state of consciousness, but in harmonious con-

246 The Psychological Critique of Mysticism

formity with the previous purely ideational process. This was a different state of awareness, not simply one state of awareness with a different feeling tone. I was aware of a content in a different way, which I believe is quite validly defined as an addition of another knowledge, even though not diverging in pattern from the original schema. Also, there was something added that was not in the original schema. I had not at all anticipated Mephisto and the wonderful car, which became novel material for my intellect to consider. In particular, the "Old Boy" poses some very intriguing problems. This greatly enhanced my interest in Jung's treatment of the transformation process, when I read the latter some years afterward. I definitely acquired something from the experience that was valuable for thought.

It is not suggested that this episode of dream experience has anything of the mystical about it, for the whole incident falls within the range of the subject-object type of consciousness. There is no ineffability other than that which is always present in the relationship between the perceptual and the conceptual orders. It is offered simply as an illustration of (1) how a conceptual series may become a perceptual series that is a schematic duplicate, yet adds new knowledge, and (2) how, in addition, such a perceptual series may react upon the conceptual to add new material for thought. The whole is a schematic pattern of the relation between conceptual and mystical knowledge.

The same principle is involved in the figure of the telescope used to verify the existence of a planet predetermined by mathematical calculation. In this case, the cognizing of the planet as a perceptual object may well have added nothing necessary for the purposes of calculation. Calculation determined a somewhat that might be called "n" and probably could establish both orbit and mass, so that n thereafter is as fully known as is necessary for all purposes of calculation alone. Nevertheless, such a knowledge of n is insufficient for the establishment of all significant astronomical knowledge relative to the new body. It would not produce data such as temperature, amount and kind of light radiation, and possible chemical composition, as the latter might reveal. For this purpose n must be realized as an object for perception, directly or indirectly. Hence, n as perceptually realized becomes a source of possible additional development of conceptual knowledge that could not have been derived from calculation alone. So, in addition to the *knowledge* of the planet through pure calculation, *experience* of the planet adds the following two increments of knowledge:

1. knowledge as perceptual cognition, and
2. physical and chemical knowledge, in the conceptual sense, that could not have been derived from calculation alone.

There is some dispute as to whether perceptual cognition may properly be called "knowledge." In common practice, the term is defined as "the cognitive aspect of consciousness in general,"* of which two forms are recognized, namely, "knowledge of acquaintance," or perceptual cognition, and "knowledge about," or conceptual cognition. Thus, "to know may mean either to perceive or apprehend, or, to understand or comprehend."† A blind person could not know light in the first sense but could know *about* light in the second sense. Yet, while this division of knowledge into two classes is a matter of general practice, Dewey challenges the correctness of calling "knowledge by acquaintance" "knowledge" at all. He calls it "experience," and restricts the term *knowledge* to the conceptual order. Of course, this is largely a matter of definition. It is certainly clear that simple perceptual awareness is distinguishable from conation or will and affection or feeling. We might follow the more general practice of classification of the modes of the mind into two or three categories:

1. Cognition and conation, the latter including affection, or
2. cognition, conation and affection.

If so, then perceptual awareness, apart from all feeling tone and activistic element in consciousness, is certainly a cognition. Accordingly, perception is a kind of knowledge. In my discussion, I am following the general practice, rather than that of Dewey, particularly as his approach exemplifies a philosophic interpretation and attitude with which I disagree.

Of the two branches of knowledge, mystical Recognition (introceptive Realization) is most nearly like knowledge by acquaintance and hence bears a relationship to conceptual knowledge analogous to that of perception. However, there are important points of departure. For instance, perceptual awareness is closer to the conceptual particulars and singulars than it is to general and universal concepts. The reverse is the case with mystical Recognition, for this kind of cognition comes into closest affinity with the most universal and most abstract conceptions. The more general a conception, the further it is from the perceptual order and the closer it lies to the mystical. In the thought that recognizes solely the perceptual and conceptual, only particular concepts have true referents, that is, perceptual existences that they mean. General concepts are viewed as lacking true referents and are regarded as valuable only as instruments in the manipulation of ideas that ulti-

---

*Baldwin, *Dictionary*, s.v. "knowledge."
†Ibid.

mately lead to concrete ideas having perceptual referents. In contrast, to the mystic, at least of the more profound sort, the reference of the most universal concept is most immediate, and therefore most concrete. The particular concept and its referent have the value of abstraction away from this concrete reality and, hence, have a greater or lesser degree of unreality. Consequently, from the viewpoint of mystical awareness, particulars possess only instrumental value.

Another respect in which mystical Recognition diverges from perceptual awareness or knowledge by acquaintance, in the usual sense, is that mystical consciousness, when developed deeply enough, is not concerned with any object. The general definition of the term *cognition* is "the being aware of an object." In the well-developed mystical state, subject and object fuse or coalesce, so that the normal relationship of experience and thought does not exist. It follows that cognition, or knowledge, in the sense of being aware of an object, as distinct from a subject, is not a mystical kind of knowledge. The term *Knowledge* in the sense of *Gnosis*, or *Jnana*, is knowledge of a different sort. It falls outside current philosophical definition. Yet, the use of the term in this sense may be traced to the ancient Greeks and East Indians, and thus has a hoary justification. 'Knowledge' in the sense of 'Nous', and the corresponding adjective 'Noetic', has the essential meaning of 'Gnosis' and 'Jnana', a nondiscursive knowledge in which the knowledge and the thing known are identical. The denial of Nous is a denial of mystical knowledge, and vice versa. This denial is equivalent to materialism in the invidious, though not in the technical, sense.

The fundamental issue here is whether we are justified in viewing a state of consciousness in which there is a coalescence of subject and object, of knowledge and thing known, as a case of knowledge? So long as the state stands in *complete* separation from relative consciousness, the response must be negative. However, we equally cannot predicate affection or conation of such a state. It is simply beyond all relative predication, so it can only be defined by universal negation. Fortunately, the pure mystical state may impinge upon relative consciousness, in greater or lesser degree, producing effects for the latter. This results in a compound consciousness in which either the mystical and relative form an impure effect, or the two forms of consciousness exist side by side. In either case, relative consciousness is affected. It is relative consciousness that experiences Bliss or Beatitude, reorientation of the will, and a new noetic orientation and content. In terms of content, relative consciousness now knows, as an object, the state of consciousness in which merge both subject and object, as well as knowledge and thing known. This is an increase of relative knowledge having most profound significance, both in the theoretical and pragmatic senses, insofar as it tends to make an enormous difference in life and conduct, and in valuation and meaning. The new orientation is like changing the base of reference in mathematical analysis. The material of relative consciousness enters into a new perspective that tends toward radical difference in theoretical organization. In this way there is addition to knowledge in the conceptual sense, with respect to content as well as altered theoretical organization.

A discussion of the foregoing sort is quite appropriate in connection with the study of Shankara. Whether or not he wrote the parallel of this argument in its entirety, I do not know, but this would be improbable, since the intellectual nexus of his time was markedly different from our own. This is rather the way Shankara would have written were he alive today.

For Shankara, the problem of Liberation is preeminently a problem of knowledge, both for the reason that knowledge is the primary means and, in the deeper sense, that Knowledge itself is Liberation. Christ gives the compound mode of affection-conation nearly exclusive emphasis, while Buddha gives it primary emphasis, at least in his popular discourses. However, Buddha also gives substantial attention to the noetic factor, particularly in discourses to advanced disciples. This difference in the orientation to the problem of Liberation, Salvation or Enlightenment, proves to be a matter of very considerable psychological and speculative interest. For one thing, it correlates beautifully with what we know of their hereditary background: Gautama was a prince; Jesus, according to the Gospel account, was a descendent of David, and so also was a prince by blood; and Shankara was a Brahmin. This would give to Buddha and Christ the normal perspective of hereditary rulers, in contrast to Shankara, who belonged to the caste preeminent in metaphysical thought. To the natural ruler, will and feeling have ascendancy and leadership over thought, but for the natural thinker the reverse is the case. It is significant that the largest extent of influence was ultimately won by Buddha and Christ, while Shankara's influence was more restricted and specialized. In terms of emphasis, the contrast between Christ and Shankara is most marked, whereas Buddha occupies an intermediate position.

We are presented here with one of the most difficult recurring problems of philosophy and psychology. Which is more fundamental in the constitution of the universe—Will or Idea? Which is more determinant in the life of an individual—knowledge or feeling-conation? There is good reason for reducing the three modes of consciousness—namely, cognition, affection and conation—to two, by combining feeling and will. Manifestly there is a very close connection between pleasure and desiring, but pure knowing may leave desire largely unaffected. Ethical consciousness as an attitude is an expression of the will and depends upon the intellect simply for the resolution of ethical problems. Hence, accentuation of the ethical is equivalent to giving primacy to the Will. Of course, in the present discussion, Will must be understood as including the whole of the activistic element in consciousness, and thus includes desire and the autonomous will to live. It is not restricted to conscious volition. The usage is close to, if not identical with, that of Schopenhauer. Buddha's emphasis on the destruction of the desire for sentient existence seems to place him somewhat closer to the emphasis of Christ than that of Shankara. However, the doctrine of the Prajna-Paramita accords more closely with Shankara.

Modern philosophy has not finally resolved the problem of the relative primacy of Will and Idea. The impact of Hegel and Schopenhauer does not destroy either contestant. The Truth would seem to be, much as Von Hartmann suggested, that Will and Idea are component parts of a more ultimate incognizable reality. Then, there is no ultimate primacy for either the Will or the Idea, but relative primacy in different contexts, in stages of processes and in individual organizations. Regarding the very practical question of which way, for a given individual, will lead successfully to Yoga, we must consider whether Will or Idea dominates the individual life. Method must be adjusted accordingly. Unquestionably, for the overwhelming mass of people, Will dominates, and, hence, affective ethical techniques are indicated. However, there is a smaller number of individuals whose cognitive development is not only large, but also occupies the commanding position in life-determination. In such cases the Will has been brought into subjugation to the Idea. Consequently, for them the problem of Yoga, as a means, becomes simply the achievement of the *right conception*, in the absence of any effective autonomous resistance on the part of the Will. For most people, right conception is insufficient, because the amount of undomesticated autonomous Will is far too large.

Schopenhauer is right when he states that emancipation depends upon the reversal of the Will, so that the will to live becomes denial of the will to live—though I do not find that he has adequately established how such a reversal is possible, if Will is all-powerful. When Will is subjugated to Idea, practically as well as theoretically, the problem of reversal reduces to realization of the conception of what is to be done and how to do it.

Shankara is not concerned with Yoga in all its ramifications as method, but primarily with the problem as it appears after subjugation of the Will to Idea has been already achieved. Explicitly, he does not view all persons as possible candidates for this at their present stage of development. They must have qualifications, the nature of which he explicitly indicates, after remarking that the unredeemed state of humanity is due to Ignorance.

Therefore it is clear that Ignorance can only be removed by Wisdom.

Q. How can this Wisdom be acquired?

A. By discussion—by discussing as to the nature of Spirit and Not-Spirit.

Q. Who are worthy of engaging in such discussion?

A. Those who have acquired the four qualifications.

Q. What are the four qualifications?

A. 1. True discrimination of permanent and impermanent things;

2. Indifference to the enjoyment of the fruits of one's actions both here and hereafter;

3. Possession of Sama (calmness) and the other five qualities;

4. An intense desire of becoming liberated (from material existence).*

Clearly one who possesses these four qualifications has already gone a considerable way along the Path. Somehow or other much self-discipline has been achieved, passion quieted, the direction of desire reversed, and the habit of discriminative analysis developed. The antiegoistic ethic is presupposed. It is possible that various technical means have been employed to achieve the four qualifications.

At any rate, from this point on, Shankara abandons all ritual, sacrifice, technical expedients—in a word, all objective sensible action, or works, as agencies that are, in principle, necessary. An intellective process of discrimination, including discussion, is well-nigh the only agency. In the end, when this discrimination has completed the final preparation, the Realization comes at its own time, spontaneously. All preparation has the value of purification or destruction of barriers but is not a magical agent that commands the Realization.

The Awakened State is not an effect of causes set up by the candidate, for it has nothing to do with conditions. It is as though at some moment in the process of preparation the optimum balance is achieved such that an obscuring curtain drops, simply revealing what has always been there—and has always been the Truth. Indifference to specific method or technique is not only allowed, it is mandatory; for by attaching importance to any means, the candidate is clouding his or her mind with the delusion of efficient causal connection. Meditation ceases to be a matter of set method or of specific periods, but becomes something spontaneous and capable of being superimposed upon reflective pro-

---

*Shankara, *Discrimination of Self and Not-Self* (*Atmanatma Viveka*).

cess, or even objective activity. The Samadhi thereby attained is the Nirvikalpa or undifferentiated Samadhi, which by no means necessarily implies blackout trance. To require trance is to impose a visible means as causally effective, which would be contrary to the primary principle that the State of Realization is not the effect of a relative cause.

It is significant that the highest state of Samadhi may appear to the incompetent observer as the most casual, and indistinguishable from ordinary consciousness. Actually, it effects an integration such that the usual and ordinary is seen as of one sameness with the undifferentiated, and the practitioner may not know the difference between meditation and nonmeditation. The practitioner has transcended the duality of *this*, as ordinary consciousness, and *that*, as Mystical Consciousness. The one sameness of the permanent and undifferentiated is known to under-lie and interpenetrate all states. The state of consciousness is peculiarly indescribable and obscure. It is no more disembodied than it is embod-ied, no more of one aspect of any duality than it is of the other. Perhaps all that one can positively say is, "It Is," but It cannot be imagined. One of such Realization is no longer identical with his or her embodiment; one is both there and not there in the body. The activities and death of the body are merely events within him or her and, therefore, not involv-ing him or her.

There is a seeming discrepancy of high importance between Bud-dhism and the teaching of Shankara. It has already been shown that the doctrine of Anatman, or the nonreality of the self, is fundamental to Buddhism. In contrast, Shankara taught the Atmavidya, or Knowledge of the Self. In fact, the name of the source of the above quotation, *Atmanatma Viveka* may be translated as "Discrimination between Self and not-Self." Shankara gives the positive value to Self-Realization, but, in other respects, the fundamental similarity between Shankara's teach-ings and Buddhism has been well recognized. Here is a subject that calls for serious investigation.

There is no reasonable ground for doubt that the Way taught by the Buddha serves as an effective means whereby an undetermined number of individuals have achieved Enlightenment. This Way, insofar as it relates to a doctrinal orientation, involves the teaching of Anatman. At the very least, this gives the teaching a pragmatic justification, since it has facilitated the primary objective of the Buddha's mission. How-ever, the same may be said of Shankara's teaching of the Atmavidya, or Knowledge of the Self, which also provides an effective Way. Further, I know that it can initiate a process that, in its final stage, gives the Bud-dhist state of the twofold ego-selflessness. The implication is that the apparent incompatibility of the two teachings does not constitute a real contradiction.

Personally, I am convinced that the apparent contradiction is actually a paradox, which is a very common conceptual form that mystics employ. Because it is also a very fruitful source of misunderstanding, it is necessary to appreciate its logical significance. First of all, the mystical state of consciousness is integrative, in greater or lesser degree, depending upon the relative depth of mystical penetration. It is integrative in the sense that elements, or phases or states that are mutually incompatible when apprehended by ordinary consciousness, actually become compatible parts of a larger whole. Just as the dynamic conception of the parallelogram of forces achieves a logical integration of forces operating more or less in opposition, such as the centrifugal and centripetal forces, so the mystical state effects analogous integration for consciousness. Yet, a purely mystical integration, without the collaboration of the intellect, is not a logical conceptual integration, in contrast to the instance of the parallelogram of forces. It is an immediate integration through what we have called the "mystical sense." It is quite possible that when the mystic attempts to express conceptually the value of the mystical insight, one finds one's intellectual capacity inadequate for the task of constructing a logically connected symbol. In this case, because the intellectual level is correspondingly inferior to that of the insight, the formulation appears in paired statements that seem to negate each other, or in the form of substantives seemingly contradicted by modifying adjectives, such as "the teeming desert," "the whispering silence," and so on. However, through competent analyses, these apparent contradictions are found not to be true contradictions, for they do not affirm that x can be both A and not-A *at the same time and in the same sense*. Usually they mean that the Realization is like a somewhat that in one sense is A, but in another sense is, or incorporates, the opposite of A—all at the same time. That which is separated, and of necessity must be separated, in ordinary experience, because of the structural framework of that experience, is united in simultaneity in the mystical state. There is no logical contradiction in this.

At times, in the development of physical science, the scientist may become aware of new phenomena that partially conform with previous conceptions, but, likewise, partially violate those conceptions. This is recognized as a sign that there is need for a new conception on a higher level that shall incorporate both forms of the behavior of the phenomena within a logical whole. The same need arises when the doctrines coming forth from authentic states of mystical insight result in an unresolved paradoxical complex. The mystical insight may have developed well ahead of the intellectual evolution of these individuals, or even of the whole human race. In that case, the paradox remains until such time that someone with the requisite intellectual development, perhaps at a

The Psychological Critique of Mysticism

much later stage of human history, deals with the problem, and who, if successful, resolves it. The development of the logical sense in modern mathematics renders possible the resolution of many paradoxes that had remained unresolved for centuries, even millennia, as is illustrated by those of Zeno.

SELF (ATMAN) OR NO-SELF (ANATMAN)

I believe that at present we have developed the necessary logical and conceptual equipment for the resolution of the seeming contradiction of the Anatmic doctrine of Buddha and the Atmic doctrine of Shankara. Even if it is incomplete, it will most likely be substantial, though far from simple. First of all, let us return to Buddha's conception of the ego, the self or the "I am" as employed in the Sutra from which our quotation was taken. From the context, the reference is primarily to the personal ego (Ahamkara), that which I mean when I speak of myself as distinct from other persons, that which has various desires, inclinations, points of view, and so on that differentiate me from other beings. It is the manifest ground of competitive activities of all sorts, including the wars of nations. It is this that Buddha affirms is impermanent and, concerning which, says is the cause of ubiquitous suffering, which can never be destroyed so long as bondage to this egoism remains. In the Sanskrit Sutras, which largely constitute the basis of departure of northern from southern Buddhism, there are at least implicit references to a higher egoism, so that the profoundest states of Enlightenment involve the Realization of twofold egolessness. Let us ignore this portion of the full conception for the moment so as to focus on the simple personal egoism.

What is the ego in the simpler sense? Kant and Jung, among other Western thinkers, provide considerable assistance here. This ego is a power of subjective awareness. It is I who sees; it is I who hears and otherwise senses; and it is I who thinks, who feels, who intuits and who wills. At least it seems so. Still, there is more than pure awareness involved in this complex process. The sensing, intuiting, feeling, thinking and willing involve *forms* of being aware. The awareness operates in certain ways that, by psychological and epistemological analyses, even we of the West have been able to study extensively. To be sure, a way or form of awareness is distinguishable from pure awareness in the abstract. Abstract awareness is without any form or conditioning whatsoever; it could not be described as thinking, sensing, intuiting, feeling, willing or as conditioned by any other possible mode. If by subjectivity we mean this, and only this, then it is not the same as the ego or the subject in the concrete sense. If we conceive of Shankara's Atman as pure subjectivity, or the bare power of awareness unmodified by any form whatsoever, then it is clearly distinguishable from the egoism treated by Buddha, both in the lower and in the higher senses. Bare subjectivity, being uncompounded, is not subject to change; therefore, it neither grows nor decays. However, the concrete subject is compounded and, thus, subject to process. Hence, bondage to the concrete subject involves unending suffering.

Full analysis shows that we must make a further distinction between the concrete subject and the ego proper. The ego appears to stand as a sort of framework or form through which the concrete subject operates upon the objective, *insofar as the process falls within the field of the personal consciousness*. There remains an indeterminate zone in which the interaction between the concrete subjective and the objective takes place without passing through the personal ego. This is the zone of the psychologic unconscious. Much of the adjustment of the individual entity to the environment in which it lives does not pass through the framework of the conscious personal ego. From time to time, incursions from the unconscious enter into the egoic field of consciousness without being integrated by the ego, often without being capable of such integration unless the egoic framework is dissolved. The literature concerning both psychosis and the transformation process is full of references to such incursions. We must, therefore, enlarge the conception of the concrete subject quite beyond the limited field commanded by the individual, personally conscious ego.

Concrete subjectivity, in addition to the abstract power of pure awareness, includes innumerable forms; for this reason, it may be deemed to have a structure. Ordinarily the individual is not directly conscious of these forms. They enter into determining the form of experience but are not immediately apparent to the objective consciousness. Seemingly, this consciousness contains only the objective content as something given from outside. This view, either naively believed, or theoretically affirmed, that the content is exclusively objectively determined, is that of materialism. Strong conviction of this sort has serious effects that we shall consider later.

In any event, analysis does not have to go very far for one to see that experience is a compound effect of a subjective and objective determination. For instance, an individual who has a defect of vision that is corrected by wearing lenses when reading or looking at the objects of his or her environment, most of the time is either not at all, or only slightly, aware of the lenses. He or she might imagine that the experience of the visible world was only objectively determined. However, let this person remove the lenses and the visual world appears altered, probably becoming quite blurred. The experience changes, but not by a change from outside. If, in addition to the ordinary lenses, he or she were to wear various colored glasses, or ones producing distorted images, the individual would find his or her experience changed in each case. From this it is easy to take the further step of realizing that our way of seeing, as conditioned by the structure of the eye, plays its part in determining the world as seen. The eye of a fly would present a different kind of world. Still, behind the conditioning imposed by the visual organ, there are determinants of a more psychical nature. Seeing, as a function, has laws other than the optical limitations of the eye. We see in the form of the visual kind of space. The objective as experienced in terms of seeing must fall within this kind of space. Whatever there may be that cannot fit within that kind of conditioning could never be seen, in the visual sense.

In general, the foregoing illustration applies to all the senses and to thinking as well. It would follow that the conscious content of our experience and our thought is the mutual product of subjective and objective factors. Additionally, in order that there may be mutuality of interaction, the subjective and the objective must have a common substratum. They cannot be of wholly disparate natures. As a result, the objective can be introjected into the subjective and the subjective can be projected into the objective—psychological processes that are well known to analytic psychology. Ordinarily this occurs solely with respect to elements of the respective contents, but once the actuality of the complementary processes of introjection and projection is recognized, it is then seen that, in principle, a thoroughgoing reversal is possible. In such a case, all that which was objective becomes subjective, and vice versa.

When the focus of consciousness is extraverted—the predominant state of most objectively embodied waking consciousness most of the time—the egoic consciousness is exclusively aware of objective content. For such consciousness, introversion into sleep is equivalent to personal egoic unconsciousness, for the field of established consciousness has vanished. Yet, falling asleep is equivalent to a fairly thorough reversal of the subjective and the objective. When the objective of waking consciousness has become the subject, this objective has become the unseen, in the same sense that the subjective of waking consciousness is unseen. Of course the extraverted consciousness is typically not conscious of the subjective determinants during the waking state and thus has not built the power of personal egoic awareness in the objective of the sleeping state. What dreams there may be then are projections of the sleeping subjective—identical with the waking objective—into the sleeping objective—identical with the waking subjective. As a result, such dreams are composed of distorted objective forms, that is, objective in the sense of corresponding to the waking state. This is the kind of dream Freud analyzed.

For individuals who are more or less familiar with conscious intro-version, either spontaneous or deliberate, the waking subjective is not an entirely unfamiliar field. The individuals are more or less conscious of the subjective structure and may have acquaintance with the archetypes of the unconscious, which Jung discussed in *The Integration of Personality*. In such cases, the sleeping state may be more than a state of personal unconsciousness or dream, but may be from slightly to wholly conscious—the latter being possible as the result of superior attainment. Accordingly, the conscious experience during sleep is not a dream, but is as objectively real as ordinary waking experience. No superior reality value may justly be predicated of the objective waking experience as compared to this.

The possibility of reversal of the objective and the subjective implies certain important consequences relative to pure abstract subjectivity and abstract objectivity. Without a common ground—that which the Hindu calls "Sat"—there could be no reversal. This common ground is pure subjectivity and pure objectivity combined. It is pure subjectivity when underlying concrete subjectivity, and pure objectivity, or the bare field of consciousness, when underlying concrete objectivity. In itself, It is neither. *Its character as subjective or objective is functional, not substantial.*

Death has the value of a more profound introversion than sleep, but psychologically it has essentially the same significance as entering sleep. However, whereas sleep is a state wherein certain unconscious psychological processes continue in the extraverted sense—namely, those which maintain the organism as a breathing and living entity—death involves the introversion of all psychological processes, both con-scious and unconscious. Then, in death the reversal of the subjective and objective is more complete. That which was objective for the out-wardly living being becomes the subjective in terms of both the con-scious and the unconscious psyche. In turn, the former subjective, just as completely, becomes the new objective. These reversals are not merely successive introversions and extraversions; rather, they are compound introversion-extraversions and extraversion-introversions. One side introverts coincidentally with the extraversion of the other side. It is both a successive and a coincidental diastole and systole.

We are now in a position to deduce certain necessities of after-death states. First, the introversion of the objective implies that, in its essential nature, the objective body becomes subjective. The visible matter of the body is not involved in this, for it simply disintegrates into physical elements or compounds. Even so, it is easy to see that the objective body is not merely the visible matter. It is known that the physical matter of which the objective body is composed does not remain with it permanently during life. This matter passes into the body and then, after remaining for a time, passes away, being replaced by other matter. Thus this physical matter may be viewed as streaming through the body. The relatively persistent factor is the form and appearance of the body, though this also changes from birth to death, but always within the limits of a recognizable human pattern. The relatively persistent element is an unseen form or paradigm, without which new accretions of matter would develop anarchically, as illustrated in the case of cancer growth. This form is an energic zone, and its pattern is essentially of the nature of an idea, objectified. This becomes subjective in the death transformation, along with other psychical elements.

That which was subjective, during objective visible existence, becomes objective after death. Henceforth the egoic state has three possibilities. It may be simply unconscious, it may be aware as in a dream, or it may be awake to relative realities that are not inferior in their reality quale to objective realities during objective life. These states depend upon the preparation during objective life. An exclusively extraverted orientation of egoic consciousness during physically visible life is not aware of the introverted part of the diastolic and systolic pulsation. Part of the pulsation is quite unconscious in the egoic sense. In a rational human, however, there is one relatively introverted activity of which he or she is conscious even when the orientation is strongly extraverted—for a rational person thinks as well as experiences. As thinker an individual is more introverted than as experiencer. In the reversal at death, this thought becomes objective as experience. As the individual has thought, he or she subsequently experiences. Hence, one who during objective life thought strongly and persistently that death was complete annihilation, experiences—so to speak—complete unconsciousness, until such time as the energy resident in the thought is exhausted. However, if without this idea, he or she was wholly objectively oriented during life, the only consciousness the individual can know after death is a dream state. Not having developed consciousness of the subjective during objective life, the only possible content that can exist for him or her in the new objective, after death—which is the old subjective become objective—is projected contents from the new subjective—which is the old objective become subjective. These contents have merely the value of dreams; they are parts of the old waking life, experienced over again but guided by the thought conceptions held in life. Hence, such a one inevitably experiences in the forms of the religious teachings, if any, what he or she had accepted and believed during life, though their nature is that of dreams. In the case of one who has become discriminately conscious of the subjective determinants during objective physical life, the new objective experience, after death, has material around which to develop that is no less real than the experience of physical life. Discrimination continues beyond death, and consequently this state becomes more than a dream.

It is said that those who have aroused into activity the appropriate mystical faculty can trace these processes after death by means analogous to physically objective observation. The preceding discussion, as far as it goes, does not depend on this. It is in the nature of deduction from primary premises. If it is called a kind of "seeing," it is so in the same sense that the mathematician saw Neptune by calculation alone. Seeing through the appropriate mystical organ would be like seeing Neptune through the telescope, so would involve the corresponding problems of mastery of technique in handling the telescope and of interpretation of the image seen. An amateur might locate the wrong object, or fail to understand what she saw even if she found the right object. Nonetheless, she would have an invaluable instrument, the functions of which can be only partly replaced by calculation.

This rather extensive digression into sleep states and after-death states serves the twofold purpose of preparing the way for a more complete understanding of the mystical function, and a clearer understanding of egoism, both in the lower and in the higher senses.

As here employed, the term *mystical* carries a compound meaning including states and functional forms of consciousness. It is recognized, even by Western psychologists, that mystical consciousness may be developed to varying degrees, and, consequently, that we must deal with more than one exclusive possibility. Certainly there are qualitative differences in different mystical states, so it is only in the most profound development that we find identity of approach to identity of meaning. In a given case the mystical sense may be of a minor order, but there is a psychological similarity in all mystical development. It is always a process of introversion that reaches a level more interior than conceptual thought. Thought stands, as it were, in the center, with the mystical on one side and the perceptual on the other. To penetrate mystically is to become conscious, in greater or lesser degree, of the subjective. It is a reversal of direction of the libido, which most commonly moves in waking consciousness toward the perceptible object. It is a turning about of the focus of consciousness. For this reason, the mystic tends to become conscious in the realm of life commonly called "sleep" and "death," and in grand mysticism the process goes very much deeper. However, the mystic differs from the nonmystic in that he or she does this while still alive, in the objective sense.

Admittedly, there is a tendency toward the trance state, since beyond a certain critical point the libido tends to burst out completely in the new direction. Be that as it may, it is possible by conscious control to keep the stream of the libido divided, in which case the objective and the subjective states can be experienced simultaneously. By comparison, in many respects someone who is in a trance is just where the ordinary human is when dead, except that self-consciousness tends to be considerably greater. Remember though, as I have stated repeatedly, trance is not essential, and undoubtedly it is easier to maintain critical self-consciousness without it than with it. In any case, the mystical movement is an exceptional introversion with respect to self-consciousness.

In one feature of lesser significance, mystical development is a preparation for death. It prepares the way for an after-death state for which there is a bona fide reality quale not inferior to the objective perceptual reality. Thus it guards against a state of mere dreaming, or one of complete egoistic unconsciousness. Preparation for death is a matter of exceedingly great importance and should be the prime interest of the latter half of life. Jung is emphatically right on this point. We of the West have been foolishly negligent with respect to this matter.

We now come to the crucial consideration of egoism. Analytic psychology has, quite correctly, differentiated the personal ego from the subject. The subject includes, in addition to the conscious field of the ego, an indeterminate zone, which to the personal ego is quite unconscious. Analytic psychology conceives of the transformation as the establishment of a new self-center in the unconscious, behind the ego, as it were. This process is fundamentally mystical. It places the personal ego in a position of objectivity with respect to the new subject. Much that was formerly unconscious to the personal ego becomes conscious. However, in order to take this step in transformation, attachment to the personal ego must be weakened, if not wholly severed. So far, this accords well with the Buddhist process. The ego that has become possessed by me is no longer a fixed determinant. Instead of taking the false valuation of a sun, it is reduced to its proper status of a planet moving in orbit around the self or the subject. The ego continues to condition the appearance to the milieu of the individual entity but is not identical with that entity. As contrasted with the objective contents of consciousness, the ego has a relative fixity and unity. It is not a true invariant, but is rather like a parameter, in the sense already discussed. From birth to death a person does not remain identically the same. In the sense of egoic continuity the individual remains the same, but his or her personal character is subject to change, generally more or less imperceptibly—though, in the aggregate, quite considerably, and at times even catastrophically. The person who arises in the morning is not quite the same ego as that of the night before. Close self-analysis, as well as observation, will disclose this.

A MATHEMATICAL MODEL OF EGO METAPHYSICS

The ego may be viewed as a continuum in time that is, at every point, the center of a flowing world of experience. Experience may thus be viewed as a continuum centering upon another continuum that, at every point, is relatively fixed with respect to the former. The conception here is schematically familiar to much of mathematical thinking. Thus, in mathematical language, experience is a locus of a locus. We may view the ego as a locus of a point that is a variable dependent upon the self behind the ego.

We may now abstract two continua, one the continuum of the stream of experience, the other the continuum of the ego. In order to represent the systolic-diastolic movement, in which the objective becomes subjective and the subjective becomes objective in a periodic rhythm, we may construct two sine curves, drawn symmetrically with respect to the x-axis, as given in figure 1. The origin, at 0 (zero), is taken arbitrarily at any point where the broken (dashed) curve *LE* crosses the x-axis from below and rises above it. The y-axis represents the Field of Consciousness, both subjective and objective: +y represents the subjective field during waking, physically embodied consciousness, while –y represents the objective aspect of the field during waking consciousness. The x-axis represents Time: –x represents time in the past with

FIGURE 1

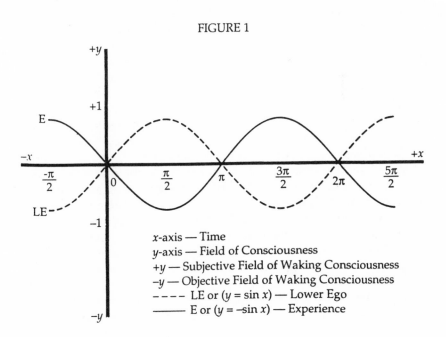

x-axis — Time
y-axis — Field of Consciousness
+y — Subjective Field of Waking Consciousness
–y — Objective Field of Waking Consciousness
– – – – LE or (y = sin x) — Lower Ego
———— E or (y = –sin x) — Experience

respect to the arbitrary point of beginning, whereas +x represents the future with respect to that same point. The broken curve LE, of the form sin x, is the continuum of the lower ego; the solid curve E, corresponding to the form -sin x, is the continuum of experience. From mathematics it is known that these curves will intersect the x-axis at 0, π and at any integral multiples of π.

The point 0 is the moment of birth of a new ego and the simultaneous beginning of experience, represented by the curve E. This is the experience of embodied objective life. The rising of the egoic curve represents the maturing of egoic consciousness, followed by its normal recession in old age up to death. The descent of the curve of experience marks intensification of experiential content, followed by a corresponding decline. At π is the point of death of the objective phase and the transition point to the reversal of the subjective-objective. Between π and 2π the curve of the ego lies in what was the objective phase of physically embodied consciousness. The experiential curve moves in symmetrical balance on the opposite side of the x-axis. The range from 0 to π covers the cycle of embodied experience, while π to 2π covers the cycle of after-death consciousness or experience. In the second cycle, that which was thought or contained in the subjective in the first, becomes objective as experience, and vice versa.

I am indebted to Mohini Chatterji for the initial suggestion that the permanent ego of an incarnation may be viewed as the time integral of all the instantaneous states of the ego through the continuum of a lifetime. I have found that the use of the definite integral in this connection brings out a fuller figure. If we take the definite integral of the curve LE between 0 and π, we get the area enclosed by this arc of the curve and the x-axis. Curiously, it has the value of 2, quite an interesting fact, since we are dealing with dualistic or subject-object consciousness. We may regard the definite integral, or the above area, as the total unified ego of the incarnation. That is to say, the "I am," which in the first instance seems like a point, fixed at any instant, but actually flowing in time, becomes as a totality, space-like. Psychologically, its significance shifts from that of the contained to the container—but it is the container of subjective psychical contents. If we take the definite integral from π to 2π, we have the same result in the reverse sense, that is, –2. So, the definite integral from 0 to 2π has the value of 0. This is the conclusion of the cycle of the given ego. The following new birth is the beginning of a new ego, which may be viewed as the offspring of its predecessor. This is in conformity with the Buddhist doctrine of the ego.

The constant factor throughout this entire process is the Field of Consciousness, which takes on subjective and objective coloring depending on whether It appears as objective, as the ground of experience, or as subjective, as the ground of the ego. In Itself, in Its own nature, It is neither subjective nor objective, but only appears as one or the other depending on the coloring given by the approach. Through the ego, It appears as Pure Subjectivity.

Shankara's approach is through the ego; hence, the Ground is reached as Pure Subjectivity, or the potential of all awareness—an absolutely permanent principle involving time. The diametrically opposite approach, by piercing through the objective, is suggested as a theoretical possibility.

To approach the Ultimate through the subject appears to me the easiest way. Pure Subjectivity, when reached or Realized, by its own nature transforms into the subjective-objective, and then to Its real nature as neither subjective nor objective, and finally there remains only the ineffable Ground of Consciousness-without-an-object and without-a-subject.

The Ground lies outside all conditioning, and therefore may not be said to develop or evolve. Evolution or development has a one-way dependence upon the Ground. The cycle of progression of the personal egoic consciousness is an endless series in its own dimension. Yet, there is such a thing as real progression. However, we must conceive of this not as continuation along the lines of the sine curves, but as a progressive integration rising in another dimension in such a way that earlier stages are embraced within the latter.

FIGURE 2

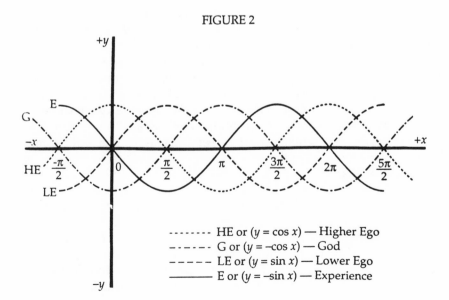

```
------- HE or (y = cos x) — Higher Ego
------ G or (y = –cos x) — God
----- LE or (y = sin x) — Lower Ego
——— E or (y = –sin x) — Experience
```

It is readily suggested to us that if we take the indefinite integral of the sine curves we would arrive at a higher integration. In performing this, and working out the consequent interpretations, I had several surprises. Some of the consequences were quite at variance from certain preconceptions that I had held, but, in studying the logic of the whole complex, I reached the conclusion that my preconceptions had been in error. A number of mystical elements began to slip into place, forming a larger, comprehensible whole. I do not by any means suggest that we have in the final effect the whole picture, even though I find the integration quite remarkable. As a thinkable schema, the whole is rather complicated, independent of the degree of simplicity of the direct Realization.

The indefinite integral of $\sin x \, dx$ is $-\cos x$. Referring to figure 2, this gives the dotted curve HE, with respect to which the irregularly broken curve G corresponds, in the same relation that curves LE and E have to each other. It will be noted that these curves are at their respective maxima and minima at the points

$$0, \pi, 2\pi, \cdots, n\pi, \cdots,$$

the precise points at which the curves LE and E intersect the x-axis. Similarly, at points

$$\tfrac{\pi}{2}, \tfrac{3\pi}{2}, \cdots, (n+1)\tfrac{\pi}{2}, \cdots,$$

where curves LE and E are at their respective maxima and minima, the curves HE and G intersect the x-axis. The curve HE represents the Higher Ego, and the curve G represents the metaphysical reality corresponding to the Divinity or God—the Higher Ego in its aspect as objective. Since subjectivity by itself is an abstraction, but no real existence, all entities are subjective-objective. This principle would have to apply to the Higher Ego as well as to the lower ego. Thus, just as the lower ego, when objectively considered, is humankind, so also the Higher Ego would have its objective counter aspect. For reasons that will become clear later, I have called this the "Divinity" or "God."

The points

$$\pi, 3\pi, 5\pi, \cdots, (2n+1)\pi, \cdots,$$

are the points in time of the death of the personal being, though in a more superficial interpretation, they are also the points of going to sleep, and in a profounder sense, they are the points of mystical death. The complex of curves in figure 2 is thus a generalized schema lending itself to major and minor interpretations. It will be noted that, fundamental to the whole interpretation, the curves stand in relationships of perfect symmetry, which indicates that they represent processes in perfect equilibrium. Hence, this symbolism is consonant with the conception that Equilibrium is the essence of Law, an idea developed in the commentaries on the "Aphorisms on Consciousness-without-an-object."*

The points

$$0, 2\pi, 4\pi, \cdots, 2n\pi, \cdots,$$

are the points in time of the birth of the personal being, of awakening from sleep, and of return from the mystic state to objective polarization of consciousness, corresponding to ordinary waking consciousness. The points

$$\tfrac{\pi}{2}, \tfrac{5\pi}{2}, \tfrac{9\pi}{2}, \cdots, (2n + \tfrac{1}{2})\pi, \cdots,$$

are the points in time of the birth of God, in the phase analogous to the birth of the personal being. The points

$$\tfrac{3\pi}{2}, \tfrac{7\pi}{2}, \tfrac{11\pi}{2}, \cdots, (2n + \tfrac{3}{2})\pi, \cdots,$$

are the points in time when the God dies objectively. It must constantly be kept in mind that birth in one phase is, at the same time, death in the opposite phase, and vice versa. The words *birth* and *death* thus refer to transition in phase, not to *de novo* becoming or to extinction.

In studying the curve *LE*, we find that when personal egoism rises to a maximum, the objective life of humankind is in its objective development. In terms of psychical energy, the libido has developed furthest into the objective. This corresponds to the lowest point of the curve *E*, which means that the visible being is then at its prime. However, at this point the curves *HE* and *G* intersect the x-axis, the point of greatest recession of psychical energy in the divine counterpart of humanity. Here, at $\tfrac{\pi}{2}$, the God dies inwardly, and thenceforth grows outwardly as the individual decreases toward outward death. At this latter death, the transference of the libido to the outwardly manifest God is at a maximum.

At the moment of personal death, the God is objectified in maximum degree. In other words, the introversion of the personal life corresponds to the infilling of the God with life, while extraversion draws life from the God. This leads to a remarkable clarification of Nietzsche's

---

*Wolff, *Consciousness*, part 2.

famous dictum: "God is dead." The God is dead whenever the individual or collective being achieves maximum extraversion. Fixation in extraversion is equivalent to killing God. This will explain the spiritual barrenness of the more extensively empirical sciences. Since Darwinism, in the philosophical sense, is the acme of materialism, it is equivalent to the death of the God, that is, loss of spiritual consciousness.

Our primary interest here is connected with the mystical processes, rather than with the ordinary periodicity of birth and death. We must generalize our conception of time represented by the x-axis. This time in some situations, such as ordinary birth and death, night and day, and so on, may well be regarded as identical with the cosmic or objective time determined by the stars. Yet, this is a sort of collective time that may not synchronize with the individual time sequence. The base of time is succession of states of consciousness. In the case of the mystic, the time sequence is not identical with the time of the objective stars. The succession of the mystic's states of consciousness introduces a periodicity of its own, which, while symmetrically balanced on its own scale, may appear asymmetrical in its relation to objective cosmic time. When the succession of states of consciousness is very rapid, in terms of the objective time, the cycle of life may appear very short, and vice versa. Hence, the oscillation of the mystic may be—indeed is—a true periodicity, even though the arrangement of phases in terms of cosmic time, as noted by the observer, may be quite asymmetrical. If in the mystic's development a certain step in transformation takes ten years, in one case, and ten minutes in another, then in the mystical sense the time interval in the two cases is the same. The life of the mystic qua mystic is to be isolated from the worldly cycles of the visible person. We shall therefore consider the complex of curves in relation to the mystic in abstraction from ordinary life.

The moment of mystical death—which is identical with the moment of inward birth—is the moment of extreme introversion, when life in the individual is reduced to a minimum, and the life of the God reaches a maximum. God is the Presence Realized by the mystic; further, with some psychical organizations, this can be a seen Presence. It is easy to identify it with the Heavenly Father of Christ, the pattern normally followed by those whose reality orientation is primarily objective. For those whose primary orientation has been to the subjective, the Realization is equivalent to identification with the Higher Ego, which is the same as being identical with the God, rather than experiencing God as Presence. Mystical records give both patterns. Christian mysticism is mainly of the former type.

If we integrate the curves *HE* and *G*, we get the original curves *LE* and *E*. This implies that the pairs, *LE* and *HE* and *E* and *G*, stand in interdependent relation to each other. The higher and lower egos are not separable and, in the last analysis, the distinction of higher and lower is not absolute. This conclusion is sound. "High" and "low" have meaning only from the perspective of a relative base. From the standpoint of the ultimate Ground, there is no meaning in this relativity. The same point applies in the relationship between God and humanity. The obvious conclusion may be somewhat shocking to some pietists, but it has strong mystical support. Significantly, it has been said that Buddha taught the Gods as well as people. Also, Meister Eckhart said, "For man is truly God, and God is truly man." Angelus Silesius said, "I am as great as God, and He is small like me; He cannot be above, nor I below Him be." It is surely true that human reality is not a whit greater than that of God, but it is as great as God's. The mystical need is mutual. Only the God-man attains superiority, for only he has attained the dual consciousness, synthesized. Only he has freed himself from dependence upon the cycle of evolution. Insofar as he continues in the interweaving of evolution, it is as a process within him, not as something that possesses him. This is the Liberated State.

From the standpoint of the Ground, all Gods and all humans, all egos, whether higher or lower, inhere in the Ultimate, which is neither subjective nor objective. Eckhart reveals his profundity in that he has Realized the relativity of God and man, but also the ultimate inherence of both in the Godhead, which is not subject to becoming. This Godhead is identical with the Ground, or Consciousness-without-an-object and without-a-subject.

Just as the complex of sine and cosine curves extend to positive and negative infinity, so also, evolution has no beginning nor end. It is a mistake to think that the evolutionary stream ceases after full Enlightenment. The Enlightened One is free just because he is consciously one with the Ground, and so the evolutionary stream flows within him, instead of he upon it. The stream remains as it always has been and ever will be, but for the Enlightened One it is no longer a source of bondage, no longer a well of sorrow, but is, as it were, the revelry of the Eternal. Neither of the two Doors of Ashvaghosha is ever closed.

The foregoing is not a metaphysical dissertation, but rather a determination of how a metaphysical reality and experience are possible. If we regard the physical as the objective with respect to ordinary waking experience, then we may regard the metaphysical as the objective in the inverse phase, or after-death consciousness. In another sense, the metaphysical is the objective aspect of the consciousness of God, but it must be remembered that God and man are interdependent phases of one entity. The Ground underlies both the physical and the metaphysical.

This discussion is psychological in the sense of metapsychology. By the term *metapsychology* I mean the study of that portion of psychical structure that is not accessible to objective empirical methods, as such. Because empirical methodology is limited by sensible determination, it is restricted within a zone of possibility, such that, although development in this zone may be indefinitely extended, it can only give a certain type of knowledge. Immediate acquaintance with the material of metapsychology is possible only through the arousal and development of the mystical faculty in the appropriate degree.

Something of indirect acquaintance with metapsychology is possible through what we might call the "eye" of mathematics. Just as through mathematics we can "see" into the structure of matter further than it is possible to follow with the senses, so may we likewise see in this same way into the more ultimate structure of the total human psychical nature. It is not a complete knowledge, much as the knowledge of Neptune through sheer calculation is not entire, but in its own dimension it may develop without limits, save that of the capacity of human understanding. Some hold the position that no science becomes truly scientific until it achieves mathematical formulation. The premathematical stage of a science might be viewed as its adolescent phase. Then, when the concepts assume mathematical form, the science achieves maturity. I have always supported this view.

Why is it that a person may think in terms of pure mathematical construction, without thought of any application beyond mathematics itself, yet this structure later proves valuable for other than purely mathematical ends? For example, the geometry of Riemann was a development from abstract theory that eventually rendered possible the conception of the general theory of relativity. Einstein supplied the necessary integration with physical determination, but independently, as pure thought, Riemann supplied the structural form. This is by no means an isolated instance of this sort. Since the development of non-Euclidean geometry, it has been evident that mathematics is not an existence beyond thought; that is, it is not a structure in an external and independent nature. It is rather the necessitarian aspect of thought. Even so, a necessity of thought is also a necessity of nature just to the extent that nature is determined by thought. Certainly nature derives a portion of its determination, as we experience it, through our thinking. So I believe we may say with justice that the eye of the mathematician sees into the deep structure of the subjective psyche, although the formal mathematician may not realize the psychical significance of her construction.

Jung calls attention to the interesting fact that the profound poet, following only an aesthetic ideal, so far as his personal consciousness is concerned, actually reveals truth of great psychological significance. It may require great psychological understanding to interpret the poem, but when this is done, meaning is revealed of which the poet-creator knew little or nothing. Thus it is also with the pure mathematician, I believe, in even profounder degree. Even though the mathematician may start with seemingly meaningless fantasy, the thought does not develop arbitrarily, but according to rigorous necessity. In this we have revealed underlying law in its nakedness. The pure thought of mathematics is actually a study of the ultimate nature of that total being, revealed to us objectively as humankind. May it not be that mathematical thought is the speech of the Divinity in our inner consciousness? If so, then mathematical thought is inner communion.

In this discussion of Christ, Buddha and Shankara I have dealt but lightly with the lives and teachings of these great beings. I have attempted to show that these outstanding fountainheads of religion and philosophy are surpassingly great exemplars of grand mysticism. Because of the lack of introspective biographical material, I have not been able to employ the methods so dear to the heart of the empiric psychologist. I have derived the evidence of the mystical quality of these figures through the following kinds of manifestations:

1. The external evidence from their biographies, so far as they exist, relative to the period prior to the beginning of their missions, is virtually silent concerning this significant part of the life of Christ. The Buddha clearly employed the method of Samadhi under the Bo tree, and Shankara had all the knowledge and training available as a Brahmin.
2. Evidence of how they lived during the fulfillment of their respective missions shows that each of them lived the typical life of the Sannyasin.*
3. The evidence from the type of influence each exerted upon his entourage establishes that their followers developed a desire for mystical Realization, which in many instances was fulfilled. The influence was only partly through the teachings, but perhaps more largely through the personality of the teachers.
4. Evidence from the inner content of the teachings is decisive. All teach the objective of otherworldliness. They taught different methods of

*[Although this term normally applies to one who is still a seeker, it refers generally to a spiritual wanderer who has renounced worldly possessions.]

attainment, but their objective was substantially the same. The conceptual interpretation of the end varied, both in form and extent of development, but I believe I have shown that all three shared an essential congruence.

My approach to mysticism as a psychological problem has been governed by two canons:

1. The understanding of any way of consciousness is better achieved by dealing first with the inner meaningful content and then proceeding to its more objective behavioristic aspects. The content, rather than the behavior that forms the material of empiric psychology, then stands as monitor.
2. It is better to look high first, before looking low, since the resulting view is the broad perspective from the mountaintop, rather than the restricted one of the valley, often a narrow ravine.

Having established our base of approach, the next task will be the consideration of detailed psychological criticism of mystical states of consciousness. This I shall essay primarily with reference to Leuba's critique.

13

Mystical Knowledge

The central interest of the present work is concerned with the noetic value of mystical states of consciousness. The preceding discussion deals predominantly with noetic content, either as native to the mystical state, or as a precipitated effect within the intellectual consciousness. Some attention, particularly in the previous chapter, has been given to a critical consideration of the problem of whether we are justified in viewing the noetic element as true knowledge or only delusion. We must now treat this problem more systematically and completely.

CRITIQUE OF LEUBA'S METHODOLOGY

James Leuba has devoted much research and thought to the problem of mysticism, and finally concludes that

> for the psychologist who remains within the province of science, religious mysticism is a revelation not of God but of man. Whoever wants to know the deepest that is in man, the hidden forces that drive him onward, should become a student of mysticism. And if knowing man is not knowing God, it is nevertheless only when in possession of an adequate knowledge of man that metaphysics may expect to fashion an acceptable conception of the Ultimate.*

This does not deny all value to mystical states of consciousness. Indeed, it confers a much higher valuation than one who is familiar with his book might have expected, since its general effect is a rather radical depreciation of the mystical state, along with its contents. Anyone who reads the present work, and its companions, *Pathways Through to Space*, and *The Philosophy of Consciousness without an Object*, and who understands their true meaning, will find no interpretation of the mystical

---

*Leuba, 318.

state as implying an authentication of an extracosmic, anthropological or personal God. The word *God* has been used here to symbolize the Supreme Value in human consciousness, but not as meaning a self-existence in the sense of a being or entity that serves as the Ground of the universe. The conception of God as a personal force that can interfere with the operation of natural law is repudiated either directly or by implication. I am quite willing to agree with Leuba when he claims that "mysticism is a revelation of man," provided that humankind has not been defined beforehand in such a way as to be prejudicial to such revelation of human nature as mystical insight may give. We must be prepared to find that it may mean as much, or more, than the theistic religions have attributed to God. In that case, we are immeasurably more than our biological classification as a "plantigrade, featherless, biped mammal of the genus Homo."

Also, I agree that it is "only when in possession of an adequate knowledge of man that metaphysics may expect to fashion an acceptable conception of the Ultimate."* However, it must, most positively, be an *adequate* knowledge. Adopting an unsound epistemology would destroy the adequacy of the knowledge gained. The epistemological assumptions of physical science are, themselves, subject to criticism. They have not been held eternally in the past but are the result of development. It is sheer egotistical conceit for the physical scientist to imagine that his or her knowledge is the ultimate product of such development. Thus, if the subject-object framework of knowledge is a distortion of Ultimate Truth, as the mystical philosopher maintains—for to know mystically is to know in a way transcending the subject-object sense—then physical science as a whole is such a distortion, as is all other relative cognition.

Consequently, to know humankind, the study of mysticism must exceed the external study of mysticism by scientific methodology, which is grounded in certain limiting epistemological assumptions. One must personally achieve the inside view of the mystical state, and not be content with conceptual reports supplied by mystics. It is as little possible to derive the state from the conceptual portrayal of it as it would be for someone born blind to know the immediate actuality of light from the conceptions related to light. Much that we know of light depends upon the immediate sensuous intuitions of the visible world, and these intuitions are a component part of most of our actual discourse concerning light. Undoubtedly, we could formulate a mathematics of light phenomena that would not involve this intuition and which could be understood by a blind person who

*Leuba, 318.

had the requisite mathematical ability. However, the mathematical signs and expressions would have no referent for him. If he imagined a referent that satisfied the mathematical definitions, and then somehow acquired sight, he would almost certainly find the actuality in its immediate quale wholly unexpected. The quale of that which he had imagined would be conditioned by his sensuous imagination *in terms of the senses he already possessed.* The experience of the immediate value of the seen world might well add nothing to the purely mathematical conception of light phenomena, though it might suggest further development. By comparison, his nonmathematical knowledge of the world of light would be vastly extended. For instance, there could be an experience of beauty that was quite other than the intellectual beauty that might be contained in the mathematical conception. Also, there could be a development of aesthetic criticism that would be quite impossible for one initially blind who has not gained vision.

Taken with the above reservations and interpretations, Leuba's conclusion is acceptable. However, before he reaches it, he develops a searching critique of the significance of the mystical state of consciousness. This ultimately results in a virtual denial of all spiritual value for it, particularly in the sense of spiritual knowledge. Further, he orients his whole approach through the phenomena of drug intoxication. Entirely apart from the methodological criticism of this kind of approach, which I have already developed, there is something in it that hits one with the force of a moral shock. From the evidence, there are mystoid states that can be induced by certain drugs and other chemical substances. Even so, to imply that these states are substantially identical with the Realizations gained by the most exacting moral, spiritual and intellectual discipline involves something that is little, if at all, less than profanation. It is rank injustice for the investigator to assume that there is no fundamental difference between a drunkard and exemplary spiritual beings, such as Christ, Buddha and Shankara. It is like classifying an honorable and upright householder with a panderer to the lusts. How must one feel who has endeavored for decades to live by the exacting moral code of a religious discipline, when he or she finds his or her ultimate Realization thus evaluated?

Remember, the price of true attainment is always high. The Way is straight and narrow. The aspirant must be prepared to offer all upon the altar of sacrifice: private yearnings and loves; ambitions and fond convictions; life and worldly honor; ultimately, even his or her hope of attaining the goal. Only in this way is the barrier of personal egoism dissolved. Then one must labor as do the ambitious, but without the urge of personal ambition; study assiduously as the scholar, yet without expectation of professional recognition; maintain a compassionate consideration for the suffering of all other creatures, while dealing sternly with his or her own private suffering. One must be prepared to pass through the valley of despair, yet persevere on the course. Indeed, on occasions, one may skirt the abyss of madness, yet never falter. Not with all is the trial the same, nor equally severe, but, always, of all labors known to humankind, it is the most exacting. In the end, after many years, perhaps near the end of life, one stands before the Gate, which opens not until the consummation of the final renunciation. This is the Realization that there is nothing to be attained, with which the seeker abandons the search, content that the Gate should never open—but at that moment he or she has turned the key. The mystic Gate has opened! Is it not the acme of unwisdom to imagine that all this brings no greater fruit than the dream of the drunkard and the drug addict? Shame on whoever suggests this. No worse did the lust-ridden monsters of Nero's Rome do to the followers of the Christic Light.

Full investigation is possible into the nature of the states of consciousness induced by narcotic and hypnotic drugs, anesthetics and alcohol only by those who have passed through them. In this I am not qualified, and am quite unwilling to pay the frightful price of qualifying by damaging the mystical function. The only experience I have had with a drug effect was from three one-quarter-grain tablets of codeine taken over a period of some nine or ten hours to relieve extreme pain from an injury. By the end of this period I decided that the pain was more tolerable than the effect of the drug. Near the end of this time I experienced psychical effects induced by the narcotic. The intellectual, judging consciousness was present, and while not capable of concentrated and precise effort, still knew that the psychical state induced was an illusion, yet was interested in it in a somewhat amused fashion. I was lying in bed when I found myself *also* outside the window by the bed. Then, continuing conscious in the bed all the while, I was over by the east corner of the house, where I saw an immense hawser lying in a somewhat serpentine line along the ground. Presently, this was the Von Hindenburg line in Western Europe during World War I. The hawser being, rather than becoming, the Von Hindenburg line seemed perfectly reasonable to the state of consciousness. Yet, all the while, the intellectual consciousness in the bed knew that this was a hallucination. Qualitatively, the state was intensely unpleasant. The feeling might be likened to the way one would feel if immersed in a mucky, muggy pool of a sticky, viscous liquid. Nothing that I know is so completely opposite the state of genuine mystic Realization as this, in its affective and noetic effect. It was a blurred, twilight kind of consciousness. If that is the sort of thing Leuba means by trance, his characterization of it as degraded is quite justified. Nevertheless, it is as little like the genuine mystical state as essence of skunk is like attar of roses, or modern swing music is like a Bach fugue. I do not consider that the true approach to the understanding of fine perfume lies in a self-saturation with essence of skunk, or that a just evaluation of lofty classical music can be attained by attending the maudlin orgies of swing. Yet, all too often, such seems to be the predilection of the physiological psychologist.

The state of mystical Realization, as I know it, is in a measure comparable with an experience, known by some, that is not generally classed as mystical. In my academic life there were occasions when I had to master, or wished to master, conceptions that I could not understand at all at my normal level of concentration. I shall describe the process involved in two instances of this sort. Once I had to prepare a paper on Kant's transcendental deduction of the Categories, and on another occasion, in a class in the theory of groups, I had to read an article in a mathematical journal to prepare an analogous paper that was possible only by understanding the article. In both cases, at first reading, at a normal level of concentration, I simply derived no understanding whatsoever. Later, in each case, I concentrated to an extreme intellectual pitch such that, in the resultant state, which had a luminous value, I was able to assimilate the articles and write my theses, which passed the criticism of my instructors. Yet, this did not mean that, at the normal level of concentration afterward, I understood either what I read or what I wrote. Some "pitching up" still remained necessary. All this suggests differences in intellectual level that may be crossed by the appropriate effort and the willingness to pay the price exacted. One gets a pain in the head, literally, and the organism takes quite a bit of punishment. Still, at the level of high pitch, certain values are known that are not realized at other times. There is a sense of light and, at times, of ecstatic beauty when integrating conceptions are born in the mind. Of anything that I know, this comes the nearest to paralleling the mystical state. The main differences are:

1. The mystical state has a much greater luminous value.
2. The intellect sees deeper and more keenly.
3. The ecstatic value is vastly greater and includes moral beatitude.
4. All of this develops in a state of relaxation, with no intellectual strain.
5. The organism gains refreshment, rather than enduring fatigue.

There is a difference between intellectual seeing under the strain of heavy concentration and "clear-seeing" with the "eye" of the mind when the intellect is relaxed but alert. In both cases, one may come to understand the same conceptions. However, in the former case, one is operating on a lower level of mind, straining to reach above himself. In the latter case, the understanding is not something forced, but is largely spontaneous. One stands on a higher level and easily uses resources below it. This is part of the meaning of mystical awakening. Something, which may be likened to a new organ, begins to function.

Here we are not dealing with the ultimate depths of the mystical consciousness nor, from the records, would I judge it a part of all mystical experiences. Robert Vaughn, in his *Hours with the Mystics*,* distinguishes between the mysticism of sentiment and that of thought. My own study has led me to acknowledge that there is justice in this distinction. It appears that the mystic Gate opens into a realm of many possibilities. Some of these I know directly, while of others, that I have found reported, I can see the possibility. For all those who know this land, there is a common basic language, the sign of a common brotherhood. Nonetheless, to be born into this realm is not enough to be master of all its possibilities. One develops within the subregion for which one is naturally best suited, and to which one's inclination leads. Doubtless, in this domain, as in the ordinary world, there are those who feel most and know little, but there are also those who value most the mystic knowledge, colored by the mystic feeling. In the far distance of that mystic land, there rise the snowcapped mountain peaks, and, among them, that vast mountain of mountains that reaches beyond the vision of relative consciousness into the sky of the inconceivable, where only definition by strict negation applies.

THE MYSTIC THOUGHT

There is a mystic thought, which is not at all the same as the objective language of words in which the mystic writes or speaks his or her thought, however crudely or well. There is a thought beyond all words that is like a stream within the mind. It has no part with definable concepts. Concerning this supernal realm, the definitive concept may be likened unto a vessel immersed in the sea. The form of the vessel is the definitive concept, while the water that it contains is its substantive meaning. By analogy, just as the water, in its inherent nature, has not the shape of the vessel, the meaning overflows the form of the concept. The concept (vessel) has truth bestowed upon it by reason of the meaning (water) that it holds, but many vessels may hold water. The thought that is of identical nature with the sea is like the oceanic currents that

---

*Vaughn.

flow from shore to shore, distinguishable as currents, yet not distinguishable from the whole ocean as water. In the end, the flow of any current mingles indistinguishably with the whole. One who finds thought thus thinking within discovers no words therein nor concepts that his or her personal understanding can embrace but knows the truth of the thought, and that remains.

Then, later, out of this thought is born another kind of thought, which partly thinks itself, and partly one thinks with contributed effort. It is all exceedingly clear and employs word concepts, seemingly as one might speak or write. However, they are not yet speakable or writable. They are thoughts of which the words are the cream of human abstraction. They fly like the royal bird from peak to peak of the best of mundane apprehension. The continuity is the flight of the bird, and for this, mundane human verbal construction fails. Once again it must be thought, this time by laborious effort, tracing the way from peak to peak through the stony valleys between, until, at last, there is the thought of words and syntax. Yet, at best, this is only a poor product, a fraction of a fraction, in which some drops of the supernal waters remain.

It is the self-moving, inarticulate, flowing thought that constitutes the primary ground of the noetic aspect of mystical consciousness. I do not see any possible means of achieving direct acquaintance with this thought, other than by deep introversion. It may well be an unseen determinant in all thinking, and it is not inconceivable that a sufficiently acute analysis of objective thinking might have to hypothesize such an unseen thought. At present, I am unable to speak more positively with respect to this possibility. In any case, by means of sufficiently profound introversion, this inner spiritual thought may be known directly. It certainly is not under the direction or control of the personal ego. At the appropriate level of mystical penetration wherein both the personal egoic thought and the higher thought are conscious, within a common zone of consciousness, the personally directed thought may query the higher thought, either by a direct question or by tentative predication. This will initiate a responsive activity in the higher thought. The effect of this process is partially assimilable by the personal mind, but it continues into depths where the latter cannot follow. Notably, the effect upon the personal mind is that of unequivocal demonstration not unlike nor less convincing than rigorous mathematical demonstration. At this level, the mystic can say he or she knows in the identical sense that the mathematician can say he or she knows after the formal demonstration of a theorem. The logic of the higher thought is, to one who stands consciously in its presence, manifestly no less conditioned by logical inevitability than is the case with the more objective mathematical thought. Is one justified in calling this "knowledge," and the determination of the thought, "truth"? Unconditionally, I would say that it is no less so than is the process of demonstration and the consequent of pure mathematics thus legitimately viewed.

Still, does pure mathematics give truth and knowledge? This question leads us into already extant philosophical controversy. In the most general sense, it leads to the perennial dispute between rationalists and empiricists. Of course, I shall not attempt to do what no philosopher has yet been able to accomplish, namely, to achieve a final resolution of the issue that would be universally acceptable. Rather, I simply take my stand with the rationalists and deny the adequacy of the empiricists' definition of truth and knowledge, letting the issue rest there. All that I seek to establish at this point is that the question as to whether mystical content is noetic is essentially identical with the issue of whether the content of pure mathematics is noetic. Hence, it becomes a question of logic and epistemology, rather than one of physiological psychology. The controversy is thus raised to a level of much higher dignity.

In the above thesis, I have affirmed direct acquaintance with a thought process that is accessible at a certain level of mystical penetration and, so far as I know, only thus accessible. From the standpoint of general discourse, it is, admittedly, unsatisfactory to introduce, as a necessary constituent, an element that is not one of common acquaintance. The higher thought is not discursively proven to be an implication from commonly known elements. Of course, as a matter of formal discourse, there is a begging of the question here. I concede this. I simply oppose to this the fact that, in the antimystical view of the physiological psychologist, analysis will also show analogous, conscious or unconscious, philosophical presuppositions that also beg the question. Every philosophy and philosopher is vulnerable before this charge. All I hope to prove is a way, if not *the* way, in which noetic mystical content is possible in principle and, in the negative sense, to refute the antimystical pretension of disproof of this possibility. Success in this project would mean that henceforth, for discourse, the issue is an open one, incapable of being closed by the methods of physiological psychology. In the zone wherein discourse must be neutral, faith or predilection has the logical right to be determinant in the personal attitude. Accordingly, the antimystical attitude is unassailable if it grounds itself in mere wishful thinking, but then the position will have forfeited all right to scientific and discursive respect.

An objectively formulated thought—that is, in terms of word concepts and conforming to the rules of syntax—that has its source and reference in the transcendental thought has only incidental relationship to sensible objects and relatives. A fertile source of confusion lies in the fact that, in large degree at least, the word concepts have a perceptual derivation and are mainly employed with a perceptual reference. Consequently, the objectively formulated mystical thought, on its surface, appears to be a statement concerning the objective world. One who assumes this kind of meaning for this thought will scarcely find anything intelligible in it. It will not have any conceivable relationship with actual objective experience. Hence, it is easier to judge it as meaningless fantasy.

The judgment that it has no relationship to empiric content is largely true, but the further judgment that it is meaningless fantasy is wholly false. Again we find a parallelism in pure mathematics. Here also we have a language that is composed, in part, of word concepts normally having a perceptual reference, though the mathematical reference is nonperceptual. Assuredly, it is for this reason that mathematics has been humorously defined as the science of simple words with difficult meanings. A mind that is in too great bondage to the empiric is hopelessly lost when it attempts to grasp the thought of pure mathematics and, for substantially the same reason, it is lost with respect to mystical thought. The weakness here does not lie in pure mathematical thought nor in mystical thought, but in the intellect that is in bondage to the empirical.

From the standpoint of active participation in the external world of affairs, the mystical thought may render little or no assistance. It may even lead to becoming disconnected from external matters. However, this is quite as irrelevant as the similar effect that pure mathematical thought has upon the mathematician. Pure mathematicians are rarely ever personally effective in worldly affairs. (In this, the German mathematician Leibniz is an outstanding exception.) Their absentmindedness with respect to the objective is notorious. From the perspective of the standard of values of the pugilist or soldier, they are apt to seem mostly like ineffective babes. Nevertheless, none of this is relevant in the estimation of their true attitude. Too much of the real power of pure mathematical thought has been precipitated through applied mathematics into the field of empiric power for the intelligent nonmathematician to deny the worth and potency of pure mathematical thought. The same power, in another dimension, exists in the mystical thought, although its demonstration to the empirically bound mind is considerably more difficult. However, the influence of the Buddhas and the Christs does constitute part of this demonstration.

KNOWLEDGE AS NEGATION

The second sense in which I affirm that mystical consciousness manifests noetic value is related to the ultimate stage of mystical penetration.

In this case, I mean "ultimate" from the standpoint of the objective witness. I do not mean that there are not still further depths, as I know the reverse to be true. From the objective standpoint, the ultimate is the point of universal negation of everything relative. To the objective consciousness, the language of the mystic at this point suggests absolute unconsciousness, though the inference that it is simply unconsciousness is neither logically necessary nor true. It will not profit us to consider whether the state of consciousness beyond the point of disappearance may be called "knowledge," for objective concepts simply have no relevance there. Yet, may it be viewed as a state of knowledge in its relation to the relative? I think we must say "Yes," quite definitely. It is knowledge as negation of everything relative. It is genuinely knowledge because to know as negation is as truly knowledge as to know as affirmation. We may take as an illustration the case of a person who perceives what in reality is a mirage, but who does not yet know its true nature. In affirmative terms, she says, "There is a lake with boats upon it and trees along its border." This is like knowledge in the ordinary empiric sense. Later, when she recognizes that the seeming objects are only a mirage, she then says, "There is no lake; there are no boats and no trees." This resembles the mystical negation of all discursive concepts and all sensible perceptions. Clearly, it is an accession of knowledge, even though, relative to the earlier state that cognized a lake, boats and trees, it is knowledge as pure negation. In our common practice in such a situation, we definitely do not regard whoever cognizes a lake, boats and trees as the person possessing knowledge. Rather, whoever realizes that it is only a mirage is the true knower and discriminator. Here attainment of knowledge is equivalent to absolute negation of the earlier state. *To become aware of the reality of the nonbeing of that which was formerly believed in as being is attainment of true Knowledge.*

SHIFT IN THE BASE OF REFERENCE

There is a third sense in which mystical orientation affects knowledge, and therefore is a knowledge determinant. To one who has had no more than passing mystical glimpses, we may properly speak of such as "experiences," since the orientation still remains centered in the personal ego. We have simply what seems a strange content that cannot be successfully integrated within the previous system. It remains as an unassimilated irritant that tends to raise doubt as to his socially inherited reality-orientation. However, one who has passed through the mystical transformation has shifted his center of self-reference. In mystical language, he has perished and been born again. Strictly speaking, this is not change of content of cognition, but change of the base of orientation to cognition, and therefore is not experience. Again, disregarding the relationship of the newborn to the *proper* content of the mystical consciousness, we have to consider the effect of the change of base of self-identity to relative cognition. Henceforth, from the time of the new birth, when thinking in terms of his essential reality thought—but not in his more or less frequent "as if" thinking from the base of the old ego— the mystic integrates the whole of relative cognition about a new center or base of reference. This is equivalent to a radical alteration in the significance of the whole body of relative cognition. Shift in significance is a noetic alteration and, hence, accession of knowledge.

May the shift in base of reference validly be called a "change of knowledge"? Excluding the real possibility of new content becoming possible directly as the result of change of perspective, we have two components that I believe are to be viewed justly as noetic: (1) change in meaning, and (2) acquaintance with the fact of base of reference and its determinant place with respect to cognitive content; moreover, there is the possibility and actuality of more than one base of reference. The question just posed has its analogues in the three following events in the history of science and philosophy:

1. Was the Copernican change in astronomy, considered exclusively as a change of base of reference from the earth to the sun, an addition to knowledge?
2. Was the analogous shift in base in the Kantian philosophy an addition to knowledge?
3. Is the concept of base of reference, and the use of change of base, in mathematical analysis properly a part of knowledge?

I can see no possible valid ground for denying a noetic accession in all three of these instances. Then if we answer affirmatively in these three cases, consistency demands an equally positive answer with respect to the effect of the mystical shift of base.

Let us consider briefly the function of the base of reference in mathematical analysis. The analytic formulation of a problem invariably depends upon a base of reference, most commonly in the form of rectilinear Cartesian coordinates. Generally, this base is no explicit part of the analytic development but is implicit in the very form of the development. The expressions and equations are what they are partly because the chosen base of reference is what it is, and partly because of the specific nature of the configurations analyzed. A transformation of base changes the analytic development. If we think of the analytic development as thought content, then the base of reference does not appear explicitly in the content. Yet, the specific pattern of that content stands in functional relationship to that base. Furthermore, if the noetic element were conceived as exclusively the content, then the base would stand apart from knowledge. However, if the noetic is understood as including its roots as well as the content, then the base of reference is part of the noetic order. I believe the latter conception is the sounder, so in that sense we may affirm that the mystical change of base is noetically significant.

So far, I believe I have established, either presumptively or definitely, three senses in which noetic value may be predicated of mystical consciousness. In summation, these are:

1. Transcendental thought that, at a certain level of mystical penetration, is Realized as a self-moving process, in terms of a stream-like cognition incommensurable with the granular relative conceptions, which are capable of definitive differentiation. Using word conceptions this thought may be precipitated in such a way as to determine a pattern of relative thought, which, however, has an exclusively or predominantly transcendental, rather than perceptual, reference.
2. The knowledge of the negation of all relative predication and of sensible presentation has noetic value. This is the noetic value, appertaining to the highest discernible ascension of mystical consciousness from the relative perspective, in its relationship to all relative cognition.
3. Noetic value grows out of the new birth, in the sense of change of base of reference, with manifold effects in the meaningful evaluation of all relative knowledge.

LEUBA'S ANTINOETIC ARGUMENT

Leuba's antinoetic argument relative to evaluation of the mystical is sketched most clearly in chapter 12, headed "Religion, Science and Philosophy." The central burden of his argument is concerned with the actuality of God as determined by experience and, more especially, mystical "experience." Leuba quite clearly views belief in such a God as central in all historic religions, and, accordingly, the ground of such religions would be undermined if the belief is shown on scientific grounds to be untenable. Leuba defines his position in the two following quotations:

> The question raised by the affirmation we are discussing is that of the relation of science to the *belief which makes the religions possible*, i.e., *the belief in a sympathetic God in direct communication with man* [italics mine].*

---

*Leuba, 301.

The God to which this dominant trend of metaphysics points is an impassible, infinite Being—a being therefore who does not bear to man the relation which *every one* of the historical religions assumes to exist and seeks to maintain by means of its system of creeds and worship [italics mine].*

Before outlining the argument, two points need clarification: one, a gross error of fact in Leuba's statement; the other, the divergence of our position from Leuba's assumed position.

First of all, it simply is not true that every historical religion assumes the existence of a "sympathetic God in direct communication with man." The teachings of Buddha and, so far as I know, of all the illumined Buddhist Arhats, affirm an atheistic (Nastikata) position. Their central religious objective is the attainment of the State of Enlightenment. Buddhism does not, in principle, deny the existence of beings invisible to the gross physical senses, but these are in no sense equivalent to the Gods of Christianity, Judaism and Islam. For Buddhism, there is no God in the sense of root causal source or as an intermediator who can intervene and set aside the action of law, either in response to prayer or otherwise. I trust that Leuba will grant that a religion five hundred years older than Christianity is a historical religion. This error is hardly excusable on the part of Leuba, who is a special student of the psychology of religion. In all history, Buddha is the outstanding psychological analyst within the religious domain.

As my position with respect to this point is in fundamental agreement with the Buddha's thesis, Leuba's argument relative to the empiric Gods is incompatible with the thesis of this work. However, schematically, insofar as his thesis is identical with the denial of noetic value in the mystical state, it thus is relevant.

I shall give the essential steps in Leuba's argument in a series of numbered statements.

1. *The Gods of religion are not beyond scientific investigation unless they are exclusively transcendental objects.*[†] No exception can be taken to this statement as it is, in principle, correct, so far as I can see; for whatever is experiential, in the strict sense of being a content determined by the senses, falls within the field of empiric or physical science, as a general possibility. Methodological difficulty may place portions of such subject matter out of the range of our science, as presently developed. However, it is always possible that the development of method will correct

---

*Ibid., 304.
†Ibid., 300.

this limitation, so we are not justified in setting an a priori limitation upon scientific possibility within this circumscribed domain. However, a transcendental object or state is, by definition, unavailable to empiric method, and therefore is not a potential object of investigation by empirical science. Also, we should recall that since the analysis of Kant it has been known that pure reason is incapable of reaching the Transcendent. Thus, if it is assumed that sense and reason are the only avenues of knowledge, then the Transcendent cannot by any possibility ever be known. There would be no logical or other right to affirm its existence or possibility. If there is a transcendent Reality that may be affirmed, then it must be recognizable by a way of consciousness that is neither sense nor reason. Such a way of consciousness, *in its purity*, would be neither empiric nor conceptual. It is my thesis that mystical Realization, or introception, is such a way of consciousness. Thus, by hypothesis, it would be inaccessible by the methods of empiric or physical science. Even so, a mixed mode of consciousness that is partly introceptual and partly empiric would be somewhat accessible to empiric science, though it would be a borderline zone in which physical science could never be sure of its determinations.

2. *Belief in God that is derived as the result of naive interpretation of phenomena and inner experience is accessible to empiric science.** In principle, no exception can be taken to this statement.

3. *"Should there be no ground of belief other than physical phenomena and inner experiences, then, for those who are acquainted with the modern scientific conceptions, there could be no belief in God."†* Superficially, this statement seems to follow from the foregoing, but as a matter of logic it does not. Merely because subject matter is available for the investigation of empiric science, it does not follow that the conceptions that the *scientific investigator* presents carry authority. The inherent limitations of inductive method are such that no conception derived through this method is ever authoritative, but only has the character of "warranted assertibility," to use Dewey's terminology. Warranted assertibility is always only tentative. There is ever the possibility that it may be so altered that, while remaining conformable with scientific determinations, it is also consonant with an extant or future God conception, without the latter being exclusively transcendental. Further, scientific investigators are as much subject to the limitations imposed by predilection as are people of religion. Repeatedly this influence is traceable in the proffered theoretical constructions. These individuals, as well as those

*Ibid., 302-4.
†Ibid., 304.

of religious feeling, have their over-beliefs. Some of them simply replace belief in God with a belief in the Darwinian ape, which they worship, as it were, in their peculiar ways. I do not see that this has any logical advantage over God, but it certainly does possess considerable aesthetic and moral disadvantages.

4. *"When one believes with the mystics that God, the Absolute, the Ultimate Reality . . . is directly experienced in ecstatic trance and nowhere else, it would seem to follow that knowledge of the trance-consciousness includes a knowledge of God."** From a study of this statement, one begins to gain a fairly distinct idea of the line that Leuba is following. However, careful study of it reveals much ambiguity, so that, as a matter of strict logic, the implications are unclear. Nonetheless, Leuba apparently means—and this is borne out by his following passages—that by the study of trance one can gain a true evaluation of the meaningful aspect of consciousness, without the investigator personally directly realizing the trance state; or else, possibly by realizing it in one way, he or she has the key to its nature as a whole. He supports this as follows: "However it may be produced, ecstasy is ecstasy, just as fever is fever whatever its cause. The truth-kernel of religious ecstasy is, as we have shown, no other than the truth-kernel of narcotic intoxication and of the ecstatic trance in general."† In discussing two ways of unification, Leuba says with respect to the second way that "the terms may lose their individual features and be degraded to a level of undifferentiated simplicity. That, as we have seen, is the mystical way of producing 'harmony' or 'unity.' It *is a way which does not secure any knowledge* [italics mine]."‡

As a matter of strict logic, the terms *trance consciousness, ecstatic-trance* and *ecstasy* are not necessarily identical in meaning, but the study of his text forces upon one the conclusion that Leuba employs them as synonyms. In the ensuing analysis, I shall assume this as his meaning. Thus the clause, *ecstasy is ecstasy*, would stand identical with *trance consciousness is trance consciousness*. The overall implication is that if one has psychological acquaintance with trance consciousness in any form, one has the key to the meaning of religious mysticism, however highly developed, insofar as its source lies in the ecstatic state. Thus the essential differences between mystics as to their doctrines, feeling valuations, moral conceptions and practices are factors from outside the trance that have colored its meaning. I believe I have justly presented Leuba's meaning in this abstract.

---

*Ibid., 305.
†Ibid., 309.
‡Ibid.

A number of his assumptions break down completely under analysis, I believe. Thus, for example, are we justified in claiming that ecstasy is always a trance consciousness and, conversely, that a trance consciousness is always ecstatic? This is like asking, "Is gold always a glittering yellow substance and, conversely, is a glittering yellow substance always gold?" One who has experience with mining placer gold will rise up and shout an emphatic "No!" By reason of an error in his conceptions in this matter, many an amateur has expended painful labor gathering worthless mineral and thrown away real gold. (I believe that this is precisely what Leuba has done in his book.) Gold may appear as a glittering yellow substance, as it does when it is perfectly pure and uncoated. However, in nature it may appear black with a coating of manganese oxide, or red with a rusty stain, or be so alloyed and even chemically combined with other minerals that it is not recognizable. Moreover, mica, in certain lights, and pyrite may look for all the world like gold. The experienced miner soon learns to discount appearances and comes to judge by fundamentals, such as specific gravity and chemical reactions. Here we are presented with the proper test. Gold is that which possesses the group of qualities belonging uniquely to gold. Likewise, mystical insight is that which gives the mystic meaningful value, whatever the appearance of the process.

To be sure, the above illustration is by no means a logical demonstration that seeming is never dependable. It is possible that there may be subjects of which the seeming is so unique that the logical propositions may be converted simply. Even so, this can never justifiably be assumed. Yet inductive thinkers do just this. The master logician Bertrand Russell has said, "What is called induction appears to me to be either disguised deduction or a mere method of making plausible guesses."[*] The aim of the inductive thinker is the justification of a universal proposition from one or more observations that lead to particular judgments. There is manifest logical error in a step of this sort. The observations themselves do not give any universal whatsoever. It is through the imagination of the scientist, working in directions suggested by the observations, that a general hypothesis is invented of such a nature that the consequences or observations may be deduced. If the hypothesis suggests further consequences that can be checked by observation, and the results of such checking are positive, then a presumption is built for the hypothesis. The only difference between a hypothesis of this sort and scientific theories and laws is that the latter have stood such checking over a wider field and for a longer time. The difference is only one of degree. There is no guarantee that the so-called

---

*Russell, *The Principles of Mathematics*, 11n.

law is truly such, that is, one having ontological character from which there could be no deviation by way of exception. From the standpoint of logic, the supposed law of science is only a lucky guess. The history of science shows that such laws often fail, even after they have withstood the tests of generations. Then the advance of theoretical science marks time until some genius comes along who can make a better guess. Nevertheless, a guess is a guess, no matter how brilliant the genius.

Quite commonly, if not always, the scientific problem takes the following form. It is desired to investigate some zone of manifest fact, which we designate by the letter *A*, but *A*, it so happens, is of such a nature that it cannot be known directly by means of scientific observation. However, it may be determined that *A* is generally associated with certain phenomena of a sort that can be observed, which we will call "*B*." We have then the initial proposition that "*A* is *B*" or, more exactly, "The class *A* is a member of the class *B*." Then instances of *B* are studied by the methods of scientific observation. Some uniformity of character is found in these observed instances. These are generalized as always true of *B*. Then the original proposition is converted simply, and we get, "The class *B* is a member of the class *A*." Of course, this is an elementary logical fallacy, but science justifies itself by securing a number of results that do work. Unfortunately, this means that the justification of scientific results is only pragmatic. Empiric science does not determine Truth and Law in an objective or ontological sense.

Leuba employs the above method with respect to religious mysticism and trance consciousness. He takes as his primary proposition, "Religious mystical insight is a member of the class of trance-consciousness." He adds, as an arbitrary affirmation, that "ecstasy is ecstasy, just as fever is fever whatever its cause." By this we have seen that he means that trance consciousness is trance consciousness. He uses the assumed truth of this proposition to justify the further conclusion: If we can explore one or more cases of trance consciousness by scientific means, then we know the nature of trance consciousness as a whole. Thus we will find the true nature of mystical ecstasy as isolated from content derived from the individual character, beliefs and knowledge of the mystic. The next question is: How can we secure instances of trance consciousness that are suitable for scientific observation and experiment? Manifestly, the moral disciplines of Yoga are far too exacting for this purpose. They would require that the scientist become a superior kind of saint before he or she could investigate, and not many scientists are such great lovers of truth that they are willing to be that heroic. For another thing, the process is generally very slow and may require not less than the whole of a lifetime. Consequently, that method of experiment is not chosen. However, the student of the appropriate literature will find that statements of certain kinds of psychotics, epileptics and some chemical users have certain similarities to the expressions of genuine religious mystics. Perhaps it is expecting too much heroism on the part of the investigator to become a voluntary psychotic, and one can hardly become an epileptic at will. Then the remaining route to the trance state, on this program, is through chemical intoxication, that is, scientific research by becoming drunk! It is easy and not nearly so heroic as becoming a saint.

Undoubtedly it is possible to determine certain neural and other physiological alterations in connection with chemical drunkenness. I am not at all surprised that Leuba should view the psychical condition as one of degradation. Any other conclusion I would have found unexpected. Nevertheless, it does not therefore follow that all psychical states that for a distance parallel these are moving toward degradation. Thus, in the case of insects and some other creatures, the transformation from the larva to the chrysalis involves a process initially appearing very much to possess the character of degradation. In reality, however, it does not have the significance of death or decline, but of transformation into a higher form. The meaning of a butterfly is not identical to that of a drunk caterpillar, nor with that of a caterpillar that is simply degenerating. The road to rebirth is not through intoxication, even though there may be a psychical parallelism for a distance. Dissolution as part of the process of a new integration means something very different from mere dissolution alone.

The important point is that the assumption that trance consciousness, as such, has a uniform significance is not justified. A person in a cataleptic state may be superficially indistinguishable from a dead body, but his state has a very different meaning. Leuba's whole process of reasoning is unsound. So obviously is this the case that one suspects that wishful thinking guided the whole research. If William James is vulnerable before Leuba's charge of wishful thinking, no less is Leuba himself, but in an opposite direction.

Two ships at sea, having quite different points of departure and equally divergent destinations, may, nonetheless, move in the same identical course for a portion of a trip. One who has knowledge only of the coinciding portion of the two courses, and the points of departure and destination of one of the ships, cannot deduce the point of departure and destination of the other. So is it true that the end of a process cannot be known without full consideration of the means. Where entirely different means are employed, resulting in passing stages that are similar, it is impossible to deduce identity of ends. One who becomes a mystic by means of protracted exacting moral discipline and keen intellectual discrimination is moving toward something vastly different as contrasted with the instance of a person who is merely intoxicated with chemicals.

Finally, based upon logic alone, we are forced to the conclusion that knowledge of any kind of trance consciousness is insufficient to give us knowledge of God or, more correctly and more generally, knowledge of the values and noetic elements of bona fide mystical states. Additionally, Leuba makes the error of confusing judgments of existence with judgments of meaning or value. Trance consciousness, insofar as it is available for study by empiric psychology, is only a temporal phenomenal existence. The inner meaningful content of the consciousness is something quite different and not at all to be judged by the state of the organism.

5. Leuba's most important argument concerns the step from an immediate state of consciousness to the predication of an objective existence corresponding thereto. For mystical states of consciousness there is no question that there are generally, at least, the following qualitative modifications:

1. sense of Presence
2. sense of Illumination
3. sense of Communion
4. feeling of Reconciliation
5. conviction of Vastness
6. sense of Repose
7. feeling of Safety
8. sense of Union
9. feeling of Harmony

The state in its immediacy is thus qualified, and this is attested so overwhelmingly that its actuality is not disputed. However, apparently more often than not, the mystic goes beyond simply reporting these immediate qualities by predicating objective existence corresponding to them. Very often he says, in effect, that all this means direct knowledge of and relation to God, or some other metaphysical existence, thus imposing upon the unquestionable immediacy an objective interpretation. Leuba contends that *the objective interpretation does not possess the invulnerability of the immediacy, and is thus subject to rational criticism.* This takes us to the heart of the problem relative to the authority of the mystical state.

On this point Leuba's criticism is just, as far as it goes. It is true enough that we are in the habit of ascribing an objectively existent cause for experienced states of consciousness. We do this continually in the field of ordinary consciousness. For instance, perhaps we feel a sensation, which we call a "blow upon the arm"; at the same time, we have a visual experience, which we call a "falling tree limb." We infer the conclusion that an external existence, called a tree limb, fell and hit us on the arm. We have thus projected an objective cause to explain a group of sensible experiences. We have explained an immediate state by a somewhat that involves more than the immediacy. Most mystics unquestionably do the same thing.

I quite agree with the statement that the predication of an objective existence from immediacy is not justified. The immediacy itself is the only certainty. The criticism is quite valid, *so long as it is applied with absolute consistency*. When it is applied to that which one does not like and not applied in the direction of one's preferences, it becomes merely vicious.

The predication of an external physical world, in the last analysis, is grounded only upon psychical immediacy. It thus rests upon the same base as the metaphysical world predicated by the uncritical mystic. The logical analysis that discredits the metaphysical existence, when applied consistently, equally discredits the objective physical world. The fallacy of hypostatization arises just as much in the one instance as in the other. Strictly, then, the only thing we know beyond all doubt is immediacy. All else rests upon an "as if" basis. We may act as if there were a physical world that serves as the cause of certain immediate psychical states. However, we may also act as if a metaphysical reality, such as God, caused other of our immediate psychical states. The logical ground of either position is equally weak.

If Leuba had been consistent in his refusal to accept hypostatization, then he would have won my respect as another Buddhist. However, he was not consistent. He repudiated the Gods of the mystics, but proceeded to replace these with his own hypostatization in the form of a psychophysiological existence. This is just another kind of god that serves the habit of seeking an external cause of an immediate state. Well, Leuba has a right to his preferred god, provided he grants equal logical right to the mystic to choose his kind of God. For my part, I do not admire the kind of taste that prefers what Shankara calls "a compound of skin, tissue and bones, filled with ordure, urine and phlegm." It smacks too much of the refuse pile.

The one indubitably sound position is to repudiate all hypostatization, whether physical or metaphysical. Then we ground ourselves upon pure immediacy. Law becomes the necessary connection between various states of consciousness, both of a more objective and of a more subjective sort. When one arrives at this position, one is in accord with Buddhist epistemology, regardless of whether he or she has ever heard of Gautama Buddha or of the Buddhist religion and philosophy. Here we have retained only that which is strictly necessary and of which we can be justifiably certain. The immediate qualities of conscious states are their own existences; they do not depend upon or hang upon either a physical or a metaphysical somewhat beyond themselves. Consciousness is the one self-existent Reality. The goal of religion and practical philosophy is not union with a metaphysical Being, but Realization of the state of consciousness known as "Enlightenment." This is the word of the greatest mystic of all, and I submit that no standpoint has ever been more logically rigorous.

In conclusion, we may say that the final knowledge of the mystic takes the following form:

1. Negatively, it is a denial of all substantial reality to all worlds, physical or metaphysical, and an equal denial of all selfhood in the same sense.
2. Positively, it affirms the indubitable reality of consciousness, and of all its immediately Realizable states. In the 'as if' sense, there may be all kinds of worlds, objective and metaphysical, with their corresponding kinds of beings and selves. This supplies everything that is necessary for innumerable possibilities.

14

Significance of Immediate Qualities of Mystical States

We know with unequivocal certainty the immediate content and toning of our various states of consciousness. When we interpret these states as inhering in, derived from, or meaning a somewhat other than consciousness itself, we are moving beyond the range of true knowledge. The states imply just that which is necessary to their existence. Beyond this, our thought is mere speculation or extrapolation of wishful thinking. These considerations are of universal validity and, as we have shown, extrapolative interpretation or explanation is as unsound in the case of the immediately given of ordinary experience as it is in the case of mystical states of consciousness. The predication of the unreality of the world, as is done in the case of the philosophies of maya, or illusion, is not a denial of the presence of immediate states of consciousness. Rather, it is a denial of the extrapolative construct, which, though occasionally a development of conscious speculation, is preponderantly an automatic habit handed down by social heredity. Among them, those philosophies that have been thought through consistently deny reality not only to the assumed physical world beyond immediacy, but to similar metaphysical existences as well. Yet, relatively few people accept this thoroughly consistent and rigorous viewpoint and orientation, both as a way of thought and as a way of life. Consciously and unconsciously, other attitudes and interpretations usually are assumed.

Beside this rigorously consistent standpoint, three or four other interpretative orientations may be isolated and classified.

1. The extrapolated physical world of things and human society may be viewed as a real existence, whereas the metaphysical order is viewed as unreal. This is the standpoint of materialism both in the technical and in the practical senses. In its more extreme and naive development, those who hold this position may regard the supposed external existence of things and of humankind as the only real existence, while the immediacy in consciousness is considered a dependent effect.

All such thinking is an effort to explain the clearly and immediately known by that which is unknown and theoretically, as well as practically, unknowable. It is thus interpretation and orientation of life through the myth of external things. This is a standpoint and attitude of extremely wide currency, which colors much of scientific thought, particularly the aspect that not philosophically self-critical. Marxian social philosophy assumes this stance both in theory and in practice. We find that this extreme position may be modified by the recognition of ordinary sensuous immediacy as it is found variously toned by feeling.

2. The extrapolated metaphysical worlds of the Gods may be viewed as real in themselves, and unreality predicated of the physical universe. This is the viewpoint of spiritualism (using this term in its original and proper sense). For those who are thus inclined, the Gods are intrinsically real, but physical human beings possess merely a shadowy existence. It would appear that not many adopt this approach.

3. Both the physical and the metaphysical worlds may be accepted as real in themselves. This is probably the standpoint of most of the religions, including Christianity. For such, both Heaven and this world are actual external existences in themselves. It seems to be the most general, naive popular view. It has the merit of being more consistent than either of the preceding views, but shares with them the error of viewing as *given* that which is really only extrapolation.

4. The other general position that may be taken is that which was discussed at the beginning of this chapter. It comprises the perspective of this whole philosophy of Consciousness-without-an-object. One who is familiar with the "Essence of Mind" to which the northern Buddhist Sutras refer will recognize the similarity of the conception. This philosophy asserts that *appearance* is the sole nature of existence of both the physical and the heavenly worlds, and of their respective denizens. Moreover, as appearance, it affirms equal reality of both orders. When truly understood, it will be found that this philosophy involves the loss of no essential value. On the contrary, it strikes away the chains of bondage and fear, which cause perennial human suffering.

Toward the close of the previous chapter, I listed nine modifications of consciousness that are, admittedly, qualitative characterizations of mystical states of consciousness. Perhaps they are not all present in a single given instance, but some always are, and in sum they characterize the state's most common features. Here I propose to interpret these qualities in the light of the present philosophy.

First of all, the reason so many efforts at interpretation of these Realizations have led to indefensible consequences is that the problem has been falsely conceived. It has been assumed that the meaning of the state of consciousness lies in something other than itself. Actually, it is its own meaning. Imagined, supposed, or seeming otherness acquires its meaning from the immediately Realized state, not the other way around. *Thus, Presence does not mean God, but the God notion or God appearance means Presence.* The Presence is real, whereas the notion or appearance is a construct. It is not necessary to interpret Presence as meaning something beyond itself. It is the superlative value itself, without the intervention of agency. One who has Realized Presence needs no God. That person is the reality that has been called Divinity. Presence is identity, not relationship. Conceiving it as relationship produces delusion. Presence is fullness of Life or of Consciousness. It is the normal condition. So, for a being that had always been normal, the idea of Presence could never have arisen. Only those who were deluded through abnormal existence could ever feel the arising of a state of Presence, because, when Realized, there is produced a contrast with the abnormal state. The Realization of Presence is the sign that an insane person has at last become sane. It is conceived as a rare and strange state of consciousness in this world, because this humanity has the perspective of the inmates of a lunatic asylum. For the truly normal it is so natural as not to be noticeable.

In our ordinary usage we think of "presence" in the sense of "presence of." It is thus conceived as the "presence to a self of someone or something." This is not the meaning of the mystical Realization of Presence, though, I must confess, a mystic who did not discriminate clearly between the mystical state per se and a subsequent complex of the memory of that state, together with the ordinary consciousness, might confuse the meaning. The mystical significance is nearer to the dictionary meaning as "the state of being present." The mystic is in the state of being present to him- or herself, that is, in concentric relationship, rather than in the ordinary state of eccentric relationship. Becoming consciously centered in the Center is to Realize Presence.

In the discussion of the subject of Presence, both James Leuba and William James correlate the mystical Realization of Presence with a "sense of presence," fairly frequently experienced, wherein the subject feels that someone or something is somewhere in his or her vicinity. Very often, perhaps typically, there is a sense of a somewhat localized somewhere nearby in space. Connected with this, there are various reported sensations of a more or less indescribable sort and, quite often, a sense of fear that may approach the intensity of terror. This effect has been produced experimentally. For my part, I do not remember ever having had an experience precisely of this sort, but there have been a few rare experiences that seem to be related. Once at night near a mountain stream, while in the company of others, I heard a distinct shout, which I thought at the time might be a call by a person who was expected to arrive shortly. The shout had not been generally heard by the others, though it had seemed very clear to me. Investigation failed to uncover any normal physical source of the sound. At any rate, the curious feature of the whole experience was an impression of a series of cold shivers passing up and down the spine, with a tendency toward terror panic, which I found rather difficult to control. Rational analysis had no effect upon the affective reaction. Only by abstracting the mind and using will was I able to achieve control. Intellectually, at the time, I did not view this as a presence of something, but as a psychical curiosity of some interest. However, autonomously, another part of consciousness seemed to feel as though something alien and inimical were present. The descriptions of the experience of localized presence include certain qualities so closely resembling what I experienced that I suspect the phenomenon was of a similar sort. If such is the case, then I can say quite definitely that it is not at all like the mystical Realization of Presence. It is more like the diametric opposite of that. It had a felt effect like invasion by the alien, or, rather, threatened invasion. It was definitely distasteful.

In contrast, the genuine Realization of Presence might be said to have the value of escape from the *alien*, and centering in the *proper*. (These words approximate Spengler's sense.) If the mystical Realization of Presence may be called "centralization," the other sense of presence had the value of "eccentralization." The first has integrative value, the latter a disintegrative tendency. The Realization had the value of being Home, in the most fundamental sense possible; of being right at last; of "being on beam" (in terms of modern technical slang); of everything being just what it should be; of at last being truly rationally attuned. In every way in all stages, at the time and ever since, it was most welcome. Thus the contrast between the two states is radical in a profound sense. Scientific research that follows the line of "sense of presence," as contrasted with Realization of Presence, is definitely off the track, so far as understanding real mystical consciousness is concerned.

Meaning and Value are achieved when the seemingly distant and alien are transformed into the near and proper. Thus explanation and other labor have performed their office when the distant and mediate are elevated to the immediate. It is not the immediate value in consciousness that needs explanation and justification. These are what they are, as given. The immediate modification of consciousness cannot possibly carry any injurious potency, since the whole support of its existence is consciousness itself. The modification of consciousness cannot destroy consciousness.

The immediate experience of the mystic constitutes its own justification and authority. Thus the Realization of Presence is the Realization
of all it implies. It is Reconciliation, Repose, Security, Union, Harmony
and the rest. It is not that in the mystical state something new is gained
or attained, but a false condition, as in the example of belief in the
mirage, is lost. It is because people have been in a deluded state in
which they felt unreconciled, restless, insecure, lost and at war with
themselves, that the mystical awakening takes on the positive values
corresponding to the opposite negative conditions of the deluded state.
Mystical Realization does not prove a metaphysically existing God, but
disproves the mirage of the world.

In much of our thinking we have confused means and ends. For
instance, food is not an end, but a means. Nutrition is the end. The relationship with another is not an end, but a means. Communion is the
end. Travel (particularly in the sense of touring or exploration) is not an
end but a means to fulfilled or enriched consciousness. God is not an
end, but a means to the Realization of Presence. So, in this manner, we
can list all the searchings and strivings of ordinary human life and find
that all of them are valuable only as they lead to an enhancement of
immediate consciousness. However, one who has found the key to all
the immediate values directly has no longer need of the means that so
occupy the thought and effort of those in the state of delusion. Genuine mystical awakening achieves just this. That is why its Assurance is
absolutely justified. It is not an assurance as to external relations that
compose all the various means of life, but rather Assurance in the sense
of Realization of all ends. The science that is competent only in the
world of means or instruments is wholly impotent when it attempts to
assail the immediate Assurance of the mystic.

It is true that when the mystic steps out of the immediate mystical
state so as to attempt to interpret its meaning in relative terms, he or she
may make errors in discrimination, and thereby develop interpretations that will not withstand objective criticism. By mystical awakening,
one has not acquired authority to pronounce what is so in the realm of
the science of means. One has a perspective from which he or she may
approach the problems of physical science that may supply superior
advantages, but he or she will have to labor with the resources of nonmystical humanity. One's pure knowledge as mystic is of quite another
order.

William James, in his search for the unassailable kernel of mystical
consciousness, found what he called a "higher power," which possessed, overshadowed or enveloped the mystic. In analyzing this, Leuba
points out that in the conception of higher power we have more than
pure immediacy. There is also involved a judgment of comparison as

between something lower and something higher. This criticism is valid. The immediate content of the *pure* mystical state does not give the sense of higher power. As the state deepens toward purity, the capacity to apprehend, in the comparative sense, tends to dissolve. I am sufficiently familiar with this tendency to be able to analyze it. It is as though there were a process in which, in intellectual terms, there was a progression in an infinite series that the intellectual side of the mind followed as far as it was capable. The conceptual side becomes more and more subtle and the concepts less and less granular or definitive, until, at the utmost limit of abstraction, the concepts, together with the process of conceiving and judging, begin to dissolve into a state wherein there is no more thinking. At this point I stopped the further process, since I was interested in maintaining intellectual continuity. In any case, the direction of the development is intellectually clear in much the same sense that the thinking mind can apprehend an infinite series from the nature of a developing progression. By such a process we are able mathematically to sum an infinite series without actually passing over the infinitely large number of terms in the series. The summation is a reaching beyond the consciousness of the concrete mind, but its truth and actuality are not thereby less certain to the mathematician. Similarly, we may liken the pure mystical Realization to the actual culmination of that which, to the intellective consciousness, is a converging infinite series. As such, the intellect can apprehend the culmination in the mathematical sense. The final term is the point wherein intellection is reduced to zero. The extent to which this process can be followed with conscious intellection depends upon the equipment of the individual mystic.

For the pure mystical state, there is neither high nor low, insofar as it transcends relativity. Evaluation is intellective. To a consciousness dwelling on earth it is natural to take the earth as the base of reference. From that base we are in quite general agreement that low is that which is in the direction of the effect of gravity, and high is that which stands up against gravity. Hence, the submarine descends, whereas the airplane rises. However, if we abstract the earth from these two objects while in their relative motion of descent and ascent, we would no longer have any ground for saying that one was going down while the other was going up. They would simply be tending in opposite directions. It is movement relative to the direction of gravity that defines the meaning of up and down. By analogy, in terms of conscious states, gravity is orientation to objects, whereas negation of gravity, or levity, is orientation away from objects. The mystical movement is away from objects, as can be observed by the witnessing intellect. Thus, in the familiar sense of the words *high* and *low*, it is movement to the higher. In terms of *power*, then, it is movement toward *higher power*, but in the absolute sense there is neither higher nor lower.

There is another sense in which we commonly differentiate between higher and lower. Consciousness that comprehends more, as compared with another consciousness that comprehends less, is higher than the latter. In conceptual terms, a concept that subsumes more is higher than a concept that subsumes less. This implies that the genus is higher than the species. Now, as the intellect joins flight with the mystical sense, it clearly soars into greater comprehension, and so the judgment of a higher consciousness is quite consonant with common evaluation.

Here I have been speaking of deepening mystical process. In the strictest sense, there is no process, but only sudden Enlightenment that is absolutely complete. The effect of process belongs to the conjunction with the intellect. Inevitably, all that can be said in these matters is valid only with respect to a sort of compound consciousness that is partly mystical and partly intellective. The only absolutely perfect "Word" is absolute silence.

Epilogue

This writing has no logical end. It is finished rather arbitrarily, in much the way that a that fugue composition is concluded. The music might have continued forever as a flight of musical voices. Similarly, the development from that base of reference that was defined by the Realization called the "High Indifference"* could have continued through all fields of human thought without any conceivable end. However, this does not mean that it is all of equal value.

In the present work there are only two points covered that are of a central importance:

1. the factuality of a third organ, faculty or function of cognition, which was called "introception";
2. the possibility, through the function of introception, of a metaphysical knowledge.

The problem is fundamental. Is a metaphysical knowledge possible?

I think we may conclude from the work of Hume and Kant that a pure metaphysical knowledge is not possible if we are limited to the cog-

---

*[The accounts Wolff provides of his second Fundamental Realization constitute the focal point of *Pathways Through to Space* and *The Philosophy of Consciousness without an Object*. In a previous characterization, I have explained that "Wolff labels the state the 'High Indifference' because it was absolutely neutral between all polar concepts (including subject-object), and all reference to what he immediately 'knew' must therefore be considered symbolic (not strictly descriptive) of THAT which is neither subject nor object. Although he alludes to It as a fusion of matter, form and awareness, as functions of consciousness, he denies that *ultimately* It was any more consciousness than nonconsciousness. Wolff symbolizes this Transcendent base primarily as 'Consciousness-without-an-object,' but employs alternate designations as well, in particular, the 'GREAT SPACE.' It constitutes both his experiential terminus in mystical penetration and the source or ultimate foundation for his philosophy" (Ron Leonard, "The Transcendental Philosophy of Franklin Merrell-Wolff" (Ph.D. diss., University of Waterloo, 1991), 74-75).]

nitive forms of sense perception and conceptual cognition. Efforts at metaphysical statement have typically been dogmatic and in disagreement with each other. Moreover, there exists no means of critical discrimination between such incompatible dogmatic statements. This has been acknowledged since the time of Kant. Not only Kant, but also Jung challenges the validity of any metaphysical conception. Jung contends, in complete conformity with Kant's position, that our conceptions concerning a supposed metaphysical subject matter are only statements concerning the structure of the mind. In the psychological commentary in his introduction to *The Tibetan Book of the Great Liberation*, he states:

> In the first place, the structure of the mind is responsible for anything we may assert about metaphysical matters, as I have already pointed out. We have also begun to understand that the intellect is not an *ens per se*, or an independent mental faculty, but a psychic function dependent upon the conditions of the psyche as a whole. A philosophical statement is the product of a certain personality, living at a certain time in a certain place, and not the outcome of a purely logical and impersonal procedure. To that extent it is chiefly subjective; whether it has an objective validity or not depends on whether there are few or many persons who argue in the same way. The isolation of man within his mind as a result of epistemological criticism has naturally led to psychological criticism. This kind of criticism is not popular with the philosophers, since they like to consider the philosophic intellect as the perfect and unconditioned instrument of philosophy. Yet this intellect of theirs is a function dependent upon an individual psyche and determined on all sides by subjective conditions, quite apart from environmental influences. Indeed we have already become so accustomed to this point of view that 'mind' has lost its universal character altogether. It has become a more or less individualized affair, with no trace of its former cosmic aspect as the *anima rationalis*.*

This would challenge any possibility of an a priori determination. Now let us turn to Kant, who recognized that the problem is not quite so simple as that:

---

*Carl G. Jung, commentary on *The Tibetan Book of the Great Liberation*, trans. Sardar Bahādur S. W. Laden La, and Lamas Karma Sumdhon Paul, Lobzang Mingyur Dorje, and Kazi Dawa-Sandup, with introductions, annotations and editing by W. Y. Evans-Wentz (Oxford: University Press, 1954), xxxii-xxxiii.

That metaphysical science has hitherto remained in so vac-
illating a state of uncertainty and contradiction, is only to be
attributed to the fact, that this great problem, and perhaps even
the difference between analytical and synthetical judgments,
did not sooner suggest itself to philosophers. Upon the solution
of this problem, or upon sufficient proof of the impossibility
of synthetical knowledge *a priori*, depends the existence or
downfall of the science of metaphysics. Among philosophers,
David Hume came the nearest of all to this problem; yet it
never acquired in his mind sufficient precision, nor did he
regard the question in its universality. On the contrary, he
stopped short at the synthetical proposition of the connection of
an effect with its cause (*principium causalitatis*), insisting that
such proposition *a priori* was impossible. According to his conclusions, then, all that we term metaphysical science is a mere
delusion, arising from the fancied insight of reason into that
which is in truth borrowed from experience, and to which habit
has given the appearance of necessity. Against this assertion,
destructive to all pure philosophy, he would have been
guarded, had he had our problem before his eyes in its universality. For he would then have perceived that, according to his
own argument, there likewise could not be any pure mathematical science, which assuredly cannot exist without synthetical propositions *a priori*—an absurdity from which his good
understanding must have saved him.

In the solution of the above problem is at the same time
comprehended the possibility of the use of pure reason in the
foundation and construction of all sciences which contain theoretical knowledge *a priori* of objects, that is to say, the answer
to the following questions:

How is pure mathematical science possible?
How is pure natural science possible?

Respecting these sciences, as they do certainly exist, it may
with propriety be asked, *how* they are possible?—for that they
must be possible is shown by the fact of their really existing.
But as to metaphysics, the miserable progress it has hitherto
made, and the fact that of no one system yet brought forward,
as far as regards its true aim, can it be said that this science
really exists, leaves any one at liberty to doubt with reason the
very possibility of its existence.*

*Kant, *Critique of Pure Reason*, 56-57.

Kant sets forth a further question: "How is metaphysics, as a natural disposition, possible?"*

In my mind, these questions are just about as fundamental as exist anywhere. If our knowledge is empiric, and only empiric, then we are helplessly enclosed within the world of phenomena, without even the faintest knowledge of law, necessity or order. We could have no certainty concerning the great problems of God, Freedom or Immortality. We could have no certainty in the domain that properly belongs to religion.

Concerning mathematics, let us consider a question pointedly raised by Einstein: "How can it be that mathematics, being, after all, a product of human thought, independent of experience, is so admirably adapted to the objects of reality?" Einstein's query carries us back into the history of the development of the general theory of relativity. He found in the work of Riemann, a pure mathematician, the mathematical pattern that could give form to that theory. Riemann was a mathematical thinker in an ivory tower, so to speak, without any reference in his thought to experience. He was concerned with a pure problem that, from the ordinary point of view, would seem very abstruse. It grew out of the question whether Euclid's so-called parallel axiom actually was an axiom, as opposed to a proposition or theorem that could be deduced from previous axioms. This effort failed, so he attempted to develop a system in which the assumption of the parallel axiom was altered. Out of this arose two systems of non-Euclidean geometry. One was attributed to Lobachevsky and Bolyai, the other to Riemann. The former assumed that through a point on a plane outside of a given line on that plane, two parallel lines could be drawn that would not meet the given line in a finite distance and that between these two lines there were an infinite number of other lines that were called "nonintersectors." He built a perfectly logical and coherent geometry upon this assumption.

Riemann followed the other course, assuming that through such a point no line could be drawn that would not meet the given line in a finite distance. His approach thus abandons the notion of 'parallelism' in the sense of two lines that meet only at infinity. This would mean that if we have two lines such that the sum of the interior angles formed on one side of a transversal are equal to two right angles, instead of these lines continuing separately to infinity, they would meet in a finite distance. This defines a conception of a limited or finite space, when the implications are followed to final conclusions. The only imaginable model we have of such a space is the two-dimensional surface of a

*Ibid., 57.

sphere, where the great circles are the analogue of straight lines. In that case you can have great circles that meet in a finite distance. This non-Euclidean system was a pure construction, a pure mathematical development, without any thought or intention of its having a practical application. Yet, many years later, Einstein found that it, along with a further generalization of geometry by Riemann, supplied the basic mathematical conception that served to integrate his general theory of relativity. Hence he began to wonder how it was possible that mathematical thought, which is purely a priori, could apply so well to the experiential domain.

I submit that the problem of how pure mathematics is possible is closely connected to the problem of whether a pure metaphysics is possible. The thought of the pure mathematician moves everlastingly to the infinite, as also does the disposition of a metaphysician to contemplate the Infinite. The call of the metaphysical is a fact of human psychology. Even so, how can it be justified? How can we attain a metaphysical certainty analogous to the certainty we attain in pure mathematics? The two problems are very closely related. The importance of the noetic thesis, that there is a third organ, faculty or function of cognition other than sense perception and conceptual cognition, is that this is a way of knowing that leads to metaphysical certainty. However, it is viewed as a function latent in the total psychology of humankind, active generally only as an unconscious influence, and that because of this influence, we have a metaphysical disposition, an urge to achieve metaphysical certainty. It is also suggested that this function lies in the background, operating and influencing the work of all genius, and thus distinguishing the thought of genius from the thought of mere talent. Furthermore, the influence of the third faculty of cognition may be active without it having been isolated as an object of cognition itself.

No doubt, the emergence and isolation of this function calls for that which we regard as Yogic Realization or Awakening. It is not generally active in most people, only the few, yet presumably potential in all. If the actuality of such a function is entertained as a possibility, then we may see how metaphysical certainty is possible, and thus the resolution of all basic philosophical and religious questions may be available, so that we are no longer dependent upon faith alone. The truth of this thesis, that there is such a third means of cognition, cannot be proven on the basis of the familiar twofold form of cognition through sense perception and conceptual cognition alone. Consequently, it is vulnerable to criticism from that point of view. Its validation depends, at least minimally, upon the assumption that there is such a thing as a Realization that gives not only affective value and moral elevation, but also essential knowledge. This point is central to the whole text.

There are frequent references in this book to mathematical analogues—and for good reason. The underlying thesis is that the factuality of pure mathematics is as much in doubt as the factuality of pure metaphysics. However, as the factuality of pure mathematics is abundantly proven, there is the presumption that the factuality of pure metaphysics may be proven equally well. In any case, unless the philosopher seriously considers this possibility, he or she has not completed his or her obligation to the determination of Truth.

I do not reject criticism, in the sense that Kant and Jung use the term, for it simply means discriminative evaluation. In fact, I solicit it. I am more concerned that this conception be given serious consideration than that it should be arbitrarily accepted. Nevertheless, to be competent, criticism involves rare qualifications. Only one who has awakened within him- or herself the introceptive function can be a competent critic. For all others, it can only be entertained as a possibility—but that is enough. I desire that the mind should not be closed in this direction. I do not wish that it should accept or reject blindly, but simply to entertain this possibility. Competent criticism would further require the mystical insight and intellectual acuity of a Shankara or a Plotinus, plus knowledge of modern epistemological and psychological criticism, as well as knowledge of pure mathematics. Therefore, not many can qualify as competent critics.

In presenting the evidence, as far as possible, for the factuality of this faculty (or "Samadhindriya," if you please, or "inner organ" of Fichte), I have included the explicit report of the events leading to the actual awakening of the function.* Such material falls within the category of subjective biography, a field that one is a bit sensitive about giving formal expression. However, it does open the door to psychological criticism and evaluation, so it seems to me that there is an obligation to render this material available, for the last thing I want is uncritical acceptance or rejection.

Recall that Jung says that our thought is only an expression of our personal limitations or subjective mental conditioning, and that it attains a general validity only by its corresponding to a similar impress in the thoughts or consciousness of others. In response, it must be borne in mind that his charge of subjectivism would apply equally well to pure mathematics as to pure metaphysics. I would point out that the authority of pure mathematics is as objective as anything we know;

---

*[See his other cited works for the preponderance of this material.]

that its truth is not determined by popular vote; that it is authentically universal; and that it works in the pragmatic domain of experience. However, I submit that the proof of its truth is not simply the fact that it works pragmatically, but lies in the fact that it follows logically from its premises. Still, I am greatly indebted to Jung, and I feel that he said much that has merit. Finally, even though his statements are pejorative with respect to the overall possibility of metaphysics, on one occasion he states that if we clear away certain things, we may find such metaphysical truth as there may be.

Truth is a complex of two determinants: form and substance. In the empiric realm, the form is logic, and the substance comes from sense experience. I contend that the same holds true on the metaphysical level—that there is a substantive Truth attained only by the function of introceptual Realization and that there is a logical form in which it is enrobed. The logical form without the Realization becomes, with respect to metaphysical material, only speculation—but, in combination with the introceptual content, it becomes a transcriptive presentation of a Transcendent Reality.

Index

absolute, 3, 17, 24, 26, 51, 74, 80, 114-
115, 119, 125, 156, 165-166, 170,
180, 207, 225, 236, 267, 280, 298
Absolute, 3, 51, 74, 88, 165, 223
Consciousness, 75, 199
-ness, 126
One, 52
absolutism, 51-52
absorption, 224n
abstract, 169, 171, 188, 247, 254-255,
257, 261, 268, 295, 297
abstraction, 169-170, 207, 226, 248,
264, 266, 277, 297
action, 31-32, 50, 76, 169, 233
activism(-tic), 48-49, 76, 143, 149, 162,
250
Advaita Vedanta, 220
See also Vedanta
aesthetic, xvi, 20, 44-45, 85, 88, 91-93,
234-235, 268, 273, 285
transcendental, 87
affection(-ive), 45, 52, 247-250, 274,
295, 303
affectionism, 45
agnostic(-ism), 17-18, 197, 204
Ahamkara, 254
Alexander the Great, 185
Allegory of the Cave, 76-77
analysis, xvii, 5, 25, 27, 37, 54, 65, 92,
104, 115, 130-131, 139, 145,
152-153, 156, 191, 195, 197, 206,
227, 230, 249, 251, 253-255, 257,
260, 277, 281, 284, 286, 290,
295-297
analytic, 238
philosophy, xiiin

psychology, x, 4, 85, 89-90, 103,
105, 129, 145, 147, 230-231, 256,
260
Anatman, 252
and Atman, 254-260
doctrine of, 242, 252, 254
annihilation, 193, 236-237, 258
antinomy(-ies), 124
aphorism, xviii, 189, 265
a posteriori, 92
apperception, 56, 73, 88
apprehension, 221-223, 297
and comprehension, 94
a priori, 16, 30, 52, 58, 64, 87, 89, 91-
92, 95, 122, 161, 173, 176, 284,
300, 303
archetypal image, 90
See also primordial images
archetype, 90, 95, 257
of the wise old man, 188
Archimedes, xin
argumentum ad hominem, 39
Arhat, 237, 283
ascetic, 229
asceticism, 229, 235, 239
Ashvaghosha, 118, 267
"as if" (thinking), 281, 290-291
assurance, xv, 6, 29, 71, 76, 87, 104-
105, 108, 189-190, 196, 219, 296
Assurance, 130-131, 192, 296
atheism, 202
Atman, 239, 254-260
Atmanatma Viveka, 251-252
Atmavidya, 243, 252
See also Knowledge of the Self
attention, xiii, 2, 54, 146

307